Contemporary Soviet Education

A Collection of Readings from Soviet Journals

Editor
FRED ABLIN

With an Introduction by
GEORGE S. COUNTS

INTERNATIONAL ARTS AND SCIENCES PRESS
WHITE PLAINS, NEW YORK

for Hanka

Acknowledgments

The material in this collection first appeared in <u>Soviet Education</u>, a journal of translations from Soviet sources that has been published by the International Arts and Sciences Press since 1958. An earlier collection, <u>Education in the USSR</u>, appeared in 1963 under the same editorship.

A number of acknowledgments are in order. The various translators who rendered the Soviet material into English did their work with care and competence. Seymour M. Rosen, the present Editor of <u>Soviet Education</u>, selected and edited several of the more recent items included in the volume. Members of the distinguished Advisory Committee for <u>Soviet Education</u> have recommended material for translation and have enhanced the quality of the journal, and hence of this collection, in other ways. This is particularly true of Professor Counts, who has been an active and encouraging Advisor throughout the years.

Of the IASP editorial staff, Esther Gollobin should be singled out for special mention since her extraordinary meticulousness and intelligence in copyediting and proofreading have set high standards for all those who work on the journal and other IASP publications.

I would add that, like other editors of IASP publications, I enjoyed complete editorial discretion and full support while I edited <u>Soviet Education</u> and the two collections. For that I would thank Myron E. Sharpe, who had the foresight to establish IASP's translation series some ten years ago.

Fred Ablin

Library of Congress Catalog Card Number 68-14428

Printed in the United States of America

Contents

PROGRAMMED INSTRUCTION

COMMUNIST UPBRINGING

ECONOMICS OF EDUCATION

STATISTICS

George S. Counts

Introduction

The time is most appropriate for the publication of these essays by leading Soviet educators on Soviet education. Just fifty years ago November 7 (October 25, according to the old calendar) Lenin and his small party of Bolsheviks, in "ten days that shook the world," overthrew the Provisional Government and in the course of four years established their rule over practically the whole of the old Russian Empire, "one-sixth of the land surface of the earth." Thus the Union of Soviet Socialist Republics was launched on its fateful course. Without doubt this was one of the truly portentous events of the twentieth century. George F. Kennan, one of our most distinguished students of the subject, both as statesman and as scholar, declares in an article in the October 1967 issue of Foreign Affairs that "one is obliged to concede to the Russian Revolution the status of the greatest political event of the present century." He then proceeds to say that "it deserves this description by virtue of the profound exemplary effect it had across great portions of the globe, of the alteration it produced in Russia's relations with the great powers of the West, and of the changes it brought to the life of one of the world's great peoples."

That the fiftieth anniversary of the Great October Revolution was celebrated in the Soviet Union as few events have ever been celebrated in the past is on the record. In the issue of Pravda for July 25 of 1967, the Central Committee of the Communist Party of the Soviet Union published a four and one-half page document of "Theses" dedicated to the anniversary. The opening sentence gives expression to the spirit of the declaration: "Workers of the Soviet Union, peoples of fraternal socialist countries, peoples of communist and workers' movements, and all progressive mankind triumphantly mark the fiftieth anniversary of the Great October Socialist Revolution." And it closes with these Messianic words: "The ideas of October, the ideas of Communism are the leading ideas of our time, the great creative force of contemporary history." The textbook in social science studied in the tenth grade, the final year of the secondary school, closes with a section entitled "The Twentieth Century—the Century of the Triumph of Communism." And the Great October Revolution is often characterized as the greatest turning point in the whole history of mankind. It is important to note also that most of our leading newspapers and journals gave a great deal of attention to the fiftieth anniversary.

It would seem desirable, therefore, to place these essays in historical and social perspective. First of all, we should note the backwardness of Russia in 1917. Although precise data on the rate of illiteracy are not available, it is generally assumed that the figure was about 60 to 65 percent. During the past year Pravda has put it much higher. Also, the country as a whole was in the early stages of industrialization and urbanization. Approximately 85 percent of the people were living on the land, with the vestiges of feudalism present in many areas. In 1929, during the first year of the First Five-Year Plan, the present writer had an unusual opportunity to observe the backwardness of the country. He took an automobile to the Soviet Union and during the months from early July to the end of October drove his car 6,000 miles through the land west of the Urals, a large part of the way entirely alone. For the most part he lived with the peasants in their villages.

The roads, with a few notable exceptions, were ungraded tracks through the forests and over the steppes. Automobiles were as rare as great ocean liners on the Atlantic, and he saw the wooden plow in use in northeastern Russia. He visited "deaf villages," that is, villages whose inhabitants could not hear what was happening in the world outside, there being no automobiles, or railroads, or telephones, or newspapers. He also saw many "dark people," as they were called, peoples who were abysmally ignorant. The backwardness of Russia was clearly recognized by Lenin in 1918, the year after the seizure of power. "History has taught us a lesson," he wrote. "It is a lesson, because it is the absolute truth that without a German revolution we are doomed. . . . At all events, under all conceivable vicissitudes, if the German revolution does not come, we are doomed."

Education must be placed also in the perspective of the triumph of Bolshevism. While we in America were not surprised by the Russian revolution, we were greatly surprised and shocked to witness the establishment of a dictatorship. We entered the First World War under the slogan of "a war to make the world safe for democracy." We were consequently totally unprepared for the establishment of dictatorships, whether communist or fascist. The word "totalitarianism," in fact, was not even in our dictionaries. We knew therefore that the Bolsheviks could not remain in power. At first we thought that they would collapse within a few days, then within a few months, and later within a few years. When Lenin launched his New Economic Policy in 1921, many were certain that Russia was on the way back to capitalism, even though Lenin stated that this was not a surrender, but only a retreat. We also knew that the Bolsheviks would not dare to launch a comprehensive system of schools, because only free societies would do this. History had proved that autocracies would never establish schools for the masses, because they wanted to keep the people in ignorance. And they would not teach them to read and write, because literacy is always a liberating force in society. Apparently Lenin and his followers did not know these things!

As a matter of fact, the development of organized education in the Soviet Union is probably without precedent in the whole history of mankind. The party has endeavored from the early twenties to marshal all the forces of organized education, including all agencies for the molding and the informing of the minds of both young and old, to achieve its purposes and advance toward its distant apocalyptic goal of communism. And here, apart from the dictatorship itself, is the key to the understanding of the growth of this mighty colossus. If this had not happened, we would not be greatly concerned about events taking place in the Soviet Union. "The Theses of the Central Committee," to which reference has already been made, includes the following statement: "Before the revolution there were 9,656,000 pupils in general educational schools of all kinds, and in 1966 – 48,170,000; in tsarist Russia there were 127,000 students in higher schools, and in 1966 in the USSR – 4,123,000. In 1966 there were 124,000 mass libraries, that is, nine times more than before the Great October Revolution. The press, the radio, the cinema, and television have received broad development, being mass means of informing and uniting the workers for cultural values, a dynamic agency of communistic education."

Communist spokesmen, whether inside or outside the Soviet Union (except the Chinese and a few others), never tire of praising in the most extravagant terms the Soviet system of education. It is the "most advanced in the world"; it expresses the most fully developed "ideological convictions"; it rests on "scientific foundations"; it assures the "harmonious development of the intellectual, moral, esthetic, and physical powers" of the individual; and it is committed without reservation to the great cause of "peace, democracy, and the liberation of oppressed peoples everywhere." And a recent edition of the approved textbook on the theory and practice of Soviet education for the training of secondary school teachers closes with these words: "The system of people's education in the Soviet Union has no equal in the entire world." It has certainly been a formidable factor in the historic struggle between two worlds — in that "most ferocious struggle," according to Konstantin Simonov, a distinguished dramatist, "between two systems, between two world outlooks. between two conceptions of the future of mankind (which) has been, is being, and will be waged in the world." In reading these essays one must realize that education is not an autonomous process, everywhere the same and governed by its own laws. In fact, unless imposed by force from without, it is always an expression of a particular society and culture at a particular time in history. Consequently, there is little in our American experience to prepare us to understand the education of the strange social order which has risen beyond the Vistula during this century. Though carrying the banners of European Marxism, it has been profoundly molded by the deeply rooted traditions of Russian absolutism and revolutionary movements of the nineteenth century. The problem is complicated further by the dynamism of Soviet education. Although the system is marked by certain enduring features, it has probably changed more swiftly and profoundly since 1917 than any other educational system in a like period of time.

Another source of difficulty, therefore, is change — change not only in quantity but also in quality or substance. So great have been the changes in the realm of curriculum content, moral emphases, methods of teaching, concepts of discipline, and pupil-teacher relationships that the observer would be justified in concluding that a revolution or counterrevolution had occurred. Indeed, certain ideas and practices during the rule of Stalin in the thirties and forties would have been regarded as counterrevolutionary in the decade of the twenties. Many of the outstanding educators of the earlier period were sent to the forced labor camps. If some Rip Van Winkle, on quaffing the favorite drink of the Russians in place of the schnapps of the ghosts of Henry Hudson and his companions, had fallen into a deep sleep in 1927 after visiting a Soviet school, had slept for only ten years, and then on waking had returned to the same school, he would have been quite as bewildered as Washington Irving's hero was on

discovering that his wife was dead, his cronies gone, the American Republic launched, and himself forgotten. Except for the Russian language, the glorification of the Great October Revolution, the commitment to a materialistic world view, the luxuriant whiskers of Marx and the neatly trimmed beard of Lenin, the enduring physical structures of buildings and desks, and perhaps the red scarves of the Young Pioneers, he would have found himself moving amid almost totally strange surroundings. Then, following the death of Stalin in 1953 and Khrushchev's secret speech at the Twentieth Party Congress in 1956, Soviet education entered a new period in its history. In November 1958, the Central Committee published a resolution containing forty-eight theses entitled "On Strengthening the Ties of the School with Life and on the Further Development of the System of Public Education in the Country." This event revived some of the ideas of the twenties and marked another great shift in Soviet education.

In spite of the changes, however, perhaps the most fundamental and distinctive features of the Soviet system of education have survived the passing of the years. These are concerned with the role of education in society, the scope of the educational undertaking, the locus of power and authority, and, finally, the distant social goals of education. Each of these features will be briefly examined.

The role of education in the Soviet Union is essentially and profoundly political. Standing on the foundations of their version of the historical materialism of Marx and Engels, Soviet authorities subscribe unreservedly to the dogma that throughout history organized education has been the handmaiden of politics; that the very idea of the school standing outside politics is, in the words of Lenin, "a lie and a hypocrisy"; that, since the dissolution of primitive society, education has always been the servant of the ruling class; that this was the condition in the slaveholding states of antiquity and in the feudal order of the Middle Ages, and that it is the condition of contemporary capitalist society everywhere, regardless of differences in political forms and ideologies. The true.

Bolshevik scoffs at the very idea of "freedom in education" in any "bourgeois state." In fact he would say that capitalism inevitably establishes some form of totalitarian rule.

The way in which education is conceived in the Soviet Union was outlined with utter clarity by Lenin in a passage which is more widely quoted today than when he was alive. "In the field of public education," he wrote, "the Communist Party sets itself the aim of concluding the task, begun by the October Revolution of 1917, of converting the school from a weapon for the class domination of the bourgeoisie into a weapon for the destruction of this domination, as well as for the complete destruction of the division of society into classes. The school must become a weapon of the dictatorship of the proletariat." Stalin, as was his habit, put the matter even more bluntly in a conversation with H. G. Wells in 1934. "Education," he said, "is a weapon whose effect depends on who holds it in his hands and at whom it is aimed." This means that the teacher is regarded as a soldier in the great battle for the ultimate victory of Communism both at home and abroad. In fact, Andrei Zhdanov, second only to Stalin in the party hierarchy at the time, told the assembled literary writers on August 21, 1946, that "all of our ideological workers are standing today in the advanced line of fire." For any one of these workers, including the teacher, to refuse to use his weapon, whether voice, pen, or textbook, would be to betray the Soviet Motherland. While conditions have moderated somewhat since the downgrading of Stalin, education is certainly viewed today in the Soviet Union as a powerful weapon. This means that education is regarded more seriously there than it ever has been in the United States.

The scope of Soviet education is a matter of great importance. Ask almost any American what education is, and he will almost invariably respond by identifying it with the work of the school. The assumption seems to be that the younger generation of the human species received no education until the invention of the school a few thousand years ago. This, of course, is nonsense. In actuality, education involves the entire process of inducting the young into the life of the group or society. And one of the first impressions gained by a visitor to the Soviet Union or a student of Soviet cultural affairs is that organized education is extremely broad in conception. As a matter of fact, it embraces the entire cultural apparatus, all of the agencies involved in the molding and the informing of the minds and hearts of both young and old. It includes, of course, the regular school system from the nursery, the nursery school, the kindergarten, the ten-year school of general education, and the university and scientific institute, as well as a wide range of schools designed to give specialized training at different occupational levels. Indeed, it includes two other systems of schools, one for the training of officers in the armed forces, and the other for training party members. It also includes universities for training Communist leaders in other countries, people's universities for the education of adults, atheist institutes or seminaries, schools for preparing young people for parenthood, etc. But it also includes the press in all of its forms and manifestations — the newspaper, the periodical, the book, the library, the bookstore, and even the lowly calendar. Then there must be added the newer media of mass communication, such as the radio and television, and the agencies of entertainment and amusement — the theater, the moving picture, the circus, the playground, the club, the museum, and the public park. It includes the works of literature, music, graphic art, science, scholarship, and philosophy. It includes the political and cultural potentialities of all organizations, and particularly professional unions and organizations for children and youth. It even includes the process of oral persuasion which, through the activities of a disciplined party membership of about 12 million, reaches the most distant villages and the far borders of the Union. One should also not overlook the role of the forced labor or "corrective" labor camps, which involved millions of persons during the rule of Stalin. Even economic institutions, factories, collective farms, mines, and so forth, are regarded as educational institutions.

This brings our analysis to the third characteristic feature of Soviet education – the locus of power and authority. Who holds this powerful weapon or battery of weapons in his hands? The answer to this question is implicit in much that has already been presented. In design, the pattern of control is monolithic. Regardless of the forms of administration, which recognize the organs of the Soviet government and the political divisions and subdivisions of the country, actual control of this vast educational system and program in all crucial matters rests squarely in the hands of the Communist Party of the Soviet Union and its powerful Central Committee. Moreover, neither the citizens nor the ordinary party members take any part in the process of decision-making, unless they are invited to do so. Teachers and educators as such are essentially technicians who translate into practice the general and specific directives formulated by the party leadership. This does not mean that they may not on occasion influence that leadership; but when they do, they must take care lest they overstep the shifting boundaries imposed by the totalitarian nature of the Bolshevik state. The history of Soviet education is strewn with the wrecked lives of teachers, leading educators, and even distinguished writers who for one reason or another found themselves convicted or suspected of espousing "counterrevolutionary" doctrines or of failing to follow with visible enthusiasm changes in the party line. To be sure, the severity of the dictatorship has varied from time to time. Certainly there has been considerable moderation of the process of control since the close of the Stalin era.

A few words should be said about the nature of the Communist Party. It is not a political party at all in terms of the traditions and practices of free societies. It is in fact a kind of political army designed to rule the country and shape its future. In the opinion of the present writer, moreover, it derives, for the most part, not from Marx and Engels, but from a Russian revolutionary tradition reaching back to the beginning of the nineteenth century. The nature of the party was clearly indicated in these words by Lenin: "There could be any number of political parties in Russia on one condition. The Communist Party must be in power and all other parties must be in jail." Certainly, the shortest road to prison in the Soviet Union would be an attempt to launch a rival political party. This conception of the role of the party was made unequivocally explicit by the Central Committee after the "downgrading" of Stalin by Khrushchev at the Twentieth Congress in February 1956. Apparently some Soviet citizens got the idea that the political system might be fundamentally changed in the direction of political liberty. Such heresies were quickly squelched by a powerful editorial in the July 6, 1956, issue of Pravda, official organ of the Central Committee, entitled "The Communist Party – the Inspirer and Leader of the Soviet People." The key sentence in the long editorial reads as follows: "As for our country, the Communist Party has been, is, and will be the sole master of the minds, the voice of the thoughts and hopes, the leader and organizer of the people in their entire struggle for Communism." Here is a typical letter from the people which appeared in the issue of Pravda, March 10, 1960: "The Communist Party correctly expresses that which the people feel, toward which the masses of the people are striving. The party marches at the head of the masses and, like a searchlight, illuminates for them the way. Its ideas are the progressive ideas of the age, the expression of the thoughts and hopes of the people. To it, as to the sun, are drawn the honest and progressive people of the entire earth." And it is stated over and over again that the members of the party are "our best people."

This brings the account to the most important question about Soviet education, or education in any country or society in the world: What are its goals? The answer to this question for the Soviet Union, at least in terms of the professed goals, is not difficult. They can be divided into two categories – the major political goals and the subsidiary goals.

The great political goals are three. The first is the building of a Communist society in the Soviet Union, the society of which the "best people in all ages have dreamed," a society in which the guiding principle will be: "From each according to his ability, and to each according to his needs." The second goal is to overtake and surpass America in science and technology. In 1927, the year before the launching of the First Five-Year Plan, the party issued the following slogan: "We must strive in the shortest possible historical period to overtake and surpass the most advanced capitalist countries and thus insure the victory of socialism in its historic competition with the system of capitalism." The present writer in 1929 asked G. F. Grinko, Vice-President of the State Planning Commission, whether they had any particular country in mind. He smiled and said: "You know. The United States of America." The third great goal is, of course, the triumph of Communism throughout the world. And this was expressed with Utopian vision in the great slogan proclaimed at the Twenty-second Congress of the Party in October 1961: "Communism will assure on the earth Peace, Labor, Liberty, Equality, Fraternity, and Happiness of all peoples." The textbook in social science taught in the last year of the secondary school devotes a section to each of these six ideals. And the slogan has been repeated continuously in both the general and pedagogical press. It is repeated in an editorial in Pravda on August 17, 1967, under the title of "The Revolutionary Humanism of October." Obviously the party is endeavoring to appropriate the great ideals of the American and French revolutions.

The subsidiary goals are designed to direct the full power of education toward the achievement of the great political goals mentioned in the preceding paragraph. They include the liquidation of illiteracy, the development of the talents of the "growing generation" ("our future"), the mastery of science and technology, and the inculcation of the doctrines of scientific atheism. That their achievements in each of these areas, except perhaps the last, have been remarkable has been clearly demonstrated. But the major subsidiary goal, a truly major goal, is the creation of the New Soviet Man, a type of man that has never existed at any time or place in the past. And this will require the transformation

of human nature. The idea has its roots in the Russian revolutionary tradition and was clearly expressed by Peter N. Tkachev (1844-1885), who was characterized by Professor Michael Karpovich, one of our most distinguished scholars in Russian history, as a "forerunner of Lenin." According to Tkachev, the revolutionary minority, after overthrowing the old order with the help of the people, would take all power into its own hands, transform or abolish all social institutions, and proceed to build a Communist society. In this process the long-time task would be "to reeducate man and change his very nature." Moreover, this task could only be performed by "people who are intellectually and morally developed, that is, by a minority. By virtue of its high intellectual development, this minority always has and always must exercise intellectual and moral power over the majority." This sounds very much like the voice of Lenin and his Bolsheviks. In fact, in response to a question by the present writer in 1929 about the purpose of Soviet education, a most distinguished educator replied, without smiling: "We are going to change the character of the Soviet people."

Uchitel'skaia gazeta, the most widely distributed pedagogical organ in the Soviet Union, anticipating the adoption by the party, at its Twenty-second Congress in October 1961, of the 50,000-word program for the future, published in red letters the following declaration on its front page in the issue of August 31, 1961:

"On the Foundation of Communist Morality Rests the Struggle for the Strengthening and the Achievement of Communism.-V. I. Lenin."

The Ethical Code of the Builder of Communism

According to the party, the ethical code of the builder of Communism includes the following moral principles:

1. Devotion to the cause of Communism, love of the socialist Motherland, of the countries of Socialism.

2. Conscientious labor for the welfare of

society: he who does not work shall not eat.

3. Care of each for the guarding and expansion of public property.

4. High consciousness of social duty, intolerance of violation of social interests.

5. Collectivism and comradely aid: each for all and all for each.

6. Humane relations and mutual respect among people: person to person – friend, comrade and brother.

7. Honesty and truthfulness, moral purity, simplicity and modesty in social and personal life.

8. Mutual respect in the family, care for the rearing of children.

9. Irreconcilability toward injustice, parasitism, dishonesty, careerism.

10. Friendship and brotherhood of all peoples of the USSR, intolerance of national and racial hostility.

11. Irreconcilability toward the enemies of Communism, the cause of peace, and freedom of peoples.

12. Brotherly solidarity with the toilers of all countries, with all peoples.

Here is clearly outlined the image of the New Soviet Man. However, a fundamental commandment usually included in pedagogical discussions of "education in Communist morality" is omitted: "Love of and loyalty to the party." The point is commonly emphasized that if one loves the Motherland, one must love the party, because the latter is dedicated to serving the former. To what extent the New Soviet Man is actually being created cannot be known as long as the dictatorship endures. But we must realize that this is, in a sense, the must crucial goal of Soviet education as conceived by the party, even more important than the mastery of science and technology. For the leaders know that, if they fail here, the creation of the ideal society will be impossible. Here is the basic challenge of Soviet education, a challenge which reverberates throughout the world.

In the achievement of its goals, the party is placing great emphasis on the social sciences. This policy is clearly expressed in a quotation from a 4,000-word editorial in the issue of Pravda for August 22, 1967, a pronouncement by the Central Committee at the Party entitled "On Measures for the Further Development of the Social Sciences and the Raising of Their Role in the Building of Communism." It concludes with the following significant declaration: "It is the duty of the social sciences to develop broad scientific and mass-propagandistic work, resting on the foundations of the decisions of the Twenty-third (1966) Congress of the Communist Party of the Soviet Union." For the achievement of its goals the party is placing ever greater responsibility on the social sciences which are based on the ideas of Marxism-Leninism, often referred to as the "science of the sciences."

A final word should be said about the importance of the essays in this volume for the development of understanding of the nature of Soviet education and of Soviet society. They have been selected with care and understanding by Mr. Ablin from a great mass of articles published over the years in Soviet Education. And they were not written for the American reader. This fact adds greatly to their value. It is to be hoped, of course, that some Soviet editor will publish a companion journal composed of articles written by American educators. More communication between the peoples of the two most powerful nations in the world today is greatly to be desired.

Soviet Youth

Literatura v shkole, 1964, No. 5

L. S. Aizerman

CONTEMPORARY LITERATURE THROUGH THE EYES OF UPPER-GRADE PUPILS

We still do not know our pupil well, his interests and his tastes, the peculiarities of his perception of works of art, his attitude toward what is done in class. And without all this it is very difficult to teach literature and simultaneously to see to the upbringing of the pupils and their instruction.

"Study of the influence of the collective on the personality should be added to the investigations of other forms of social influences on the masses, such as, for example, the influence of belles-lettres, periodicals, movies, radio, television, and propaganda lectures. This has particularly great significance for pedagogy, for the work of rearing the rising generation. Not knowing exactly what radio programs the students listen to, what television programs please them, and how they perceive movies, it is difficult to mold esthetic tastes and a scientific world outlook, and to bring them up as collectivists." (1)

Compositions by Moscow students on the theme "Which of the Works of Contemporary Soviet or Foreign Literature I Like the Most and Why" provide interesting material for characterizing the literary sympathies of upper-grade pupils, their attitudes toward contemporary literature and their understanding of it.

This theme, among four others, was proposed in February 1964 by the Moscow Department of Public Education and the Moscow Advanced Teacher Training Institute as a city composition in the 9th to 11th grades. The compositions were written in all the districts of the city and in several schools of each district.

Written with the passionate directness peculiar to youth, these compositions also make it possible to judge the quality of the teaching of literature in the schools. Its task is to develop artistic taste, to teach the students to read literature, and to understand it fully. The extent to which the pupil studied and understood Gogol and Tolstoy can best be judged by how he perceives and evaluates the work of K. Simonov, A. Solzhenitsyn, K. Paustovskii, and D. Granin. Knowledge is tested in practice. And in our work, practice is independent reading.

At our disposal are 1,139 compositions on the theme "Which of the Works of Contemporary Soviet or Foreign Literature I Like the Most and Why." We shall try to be brief in our comments. Let the pupils speak more for themselves. And we shall not argue with them on each occasion: this must be done in class. Our main purpose here is to understand the pupils: what they like in literature and why.

Discovery of the World

What does the upper-grade pupil look for in a book? What does he expect from it? "I want to know life, people and myself"; this expresses concisely the thought of a great many of the authors of compositions. To see, unnoticed, to understand while still not being clear, to investigate one's surroundings and one's self — this is what the young reader wants; for him, a book is first of all an artistic investigation of reality.

"What do I seek in books, what interests me? Oh, many, many things. And, certainly, you can't enumerate them all. In the first place, of course, people. What are they like? How do they relate to each other, what do they think about, what do they live for? What are 'good' people and what 'bad'? Which should be taken as examples and which not? And, in general: 'Just what is good and what is bad?' And again: Why are they so?" (2)

"Each literary work pursues two aims: first, to make the invisible visible, and, second, to make men think about these invisible or, often, simply unnoticed aspects of life."

That is why, when the upper-grade pupils give their reasons for naming a particular book as the work which they liked most of all, they write first of all about what they learned about life from having read it.

"I read many books about the war and saw many movies. But only after having read The Living and the Dead [Zhivye i mertvye] did I understand at what price victory was gained."

"To read the novel (the reference is to Silence [Tishina] — L. A.) is an extraordinarily interesting experience. And not only because the subject and the fortunes of the heroes are interesting, but because the times themselves are interesting too; one wants to learn more about them, to understand them better."

"I could not conceive until then (until having read Salinger's novel Catcher in the Rye [Nad propast'iu vo rzhi] — L. A.) of a young American who could love Burns. I thought that they all loved baseball, that in the evenings they sat in bars and paid very little attention to the fact

that poetry and young children exist in the world."

In a composition about Paustovskii, a pupil wrote emotionally and poetically about the significance of a book which reveals the world and teaches one not only to look, but also to see, not only to listen, but also to hear.

"A man lived in a great city. Each day he walked along the streets. The man hurried; he had no time to look around him. He, of course, knew that there were strange lands in the world and fantastic plants. But he was a serious man; he had no time to think about that. But then Paustovskii enters his life. He brings with him the white nights of Leningrad, the white and transparent woods of Scandinavia, the warm, caressing mists of the Baltic, the gaily colored days and the nights, black as soot, of Odessa, the quiet bashful nature of Meshcher. He brings people with him: fishermen and writers, meteorologists and pilots, sailors and artists, gardeners and actors, urchins and scholars — all such romantics as he himself. And the serious man can no longer go along the streets, hurrying and not looking about. He is infected by romanticism. He sees how deficient his life was, how much of beauty he cast out of his life; he cast out that without which in the end it is impossible to be happy...."

"It is a shame to admit, but previously I skipped over the descriptions of nature in books. But reading Paustovskii, you sense the salty smell of the sea, you hear how 'the first drops of rain beat upon the elastic leaves of the lilac,' you feel the piercing Northern wind. Perhaps this sounds too grandiloquent, but, on my word of honor, my heart stops beating at such words as these: 'All the beauty in the world I would give away for the willow bush, wet from the rain, on the sandy bank of the Oka.' I have never been on the Oka, but this willow bush, this sandy bank, I see as clearly as if I had passed my whole life on this bank.... My life can be divided into two parts: the period up to the time I read Paustovskii, and my life after."

To see the world in all its complex diversity, to understand people, to introspect — this is not only a natural desire of youth to understand their environment. To see the world in order to make it better; to understand people in order truly to be friends with them and passionately to struggle with them; to look into one's self in order to develop oneself — this is what the students write about in their compositions, which distinguishes the citizen's personal involvement, the citizen's enthusiasm for personal participation and personal responsibility. In this respect, the compositions on the narrative by A. Solzhenitsyn, One Day in the Life of Ivan Denisovich [Odin den' Ivana Denisovicha], are characteristic.

"In order to truly understand what a terrible thing it is when people begin to create gods and what a tragedy this can become for the nation, the youth need such books as One Day in the Life of Ivan Denisovich. They evoke many arguments, thoughts and conclusions, and the main one is: 'This must not happen again!'"

"I will say honestly that for me this narrative was not only a revelation, but, to a certain degree, a blow. Perhaps I am not right, but it seems to me that this narrative, One Day in the Life of Ivan Denisovich, is an appeal directly to us, to the youth. We must not allow this a second time; we are obligated to know where this can lead."

To understand in order to construct life better; to know in order to be able to organize it wisely and humanely:

"In a year and a half we tenth-graders will finish school, our childhood will end, the time will pass when adults decided all matters, big and small, for us. We will enter into an independent life. It is said that a life to live is not a field to cross over. But, surely, even a field can be crossed in different ways: it is possible to walk along the edges of pits and hummocks, or one can go straight across. And so with life: one wants to set a direct course, so that the conscience may never be tormented that somewhere the soul was twisted.

"A great many works are devoted to the young generation. We will learn from them; they will help us in the future not to make mistakes and to go along the right path, to find our 'place in life.' For this, I like the writers who tell of boys and girls who are entering or have already entered into life"; thus begins a composition on the story

by V. Aksenov, Colleagues [Kollegi]. This approach to literature determines the attitude not only toward books which deal with yesterday's students entering into the larger world. Here are some interesting reflections from a composition on K. Simonov's novel The Living and the Dead.

"Before this, I had read a great deal about the war, but I imagined it to be completely different .... Simonov's book changed my attitude in many ways toward that terrible grief through which the whole nation, the whole land, lived while repelling the barbaric attack of the fascists.... I have often heard it said by people of the generation that lived through the revolution and then through the war, that modern youth does not value and cannot evaluate the great feat which our fathers performed. In my opinion, this is not true. It is simply a prejudice. I do not doubt that we, too, are capable of such feats.... Among us there are petty bourgeois, scoundrels and Philistines, but, indeed, when didn't they exist? And how would it be if all books brought as much to us as the books by Simonov!"

The author of this composition did not express his thought with sufficient clarity. But this thought is comprehensible: it is not true that the Philistines, the petty bourgeois, and the scoundrels define the character of our generation; it is not true that we cannot evaluate our fathers' feat; but we would value it all the more if it were always recounted to us as truthfully and convincingly as Simonov did.

The students' aspirations and ideals also characterize their attitude toward the heroes to whom they have given their sympathies in the books they have read. Our upper-grade pupils are attracted to strong, honest, manly, noble heroes. Serpilin, Bakhirev, Krylov, Sasha Zelenin, Andrei Sokolov, Sergei Vokhminstev, Naval Captain Buinovskii — these are the ones they named when writing about heroes close to their hearts. This list, of course, could easily be expanded. The principle upon which the favorite hero is selected is important.

And here is something interesting. Even when the students write about people very far from us in many ways, they speak first of all of the genuinely human things that are close to them, the youthful readers of the Soviet Union. In this respect, the compositions on the novels of E. M. Remarque are characteristic. "Oh, Remarque," I have heard a number of times, "why do they even publish him! Constant carousals. All the time bars, wine, women. This arouses an unhealthy interest in him." I read everything that was written by the students about Remarque: the interest in the writer is healthy and the understanding is correct.

"The friendship of the three comrades arouses admiration. True friendship, without superfluous words, without loud protestations! A friend is having a hard time of it. And they help, they help, whatever it may cost them. Pat has to be taken to the doctor, and Kester does the impossible, but he carries out his mission. Pat is doing poorly, and Robbie should be with her, but for this money is necessary. The friends sell 'Karla,' their own creation and, perhaps, the only thing remaining to them. Really, is this not healthy? Indeed, let us look at many things in different ways; let us live in different worlds. This does not prevent us from valuing genuine people in whatever country they live and regardless of what language they speak. We can love, we can be friends, we can stand up for ourselves and for our friends; therefore, the heroes of this work are close to us."

No, it is not calvados and not bars that attract our children to Remarque; they seek in a book first of all positive spiritual values. Here is yet another characteristic meditation. This is about Hemingway's The Old Man and the Sea [Starik i more].

"An old emaciated man, weak and alone; it seems that he needs nothing from life, and life nothing from him. Everything has been experienced, everything has been tried, in everything there is a bitter aftertaste. But this old man, it turns out, puts up a real struggle with what he understands as his place and role in life. He is old and weak, and he envies the power and dexterity of a fish he has caught, but he firmly believes that in the end he will triumph because he is a man. Don't you experience a true feeling of pride in this understanding of the power of man? And in the words of the old man that it is possible to kill a man, but impossible to conquer and to subjugate him? Is this not a principle of life? Can't this be the program of every real man?"

And, here, in another's experience, the youthful reader seeks his own; in remote experience he finds what is close to him. This personal identification with the heroes is characteristic of many of the compositions. It is not surprising that many compositions on the works which the students liked most became not only analyses of these works, but also meditations on the times and on the students themselves. Even if these reflections are often debatable, even if the comparison of the book with their own lives is not always justified, still it is a natural desire to think of oneself when reading.

Here is a composition on Salinger's novel Catcher in the Rye.

"I feel very sorry for Holden, because he is essentially a very good person. Behind his outward display of carelessness and undue familiarity, one senses an unusually fine and tender soul, a purity of thought. It enrages him that a scoundrel corrupts the pure souls of children and disturbs their peace. He erases some obscene words written on a wall, but they appear again elsewhere. He wants to rub them off but he is unable to do so. He is indignant because he doesn't want little ones to be touched by this depravity. But this, most likely, will lead to nothing. For Holden is alone and there are hundreds of scoundrels. Looking at his conduct, it is difficult to imagine that he can change anything. He should find effective methods of struggle. But, perhaps, he will not find this path and will go downhill and become a habitué of some bar or other and, there, will cry about the vices of society.... To be truthful, I do not think he will become a scoundrel, but, as he himself says, he is a coward, and this trait could lead him to baseness. Besides that, his complete skepticism has a rather unpleasant effect. I cannot say about myself that I am distinguished by a kind of special esteem or respect for my elders, or that I am possessed by a sacred trembling when I see historical relics. But such a scornful attitude, in my opinion, is also intolerable. Most likely, this scornfulness is basically a pretense, but, nevertheless, a person should have something which he is unable, which he does not have the right, to respond to casually."

Here is a composition on the novel Goodbye, Boys [Do svidan'ia, mal'chiki] by B. Balter.

"Involuntarily, you compare yourself with those boys and girls, and, it seems, our generation matured earlier, perhaps because we saw and heard more. We know more about life than Balter's hero, and our complex understanding of life does not boil down to simple concepts of good and evil, it does not fit into a ready-made scheme — 'our generation has grown up.'"

Here is a composition on Aksenov's novel Colleagues.

"When you read about them, you think: 'But we are their contemporaries, we are younger than they by some five or six years, and we are just like them, you know. But why are we so bored? We are not dawdlers; we are interested in many things; we burst into performances of plays, even without tickets; we are carried away by literature, English, technology; we run to the exhibitions and the creative evening get-togethers; we read newspapers and...we are bored. We are bothered by our studies and by idleness; we want to live with a KPD [efficiency coefficient] of 100 per cent. We want to do something, to do something useful for our Motherland, for people. You know, we, 'the light-headed' youth, love people...."

One can disagree with what is written in these and many other papers, and, possibly, sometimes one should take issue with them. But one thing is beyond question: it is important to know not only what our student reads (this, by the way, is the easiest of all to learn), but also how he reads, how he relates to what he has read, what he ponders over, and what thoughts the book arouses in him.

"In educating the youth, it is necessary to know with what they live, with what thoughts, and what attracts them and what repels them" — this I read in one of the compositions. What is said is provocative and controversial, but essentially correct.

Reading these compositions, you understand especially well why a study of classical literature does not always satisfy our pupils. It some- times happens that for the students, classical works represent only knowledge of the past, and that during their study in school, there is no spiritual contact between the writer and his modern readers. But without this there is no genuine contact with art.

Only the Truth

One concept is encountered more often than any other in the compositions in which the boys and girls ponder over the merits of a literary work. This concept is truth. But what does truth mean to the young reader? What connotations does this concept have for him? To write truthfully, as he sees it, means not to embroider upon life.

"When you are only seventeen, you are just entering life, you still judge everything in your own way.... And, for all that, you seek answers to many questions; you seek a man no less fine than the heroes of past years, but alive and contemporary. You always expect a great deal from books. Each person has his own needs, but all expect honesty from a writer. He should just not embroider on life."

"The novel The Living and the Dead attracted me because, in it, a difficult period for the Soviet people is described directly and honestly, without any embellishment."

The upper-grade pupils believe that to write the truth means not to describe life in a facile way. This is what particularly attracted them in D. Granin's novel I Go into the Storm [Idu na grozu].

"It pleased me that the author did not go overboard when he wrote about Agatov. It seemed that at any minute the crime would be discovered, good would triumph, the guilty would be punished, and the whole effect of the work would be ruined. But here is the end, and Agatov remains with a stain on his conscience and, perhaps, no one will learn what he did."

"Having read the novel, many will most likely be astonished. What is this? Agatov at liberty and still going strong? But this is what I liked most of all in Granin's novel. We are all accustomed to the fact that, at the end of a book, good triumphs and evil is punished. This is not so in the novel I Go into the Storm. The writer as much as warns us: 'Be on guard, such Agatovs still walk among us, ready to make their way under communism, without difficulty, at someone else's expense!'"

To write the truth, in the opinion of the girls and boys, means to speak honestly and directly about the most bitter and difficult aspects of life.

"This book (One Day in the Life of Ivan Denisovich — L. A.) is difficult and terrifying to read; you do not want to believe that these things ever happened. You don't want to. But all the strength of this book lies in the fact that you believe everything in it, right up to the end — from the first to the last line."

"Steinbeck (in the novel The Winter of Our Discontent [Zima trevogi nashei] — L. A.) shows the destructive, poisonous influence of capitalist morality. It penetrates everywhere, spreads throughout the whole country, and gets into the narrowest and most remote crannies. I liked his candor in portraying his native land and the bitter truth about it. Indeed, a man must have fortitude to write in such a way about his native land."

To write the truth means to give a full-bodied, three-dimensional portrayal of life in all its variety and contradictions. It is precisely this which attracts the youth to the works of Sholokhov: "With Sholokhov everything is natural, like life itself." This is, for them, the merit of Granin's I Go into the Storm. In connection with this, it is interesting to note how the present-day student relates to the portrayal of Germans in the war. He wants to learn how the German became a fascist, why he came to wage war against us, whose son he is and whose father. That is why many of them write on The Adventures of Werner Holt [Prikliucheniiakh Vernera Khol'ta], the novel The Bridge [Most], the narrative The Passenger [Passazhirka], and the poem "The Court of Memory" [Sud pamiati].

The students strive for a many-sided cognition of the world in all its complexity and contradictions. And from us, their literature teachers, the students also expect a many-faceted investigation into life and its reflection in art (both the art of the past and of the present). Therefore, they are not satisfied by a schematic and simplified presentation of literature, in which the good and evil of the world are fitted neatly and thoughtlessly into standard pigeonholes.

One's Point of View

"There are a great many problems about which one can think and argue and this is one of the merits of Granin's novel I Go into the Storm."

"Many parts of the book are very debatable, and this is also to the author's credit. I have had occasion to argue with many persons who have read this book, and I am glad that it provoked arguments and disagreements. This means that it is real, this means that it is powerful." This is about the novel Death Calls on Engel'khen [Smert' zovetsia Engel'khen].

These statements are symptomatic. The authors of the compositions like literature which compels them to think and to debate. For them, good books are not ones that leave their spirits calm, that do not disturb their intellects or incite interesting debates and discussions.

And this is not accidental. Youth, which Pushkin so aptly named "restless," is the time for assertion of the personality, the years when, as never before or after, it is desired to unravel all the contradictions in the world, to find the exits of the labyrinths of life.

But there is more to this than just age. In the compositions, "the era and contemporary man are reflected." The aspiration for independence, the defense of one's position, and disputes with what is read and heard — all these things are a reflection, in the school compositions, of a time of good changes in our life, of its renewal and purification.

There are constant references in the compositions to newspaper and journal reviews and to opinions heard in debates and discussions. The children pay careful attention to what is said or written about books which have interested them. They listen, but they by no means always heed what they hear. When I read the compositions,

I constantly felt the passion of the arguments and discussions. The compositions defended, the compositions attacked, the compositions upheld.

"Balter, in my opinion, writes so warmly and purely about the love of Inka and Volodia. But many, on the other hand, find this thing immoral and think that it 'will corrupt our Soviet youth.' In my opinion, this is absolute nonsense. Only people with dirty minds can see anything bad in this book."

"Let us remember his touching love for Tina Karamysh. Some will object: 'Really, what love can there be between a married man and a married woman?' But G. Nikolaeva depicted this love as so touching, so pure and bright, that even the most violent opponents of this love should, in my opinion, show some feeling of sympathy for these good people."

Especially heated arguments were provoked by Solzhenitsyn's One Day in the Life of Ivan Denisovich. (But let us not forget that no matter what point of view is expressed by the students writing about Solzhenitsyn, they all named the narrative as their favorite work. We should also remember that the compositions were written at the beginning of February, when many of the things that are now said about One Day in the Life of Ivan Denisovich had not yet been printed.)

"Shukhov is a most commonplace person," we read in one of the compositions. "His range of interests is very narrow. Only one thought occupies Ivan Denisovich: to survive, no matter what happens. Life outside the camp seems to him strange and incomprehensible. Shukhov doesn't even think about why he is serving a term. This is an ordinary punitive camp. And such a man became the main hero of the tale. I can't completely understand this.... Nor is Shukhov's spiritual world rich. And here is how that day ended. What gladdened Ivan Denisovich so? He received two servings of watery soup, bought some tobacco, was not caught with a hacksaw at the gate search. These are all the cares of the main hero."

And the author of the composition contrasts Ivan Denisovich to Naval Captain Buinovskii.

"In the camp, where the wardens mock a man's will, Buinovskii found the strength in himself to defy Lieutenant Volkovoi. In this hero, Solzhenitsyn depicted a real Communist, a real fighter."

We encounter similar contrasts in other compositions, but not all share such a conception of Ivan Denisovich:

"Ivan Denisovich is not a fighter; he does not come forth with disclosures and protests. He simply remains a man. But under camp conditions this was not simply a great deal, this was everything."

And in another composition:

"I saw the people imprisoned in the camp on the most absurd, unsubstantiated charges. Some of them became despondent, lost their dignity, their human appearance, became 'bootlickers'; others mastered themselves and remained people. Shukhov is an example of such a man. He remained the same as he was before imprisonment in the camp. His sense of personal worth did not fail him. He did not start begging cigarette butts as did Fetiukov, who was the director of some enterprise. I especially like the episode of the work of the 'Zeks' during the construction of the thermal electric power station. Shukhov and the other bricklayers no longer felt the frost and the wind rushing over their heads. Ivan Denisovich worked profitably, smoothly, surmising in advance where the most mortar should be put and how to place the bricks sideways. Now everyone had only one concern — to bring in the mortar and bricks in time, so that the bricklaying would not be brought to a standstill...."

The students think, the students argue, the students talk about their opinions, their attitudes toward what they have read, and their understanding of it. Behind all this stand good changes in the teaching of literature.

That is why it is impossible to agree with those articles in which it is asserted that teaching literature in school kills independence and thinking and condemns thoughts and words to standardization.

There are hundreds of compositions. One cannot agree with the evaluations of many of them; you can dispute the teachers' reviews.

But surely this is a fact: in no case has the evaluation of a composition been lowered because the student expressed his thoughts in a nonstandard way, wrote provocatively and combatively, or defended positions which the teacher does not share.

Here are 9th-graders defending modern literature, contrasting it to the classics: "These books, which had a revolutionary trend in their time, are read now only for an understanding of the past or because they have become part of the school work. And it seems to me that I would not have lost anything if I had not read Woe from Wit [Gore ot uma]."

"At the beginning of the composition," writes a teacher in a review, "very strange views were expressed on classical literature which could serve as a basis for argument." The evaluation was not lowered.

This from two more reviews: "Interesting, although one would like to argue with you. 5." "I do not share your tastes. The narrative... does not seem to me to deserve such a high evaluation. But you wrote well, frankly, and simply. 5."

Of course, the students' independent thinking is not always and everywhere treated both with exactingness and respect. However, there are more and more thinking teachers who are educating thinking students.

* * *

A considerate and respected attitude toward the student's own opinion not only does not exclude but often presupposes the necessity of arguing with the student in a rational and convincing way; for the upper-grade pupils have not always examined the complex phenomena of life and their (also far from always profound and faithful) representation in art.

In this connection, the compositions devoted to V. Aksenov's Star Ticket [Zvezdnyi bilet] went into more detailed discussion. For our critics and, in truth, for the author himself, Star Ticket is already past. In any case, in filming the novel, the author shifted many accents. But the book lives, it is read, it is debated. And so for us, the teachers, it is not past, but present.

What in Star Ticket attracted those students who selected it as their favorite work? First of all, there was the fact that the author described characters whom the students had had occasion to meet more often in life than in art.

"A great deal has been said about the narrative Star Ticket by V. Aksenov. The thirty-year-old critics wrote about it in the same way as the forty-year-olds. They wrote with bitterness: 'The book does not reflect reality; 'the hero of the book is not a hero of our times!' And what do the seventeen-year-olds think? Did they like it? I will say directly: 'Yes — I did.' The reason is that Dimka, Galka, Iura and Alik live next door to us, they study in our school. The author showed the life of some Moscow kids who are about seventeen with startling exactness."

But it is not only, and not so much, a question of whom the author described as of how he described his heroes. Strictly speaking, we have met them before, most often in the newspapers: teddy boys [stiliagi], scum, riff-raff. No, said Aksenov in his novel, this is not all (and in many respects he is correct in this). Often all this is only external, superficial; look deeper — these are good kids. It is this rehabilitation, I would say more — this idealization — of the character which attracted part of the students. There is enthusiasm in their compositions in defense of the heroes of the narrative:

"Aksenov very correctly understood our youth. He knows that we love the sun and music, that we want to work, that we have the strength to do a great deal. To those who say that the youth of the sixties are not able to do anything, I would like to ask a question: 'Do you know anything about us, about the youth?'

"They go along the right path in life, they make mistakes, but by their actions, their views on life, it is clear that from them come real Soviet people."

"Victor was killed, but in parting he left Dimka his punched ticket. I think that whatever road in life Dimka chose, the star ticket left him by his brother would permit him to go along it with honor, and he was worthy of this gift because, despite his boyishness, he took from his brother all his best traits."

As regards the external appearance, the language, conduct and manners to be adhered to, the students' opinions differ. Some students consider that in this there is much that is superficial, temporary, on the surface:

"Here is the environment of the heroes, the inhabitants of 'Barcelona': the troublemaker Aunt El'va, the speculator Tima, the perpetually drunk yardkeeper, and the other Philistines. Such an environment gives rise to a completely legitimate protest: 'You do not recognize modern dances? Then we will dance to spite you! You object to narrow pants? Then we will wear only narrow ones,' and so forth. A primitive protest, the antithesis, gives rise to that appearance which is 'alien to us' and to an imaginary spiritual emptiness."

Other students see in everything the signs of the times, the traits of the generation:

"The awareness that it is not for nothing that they eat their bread fills their souls with pride. The fact that they, having received a secondary education, work with simple stevedores does not antagonize them. For them the consciousness of their own independence, of their own strength, is important. They are proud of their tired hands. And the fact that they look like 'fops' as usual, go to cafes in the evening and drink wine there does not lower the significance of labor in their lives. This, in my opinion, is a distinctive trait of our generation: the youth do not want to renounce pleasures, good, stylish clothes, and at the same time they do not avoid work, but, on the contrary, they seek it. It is always pleasant to realize that you are of use to people and do not live in the world for nothing."

However, even those who think that the skeptical attitude toward adults and the nihilistic perception of established traditions and views are all only temporary and superficial (and this is exactly what is shown by the hero of the novel) arrive at peculiar conclusions:

"In our house there lives a fellow. Formerly, he was the terror of the whole house. He was just like the hero of Star Ticket; once he fell in with a gang of 'fartsovshchiks.' He discussed everything with such cynicism that it was disgusting to listen to. Everyone said that this was an 'arrant type.' But, look, he finished school. He became tempered in the virgin lands. And, arriving in Moscow, he entered the Bauman Institute. I am sure that exactly the same fate awaits the hero of this tale."

Thus, there is no need to be disturbed. Foppishness, cynicism, a nihilistic attitude toward suffering humanity, a caddish impertinence — there is nothing terrible in this; it is a childhood disease and will pass.

And there is more. Authors of the compositions affirm that the "star boys" represent not only a portrayal of certain characters who actually exist, which is, of course, a correct description, but also a portrait of the better part of our youth (can it be shown that this is not so?), more than that — a picture of the life of all young people:

"The author revealed to us the real side of the life of the youth. He revealed their thoughts, aspirations, and desires. Aksenov showed the youth as they really are; nothing is omitted, nothing is concealed."

As far as criticism of the novel is concerned, it did not convince the authors of these compositions. Here is a characteristic statement:

"It happened that when I was in the library this year, I came across an article, more correctly, a review of the novel in which it was criticized in every possible way. Since I was of a completely contrary opinion, I decided to read everything that other critics had written about it. I read four or five articles; in all of them the novel is abused. These articles even outraged me a little. I reread the novel. I went more deeply into the events occurring in it, and, nevertheless, I held to my own opinion.... Judging by the articles, one might think that the critics do not know life, that they were never young or that they now have no young acquaintances, and that they do not go out on the street and never look about them."

We are speaking now about the students' perception of the novel and not about the novel itself. Of course, a one-sided and often incorrect understanding comes, in large part, from the book itself. But now it is important for us to emphasize the other aspect: the independent judgment of the students is not always a true judgment. And in order to instill genuine independence, it is not enough to teach the students to say what they think, to "have their own opinions." N. D. Moldavskaia wrote well about this: "The students' independence of judgment and appraisal of artistic works can be formed only on the basis of literary development, the development of figurative thinking, powers of observation, imagination, and a feeling for poetic language, on a firm foundation of historical and historical-literary knowledge and concepts, on the basis of a serious orientation in the already existing points of view that have been shaped in science (at the present level of its development) and in the collective experience of Soviet readers." (3)

What Is Most Popular

"Which of the Works of Contemporary Soviet or Foreign Literature I Like the Most and Why." This was how the theme suggested to the upper-grade pupils was formulated. Hitherto we have talked about how they answered the second part of the question — the why. Now that we have become clear about the criteria from which the students proceeded in naming the works which they liked most, we should speak about the books that they have named. Let us begin with the poetry.

Comparatively few wrote about poems. Of the 1,139 compositions, only 110 were devoted to poets. But two factors must be taken into consideration here. It is very difficult to write about a poet, without having his poetry at hand. And, secondly, it is more difficult to discuss poetry in a composition than prose.

About whom were the compositions written? Sixteen poets were named. There were 3 compositions on A. Voznesenskii, 3 on E. Yevtushenko, 8 on E. Mezhelaitisa, 15 on A. Tvardovskii, 17 on R. Rozhdestvenskii, 22 on the poem by E. Isaev, "The Court of Memory" [Sud pamiati],

and 32 on the poetry of E. Asadov. Let us see how the upper-grade pupils substantiated their choices.

Students were attracted to Rozhdestvenskii's poetry because it expresses "an ardent civic concern in feelings and thoughts, an aggressive romanticism." "They have in them something of Mayakovsky. But this is not the main thing. The main thing is the very great and unaffected feeling of the poet, who unites in himself both feelings of love for our motherland, and for our Revolution, and a tremendous sense of responsibility to our contemporaries, in particular, to contemporaries of our own age.... I cannot say exactly what pleases me in Rozhdestvenskii's poetry. Most of all, perhaps, I like the crystal honesty and lofty civil courage in the poet's verses."

The girls wrote about the verses of Eduard Asadov, and they wrote rapturously:

"Softly the pages rustle. Around me the words ring, fate takes its course, and feelings are expressed in song. I discover a new world, the soul of man, I am lost in reverie. Softly the pages rustle... "In the Name of a Great Love" [Vo imia bol'shoi liubvi]. Eduard Asadov."

What is attractive in the poetry of E. Asadov was described best of all by a boy — the only one among the writers on this poet:

"Why do the majority of the people, in conjunction with the word love, use the words morals, ethics? What is this? If we begin to speak about love, then, in my opinion, it is worth talking about morals too, as one newspaper did. It seems to me that morals, in the sense in which this word is now used, is a congealed and atavistic conception. Morals — most often this word can be heard from the petty bourgeois. He was born, grew up, loved, married, had children, the children grew up — this is how this citizen pictures to himself real love. This, of course, is all good, even very good, when everything turns out this way, but surely it is not always so simple. So why is it considered immoral to be divorced and moral to live with a man whom you do not love? This, perhaps, is everything and nothing, but the whole trouble is that often scoundrels and vulgar, petty people take refuge in these words. And they will say all these words with such ardor that you can't distinguish them from real men. And it is here that the concept of morals is lost. It seems to me that for morals there should be substituted sincerity. In our society, moving towards communism, sincerity is needed in everything, and first of all in love, in the relation of one person to another....

"Sincerity in everything: in poetry, in thoughts, in feelings, in actions — this is the main theme of Asadov's poetry. In his poetry, Asadov carries on an open conversation with the reader. He does not flatter, he does not embellish, he does not idealize love. But, despite this, his poetry breathes with spring and life and optimism."

It does not have to be proven that the author of this composition was taking a stand not against morals, but against the morals of the bigoted, the morals of the Philistines, the petty bourgeois representation of respectability. He is for purity and sincerity in human relations. And this sincerity is what he values in Asadov's poetry. Others also write about the same thing. That is why the students forgive the poet (or, perhaps, simply do not see?) for the artistic shortcomings of his poetry.

Now let us turn to prose. Here are the Soviet writers about whom more than ten students wrote:

M. Sholokhov — 58 (of which, 34 — Virgin Soil Upturned [Podniataia tselina], 20 — Fate of a Man [Sud'ba cheloveka], 4 — Silent Don [Tikhii Don]).

D. Granin, I Go into the Storm — 53.

Iu. Bondarev, Silence [Tishina] — 49.

V. Aksenov — 47 (of which, 28 —Colleagues, 18 — Star Ticket, 1 — Oranges from Morocco [Apel'siny iz Marokko]).

K. Simonov, The Living and the Dead — 36.

A. Solzhenitsyn, One Day in the Life of Ivan Denisovich — 34.

B. Balter, Goodbye, Boys — 29.

Chingiz Aitmatov, Tales [Povesti] — 27.

A. Fadeev, Young Guard [Molodaia gvardiia] — 23.

N. Ostrovskii, How the Steel Was Tempered [Kak zakalialas' stal'] — 22.

G. Medynskii, Honor [Chest'] — 18.

K. Paustovskii — 18.

G. Nikolaeva, Battle on the Way [Bitva v puti] — 18.

A. Andreev, Judge Us, People [Rassudite nas, liudi] — 18.

Iu. German, My Good Man [Dorogoi moi chelovek] — 15.

A. Chakovskii, Light of a Distant Star [Svet dalekoi zvezdy] — 14.

I. Efremov — 13 (Nebula of Andromeda) [Tumannost' Andromedy] — 11, Razor Blade [Lezvie britvy] — 2).

A. Kuznetsov, Continuation of a Legend [Prodolzhenie legendy] — 12.

B. Polevoi, On the Wild Shore [Na dikom brege] — 11.

As regards compositions on foreign literature (203 in all), most of them were written on the following authors:

E. M. Remarque — 30 (wrote about Remarque "generally," but in the first place named Three Comrades [Tri tovarishcha] and All Quiet on the Western Front [Na zapadnom fronte bez peremen]).

Dieter Noll, The Adventures of Werner Holt [Prikliucheniia Vernera Khol'ta] - 30.

D. Kiusak, Hot Summer in Berlin [Zharkoe leto v Berline] — 26.

John Steinbeck — 15 (of which, The Winter of Our Discontent [Zima trevogi nashei] — 13, Of Mice and Men [O myshakh i liudiakh] — 2).

Harper Lee, To Kill a Mockingbird [Ubit' peresmeshnika] — 12.

J. D. Salinger, Catcher in the Rye [Nad propast'iu vo rzhi] — 10.

As is evident from the data given, the majority of the books named by the upper-grade pupils are really good, high-quality books (this is also true of those works which are not mentioned here). In any case, the compositions completely refuted the opinion that contemporary upper-grade students prefer The Copper Button [Mednaia pugovitsa] and not The Copper Horseman [Mednyi vsadnik]. Only three compositions were devoted to Sergeant of the Militia [Serzhant militsii], and three to the novel And One in the Field Is a Warrior [I odin v pole voin]. Not more than ten votes were given to all the books of this type. And the very choice of the book says a great deal about the taste of the writers.

Especially pleasing were those compositions in which an endeavor was made to speak about the artistic originality of the work, about the peculiarities of the author's creative style. Here a girl writes about the novel Catcher in the Rye:

"The book is written in a very original and interesting manner. The story is told in the first person, and all the people and the events are interpreted through the eyes of Holden.... Not once in the whole narrative does the author attempt to evaluate Holden. He simply portrays some mad days in his life, filled with petty, seemingly disconnected events. But from these events and from fragmentary memories, Holden rises before us as a man. The language of the novel is rather coarse. It shocks respectable readers who are sure that their children do not speak and think like that. But, along with this, the book is unusually poetic, and the whole book somehow warms one inside. There are no landscapes, no vast descriptions of the city at night, no tearful scenes by the fireside. But the poetry of the novel is concentrated in Holden's soul, a pure, sensitive and easily wounded soul, which he hides behind an affected coarseness and cynicism. At first, when you are just beginning to read, the brokenness of the thoughts and details, to whose description whole pages are devoted, is somewhat startling. But then you understand: so it is in life, exactly so. The teacher talks with Holden about life, and Holden thinks about ducks on a lake and about how repugnant it is to see the white legs of an old man. Real detail, and in such quantity in the novel, and the character of Holden becomes ever more clear ...."

Here is a composition on V. Tendriakov's Short Circuit:

"Tendriakov's method of portraying events and heroes is interesting. I would like to make a small digression in order to compare various literary methods. Take Sholokhov, for example. He lives alongside his heroes. We get to know them through their deeds, through their interactions. The characterization of the hero is shaped by the hero himself. The author does not impose anything on us. Fadeev has another method. Fadeev himself judges his heroes, gives them the author's characterization, and then, as if for confirmation of their thoughts, adds their actions and interrelations. Tendriakov proceeds in quite a different way. He characterizes his heroes at the beginning with a few strokes. It is as if he himself does not know what will happen later. The characters of the heroes are completed for him by the events, in which the complete essence of the people is manifested. And only in the end do we hear the voice of the author, who judges his heroes as if passing sentence on them. All their subsequent life is absolutely clear for him and for us. I like this method very much. He compels the reader to participate actively in events."

And here is something interesting. Sometimes the student says nothing about the peculiarities of the author's style, about the peculiarities of his poetics, but by the way in which the student himself writes, by the style of his composition, you see that he really sensed the creative style of the artist to whom his composition is devoted.

"Reading these books, you become aware of the scent of fresh breezes, the riotous display of blooming lilacs, the somber beauty of the cliffs of Kara-Dag, the dazzling snow of Scandinavia, the rusty ancient earth of the Crimea, the eternal roar of the sea" — this is from a composition on Paustovskii.

"And Holden's life is not at all sweet! It seems his parents are well-off and they love their son, but there is no pleasure in life. Why is this? Even Holden cannot answer this question. He's simply very sad and depressed. He has not yet entered the mendacious and hypocritical world of adults, but he is standing on the 'precipice,' one step more and — the fall....

"Everyone who surrounds Holden, even the children, is infected with either skepticism or cold calculation. Take Sally, for example. She seems to be a gay, joyous girl, but actually she is a calculating, fully adult and prudent person. When Holden proposes that they marry and go far away to live somewhere by the side of a stream, she answers very judiciously that they will have time to marry when Holden has finished the university, and that they will go on a honeymoon somewhere more pleasant than living 'somewhere by the side of a stream.' But, please, do not think that Holden is in love with Sally!" — this is from a composition on the novel Catcher in the Rye.

However, there are comparatively few compositions in which an understanding of the artistic peculiarities of the work is expressed in some form. Perhaps this is not so strange in the present case: the theme of the composition was not announced ahead of time, and the majority of the writers did not have at hand the books which they analyzed. It is very difficult to write about the poetics of a novel without having the novel itself.

* * *

Reading the compositions, you see how much we still have to do. And together with this there is a great deal which is heartening.

The civic maturity of many of the students' papers, the good taste, the free and unfettered quality of the exposition, the honesty of thought, the picturesqueness of language — all these things give one pleasure.

A young Philadelphia teacher, David Mallory, decided to find out how the personality of a student in a contemporary American school is formed, and what influence the school has on his life and the form of his thinking. He talked with the students in a relaxed setting and, on the basis of his investigations, he wrote a book.

While talking about teaching literature and independent reading, Mallory observed "how assiduously the students discriminated between reading for school and reading for themselves." When the talk got around to what the students read for themselves, "sometimes, with an apologetic smile, someone would introduce (in a list of books which were not read for school — L.A.) such books as A Farewell to Arms [Proshchai, oruzhie] by Hemingway or Catcher in the Rye by Salinger. I asked the question: 'Why do you name these books in such a way as if to ask

forgiveness?' Some answered: 'In them, things are written about which have no place in school'; others: 'These are contemporary books; I mean to say, they are written in our times. These books are not for the ages'; still others: 'The teacher does not suggest such books.'" (4)

Mallory was acquainted with teachers who paid a great deal of attention to out-of-class reading. But, in his words, "more often. . . the students maintained that school was not the place for conversations about personal interests."

The article from which I took these statements is entitled "High School Students Speak" [Govoriat ucheniki srednikh shkol]. If you like, our account of the compositions of Soviet students might have been called the same thing. And it is pleasing that our school has become a place for conversations about personal interests, and that a teacher suggests for reading and talks those books that are close to the student and excite him.

I am glad that the study of classical literature has improved in the school. Classical? But all the compositions are about contemporary literature. Yes, but here is what the students themselves say about this:

"The main thing is that the study of literature in the school helps us to understand not only the works in the curriculum, but also all the books which we read. You are reading something quite unrelated to school work and suddenly you begin to think: 'What is unconvincing in this, why did he act in that way? How can she do this? You think about the milieu in which the heroes live, about their interrelations, and about what kind of a man the author was and what his views were on various things."

"Would I have understood all of The Living and the Dead if at the literature lessons we had not studied Tolstoy's novel War and Peace?"

"The truly excellent works of Pushkin, Lermontov and Tolstoy enabled me to examine contemporary literature and poetry." And this is actually so.

More than a thousand compositions were written. There is a great deal in them that does not satisfy, that disturbs and saddens one.

14

But it is impossible not to see the main thing: they reflect good changes in the teaching of literature in the school.

Footnotes

1) L. F. Il'ichev, "Metodologicheskie problemy estestvoznaniia i obshchestvennykh nauk," in Metodologicheskie problemy nauki, "Nauka" Publishing House, Moscow, 1964, p. 175.

2) All the compositions are quoted without stylistic corrections.

3) N. D. Moldavskaia, "Znaniia, opyt kollektiva i sobstvennoe mnenie," in Literatura v shkole, 1964, No. 2, p. 30.

4) David Mallory, "Govoriat ucheniki srednikh shkol," in Amerika, 1964, No. 92, p. 50.

Sovetskaia pedagogika, 1965, No. 8

Iu. V. Sharov

THE SPIRITUAL NEEDS OF STUDENTS IN THE UPPER GRADES

The Department of Pedagogy and Psychology of the Novosibirsk Teacher Training Institute is investigating the basic regularities in the formation of the cognitive, labor and esthetic needs of students in the upper grades, and of their attitudes toward social activity. A high level of spiritual needs is not only the most important characterological [kharakterologicheskaia] feature of a comprehensively developed and well-balanced personality, but is also the most important condition for its formation.

Marxism proceeds from the position that man's needs are formed under the influence of all aspects of social life, of which production is the decisive one. The satisfaction and development of man's needs proceed according to the degree of development of material production and social relations, including production relations in the first place. The aim of socialist production is to satisfy the material and spiritual needs of man as fully as possible. This in itself creates the objective conditions for the all-round development of the personality, of its

_____

The author is associated with the Novosibirsk Teacher Training Institute.

physical and intellectual powers.

It is known that the development of the personality is realized in the process of activity. The more intensive this activity, the more intensive is the development of the personality. An understanding of needs as felt needs, which are satisfied in the sphere of social relations, necessarily assumes their examination as a source of the personality's activity. "No one can do anything, without at the same time doing it for the sake of some of his needs" (K. Marx and F. Engels, Works [Sochineniia], Vol. 3, 1955, p. 245).

The contradictions between the child's ever growing and developing needs and the available possibilities for satisfying them are some of the most important sources of personality development. Highly developed cognitive needs stimulate the student's lively cognitive activity and his aspiration for the enjoyment of beauty; they compel him to attend concerts and the theater and to become involved in artistic groups. The higher the level of needs, the more lively and intense is the activity directed toward their satisfaction. Consequently, in taking the path of the development of the students' spiritual needs in every way possible, we thereby stimulate their activity in various types of endeavors, and this is the basic condition for the all-round and harmonious development of the personality.

In the principle of communism — "From each according to his abilities, to each according to his needs" — the interrelation and organic unity of needs and abilities are emphasized. Psychology establishes the nature and basic regularities of these ties. In his book Being and Consciousness [Bytie i soznanie], S. L. Rubinshtein emphasized that in order to form any significant abilities it is first of all necessary to create a vital need. In practice, abilities are understood precisely as those psychological features which are needed for the successful fulfillment of certain activities. Their development is realized, first of all, in the process of that activity for which they are needed. But we have already noted that needs are a source of activity and determine man's activity. This means that the presence of corresponding needs is a necessary condition for the development of abilities. Forming and developing spiritual needs, we thereby promote the development of abilities also.

Class society, the basis of which is private property, gave rise to antagonistic contradictions in the development and satisfaction of material and spiritual needs. "Greed begins," wrote A. S. Makarenko, "when the needs of one man conflict with the needs of another and when one must take joy and satisfaction away from his neighbor by force, cunning or theft" (Works [Sochineniia], Vol. 4, 1957, p. 334). Poverty, hunger, and a constant struggle for existence prevented the development and satisfaction of the toilers' spiritual interests and doomed them to darkness and ignorance. The problem of developing spiritual needs was connected with the problem of inhibiting the so-called quasi-needs, with the creation of impediments that would prevent the development of these needs in such a way that they would be in contradiction with the resources of society.

Communism envisages the development, in every way possible, of the material needs of the broad masses of people and the creation of the means for their satisfaction. However, the development of personal material needs should be realized within definite reasonable limits; they should not come into contradiction with the actual resources of the society, with the level of material and spiritual development attained. "In the beginning we must learn to work according to our abilities and to take care of the social good, and when we are producing enough and have learned to care for what we have made, then we can allow everything to go according to needs," said M. I. Kalinin (On Communist Upbringing and Instruction [O kommunisticheskom vospitanii i obuchenii], 1948, p. 61). It is precisely the unwise development of material needs that engenders money-grubbing, a craving for more wealth, parasitism, etc., which are alien to socialist society. In the period of the full-scale building of communism, the role of spiritual needs, which act as a distinctive regulator of the development of material needs, is heightened.

The communist person seeks the meaning, content and joy of life in creative labor and in the aspiration to give all his knowledge and abilities to the common good; therefore, his spiritual needs are an enormous moral force, directed to the development and perfection of man's physical and moral qualities. Consequently, the development of the Soviet student's spiritual needs is the most important means of forming him in the spirit of communist morality.

In order to develop further the spiritual needs of the growing generation, it is important to know where we must first direct our efforts, and this requires that we have data characterizing the basic tendencies in the development of the Soviet students' spiritual needs. This article presents research material that characterizes the developmental level of the spiritual needs of students in the intermediate and upper grades.

Methods of Studying the Level of Development of the Students' Spiritual Needs

In our investigation of the students' spiritual interests, we combined the methods of collecting mass material accessible to statistical treatment (questionnaires, compositions, questionnaires on daily routines, indices of school progress, examination work) and lengthy monographic observations of the students in the course of experimental work in the school, individual and group conversations, and the study of subscriptions and the students' creative work. The application of various methods made it possible to reduce the influence of accidental circumstances to a minimum, helped to disclose cause-effect relations, and strengthened the objective significance of the research itself.

In 1964 we conducted a mass survey of students, as a result of which we collected a great deal of material revealing the general level of development of the spiritual needs of students in the secondary school. In a number of schools in Novosibirsk and the Cherepanovo District, a questionnaire on "My Interests" was filled out, in order to ascertain the students' attitudes toward various school subjects and their vocational and reading interests.

In the autumn of 1964 a questionnaire on "The Student of 1964," compiled by the Laboratory of Labor Upbringing of the Institute of the Theory and History of Pedagogy of the RSFSR Academy of Pedagogical Sciences, was filled out in a number of Novosibirsk schools (with certain additions and changes). This made it possible to gather material that characterized the students' spiritual interests as a complex (cognitive, social and political interests, vocational, attitudes toward art and problems of morality, and others).

The questionnaire on "My Interests" was filled out by students in the 6th-11th grades of the Novosibirsk schools. The questionnaire on "The Student of 1964" was filled out in schools of various districts of Novosibirsk; the schools differed as regards the social makeup of the students (in Schools No. 10 and 127, children whose parents are mainly occupied with intellectual work predominate; in Schools No. 137, 157 and 110, the predominant group is children of workers from the railway junction and the large industrial enterprises). Schools No. 3 and 4 of Cherepanovo, which is essentially a

large settlement, and rural eight-year schools situated in the collective and state farms were investigated in the Cherepanovo District (in all, six schools of the district were investigated). This permitted us to compare the interests of city and rural students, brought up in families of different cultural levels, and to level, in some measure, the influence of subjective factors on the formation and development of the students' needs. In all, we processed 1,450 questionnaires on "My Interests" and 1,200 on "The Student of 1964."

The mass survey of students was usually conducted in those schools in which the department systematically studied the state of the educational and upbringing process or in schools in which student teachers practiced. Besides that, in the 1963/64 school year we collected 485 questionnaires and compositions which characterized the esthetic development of the upper-grade students and about 5,000 questionnaires on their attitudes toward professions.

In the course of processing the material collected, the necessity arose to supplement it with conversations with teachers and students and to compare certain conclusions with the observations, made over many years, of experienced teachers and of the students themselves. In the city department of public education, a discussion was conducted with a group of teachers on the theme "Do We Know the Spiritual Interests of the Students?" Certain questions were sent around beforehand as suggested topics for discussion. Twenty-five teachers participated in a relaxed exchange of opinions. After a few days, a group of 10th- and 11th-grade students was gathered from the schools of the leaders and teachers who had participated in the discussion. It was important for us to compare the views of teachers and pupils on the questions of interest to us about the formation of the students' spiritual world. Developed and active students were invited to participate in the discussion; questions analogous to those given to the teachers were suggested to them beforehand. The discussion in the city committee of the Komsomol was also frank and relaxed, and the record of it is a valuable document. Thus, plentiful material and (which is very important) material of a varied nature was collected. Analysis of it created the opportunity to reveal typical tendencies in the formation and development of the students' spiritual needs. It is very important that this material was supplemented by long-term observations made by the department personnel.

The Students' Cognitive Interests

The formation of the need for knowledge is one of the most important tasks of pedagogy and the school. The development of the growing generation's intellectual abilities depends in large measure on its successful solution, as does the rearing of an active and energetic citizen and member of communist society, and the overcoming of the school's chronic disease — the repeating of grades. Starting in 1959, the Department of Pedagogy and Psychology of the Novosibirsk Teacher Training Institute has been systematically studying the students' attitudes toward various school subjects and the paths of development of their cognitive interests. (1) What characterizes the general educational interests of the modern Soviet student? What are the students' attitudes toward various school subjects and what motivates these attitudes?

The questionnaire on "My Interests" gave basic material on this question. In addition to revealing interests in general educational subjects, the questionnaire was also designed to elucidate the students' vocational interests and their relation to cognitive interests. The questions were composed in such a way that the students did not give simple answers, but disclosed their motives. The questionnaire included the following questions:

1. What school subjects interest you the most and why?

2. What school subject does not interest you and why?

3. What subject would you like to have more information about than is presented in the textbook? Why?

4. In what branch of knowledge (or activity) would you like to work in the future? Why?

5. When did your interest in this branch arise, and in what connection? Is your choice final?

6. Why did you come to study in the secondary school, and not in a technical school [tekhnikum] or college [uchelishche]? If you entered a technical school (or college), which would it be, and what would prompt you to enter it?

7. What pursuits do you like to engage in during out-of-class time?

8. What study groups do you, or would you like to, participate in?

9. What do you like to read about?

If the question was posed to the student: "What school subjects interest you the most?," he had to explain why. If the student reported that he entered secondary school or a technical school after completing the eight-year school, he had to explain why he made that choice. Posing the question in this way conditioned a serious attitude on the part of the students toward filling out the questionnaire and encouraged detailed answers.

It is very important to emphasize the interrelation of the individual questions: each question supplemented and corrected the preceding one. Nor is it difficult to notice that the questions revealed the general direction of the students' interests and the interrelation of general-educational and vocational interests and inclinations. In all, 930 questionnaires were analyzed (the remaining 500 were eliminated); 310 questionnaires of students of each grade (6th, 8th and 10th) were taken for comparison. In addition, material presented in the questionnaire on "The Student of 1964" was utilized (8th, 9th and 10th grades of Schools No. 7, 10, 110, 127, 137, and 157).

The questionnaire on "My Interests," which contains a limited number of questions directed toward ascertaining cognitive and vocational interests, gave the more valuable material for revealing the sources and causes of the origin, development, or abatement of interests. (The results obtained from processing these questionnaires are presented in Table 1.)

Analysis permits us to reveal the basic

Table 1

Dynamics of the Development of Students' Interest in Individual School Subjects*

Subjects	Grades											
	6th (310 students)				8th (310 students)				10th (310 students)			
	+	·	−	0	+	·	−	0	+	·	−	0
Russian language	24	5	5	2	15	2	4	0.6	-	-	-	-
Literature	29	10	1	2	47	19	-	9	48	21	6.5	-
History	32	18	3	3	26	8.5	6.5	1.6	32	15	10	-
Geography	26	13	9	4	25	13	3.6	4.3	10	1.6	18	-
Biology	27	6	6	8.5	9.5	3.5	26	3.6	8	3.6	1.6	-
Chemistry	-	-	-	-	24	15	5	10	29	14	14	-
Physics	24	15	4	10	40	23	16	19	40	30	2.6	-
Mathematics	44	13	12	10	30	10	5	9.5	55	20	6	-
Foreign language	18	8	22	4	16.6	6	19	3	12	6.6	6.5	-
Drafting	-	-	-	-	5	1	4.5	0.3	-	-	-	-
Drawing	5	0.3	13	0.3	0.6	-	0.6	-	-	-	-	-
Singing	6	-	9.5	1	4.5	-	8	0.3	-	-	-	-
Physical culture	18	1	2.5	1	23	0.3	3	1	20	2.6	4	-
Labor; production training	6	-	1	1	6.5	0.3	1.6	6.6	13.5	1.6	23	-
Astronomy	-	-	-	-	0.6	0.9	0.3	0.3	-	-	-	-

Conventional signs: Elementary academic interest — " + ". Subjects which interest the students (they would like to know more than is given in the textbook) — " · ". Uninteresting subjects — " − ". No answer — " 0 ".

Remarks. Calculations made in percentages of the number of answers (approximately).

*Statistical processing done by V. P. Gribanov.

tendencies in the attitudes of students in the 6th, 8th and 10th grades toward different school subjects:

1. A comparatively high level of interest in physics and chemistry is noted, and it increases in the upper grades. There is an upward trend in the number of students who indicate that physics and chemistry are the most interesting subjects and of those who want to go more deeply into these subjects than the school does. Thirty percent of the 10th-graders write of their desire to study physics more deeply.

2. Literature and mathematics occupy first place among other school subjects in the 8th, 9th and 10th grades, while there is a noticeable tendency for the students' interest in literature to rise from the intermediate to the upper grades (from 29% in the 6th grade to 48% in the 10th grade; in the questionnaires on "The Student of 1964," the number of such testimonials increased up to 55% in the 10th grade). The growth of interest in literature is also corroborated by the answers to the question concerning the school subject which the students would like to have more information about than is presented in the textbook. The number of students who wish to study literature more intensively than the lessons and textbooks allow also grow steadily from the 6th to the 10th grades (from 10 to 21%). There are very few students who regard

literature as an uninteresting subject.

3. Interest in history is maintained at approximately the same level (6th, 8th and 10th grades, respectively — 32%, 26%, 32%). However, in some schools the interest in the study of history declines in the upper grades. The number of students who wish "to know more than is presented in the textbook" decreases (from 18% to 8.5% in the 6th and 8th grades, respectively), and the number of students who declare that history is an uninteresting subject increases (from 3% to 10%).

4. The lowering of interest in biology (from 27% in the 6th grade to 8% in the 10th grade) is even more distinct. It is characteristic that the number of students in the 9th grade who are interested in biology falls to 0.8% (according to data from the questionnaires on "The Student of 1964"). The decline in interest in biology is accompanied by a sharp growth in the number of students who regard biology as an uninteresting subject (6% and 27.7% in the 6th and 8th grades, respectively).

5. The number of students who have a great interest in foreign languages is insignificant, and even here there is a more or less distinct tendency toward a lowering of interest from the intermediate to the upper grades (from 18.3% in the 6th grade to 6.5% in the 10th grade). The group of students expressing an opposite tendency is also significant: in the 6th and 8th grades about 20% of the students put foreign languages among the uninteresting subjects; however, the number of such students decreases by the 10th grade.

6. The level of interest in subjects of the esthetic cycle is generally low. In the 6th grade, only 6% of the students noted their enthusiasm for singing lessons, while 10% put singing among the uninteresting studies. Only 15 of 310 students in the 6th grade (5%) noted a heightened interest in drawing, while 41 persons (about 13%) declared a negative attitude toward it. In the 8th grade, only two students called drawing an interesting subject.

7. The number of students who regard the lessons in labor and production training with interest is also not great (approximately 5% in the 6th grade and 8% in the 10th grade).

What are the reasons for the students' various attitudes toward the subjects studied? They are revealed through the motives by which the students explain their positive or negative attitudes toward them. Let us dwell, first, on the motives for the students' positive attitudes toward given school subjects. Through a sampling of questionnaires, we succeeded in establishing the following groups of motives: the cognitive-educational and practical significance of the subject studied; the fascinating content of the school subject itself; good teaching; the social significance of the science.

We compared the answers of 6th- and 8th-grade students from Schools No. 3 and 4 in Cherepanovo, from the Mamonovo Eight-Year School in the Cherepanovo District, and from Schools No. 42 and 172 in Novosibirsk (213 questionnaires). Analysis established that there is no fundamental difference in the nature of the cognitive interests of students in city, city settlement, and rural schools. Besides that, the answers of all 10th-graders were analyzed.

Most often, the students' positive attitudes toward a subject are motivated by its cognitive-educational and practical significance and the prospects for the development of the science. This motive is advanced mainly by students manifesting a special interest in the physical and mathematical sciences. These are the most typical expressions by students of various grades: "Chemistry interests me because it has a great future and life demands the general application of this science" (School No. 4, Cherepanovo, 8th grade). "Physics interests me especially. All modern technology and all production are constructed on the basis of physics. And radioengineering? And conquest of the cosmos? And atomic energetics? A science with the greatest prospects!" (School No. 42, Novosibirsk, 10th grade). It is characteristic that many students maintain an interest in physics, chemistry, and mathematics even when the level of teaching in these subjects is not sufficiently high. There is no doubt that all this is explained by the influence of the enormous achievements in these fields of science.

Many students explain their interest in the subject studied by the content of the science itself. Such a motive is most frequently advanced by students with a heightened interest in the humanities, and, above all, in creative literature. The answers indicate that literature interests present-day students to a greater degree than students of 1959, that they often find answers to the problems of life which are bothering them in creative literature, and that it has become, to a greater (although evidently inadequate) degree, a source of esthetic enjoyment for them. Whereas in the first years of the school's reorganization the overwhelming majority of students noted a positive attitude toward physics and mathematics and a minority wrote of a positive attitude toward literature and history, now the situation has changed.

The majority of students in the upper grades realize the enormous and vital significance of the humanities and their role in man's spiritual life. The students' answers speak of this: "I love literature. Why? This is difficult to answer, of course. Perhaps because it is a very vital subject that reflects the epoch and people's views, that helps one to understand life, and that reveals human nature more than other subjects. A man of letters must know everything; he should be roundly developed" (School No. 10, 10th grade). "Social science, literature, and history prepare us for life much more than the other subjects" (School No. 120, 10th grade). There is no doubt that this change is a consequence of the abandonment of "sociologizing" [sotsiologizatorstvo] in the teaching of literature and, also, of the students' greater acquaintance with modern Soviet creative literature.

One of the reasons given by students for their heightened interest in a given subject is good teaching. Most unfortunately, the number of students giving this reason is small. They regard the teacher's attention to the development of the students' independent thinking as one of the essential signs of good teaching.

The absence of interest in the study of a subject is usually explained by: a lag in the study of programmed material (55 responses in the 6th grade, 44 in the 8th, 25 in the 10th); poor teaching (37 responses in the 6th grade, 59 in the 8th, 92 in the 10th); unattractiveness of the subject itself (39 responses in the 6th grade, 54 in the 8th, 64 in the 10th); difficulties in comprehension, "the absence of abilities," "unwillingness to cram" (45 in the 6th grade, 20 in the 8th, 5 in the 10th).

The figures cited (see Table 2) allow us to note the following characteristic tendencies in the motivation of the students' negative attitudes toward school subjects. The older the students, the more often they advance poor teaching and lack of correspondence between the school subject and their inclinations as causes for lack of interest in the school subject. Such a tendency is natural: it reflects the growth of consciousness, the ability of the older student to appraise the phenomena of his environment critically, and, in particular, the quality of the teaching, of the textbook, etc. There is no doubt that a lowering of interest in a school subject for such reasons as "I am incapable" and "it is difficult" (this motive is advanced by students of the lower and, more rarely, of the upper grades) also depends on the teacher to a significant degree.

In many cases the absence of interest in the study of a school subject is caused by the nature of the program and textbook. Students of the intermediate and upper grades especially do not like those sections of the program which must be mastered mainly through memorization, as well as school material which has little connection with practice and the vital importance of which they do not realize. We have noted the sharp decline in the students' interest in biology from the lower to the upper grades. The 8th-grade students especially do not like the anatomy and physiology of man. Such answers as the following testify to this: "I like anatomy least of all. It is somehow uninteresting to analyze different intestines and extremities" (School No. 172); "I do not like anatomy. You get tangled up in these fibers. You do not remember anything and simply cram" (Cherepanovo School No. 4).

A decline in the students' interest in the study

Table 2

Students' Attitudes Toward School Subjects

Reasons for negative attitudes toward school subjects	6th-8th (620 students)		6th (310 students)		8th (310 students)		10th (310 students)
			schools				
			city (113)	rural (197)	city (130)	rural (180)	
"Not useful," less important	8	7	3	5	6	1	25
Poor teaching or poor textbook	37	59	17	20	22	37	92
Do not like "cramming"	4	5	1	3	4	1	13
Behind in the study of material	55	44	15	40	24	20	25
Subject itself uninteresting ("do not like it")	39	54	18	21	26	28	64
"Do not know why"	6	10	2	4	4	6	11
"Not able," "Do not understand," "No abilities"	45	20	7	38	5	15	5

of general educational subjects is often caused by concentricity in the construction of the program. Familiar material does not arouse a feeling of "wonder." I. P. Pavlov wrote of its significance in cognition. The students write: "I do not like history especially. We repeat a great deal of old material, which we already have learned" (8th grade); "You know, we studied the geography of the USSR, and we are studying it again" (10th grade); "I have little interest in economic geography; we repeat the same thing" (10th grade). The sharp criticism expressed by the upper-grade students with respect to the textbooks and programs is very symptomatic. They mainly criticize their lag behind life and the inadequate illumination of real scientific problems: "There is a great deal of scholasticism in the physics textbook, but little practical data. We have to search in other literature. Physics is poorly presented in the textbook" (10th grade); "The material on physics is presented too dryly. The compilers of the book should be concerned about making it more popular and comprehensible" (10th grade); "I

love physics and chemistry, but the present textbooks are outdated. The most recent achievements of science and technology are not reflected at all in them. The achievements of our native land in the field of the mastery of the cosmos and many other things must be related in the textbook which was written long ago" (10th grade); "The literature textbook contains no information about the works of our time. But such works as Young Guard [Molodaia gvardiia] and How the Steel Was Tempered [Kak zakali-alas' stal'] are studied several times. In the upper grades, we should be more acquainted with modern times, with the writers and poets of our day, but some students completing school have almost no idea of them (of course, this is rare)" (10th grade).

The facts cited allow us to draw the following conclusions: the level of our students' cognitive interests rises with each year. The growing demand for knowledge is stimulated, to a significant degree, by the successes of Soviet science and technology, and also by the reorganization of the educational process. An undoubtedly positive fact is the change, which has begun to show up, in the students' attitude toward the humanities (first of all, toward literature). The diversity of the students' cognitive interests testifies to the growth of their spiritual needs.

The above-noted shortcomings in the development of the cognitive interests of upper-grade students are explained by the deficiencies that remain in the content of education and, to a still greater degree, in the organization of the educational process.

Need for the Beautiful

The development in the rising generation of a need for the beautiful is becoming a task of paramount importance. It is in no way exhausted by the development of a need for purely esthetic activities or an enjoyment of works of art. The development of esthetic needs is part of a broader task — the cultivation in Soviet students of an esthetic attitude toward life. It is manifested in man's ability to see beauty in his environment (in nature, in labor, in social relations) and in art, and in the ability to enjoy beauty, to judge it, to introduce the beautiful into his life and labor, and to feel a constant need for beauty.

The need for the beautiful is connected not only with the sphere of feelings and emotions, but also with many manifestations of the human intellect. We can judge the character and level of development of an individual's esthetic needs by his tastes, his esthetic views and judgments. That is why the esthetic need should be understood as "the aspiration to live and work according to the laws of beauty."

Esthetic upbringing is the development of esthetic feelings, of artistic taste and horizons, of views and needs, and abilities and skills for creative activity.

The esthetic need is expressed, first of all, in the aspiration for esthetic enjoyment. Like any other need, it passes through several stages of development, from an unconscious and vague aspiration for beauty to a conscious and steadfast interest in a certain form of art and esthetic activity. It is generally known that the depth of esthetic experiences and the versatility of man's emotional responses to the beautiful are determined not only by the esthetic qualities of reality and of works of art, but also by the degree of development and cultivation of esthetic perceptions. The more developed is his capacity for esthetic perception, the easier it is for a person to understand art and, consequently, to distinguish the truly beautiful from the counterfeit. A true work of art, beautiful in reality, affords enjoyment to a man with a developed esthetic sense and, on the contrary, everything false and vulgar offends and revolts and even elicits a feeling of suffering. Consequently, the presence of a need for true beauty and the aspiration for esthetic enjoyment are expressed, first of all, in the level of development of esthetic feeling.

But the capacity for esthetic receptivity is not given from above; it demands a certain training, culture, and artistic education. Indeed, the perception of the phenomena of art involves more than sensual, visual, and auditory sensations. Trying to understand also is an important link in comprehending the beautiful. Consequently, the development of the ability to understand the phenomena of the beautiful functions as a condition for the development of a conscious need for the beautiful and of an interest in art. Esthetic taste is man's ability to understand beauty, to make an esthetic appraisal of the reality surrounding him, of natural phenomena, of works of art and the conduct of people, and the ability to investigate what is beautiful and what is not beautiful from the positions of the dialectical-materialist ideology. Developed esthetic taste is also characterized by an ability to enjoy genuine beauty and a yearning for it. Everything that has been said provides grounds for asserting that the level of development of the need for beauty is expressed in the capacity for esthetic interests.

Studies of the students' esthetic needs, artistic tastes, and artistic horizons have been conducted by our department repeatedly (1955, 1957-1958, 1959-1960, 1961-1962, 1963-1964).

It was important to observe what influence the reorganization of the school exerts on the students' esthetic development. (2) The investigation of the level of the students' esthetic development in 1963-1964 was thorough. The methods elaborated by the department provided a collection of mass material accessible to statistical treatment (questionnaires, tests, compositions), supplemented by the methods of individual study of the students (conversations, observations) and by the study of school records and the children's work. A number of questions illuminating the students' attitudes toward art and their tastes were posed in the questionnaire on "The Student of 1964." (What do you like: your favorite subject, pursuit, entertainment, film, book, song, musical work, and dance? Who are your favorite heroes in literature and in the movies? How many times a week do you go to the movies, the theater, and concerts? Do you watch television? In what clubs do you participate?) Twelve hundred questionnaires were analyzed.

The students were also asked to tell how many hours per week (approximately) they spend in leisure-time reading, sports, art, technical work, social work, and preparation for lessons. Such an inquiry helped elucidate the place of various forms of activity in the lives of the upper-grade students, the degree to which they are loaded with home assignments, and the possibility of satisfying versatile needs.

The investigation indicated that art is beginning to play an ever more significant role in the students' spiritual life. The following facts testify to this. Approximately 30 percent of the students in the 9th and 10th grades of the Novosibirsk schools called the lessons in art their favorite pursuit. The overwhelming majority of the upper-grade students regularly attend the movies (on average, twice a week); many watch television daily; some attend the theater more or less regularly. Unfortunately, only an insignificant proportion of the students attend the philharmonic concert halls. In the schedule of time spent on various forms of studies, art lessons also occupy an important place for the overwhelming majority of students.

The students' compositions also testify to the growth of their esthetic needs. The very fact that some of the students took such themes as "My Attitude Toward Operatic (Symphonic) Music" and "The Most Interesting Performance in the Novosibirsk Theaters" (and some of them presented serious and profound compositions) shows that music, theater, and the movies are a source of great esthetic enjoyment and a means of learning about life for a definite (although, unfortunately, still insignificant) group of students.

A comparison of materials from 1963-1964 with the data of 1956, and even with that of 1959-1960, leads to the conclusion that there has been definite growth in the students' artistic horizons and tastes. It is to be noted that the students are highly versed in the history of their country's art. They are acquainted with the most significant works of Russian artistic genius of the 19th century. If in 1956 the students' knowledge in the field of Russian fine arts was limited to the names (and best known works) of Repin, Surikov and Shishkin, now many of them also name Perov, Vrubel', Levitan, Kuindzha, Savrasov, and many other Russian artists. If in the 1956 questionnaires many students could include Rubinstein, Rachmaninoff and even Khatchaturian in the "Moguchaia kuchka" [a group of Russian composers of the second half of the 19th century who sought the development of a national musical culture — Ed.], now there are few who do.

It may be said with confidence that the formation of the upper-grade students' artistic tastes is being realized in the correct direction. The majority of students note their need to listen to classical music (95% in School No. 10). Their favorite composers are Tchaikovsky (108 out of 155 persons), Beethoven (29 out of 155 persons), and Strauss. Among the musical works named by the students, the ones most often encountered are: Tchaikovsky's "Concerto No. 1 for Piano and Orchestra," Beethoven's "Moonlight Sonata," Rachmaninoff's "Concerto No. 2 for Piano and Orchestra," and the Strauss waltzes.

The great majority of students are working out correct criteria for the evaluation of modern works of art. The students seek lofty ideas and artistic truth in movies and theatrical performances; they distinguish a low level of skill without much difficulty. It is no accident that the students cite first, among the Soviet and foreign works of artistic cinematography in recent years, the films "Hamlet" [Gamlet], "An Optimistic Tragedy" [Optimisticheskaia tragediia], "Silence" [Tishina], and "The Living and the Dead" [Zhivye i mertvye], and only a few recollect such mediocre and unartistic films as "Seven Brides for Seven Brothers" [Sem' navest dlia semi brat'ev], "Look out, Grandmother!" [Ostorozhno, babushka!], and so forth. Of course, many students note "The Three Musketeers" [Tri mushketera] and "The Count of Monte-Cristo" [Graf Monte-Kristo] among the films they especially like. This can hardly surprise or alarm anyone. Young people have always read the fascinating works of A. Dumas, and they will continue to do so; interest in their filming is completely natural.

One could multiply the number of examples testifying to the unquestionable growth of the students' esthetic needs, artistic horizons, tastes and judgments. However, this general and pleasing conclusion still does not constitute evidence that all is well in the matter of the students' esthetic upbringing. Along with the positive facts, the research material revealed a number of substantial shortcomings in the students' esthetic development. For a significant number of students, interest in art is of a passive and contemplative nature. As of now, one can speak only of the presence in the overwhelming majority of students of a more or less stable need for esthetic enjoyment. Unfortunately, significantly fewer students (8 or 9% of the students questioned in the 9th-11th grades) of the Novosibirsk schools attend art studios, music schools, out-of-school institutions and amateur talent groups, or are engaged in art at home. At present, the number of students who own musical instruments, take a great interest in creative reading, drawing and sculpture, and participate in dramatic groups is still very small.

This is explained, to a significant degree, by the level of the schools' work in the field of esthetic upbringing. In November 1963, there

were, for example, 185 choral and 193 theatrical groups and 68 dance and choreography groups in 193 Novosibirsk schools. If a school has a drama club involving 20-25 youths, or a chorus of upper-grade students, in which the students of the primary grades cannot sing, this can hardly satisfy us. If there is one dance club at three of the city's schools, then it is useless to complain about the students' lack of cultivation in dancing.

The students willingly read, listen to music, and go to the theater and movies. This is an important stage in the formation of esthetic needs and the need to enjoy the beautiful. In this case the individual acts as a consumer of beauty, and the demand for the beautiful depends on the level to which this need is developed and on the individual's ability to perceive the beautiful. But the school is by no means doing everything possible to further the development in the students of the need for artistic creativity and active creation of the beautiful. Research has shown that the esthetic needs of boys and girls are not equal. Art occupies a significantly greater place in the interests, life plans, and out-of-school activities of girls. It is characteristic that it was primarily girls who wrote compositions on the themes "My Attitude Toward Operatic and Symphonic Music," "My Favorite Book," and "The Most Interesting Performances in the Novosibirsk Theaters."

The youths' attraction to individual art forms is extremely uneven. The majority of those who talk about their enthusiasm for art write first of all about movies, music, dances, and poetry; a significantly smaller number write about theatrical art, and only a few about the fine arts (no one writes about sculpture). And this fact testifies to serious flaws in the work on arts education in the Soviet school.

Although we have noted the unquestionable enhancement of the students' artistic taste in recent years, nevertheless the level is still not high. This is especially true in regard to the rural students. The range of their favorite musical works is usually limited to popular songs of a lyrical nature and to two or three works of classical music (for the most part, these are Oginskii's "Polonnaise" and the dance of the little swans from the ballet "Swan Lake" [Lebedinoe ozero] by Tchaikovsky). The rural students are very poorly acquainted with operatic music, and they do not know symphonic music at all. But, indeed, the range of favorite musical works of the majority of students in the schools of Novosibirsk, a city of great musical culture, is also very limited and is exhausted by several of the more popular musical works. Matters are still worse with the plastic arts. Of 155 Novosibirsk students who were asked to name representatives of contemporary fine arts and their works, 102 could not give one name. Despite an enthusiasm for poetry, the upper-grade students have a completely inadequate knowledge of the representatives of Soviet poetry and drama. It is characteristic that the names of the poets Rozhdestvenskii, Smeliakov, Aseev and Isaev were given, mainly, in School No. 10, in which the students were specifically acquainted with modern Soviet poetry at the literature lessons. Of 155 students who were asked to name their favorite composers and their works, only two named the Soviet composer Shostakovich. These data indicate that the students evidently are insufficiently familiar with modern Soviet musical and fine arts.

On the Students' Need for Social Activity

The problem of developing moral needs is extremely complicated, for it involves a whole complex of problems on the formation of the personality and, essentially, has been investigated very little in pedagogical science. Here we will be concerned only with the problem of developing the students' interests and inclinations in social activity and in the problems of internal and international politics.

The formation of the students' social and political interests is organically connected with the formation of their consciousness and the feeling of responsibility and duty. "With us, need is the sister of duty and responsibility, of abilities; this is the manifestation of the interests not of a consumer of social goods, but of the active man of socialist society," wrote A. S. Makarenko (Works [Soch.], Vol. 4, pp. 40-41). It stands to reason that an interest in social and political life reflects the new social relations and the intense and eventful life of our people.

The active social orientation of the Soviet student is generally known. It finds its expression in many phenomena of great social significance: the pupils of the Soviet school bring virgin lands under cultivation, go into construction, and master the cosmos. But we cannot be limited to a statement of these facts. Our investigation of the social and political interests of the older students has only begun, and therefore we can speak more readily about the suppositions that have occurred to us in the process of this study, than about conclusions.

In the questionnaire "The Student of 1964," we asked the students to name the best-remembered events of the past year in the world, in our city, and in the school. The flight of "Voskhod-1" occupied first place among events on a world scale (62 students of the 92 answering this question in Schools No. 110 and 157); several students mentioned Kennedy's assassination, the Olympic games in Tokyo, the Youth Festival in Moscow, new discoveries in science, and so forth.

The greatest impressions in the city were made by the arrival of W. Ulbricht (in all the schools), the opening of the exhibition on "Socialist Siberia" (in one school), and the arrival of the king of Afghanistan. The students also mentioned such facts as the starting of a bus line on Bogdan Khmel'nitskii Street (School No. 110), the opening of a skating rink (School No. 157), and others. Among the school events remembered, the students noted first of all those which were connected with the life of the collective, the Komsomol organization. Such an event for the students of School No. 137 was the introduction of self-government; in Schools No. 110 and 157, it was entry into the Komsomol and getting a passport; and in School No. 127 it was a journey to Moscow and Leningrad.

Along with this, many very important events in our country, in international life, and in the life of the city are overlooked by boys and girls in the 9th and 10th grades. A certain proportion of the upper-grade students display a definite indifference to that which occupies the minds and feelings of their contemporaries. In a number of schools, the social activity of some of the students is noticeably weak; there is a secret and, at times, even obvious unwillingness to engage in social work; in individual cases there is even a skeptical attitude toward it. In the questionnaires, some of the upper-grade students noted the collection of scrap metal and the harvesting of potatoes as the most memorable events. The ironic undercurrent of these answers is scarcely in need of deciphering.

It turns out that far from all the students have social assignments and fulfill them eagerly. This is most often noted in the classes with special contingents of students (for example, computer programmers). The most typical student here is the one for whom the mastery of scientific knowledge is most important, and everything else, which is not directly connected with his chosen path, is supposedly unworthy of attention.

The school still does little work on the formation of the students' moral and esthetic ideals. In answers to questions about ideals and about persons whom they would like to take as examples, the students name literary heroes (in the first place, Ovod) and heroes from movies, and they very seldom name our contemporaries as models that they would like to imitate.

Analysis and comparison of the collected materials, which characterize the level of development of the students' spiritual needs, reveal a definite lag in the development of esthetic needs and, in some of the students, of the need for social activity. The fact that part of the upper-grade students are not occupied with social work reveals the emergence of a serious contradiction in the personality development of some of the boys and girls, a contradiction between social duty and personal interests. And yet the aspiration for social activity should become one of the supreme spiritual needs of man.

We must seek the causes of the unequal development of given spiritual needs, first of all,

in the shortcomings of the content of education and upbringing in our school. We cannot forget that the significance of the society's ideological and upbringing functions grows as the transition from socialism to communism proceeds. In connection with this, the role of education in the humanities, as the basic means of the ideological, moral and esthetic upbringing of the youth, inevitably grows also. In recent years, however, the relative importance of the humanities subjects in secondary education has been reduced; they have been crowded in the curriculum, and some men of science have even begun to propose that the humanities be studied in out-of-school time. But this is only one side of the question. The other has to do with the defects of the humanities education itself. It reflects the contemporary epoch inadequately and, therefore, does not always answer the vital problems that are agitating the Soviet students.

The contradiction, noted above, between the upper-grade student's cognitive and social activity is caused by a contradiction between his growing spiritual needs and the content of out-of-class upbringing work, which has taken shape in many schools over the years. A certain stereotyped pattern in the organization of out-of-school work and the limitation of socially useful work to such forms as, for example, the collection of scrap metal undoubtedly lowers the students' interest in social activity. The absence of a system in the organization of out-of-class and upbringing work also has an effect.

The basic path for the further development of the students' spiritual interests and for the elimination of contradictions in the formation of their needs lies, in the first place, in heightening the social significance of knowledge acquired in school in every way possible; second, in raising substantially the intellectual content of all social and labor activity of the upper-grade students; and, third, in further reorganizing the educational process, stimulating intellectual activity, and securing a differentiated approach to the students' instruction and upbringing.

Footnotes

1) Results of the research were published in

28

the journals <u>Sovetskaia pedagogika</u>, 1961, No. 1; <u>Narodnoe obrazovanie</u>, 1963, No. 1; <u>Sibirskie ogni</u>, 1962, No. 9.

2) Results of the research were published in the journals <u>Sovetskaia pedagogika</u>, 1956, No. 9 and 1962, No. 6; <u>Sibirskie ogni</u>, 1962, No. 9; Uchenye zapiski NGPI, 1962.

* * *

Educational Psychology

Sovetskaia pedagogika, 1967, No. 10

N. A. Menchinskaia

FIFTY YEARS OF THE SOVIET PSYCHOLOGY OF LEARNING

I

Soviet psychology of learning has as its subject matter the distinctive features of psychological function in the process of learning and the laws of the learning process itself. But inasmuch as instruction is an important requisite for an individual's development during his entire lifetime, the considerable importance of that branch of psychology for the discovery of general psychological laws is quite clear.

I. M. Sechenov stated, justly, that "scientific psychology cannot, in its entire content, be anything but a series of theories on the origins of psychological functions." In a number of these theories, the branch of psychology we are examining has come to occupy an important place.

Soviet psychology of learning differs significantly from the prerevolutionary, both in its subject matter and its methods. Suffice it to say that works on educational psychology of the prerevolutionary period set forth data on individual

_____

The author is associated with the Scientific Research Institute of Psychology, USSR Academy of Pedagogical Sciences.

psychological functions derived from studies in general psychology, and an attempt was made to apply these data to circumstances of school life, teaching, and training by purely deductive procedure. The very process of learning itself, and the features of psychological activity implemented under concrete conditions of training and teaching, were themselves not studied at that time.

It does not follow that the materials set forth in the manuals on educational psychology coming from the press in the late 19th and the first quarter of the 20th centuries (P. K. Kapterev, M. M. Rubinshtein, A. P. Nechaev, and others) lack interest for us. But it does mean that studies in the psychology of learning conducted during the Soviet period were no mere continuation of the work done in Russia prior to the Revolution, but signified the appearance of new subject matter and new paths of investigation.

Extensive application of the genetic mode of research was required in order to study the changes occurring in psychological functioning under the influence of learning. However, employment of this method in the psychology of learning has certain specific characteristics.

The changes may be traced on two planes: first, studying changes in the learning activity and development of the pupils as they progress from one stage to another, from one stage of learning to the other (for the sake of convenience , let us call that the macro-plane), and, in the second place, tracing the passage from ignorance to knowledge, from one, less perfect mode of learning activity to another, more perfect, in the case of a given pupil (the micro-plane). Both aspects are characterized by changes in two opposite directions. On the one hand, there is an enrichment of knowledge and a complication of the modes of learning activity applied, while on the other hand there is the inverse process of "short-cutting," of simplification of the techniques employed. It is precisely thanks to this second type of change that uninterrupted improvement in learning activity becomes possible, as does passage, on the part of the pupil, to higher levels in the mastery of knowledge.

For implementation of this genetic approach, there has been a need for a significant modification of the principles and methods formerly applied and for the creation of new ones. For example, the "cross-section principle" once widely employed (involving comparison of data from children in different age groups) was changed to accord with the new problems. People began to study the psychological activity of a single child at different stages of education. This brought the possibility of arriving at a better founded judgment of the changes occurring in psychological activity as the result of education. Further, a new form of natural experiment was developed, an "experiment in learning," in which research is combined with the exercise of influence by the teacher. Here, in the course of the experiment, the researcher develops in the child the required knowledge, skills, habits, and modes of functioning. Thereby he is able to discover the psychological characteristics of the pupils as they come into being and change.

The utilization of experiments in learning required the introduction of preliminary stages of investigation, at which the initial state of the knowledge, abilities, and habits required for assimilation of new material was identified, and these characteristics were "brought into line" with each other.

Finally, recent years have seen the beginning of the employment of a new form of large-scale experiments in learning, in which the experiment is conducted with entire classes and over a term of years, and it is not only the methods of teaching but also curriculums that are changed.

Also common in psychological research today is the utilization of transitional and intermediate types of methods. Thus, for example, wide employment is made of an intermediate form between observation and experiment ("experimental observation"), under which phenomena are induced at will (inasmuch as a given task is posed before the subject, and the material is chosen in accordance with the concept of the piece of research), but at the same time the mental process thus induced is observed in its natural sequence. The elements of the experiment are incorporated in other methods as well. In written works, for example, the elements of the experiment manifested themselves in the fact that problems according with the intent of the experimenter were chosen with a special purpose in mind (in "experimental dictation," for example, particular words were employed; and, in work in mathematics, examples and problems). There is also the fact that a particular procedure for presentation of the material was established.

A set of methods was often employed in which intensive techniques were combined with extensive ones. Thus a clinical or "experimental" conversation or individual experiment (in its various forms) would be combined with filling out a questionnaire, or a method of writing calculated to serve a large number of cases would be used.

As in every other branch of psychology, the course of the investigation is subject to extensive modification, in accordance with the nature of the problem under study.

II

The treatment of problems in the psychology of learning has gone through a number of stages in the course of the half-century.

In the first stage (late 1920s to early 1930s), the fundamental principles of Soviet psychology of learning were established. This period is associated primarily with the names of L. S. Vygotskii and P. P. Blonskii.

Vygotskii, in his book Pedagogical Psychology [Pedagogicheskaia psikhologiia], published in 1926, wrote that it is a waste of effort to attempt to transfer into pedagogical psychology chapters already written in general psychology. He demonstrated that the subject matter of this branch of the discipline was independent, and showed the need for special research in it.

That period witnessed the formulation of certain important new problems, and studies of them were carried out. Thus, Vygotskii was the first to pose, in our country, the problem of the relationship between instruction and intellectual development, and he subjected this to profound theoretical analysis. He himself directed concrete studies that served to reveal the process whereby scientific concepts were shaped in pupils. The formation of scientific concepts was regarded as a component of the entire process of learning, which was interpreted as familiarization with culture, the mastering of a system of artificial means and signs created in the history of mankind and fixed in the oral and written language.

The development of mental activity in the process of instruction was examined in the light of this theory of cultural history. This development was characterized as a reorganization of the direct, "natural" forms of mental functions, and the assimilation by them of "cultural" forms subsuming the performance of operations with symbols (initially external but later internal).

A new concept of learning also made its appearance in the writings of Blonskii, who interpreted this as a complex activity on the part of the pupil. Therefore, in studying the process of learning the material, Blonskii strove to obtain data on how these functions related to each other in the learning process, and particularly how memory and thinking related to each other, rather than how each independent psychological function was implemented.

Blonskii ascribed a significant place to the features of the manner in which pupils organized their own learning activity, and, above all, to self-control as a component of this organization. It was precisely the features of self-control upon which Blonskii based the division of the learning process into consecutive stages. It is in this way that his research uncovered a new and very important aspect of the process of learning: it was interpreted as a complex form of man's activity reflecting the distinctive features of his personality.

The propositions formulated during that period, and the results of research, although few in number, exercised a decisive influence upon the further development of the psychology of learning in our country.

Second stage (late 1930s, and 1940s). This period was typified by two characteristics: a considerable expansion of research into problems of the psychology of learning, and differentiation of investigations by the object under study.

During this stage, psychology "swung" toward isolated special techniques for teaching the respective school subjects. The differentiation was based upon study of concrete forms of learning activity and the differences in the process of acquiring knowledge, depending upon the school subject. Naturally, the working out of general problems of instruction also progressed, but this was not unique to the second stage.

Changes in the content of research in the psychology of learning were directly associated with the resolution of the Party Central Committee, "On Pedalogical Distortions in the System of the People's Commissariats of Education" [O pedologicheskikh izvrashcheniiakh v sisteme Narkomprosov] (1936), which condemned the theory and practice of pedology, which was then dominant and was holding back the development of scientific psychology. Overcoming the concept of development held by the pedologists, who believed that stages of development succeed each other by virtue of the laws of maturation by age, independent of the content and methods of instruction, Soviet psychologists directed their attention to the study of those changes in the mind and in learning activity that occur under the influence of various kinds of content in the material to be assimilated, and diverse methods of instruction. They proved that age-group limitations are labile, and that age characteristics depend upon the conditions of upbringing to which the child is subject. All these questions were examined by means of theory and experiment (the writings of A. N. Leont'eva, published in 1937 and 1945, of S. L. Rubinshtein and his associates, published in 1939, and of others).

Important modifications were made in the previously held view on the relationship between psychology and pedagogy. It was emphasized that not only must pedagogy rest upon psychology, but that pedagogical psychology must in turn rest upon pedagogy inasmuch as it studies the mental activity of children under the conditions of upbringing and instruction. The goal was set of not displacing the pedagogues, as was the case in the period when pedology held dominance, but of helping them by developing the scientific foundations of rational organization of the process of teaching and upbringing.

Writing and reading were the first forms of learning activity to be studied as early as the 1930s (by M. P. Feofanov, N. A. Rybnikov and, somewhat later, L. M. Shvarts and others). Study of these made it possible to provide for a much deeper theoretical interpretation of the problem of habit, and of demonstrating its origin from the first cognized activities, and to reveal the automation of habit as a secondary process, differentiating it from involuntary automatic activity. Special attention was given to qualitative analysis of the structure of habit, with consideration of its origin and prospects of development. "The development of habit," wrote Shvarts, "is nothing but the replacement of certain techniques by other, more improved ones, with the consequence that habit undergoes qualitative change." It was demonstrated that the transition to a new, more perfect technique could often be accompanied by temporary impairment of the results of learning activity (the appearance of errors and slowing of the process).

These studies by Soviet psychologists were of major theoretical significance, inasmuch as they validated the principle of consciousness in learning and comprised a sharp critique of behaviorism, then dominant in the United States, and particularly one of the variants of the latter, connectionism. (The founder of the latter was E. Thorndike, who reduced the learning process to a purely quantitative accumulation of connections between stimulus and response, and interpreted exercises as mechanical training).

The sphere of studies in the psychology of learning became broader and broader. This was facilitated by the founding, in 1943, of the RSFSR Academy of Pedagogical Sciences, into which was incorporated the Institute of Psychology that had existed since 1912. Studies began on mastery of the operations of calculation and solution of problems in mathematics (N. A. Menchinskaia), assimilation of grammar and orthography (D. N. Bogoiavlenskii), and mastery of the graphic habits of writing (E. V. Gur'ianov). Studies of the process of mastering the habit of reading were continued and expanded (T. G. Egorov).

These new researches were characterized by interest in a wide age range, making it possible to trace the process of mastery of a particular form of learning activity, starting with the preschool stage of development and terminating with the culminating levels of education in school. A multiplicity of new data was discovered, revealing the complexity and qualitative distinctiveness of conscious mastery of the material to be learned.

Study of the process of mastering reading, grammar, spelling, and arithmetic confronted the investigators with complex forms of thought. They faced, above all, the problem of shaping concepts: the uniqueness of this process was discovered, relative to the nature of the material to be learned, and its general laws. In this connection, particular attention was given to analysis of the general conclusions that the schoolchildren arrive at in the process of instruction, and to obtaining a clear picture of the pedagogical conditions that promote the shaping of correct generalizations. Major attention went to the study of the psychological nature of erroneous generalizations and errors in general, inasmuch as errors revealed most clearly the character of that process of thought that existed in schoolchildren in the solution of learning problems.

Analysis of the different kinds of errors served as the basis for recommending diverse techniques for coping with them.

Thus, in study of the mastery of grammar and spelling, there were discovered difficulties unique to these subjects and psychologically very interesting, having to do with the pupils' need simultaneously to consider two aspects of linguistic phenomena: the semantic (word meanings) and that of formal grammar. It was found that pupils who experienced difficulties in mastering language either committed errors of naive semanticism, ignoring criteria of formal grammar or, on the contrary, erroneously guided themselves only by the similarity of the external forms of words, ignoring their semantics.

The difficulties children encountered in the study of arithmetic are again specific and associated with the abstract nature of the concept of number. As research has shown, these are overcome along two different lines: by operating with objects via a process of step-by-step abstraction from them or, conversely, by grasping at the undifferentiated and most universal relationship and then gradually approaching an adequate concept through a process of concretization. For example, the concept of a quantitative total arrived at as the result of calculation takes shape on the basis of enumeration of real objects, as well as of the most general notion to the effect that the result of calculation must be denoted by "some" number.

The third stage in development of Soviet psychology of learning was also marked by differentiation of research, but this time on the basis not of the object of research but of the approach to the process of learning. A number of different trends treating the process of learning from diverse standpoints and propounding a variety of concepts to explain its laws were clearly definable. The existence of these trends and their interactions made possible a theoretical interpretation of the learning process in its various connections and mediated forms.

Major attention was given (unlike the situation in the preceding period) to discovering the general laws of learning activity, the acquisition of knowledge.

An important role in this regard was played by the 1950 scholarly meeting devoted to the physiological doctrine of I. P. Pavlov. Pavlov's ideas on the analytical and synthesizing function of the brain, the laws by which temporary connections were established, the systematism of brain function, and the intimate interaction of the first and second signal systems were of direct significance in uncovering the laws of learning activity and for understanding some of its physiological mechanisms.

In the period under discussion, Soviet psychology of learning came closer to didactics, and to solution not only of special problems of technique but of general questions in the field of instruction.

It is necessary, further, to note that at this stage, as during the two previous ones, it was primarily the intellectual aspects of mental activity in the process of instruction that were subjected to investigation. There was still a significant gap between the psychology of learning and the psychology of education. But within the third stage, which includes the research now in progress, one can see signs of a new stage characterized by two features: the appearance of certain common attitudes on the part of psychologists of various trends, and emergence beyond the limits of study of the purely intellectual aspects of mental activity.

The rest of this article is devoted chiefly to a survey of the research conducted during the third stage. It does not remotely constitute a complete survey of all the problems presently under study.

III

Among the regularities of cognitive activity manifested in the process of acquiring knowledge, the laws of analysis and synthesis hold an important place. Their significance is determined primarily by the fact that they are regarded as leading laws underlying other operations of thought. This postulate has found wide application not only in general psychology — in the writings of S. L. Rubinshtein and his associates — but in research into the psychology of learning. Analysis and synthesis were studied in children of various ages and in various types of learning activity: reading and writing (A. A. Liublinskaia), assimilation of the disciplines in the physics and mathematics group, biology, and the humanities (M. N. Shardakov, G. S. Kostiuk, D. N. Bogoiavlenskii, N. A. Menchinskaia, as well as the collaborators of these researchers), plastic arts (E. I. Ignat'ev), etc. Various processes playing a significant role in the assimilation of knowledge — the understanding of textual material, the shaping of concepts, the solution of problems, the development of habits were subjected to study.

As these researches demonstrated, not only is the level of performance of each operation improved as one learns to analyze and synthesize, but there is also a change in the degree to which their levels correspond to each other. The relatively autonomous nature of these operations at early stages is then replaced by intimate interaction on their part. It is precisely this that characterizes, above all, progress in mastering analytical and synthetic thinking activity. Thus, the decisive step in shaping the concept of numbers occurs when the breakdown of a set into elements (units) is combined with an integrated grasp of the total quantitative result as a whole. Likewise, success in depictive activity is attained if a child, drawing from nature, learns to see not only the very finest details but the object as a whole, and if his attempt to render the object as accurately as possible is subordinated to a unified notion.

The replacement of various levels of analysis and synthesis in a single schoolchild is exceedingly dynamic. It is conditioned not only by the general level of development of the pupil and the level of his preparation, but by the character of the material and the degree of difficulty and novelty of the problem to be solved. As studies have shown, in the solution of an easy problem analysis and synthesis are performed almost instantaneously, in the very process of perception of the condition. In the solution of difficult problems the same operations occur in extended fashion, and the correspondence between analysis and synthesis is often broken once again: before comprehensive analysis is performed, synthetic operations are performed or, on the other hand, a detailed analysis fails to culminate in the necessary synthesis.

In arriving at a description of analysis and synthesis, researchers gained the opportunity to disclose more precisely the psychological structure of other intellectual operations that also play a significant role in learning activity: the drawing of conclusions, abstraction, and concretization. Thus, the uniqueness of the conclusion-drawing process is, in substantial measure, determined by the level of analysis that underlies it. If analysis is incomplete and certain similar (and often nonsignificant) characteristics are grasped at, what occurs is generalization (a sort of "surrogate" for conclusion-drawing), and it is only on the basis of comprehensive analysis and then combination of similar criteria that a general conclusion is drawn.

In defining the laws of assimilation of knowledge, the question of the relationship of visual-active (sensory) and detached (abstract) thought has great importance. We know from writings on child psychology that visual-action forms of thought precede the abstract in the child's intellectual development. However, merely to point to this is quite insufficient if we seek to characterize the development of thought in the process of instruction. As investigations have shown (B. G. Anan'ev, G. S. Kostiuk, D. N. Bogoiavlenskii, N. A. Menchinskaia, E. N. Kabanova-Meller, and others), concrete thought is not merely the initial form, playing the role of a temporary base for abstract thought. It itself develops in the course of instruction at school, acquiring new functions, inasmuch as instruction in geography, for example, demands of pupils the development and corresponding modification of a "mental picture." In order to develop projections of geometrical bodies in learning to draw, it is necessary to possess the skill of transforming images. In order to resolve problems of technical design successfully, the development of more complex forms of the sensory-motor intellect is required, and so forth.

This is how matters stand with the principal

direction of development of pupils' thought in the learning process. The question of the concrete and abstract as applied to stages in the acquisition of one or another kind of knowledge is even a more complex matter to decide. In that situation, the proposition that the former "precedes" the latter is applicable only to certain categories of knowledge, the essence of which may be entirely revealed only through the perception of objects and often also through operations with them. In many other cases knowledge is created on the basis of concepts that take shape as the result of verbal description.

Finally, that knowledge, the essence of which is generally incapable of being disclosed visually (shown or even described) but is expressed in a word or definition containing a conclusion, is acquired in a very special fashion. In such cases the formation of concepts by the schoolchild proceeds from two opposite directions: from the abstract and from the concrete. First the most general and as yet undifferentiated criterion of the concept is detected (for example, "poor" in mastering the concept "slave") and, along with this, some special, external, and insignificant criterion is mastered, which is singled out upon perception of a corresponding image illustrating the concept. As the result of accumulation of concrete facts, a hierarchy is established among the criteria, and the most significant of them are singled out. The most general criterion, which is initially not differentiated, becomes so, and it is only then that genuine assimilation of the concept occurs (A. Z. Red'ko and others). In that sense the word expressing the basic thought in the given category of phenomena would, as it were, regulate and direct the concrete experience of the child, and the latter serves as the "soil" on which its genuine assimilation becomes possible. It is here that there occurs that merger of the products of "the experience of others" (the sociohistorical product of human thought) and the indications suggested by one's own experience, of which Sechenov wrote in his Elements of Thought [Elementy mysli], in revealing the meaning of "to assimilate."

Research in the mental development of the child in the course of the learning process also revealed another fact of important fundamental significance: the relativity of differences between the concrete and abstract, which is also seen in dialectical logic. These operations which, at earlier stages, bear an abstract character, and rest in their shaping upon concrete operations, subsequently themselves gain concrete meaning and are capable in turn of serving as a foundation for more abstract operations. Consequently there is constant interaction between the concrete and abstract, occurring, moreover, on higher levels as well.

The psychological function of particular forms of intellectual activity also changes under the influence of tasks posed in the process of instruction. Thus, in a problem posed for application of knowledge (when what is required is to recognize a previously known general principle under new concrete conditions), the concrete material at hand not only does not assist in the solution but even makes it more difficult (as distinct from problems having to do with the shaping of concepts), inasmuch as the concrete details would appear to "mask" the principle being studied (E. A. Fleshner and others).

IV

The effectiveness of the fulfillment of intellectual operations depends not only upon the external organization of instructional activity (rational design of the syllabus, the textbook, teaching methods), but also upon the level to which the "subject being instructed," the pupil, is himself organized. This is determined to a substantial degree by whether the pupil possesses effective means or devices for performing the operations. A method does not begin to be applied automatically from the moment when a particular form of mental activity is engaged in. This was demonstrated at an even earlier date in studies of the processes of memorizing (A. A. Smirnov, P. I. Zinchenko, and others). Thus, Smirnov demonstrated that a given operation — for example, grouping by meaning, which serves subsequently to facilitate memorizing — may in itself be entirely within the capabilities of a schoolchild in the early grades, but it becomes a memory device only under specific circumstances and, above all, if the pupil himself has come to recognize the need to employ it.

The problem of developing techniques for intellectual activity in the course of learning constituted a large section of the work on the psychology of learning and was worked on by several groups of psychologists (primarily among those already listed). A study was conducted, at the Psychology Institute of the Education Ministry of the Ukraine, of the process of mastering techniques of analysis and synthesis in working with a text, and the considerable importance of these techniques for improving the effectiveness of understanding was demonstrated. Studies of shaping methods of thought were also extensively conducted by a team working on general problems of psychology of thought (under the guidance of S. L. Rubinshtein). A considerable portion of these works is of direct significance to pedagogical psychology.

A number of studies were carried out in the Laboratory of the Psychology of Learning at the Psychology Institute, USSR Academy of Pedagogical Sciences, which revealed the role of the shaping of techniques of intellectual activity in the successful solution of learning problems and the mastery of knowledge in various fields of science. In so doing, the researchers did not confine themselves merely to identifying the techniques of thought employed by schoolchildren and adults, but themselves shaped those techniques under conditions of experimental instruction.

The classification of techniques of intellectual activity has not yet been worked out in full, but the following clearly emerges from the research: general or "broad" techniques (as distinct from special or "narrow" ones) are of importance to the overall intellectual development of the pupil. Special investigations devoted to that latter problem have been conducted by E. N. Kabanova-Meller, who studied such "broad" techniques as, for example, examination of an object (or phenomenon) from various viewpoints, abstraction of the significant, etc. A method was developed

for a successively broader generalization of a technique, based upon gradual expansion of the sphere of its application. Kabanova-Meller regarded as the principal indicator of a step forward in intellectual development the fact that techniques begin to perform "many-sided functions," that is, they not only help to resolve new problems, both in learning and in practical matters (i.e., there is not only a transferrence of the technique), but also a change in the attitude toward the work of learning: intellectual initiative and independence are increased, and interest in mental activity as such is assured.

In these investigations, one of the concrete means of going beyond the limits of studying only the intellectual aspects of the learning process was taken note of.

V

It is common knowledge that pupils differ noticeably from each other in rate of accumulation and systematization of knowledge. Psychological studies have shown that they also differ in the ease with which they master the techniques of intellectual functioning. These characteristics, taken together, comprise what might be called the schoolchild's "learning capacity," or "receptivity to instruction" (B. G. Anan'ev). It would appear that "learning capacity" is evidence of the degree to which particular qualities of intelligence have taken shape in the schoolchild: independence, flexibility, powers of criticism, etc. There is every ground to assume that it is precisely these qualities of the intelligence that are capable, in the final analysis, of serving as indicators of a pupil's intellectual development.

The correctness of this hypothesis is testified to by a number of studies done by the Instruction Laboratory of the Psychology Institute, USSR Academy of Pedagogical Sciences, which have revealed that manifestation of a given quality of intellect (effectiveness of pupils' work, for example) may be quite stable and broad. Moreover, one and the same feature of intellect is manifested in various forms of thought activity — both in visual operative and abstract forms.

The research done by personnel of this laboratory and by teachers, in which the psychological capacities of schoolchildren with low instructive capacity (in arithmetic, geometry, grammar, physics, etc.), were discovered, showed that when children in this category were given additional exercises, it was not difficult to get them to the required level of assimilation of the material. However, subsequently, when new material had to be learned, their low instructive capacity was manifested again, and this quality yielded to change only as the result of long-term targeted activity based on consideration of differences in individual psychology and assuring that influence would be brought to bear not only on properties of the intellect but upon the personality as a whole.

Along with treatment of the question of the development of pupils lagging behind their age group, a problem of more universal significance arose — that of accelerating children's development and of the greater capabilities by age group that might be disclosed under the influence of change in methods of instruction and then in the programs. This problem was resolved chiefly with respect to children of the younger school group.

In this connection we cannot fail to direct attention, above all, to the experiment with 3rd grade instruction organized at one time by the Leningrad Institute of Pedagogy under B. G. Anan'ev. The experiment consisted of maximal increase in use of initiative in mastering knowledge and habits; this was, in turn, accompanied by a rise in the rate at which the class worked.

Experimental instruction was organized on the broadest scale by L. V. Zankov (Institute of the Theory and History of Pedagogy, USSR Academy of Pedagogical Sciences), which combined research into didactics and psychology. First, teaching methods were changed (to bring about more active participation by the pupils), and later the syllabus (more complex material was presented). The schoolchild's development as he moved from class to class (from the 1st to 4th grade) was followed. As the result of studies pursued for many years, Zankov came to the conclusion that the primary school curriculum could successfully be covered in three years rather than four, inasmuch as the cognitive abilities of the youngest schoolchildren are greater than we have been accustomed to think.

Experimental teaching of the Russian language (involving a study of syllabus and techniques) to an unchanging group of pupils, from the 1st through 4th grade, made it possible for S. F. Zhuikov of the Psychology Institute, USSR Academy of Pedagogical Sciences, to provide a detailed analysis of the shaping of grammatical concepts and orthographic acts, and this also demonstrated that the possibilities of child development were broader than had been believed. He also revealed the specific features of the process of mastering the Russian language, in accordance with the individual psychological differences among schoolchildren.

Three subjects — Russian, mathematics, and shop — were selected by D. B. El'konin, V. V. Davydov, and their associates at the Psychology Institute, USSR Academy of Pedagogical Sciences, for the purpose of carrying out a broad experiment in psychology and education, in which the principal accent was placed upon the rebuilding of school syllabuses. Knowledge hitherto regarded as "overly difficult" was introduced into the syllabuses, and the researchers sought such means of building the subjects and such techniques in the children's learning activity whereby knowledge difficult in the theoretical aspect would come to be within their reach. The principal result arrived at by this group of researchers is that younger schoolchildren have greater capabilities in the realm of theoretical and abstract thought than is usually presented in the traditional age group characterizations of younger schoolchildren.

The results of all these researches (on the age group capacities of young schoolchildren, and on the features of assimilation of various school subjects by secondary school pupils) have found practical application in considerable measure in the participation of a number of Soviet psychologists in drawing up new school syllabuses (S. F. Zhuikov, A. I. Lipkina, N. A. Menchinskaia, E. A. Faraponova in the primary grades; E. N. Kabanova-Meller in geography;

G. G. Saburova in foreign languages).

VI

In connection with the task of increasing the effectiveness of instruction, the question of the diagnostics of intellectual development has become very pressing.

It should be noted that in the past three decades the attention psychologists have given to that problem was greatly diminished, and the development of testing (diagnostic) methods lagged considerably behind that of methods of investigation. This is explainable by the fact that the intelligence tests popular abroad did not satisfy Soviet psychologists (in the West, too, including the USA, they are presently being subjected to considerable criticism). The need, however, was not merely to develop new tests in place of the old, but to review the principles on which they were built. In that respect, too, the development of research techniques, which has made considerable progress in our country, is of the most direct value in working out new methods of determining intellectual development. The studies conducted under the direction of B. M. Teplov are of particular importance, as are those of V. S. Merlin. These have led to the development of definitions of the properties of human higher nervous activity and have provided materials on the basis of which it is possible to compare indices of these properties with various psychological manifestations.

Other quests for means of identifying the level of intellectual development are also of interest. In one such study, the authors (Z. I. Kalmykova, V. I. Zykova, A. M. Orlova, and others) chose the schoolchild's instructive capacity as an index of intellectual development, and judged this capacity on the basis of the degree to which the pupil manifests the ability to acquire knowledge on his own, i.e., the success he has in independently analyzing a particular general law and in expressing it in words. A distinctive feature of this indicator lies in the fact that it is not static but dynamic in nature. Other psychologists (L. V. Zankov and his associates) have found it necessary, when defining general intellectual development, to study modes of activity differing in nature. In this connection different forms of mental activity were chosen for testing: powers of observation, abstract thought, and practical (work) activity. At the same time L. V. Zankov emphasizes the presence in these of universal intellectual components — namely, operations of thought of an analytical and synthetic nature. A third group of psychologists (D. B. El'konin, V. V. Davydov, and Ia. A. Ponomarev) has chosen, as index of intellectual development, the capacity to operate mentally, "in one's head" (or ability "in the internal plane of activity"). Finally, a number of psychologists (B. G. Anan'ev, Iu. A. Samarin, and others) have emphasized the significance of systematic knowledge and the ability to operate flexibly with shaped systems as criteria for judging intellectual development.

The problem facing future research is to determine the significance of each of these indices in the system of criteria that characterize intellectual development in the process of instruction.

Along with the problem of overall intellectual development, the question of special abilities is of great interest to educational psychology, inasmuch as instruction should be such as to promote the development of the personality in all the richness and uniqueness of its individual manifestations.

The problem of development of special abilities began to be worked on intensively in the 1940s, with the appearance in the press of writings by B. M. Teplov. The propositions formulated in these writings underlie most of the studies that followed. Among these it is necessary to list, above all, the treatment of abilities as the result of development and not as inborn capabilities of the individual. What are inborn are not capabilities, but those anatomical and physiological characteristics, i.e., gifts, upon which capabilities are built.

The postulate developed by B. M. Teplov, to the effect that the problem of capacities is primarily a qualitative rather than quantitative one, was of much importance. Teplov himself demonstrated this through the example of musical abilities and revealed that they were qualitative in structure. Later, V. I. Kireenko published a book devoted to the problem of abilities in the plastic arts, in which he uncovered the most important components of abilities in that form of activity, associated primarily with qualities of visual perception and visual imagination. In describing the traits of personality and behavior of children displaying ability in the plastic arts, the author notes that they have a great deal of endurance in that sphere.

N. S. Leites ascribes much significance to this quality in his studies of the gifted intellect. He emphasizes that a fondness for work is not something external and supplemental relative to ability, but is a component of talent.

V. A. Krutetskii, who studied manifestations of ability in mathematics, wrote of that same personality trait. He observes that children showing a gift for mathematics are characterized by a distinctive "mathematical turn of mind," manifested above all in a tendency to introduce a "mathematical aspect" into perception. When Krutetskii, in his research, analyzed the qualitative features of mathematical capabilities, he made extensive use of comparative studies of various groups of schoolchildren: those who were successful in mathematics and those who were unable to cope with that form of learning activity. He singled out the features that most sharply distinguished the two groups from each other: the manner in which mathematical material was generalized in the solution of problems, the process of switching from a direct to an inverse mode of thought, and "shortcutting" — the reduction of operations in learning activity.

VII

The question of reducing the number of operations (or actions) in operating with knowledge has a significance of its own. It was studied by P. A. Shevarev and his associates. It must be noted that the fact of abbreviating the process of reasoning and eliminating a number of links, as the result of processes becoming automatic, has been quite familiar from the extensive literature devoted to habits. But precisely what

mechanisms underlie this development of short cuts remained unclear. P. A. Shevarev demonstrated that that phenomenon was based upon the appearance (and implementation) of a special category of associations: "generalizing" or "variative" associations, which operate in accordance with a particular rule (grammatical, mathematical, etc.), even though the rules are not called to mind at the time they are actualized. (Therefore yet another term, "rule-conformable," is also applied to such associations.) Shevarev classes these associations with connections based on adjacency, emphasizing however that the reason they arise is not merely because two processes abut upon each other. There is also needed a "combination by thought, into a single whole, of the things or facts cognized in these processes." Thus, we are discussing not external connections, but connections by content.

Employment of the content of the rule-conformable association and detailed analysis of the composition of the connections shaped have made it possible to establish, with ample adequacy, which components of learning activity are not cognized and which are cognized and serve as condition for implementation of the required associations. Thanks to the concept thus introduced, psychologists and educators acquire an implement for analysis of the materials in exercises and are able to explain the appearance of quite a number of errors that arise despite the intentions of the learner, and also to carry into effect methods of preventing such mistakes by recourse to an appropriate reorganization of the exercise material (by changing the frequency and sequence of the exercises).

Iu. A. Samarin also had recourse to the concept of association in explaining the process of formation of systems of knowledge. As distinct from Shevarev, who revealed the psychological nature of various types of associations, Samarin employed a psychology-of-education approach and proposes the classification of the associations forming the substrata of the degree of breadth of the connections (and, accordingly, the degree of difficulty the pupils encounter in systematizing knowledge). The author distinguishes, in the first place, "local" associations effectuating connections between individual phenomena, regardless of the systems to which they belong; second, "system-limited" phenomena confined within the bounds of the given subject matter; third, "intra-systemic" connections, by means of which the combination of a number of associations by one or another principle is implemented (for example, the combination of historical events by the criterion of chronology); fourth and last, "inter-subject" or "inter-systemic" associations, by means of which relationships among kinds of knowledge belonging to different branches of science are established.

The Leningrad Institute of Pedagogy (B. G. Anan'ev, Director) has prepared a series of books devoted to analysis of the interrelationships among various school subjects during a single year of instruction, as well as to the continuity in instructional and educational work from the earliest to the upper grades. The establishment of these interconnections created the possibility of shaping a system of knowledge that would constitute the basis for development of an integrated personality.

VIII

The discovery of the laws of mental activity in the instructional process, as set forth above, is one of the preconditions for developing the most effective forms of learning activity. Thus the discovery of the successive stages in analytical and synthetic mental activity, the features of interaction of concrete and abstract thought, and the process of formation and actualization of associations makes it possible to bring a variety of indirect influences to bear upon learning activity. This can be done via the teacher's presentation, the selection of material for exercises, and so forth. At the same time direct influence is assured upon the "subject in instruction" himself, the pupil, who is taught rational modes of thinking activity.

In addition to this approach, under which indirect influence upon learning activity is combined with direct influence upon the subject in instruction, there was also another approach, characterized by a striving to assure direction to learning activity and to those intellectual activities that have to be shaped by means of direct, immediate influence upon the very process of assimilation of knowledge. In the early 1950s, P. Ia. Gal'perin, N. F. Talyzina (Moscow University), D. B. El'konin and V. V. Davydov (Psychology Institute, Academy of Pedagogical Sciences) and their associates undertook this approach.

The goal was set of identifying and building (with special emphasis upon initiative in this building process) a system of conditions that would "compel" the pupil "to function correctly and only correctly, in the required form, and to score the desired indices" (P. Ia. Gal'perin). To attain this objective, not only was the study material to be mastered "programmed," but so were the operations the pupil was to perform with it. What was envisaged above all was the creation of conditions necessary and sufficient for performance of operations (in the authors' phrase, "to construct a complete orientation base for actions"). Moreover, as was emphasized in a number of writings, the pupil was to adhere strictly to the instructions given him. If he commits errors, this means that the system of instructions contains certain lacunae or that certain "necessary guideposts" have not been provided.

Gal'perin advanced, as a significant condition making possible control of the learning process, the idea that actions take shape in stages. Initially, the effort of the pupil is implemented in external, material (or "materialized") form. It is then transferred to the plane of externalized speech, and only in the final stage does it become an internalized mental operation.

While suggesting that sequence, Gal'perin also emphasizes in his most recent writings that, in fact, there are always a variety of short cuts in movement along that route, depending upon past experience and the existence of similar forms of other acts. However, with respect to the first stage (of material action, i.e., action with things), Gal'perin observes that in the total set of knowledge about things, "such directly 'muscular' knowledge comprises only a very insignificant portion of the whole." This last observation is entirely in accord with the data of other authors (discussed above) to the effect that the course by which knowledge is acquired is not unambiguous, but is determined by many conditions, particularly the character of the knowledge itself.

Much attention in this group of writings (particularly those done under the guidance of El'konin and Davydov) is given to the shaping of intellectual operations which make it possible for pupils to master concepts fundamental to science and reflected in the subject of the course, the assimilation of which facilitates the development in schoolchildren of a distinct "cognitive" attitude to the content of the material. For example, in teaching mathematics to 1st graders (research of V. V. Davydov), the concepts of inequality and equality are selected, and in order tc enable these concepts to be assimilated, the children are taught operations that make it possible gradually to reveal abstract mathematical relationships to them.

In the entire group of psychologists referred to, that which is distinctive in the character of their approach to the learning process emerges clearly in the characterization and evaluation of various types of learning offered by Gal'perin in a number of his writings. He identifies three types of learning. The first, he believes, occurs in the course of instruction at school, and is characterized by the fact that assimilation occurs spontaneously and is an uncontrolled process. In this situation the development of new actions proceeds by trial and error, and the conditions of experiment do not manifest themselves adequately. Correct action takes shape gradually as the result of reinforcement (monitoring of the final result). Transferrence to different problems does not occur.

In the second type of learning (which occurs in a number of the studies by Gal'perin, Talyzina, and their associates), the pupil performs all operations on the basis of consideration of the objective conditions. He obtains all the required instructions; there is direct monitoring of his activities from without. Therefore the shaping of the actions occurs without significant errors (or without error). Transfer to new problems occurs, however, only if the problems have elements in common with those utilized in instruction.

Finally, in the third type of learning, all the advantages noted in describing the second type are retained, and new ones are added. The mode of operation also takes shape without trial and error, but the level of operations in this case is higher inasmuch as the pupil not only takes the conditions into consideration but understands on what the selection and composition of these conditions is based. Much of what is thus learned is transferred to new problems. This type of learning is also associated with a higher level of motivation of learning activity, and with the appearance of a cognitive attitude to the material that has to be mastered.

It is not difficult to see that this type of learning presumes direct influence not only upon the process of acquisition of knowledge (as was the case in the second type), but also upon the "subject in instruction" himself, the pupil, inasmuch as the situation is one in which the pupil has already mastered a number of more general methods (or techniques) of learning activity, and this makes possible extensive transferrence to other problems.

It should be noted that employment of the course that Gal'perin classifies in the third type is encountered in the writings of psychologists of various tendencies: both those who pose the task of developing techniques of intellectual activity and those who propound the need for "stage-by-stage shaping of intellectual activities."

Certain Soviet psychologists also suggest another path for giving direction to the learning process: reducing the learning process to algorithms.

L. N. Landa and his associates are working on that problem. They employ the term "algorithm" not in its rigorous mathematical meaning, but as a synonym for a prescription of an algorithmic type. Such prescriptions are based on careful analysis of the logical composition of the operations being shaped, and this is indissolubly associated with their "rigidity." At the same time they make it possible to resolve problems of various classes, inasmuch as the logical structures of various types of learning activity have much in common. Landa offers a classification of algorithmic prescriptions which he bases upon a number of conditions (type of problems, character of information, etc.). He offers a particular justification of two of his categories (based on a criterion for the purpose of applying them): the algorithms of transformation and of identification.

In the work that Landa performed, algorithmic prescriptions of the second type (in learning the syntax of the Russian language) were subjected to experimental verification. Moreover, the algorithms were not introduced in the form of ready-made prescriptions, but the pupils learned to identify the characteristics of phenomena and to build algorithms on their own. Toward this end, a lesson in "logic" (preliminary to the teaching of the specific algorithm) was conducted, during which the teacher disclosed the concept of criteria for phenomena and the logical structure of the criteria, demonstrating with the aid of examples why it is necessary to know this and developing in the pupils the ability to ascertain the logic of the criteria and to identify the dependence of the means of identifying the object or phenomenon upon their features.

Landa emphasizes that the use, in the course of the lesson, of problems from various spheres (everyday life, mathematics, grammar) had the purpose of attaining maximum generalization of the methods of thought (reasoning) employed by the pupils.

IX

The researches described above dealt primarily with the intellectual aspects of learning activity. The studies were primarily analytical in nature and sought to uncover the distinguishing features of the process under examination. However, as early as the 1930s and 1940s, works were published that incorporated questions of the psychology of learning into the broad context of the problem of the personality. This is true, for example, of a study by B. G. Anan'ev

in 1935; in it he advanced the goal of developing "learning self-awareness," a term he defined as an understanding by the pupil of the motives, goals, and techniques of learning, recognition of himself as the subject in learning activity, in organizing, directing, and controlling the learning process.

In analyzing the course followed by research until now, it must be stated that this task is as a whole not yet resolved, and that questions of the pupil's organization and control over himself in the learning process require special investigation. Investigations of individual psychological differences manifested in the process of instruction do provide some material for resolution of these questions. However, as a rule, they remain purely descriptive works thus far, and the question of reducing these differences to types is as yet far from solution. It will have to be the subject matter of intensive research in the future.

Also deserving attention is the attempt by Iu. A. Samarin in 1948 to study the style of intellectual work by upper-grade schoolchildren. In characterizing that "style," the author reveals not only the uniqueness of intellectual operations (and properties of mind), but also the special features of volitional and emotional processes. He shows that the pupil's "self-organization" depends directly upon his general sense of direction, his interests, his outlook for the future, and the world view he has formed.

The study by Volokitina of younger schoolchildren (1955) also falls into that category. The author divides pupils into groups and bases her division upon the degree to which the sense of duty with respect to learning requirements has taken shape. Each pupil is given an integrated characterization demonstrating how the various personality traits of the individual are "cemented" (this includes the distinguishing features of his learning activity), as well as his overall moral direction.

Unfortunately, it must be stated that studies such as Volokitina's are still few and far between in psychology. Most of the writings on the psychology of learning described above are characterized by inadequate attention to the moral direction of the personality. It is precisely for this reason that the problem of converting knowledge into convictions, into a world view system, has thus far had virtually no psychological study.

The significance in learning processes of that aspect of the personality that is characterized by attitude toward learning — motivation — has had considerably wider study than that of moral direction. A. N. Leont'ev posed the question of the fundamental significance of these aspects of the personality as long ago as 1947. In an article entitled "Psychological Questions of the Consciousness of Learning" [Psikhologicheskie voprosy soznatel'nosti ucheniia], he protested against a purely intellectualist treatment of consciousness as knowledge, and advanced the thesis that consciousness is also an attitude. The conscious character of knowledge, Leont'ev observed, is characterized specifically by the meaning it acquires for man, and the meaning of a cognized action, in his interpretation, is determined by the motivation of the activity of which the individual action is a part. These postulates had a pronounced influence upon the development of research on the problem of the motives of learning. The latter was implemented within the confines of educational psychology and at the same time made an important contribution to treatment of problems of learning (writings of L. I. Bozhovich, L. S. Slavina, N. G. Morozova, and others).

A special group of studies (by N. F. Dobrynin and his associates) is devoted to the role, in processes of assimilation, of the cognition by pupils of the significance of the knowledge they acquire in school. In this research one may follow the transition from awareness of social meaning to the appearance of a personal feeling of need to gain knowledge.

The question of the teacher's pedagogical tact occupies an important place in the shaping of the motivations for learning activity, as does his ability to control his own psychological state as he conducts his lessons (this has been studied by N. D. Levitov, I. V. Strakhov, and others). (1)

In recent years the motivational aspect began to be introduced into research devoted to the intellectual aspects of learning activity. Primary importance attaches not to whether this is associated with the mastery of rational modes of thought or with higher types of learning, in which a higher level of orientation in the problem is obtained, but to the very fact that the problem of personal need and motivation has been incorporated into the makeup of research pertaining to mental operations. This incorporation occurs inevitably when the problem is posed more broadly, as a question of a higher type of learning or as a problem of mental development in the process of instruction. G. S. Kostiuk, who asserted that the mental development of the personality is characterized by a unity of knowledge, operations, and motivations of mental activity, was quite right in this contention.

At present, certain concrete lines of investigation of intellectual development, not only in unity with motivations, but in conjunction with the moral direction of the personality and its world view, have already been plotted out.

X

In Soviet psychology, as is evident from the foregoing, the outlines of a theory of learning have clearly taken shape. Despite the existence of diverse trends emphasizing one or another aspect of learning activity, they all agree that learning has to be closely associated with development, that it must lead development forward, that it is a constantly changing process determined by external conditions operating through the internal, and that the pupil's initiative in the process of cognition plays a role of the greatest importance. All researchers seek to guarantee the most effective influence upon the learning process, viewing as necessary the existence, in one or another form, of a standard on which the learning activity should be built; and they break this latter down into individual elements ("steps," individual actions, or various stages in the shaping of a technique). They all recognize that the more particular modes of action undergo combination and are transformed into generalized methods which then become universal techniques of rational thought. Rich material has been obtained on the question of changes in intellectual activity in the process of learning, and these changes have been traced in various directions. Here we have motion from ignorance to knowledge (i.e., change in the results) and change in the quality of the operations of thinking, by means of which one attains the result (although this too has had less study), as well as change in the very properties of the intellect, which develop in the course of instruction.

In summarizing the above, one cannot fail to observe that the contours of the theory of learning that we have noted in Soviet psychology do not yet mean that this work has in any way been brought to completion. There is need for further and deeper treatment of the principal concepts, broad study of facts and laws, further discovery of shared positions, which are often concealed behind differences in terminology. There is need for intensive study of the pupil as "the subject in instruction," of his personality, which develops in the process of instruction, of his attitude toward reality, of the system of views, and of communist morality taking shape in him.

The Marxist-Leninist theory of learning presumes that the activity of learning will be revealed in all its connections and mediated forms. It must be built on the foundation of genuine synthesis of knowledge about the learning activity of the developing person.

At the present stage of its development, the Soviet psychology of learning has become a widely ramified branch of educational psychology.

On one side (to the degree that it reveals universal laws of learning) it faces toward didactics, while on another (directed toward study of particularized laws of learning manifested when instruction in the various school subjects occurs) it is directly connected with the special subject techniques. In various areas of its subject matter, the Soviet psychology of instruction has already approached introduction of its research findings into the practical work of the schools. Methods manuals, in which psychology is an integral component, have begun to be published. Psychologists are taking part in the work of improving school syllabuses.

There can be no doubt that in the future, when the psychology of learning comes closer to the psychology of character education, the practical effectiveness of research in this field will become even higher. The results will be incorporated into the everyday life of the school, and those broad opportunities that are open for development of the psychology of learning in our country will be realized to the full.

Footnote

1) It is not possible, within the confines of this article, to treat a special and very important branch of the psychology of learning: the psychology of the teacher. N. V. Kuz'mina and F. N. Gonobolin have also made an important contribution to the elaboration of that problem.

* * *

Preschool Education

Sovetskaia pedagogika, 1967, No. 5

A. P. Zaporozhets, T. A. Markova, and E. I. Radina

FIFTY YEARS OF SOVIET PRESCHOOL PEDAGOGY

In its fifty years of existence, Soviet preschool pedagogy has traversed a long and complicated road. Of great importance in its development have been the achievements of related sciences — child psychology, developmental physiology, and pediatrics.

Regarding preschool education as an important link in the overall process of forming the new man, Soviet preschool pedagogy has spent a number of years in working out problems for the successful further development of pedagogical theory and practice.

The problem of the aims of education, the cornerstone of any pedagogical system, is the most important one.

Soviet pedagogy, including preschool pedagogy, is based on the Marxist tenet that the aims of education are determined by the needs of society and assume a different character at different stages of society's development. In describing the goals of Soviet preschool education, N. K. Krupskaya used to say that this education should be communistic and indissolubly connected with the construction of a new society. The aims and tasks of education consist in developing in the children those creative abilities and moral qualities which are needed by socialist society.

As regards the aims of education, the prominent Soviet pedagogue A. S. Makarenko justly emphasized that the goals of pedagogy cannot be borrowed from either psychology or physiology, but that they are determined socially, by the tasks and developmental prospects of our society.

Indissolubly connected with the problem of the aims of education are the problems of indoctrinating preschool children with collectivism, developing collective activity during play and during such work as they can perform, organizing elementary forms of the children's collective, and linking kindergarten to contemporary life. The new social life, of course, raised the problem of training collectivists from their earliest years and of creating conditions that would make it impossible for the child to display selfishness ["individualism"] and egoism. The task of linking kindergarten to contemporary

---

The authors are affiliated with the Research Institute for Preschool Education, USSR Academy of Pedagogical Sciences.

life came to the forefront because the work was not confined within the walls of the institution, but was closely connected with the social life of the country.

Study of the aims, tasks, and content of education is closely connected with working out programs of education. If the aims of education are "dictated" by society, then we can and must program the knowledge which the child acquires, the totality of skills which he develops, and a system of abilities and personal qualities which he forms.

Conventions and conferences on preschool training have played a large role in posing and studying all the above problems. At the very first convention (1919), there was a discussion of the aims and tasks of Soviet preschool training in connection with the new forms of social life, although primary attention was given to a concrete definition of the types of preschool institutions, the organized forms of preschool education. Participants in the second and third conventions (1921 and 1924) and in the third conference on preschool education (1925) debated the aims and tasks, the content and methods of preschool training from all angles. At the fourth convention (1928), the basic principles of constructing a program of communist training for preschool-age children were laid down.

In the work of the conventions, which were led by N. K. Krupskaya and A. V. Lunacharskii, the preschool workers were actively joined by important figures in the fields of general pedagogy and psychology (P. P. Blonskii, K. N. Kornilov, S. T. Shatskii), pediatrics and child hygiene (E. A. Arkin, V. I. Gorinevskii, L. I. Chulitskaia), the arts and art education (G. I. Roshal', V. N. Shatskaia, E. A. Flerina, M. A. Rumer, et al.).

The conventions united practitioners and theorists of preschool education for the struggle against various bourgeois and petty-bourgeois tendencies. A sharp debate flared up at the third convention (1924) with regard to the ideological content of the educational process in kindergarten, as well as the connection between the formal and material aspects of this process. In their reports, R. I. Prushitskaia and A. V.

Surovtseva justly criticized the biologizing theories and the formal didactic systems which sever preschool training from life and isolate the child from surrounding social reality. Progressive theses were advanced about linking kindergarten with contemporary life, about the ideological orientation of Soviet preschool training, and about inculcating the children with collectivism and love of labor. In analyzing the activity of community children's institutions during these years, M. M. Vilenskaia has pointed out that the content of work with children was closely linked with the overall tasks of the working class, and that three "isms" came to characterize these institutions: materialism, collectivism, and activism.

At the same time it should be emphasized that in practice, alongside the great creative achievements of advanced pedagogues, the children were considerably overburdened with cognitive material (about the social and political life of the country) and practical activity. Preschool children were enlisted in various social campaigns (the struggle for the Industrial and Financial Plan, and antireligious propaganda); instructions about polytechnical education addressed to the [primary] schools were often mechanically transferred to kindergarten work, thus encouraging complicated types of labor of an allegedly "polytechnical" character. Play as a specific children's activity was underestimated; it was understood as a "free" form of children's life, completely undirected by adults, and merely reflecting the influence of the environment.

The creation of a kindergarten curriculum was discussed at the fourth convention on preschool training. Due attention was paid to the role of work and play in developing collectivism and in solving other problems of proletarian training (report by S. S. Molozhavii). The importance of posing all these questions is obvious. But the specifics of different types of activity were regarded from positions of pedology. Labor was called "a life-adapting activity"; the surrounding milieu was inevitably supposed to call forth certain forms and content even in the labor of preschoolers. It is not surprising that it was proposed to connect the work of small children with "the shock tasks of socialist reconstruction," "the industrial plan," etc. On the other hand, play was opposed to work as a "free" activity; the close link between them, so characteristic for preschool-age children, was not seen. These directions, proclaimed at conventions and later propagandized by the press, influenced the development of the theory and practice of play and work for a number of years.

The first draft curriculum for the Soviet kindergarten was issued by the Department of Education in 1932. Despite its defects, it played a great role in creating a single system of Soviet preschool education, defining its aim and basic content, and solving the problems of the comprehensive development and communist training of the children attending kindergarten. The section "Physical Training," by A. A. Nevskii, was presented first. The section of the curriculum on social and political indoctrination directed the teacher's work in bringing the content of kindergarten education into line with contemporary life. However, although the curriculum attached an explanatory note containing a critical analysis of the mistakes which were often made in practice, the curriculum itself repeated many of them. It overloaded small children with social and political information beyond their comprehension, and with labor skills beyond their abilities. Lack of comprehension of the age characteristics of preschoolers was expressed in underestimation of so remarkable a form of children's literature as the fairy tale, which was allegedly a relic of the past, distracted the child from contemporary Soviet reality, and prevented him from developing materialist thinking.

The 1934 decree of the CPSU Central Committee, "On the Overburdening of Schoolchildren and Pioneers with Social and Political Instructions," also helped preschool personnel to discover and eliminate errors in the kindergarten training of that time.

The 1934 kindergarten curriculum represented a further step forward in developing a system of Soviet preschool education. Certain defects of the first draft curriculum were overcome. In developing the program, a positive role was played by the advanced practical experience accumulated during the years of Soviet power and by the ever expanding research in the fields of preschool pedagogy, child psychology, developmental physiology, and other related sciences. The new curriculum particularly underscored the need for concern about the health and physical training of the child; the need to take account of age characteristics was indicated, and the range of information and skills to be mastered was considerably narrowed. But one should also note that this curriculum also reproduced, in part, the errors of the 1932 curriculum. The range of skills and knowledge taught to the child was still extremely broad, resulting in the (purely) formal mastery of the program content. The educational role of play was emphasized everywhere, but the proposed methods of "stimulating" play activity exaggerated the importance of prepared materials and toys or of a created pedagogical milieu. It was recommended that creative role playing be planned ahead of time. In practice, all this resulted in excessive regimentation of play and interfered with the development of children's initiative, although we can approve the idea of stimulating play since it tended to combat the then widespread attitude toward play as a free, spontaneous activity.

The negative influence of the then popular pragmatic pedagogy is seen in the grouping of curriculum material around "organizing moments," which introduced a certain artificiality into the educational process, depriving it of system and consistency. However, one cannot ignore the positive aspects of this method of work, recommended in the curriculum of the GUS [State Scientific Council]. Excessive verbalism in education was overcome; ways were sought to enlist children in practical activity, important in developing new social feelings and attitudes.

The first planners of the draft curriculum included a fairly wide range of preschool pedagogues: the scientific workers and leading methodologists A. V. Surovtseva, R. I. Prushitskaia, M. M. Vilenskaia, E. A. Flerina, A. A. Nevskii, A. M. Leushina, E. A. Arkin, L. K. Shleger, E. G. Levi-Gorinevskaia, N. A. Metlov, F. S. Levin-

Shchirin, F. N. Blekher, S. Ia. Fainshtein, and many others. Leading educators took an active part in preparing the curriculums; they were led by the staff of the "Komintern" kindergarten (the methods base of the Department of Education), where methods work was headed by D. V. Mendzheritskaia and the teachers were Z. A. Sergeva, L. A. Pen'evskaia, and others.

In the period under review, Soviet child psychology and, to a certain degree, developmental physiology of higher nervous activity could not as yet provide pedagogy with sufficiently precise scientific approaches to defining the child's age characteristics. There were insufficient reliable factual data, and certain advanced psychological ideas regarding the ontogenesis of the human psyche advanced by L. S. Vygotskii and others were not yet widely accepted and exerted no palpable influence on pedagogical theory and practice. This made it possible for pedology to penetrate the theory and practice of preschool education. Pedology had borrowed the concept of the maturation of innate abilities from various kinds of bourgeois idealist and biologizing theories about human ontogenesis, and it employed unscientific methods of testing the level of the child's intellectual development. The negative influence of pedology is seen in the 1934 curriculum. In a number of cases it advised the educator to base the content of a lesson not so much on pedagogical tasks and requirements as on the interests and psychophysiological characteristics of the child — moreover, falsely interpreted.

In 1936, the Central Committee of the All-Union Communist Party (Bolsheviks) issued a decree censuring pedagogical misinterpretations in the system of educational commissariats. The overcoming of pedological errors played an important role in the development of the theory and practice of Soviet preschool training. The rights of the pedagogue and pedagogy were reinstated. The leading role of the educator in the pedagogical process was realized in practice and acknowledged in theory. Soviet preschool pedagogy became able to define the object of its research more precisely and began to develop as an independent branch of pedagogical science.

Pedological test measurements of the child's allegedly congenital intelligence were replaced by psychological and physiological studies of the laws of the formation of the child's psychic processes under the influence of the conditions of life and education.

Implementation of the decree on pedology was, in addition to the above-mentioned positive results, also accompanied by certain negative phenomena.

In 1938 a new curriculum and methods document, "Handbook for the Kindergarten Teacher," was drawn up. The July 4, 1936, decree of the Central Committee of the CPSU(b), "On Misinterpretations in the System of Education Commissariats," served as a basis in the handbook for a clear definition of the teacher's leading role in the kindergarten pedagogical process and in carrying out the tasks of communist training. In addition to the handbook, the first "Kindergarten Regulations" in the history of socialist preschool training were published, defining the aims of kindergarten as a state institution, its structure, and characteristics of educational work. A serious defect in these curriculum and methods regulations was the omission of such pertinent sections for the Soviet kindergarten as child labor and a link with the surrounding social life. This was evidently due to a fear of repeating previous mistakes such as a burdensome program, complicated materials, etc.

The "Handbook for the Kindergarten Teacher," which appeared in 1953, represented a considerable improvement based on scientific research into the problems of preschool education, conducted by the preschool education section in the Scientific Research Institute of the Theory and History of Pedagogy, RSFSR Academy of Pedagogical Sciences. It defined more precisely the tasks and methods of preschool didactics, raised the overall level of requirements for the children's development, and elaborated a curriculum content aimed at training the children and preparing them for school.

The tremendous activity of the CPSU and the Soviet state in building communism in our country is indissolubly linked with solving the problems of increasing the role of education in forming the personality of man. The communist system of national education, as the CPSU Program emphasizes, is based on the social training of children in conjunction with family training from the first years of their life. In this situation there is a sharp increase in the need to develop the network of children's institutions as social and educational institutions, to improve scientific research, and to construct programs aimed at a more successful solution to the problems of the harmonious, rounded training of the new man.

The May 21, 1959, decree of the CPSU Central Committee and the USSR Council of Ministers regarding measures for the further development of children's preschool institutions presented scientific workers with the task of creating a new curriculum that encompassed educational work with children of both early school and preschool age. A joint commission of the RSFSR Academy of Pedagogical Sciences (APS) and the USSR Academy of Medicine was created for this purpose, headed by Professors A. P. Usova (chairman) and N. M. Shchelovanov (vice-chairman). All the laboratories of the newly organized (September 1960) Institute of Preschool Training of the APS RSFSR took part in preparing this document. The curriculum is based on the considerable experience in educational work and the many years of research by the scientific institutions of the Ministry of Education and the Ministry of Public Health; it represents the first curriculum in the history of pedagogy which defines the basic content and forms of training children from infancy until they enter school.

Drawing up the new curriculum required eliminating the break in educational work with children of early school and preschool age. The curriculum material is arranged by types of child activity, taking account of the children's age characteristics and making the teacher's work more versatile. Considerably more attention is given to play — the main preschool activity — and to the pedagogical supervision and organization of play.

A special section called "Labor" was introduced into the curriculum for children in the senior and preparatory groups after it had been incorrectly dropped from the preceding two curriculums; increased attention was also paid to this form of activity in the other child groups.

In order to improve the preparation of children for school, the curriculum provided for teaching elementary grammar and arithmetic to the preparatory group (six-year-olds). At the same time, broad educational work was planned to teach the children diligence, discipline, habits of cultural behavior, the ability to follow the teacher's directions and to work independently, all of which are of great importance in preparing children for study activity in school.

The "Kindergarten Education Curriculum" was approved and issued by the Ministry of Education in 1962 (reissued in 1964); at present it is followed by all kindergartens and nursery schools in the Russian Federation. The curriculum testified to the growth of Soviet preschool pedagogy, its movement forward in the matter of solving important key problems in the theory of preschool education. However, the curriculum formulated certain pedagogical tasks, especially in the field of training, in an overly general way, without sufficient clarity and concrete definition. The content of some of its sections does not rely sufficiently on the corresponding scientific research. The curriculum does not yet guarantee the genuine optimization of the process of preschool training or the maximally favorable conditions for comprehensive development of the child's personality. The reasons [for this] must be sought in the incomplete elaboration of the theory of preschool training This requires a sharp increase in research devoted to studying the laws governing the education and development of preschool-age children.

* * *

The demands of life and the party directives have increased the role of education and of the teacher in the pedagogical process of the kindergarten. This trend became especially manifest in the second half of the 1930's. The works and theories of N. K. Krupskaya had tremendous importance in the development of the theory and

50

practice of Soviet preschool training. At that time the works of the remarkable Soviet pedagogue A. S. Makarenko were also being published. Hypotheses advanced by pedagogy concerning the aims and methods of the communist training of the young generation, the role of family training and of the collective in forming the child's personality, and the pedagogical importance of play, exerted much influence on the creative searches of educators and scientific workers in the field of preschool pedagogy. The book of the famous Soviet preschool pedagogue E. I. Tikheeva, Speech Development of the Preschool Child [Razvitie rechi doshkol'nika], appeared in 1937; it summarized scientific methods experiments in the kindergarten of the A. I. Herzen Pedagogical Institute. E. A. Arkin and L. I. Chulitskaia prepared valuable handbooks on the physical education of preschool-age children. Scientific problems of art education (E. A. Flerina, N. P. Sakulina, N. A. Metlov), child speech development (A. M. Leushina), pedagogical guidance of play (A. P. Usova, R. I. Zhukovskaia, D. V. Mendzheritskaia), etc., were elaborated.

In the field of child psychology, A. N. Leont'eva, S. L. Rubinshtein, and others elaborated general problems of the motive factors in child psychic development and conducted detailed research into the laws of formation of various psychic processes in relation to the child's living conditions and the nature of his activity. The first works on the history of Soviet preschool pedagogy appeared (L. I. Krasnogorskaia). F. S. Levin-Shchirina and D. V. Mendzheritskaia published the first textbook on pedagogy for preschool teacher training schools. Dissertations were defended on subjects of preschool training.

The RSFSR Academy of Pedagogical Sciences, established in 1944, played a large role in the development of the theory of preschool training. Preschool sectors were organized in all institutes of the academy to work on problems in the theory of pedagogy, physical education, art education, and psychology. Then, at the end of 1960, the Scientific Research Institute for Preschool Education was founded.

Scientific work in the departments of pre-

school pedagogy of the pedagogical institutes became considerably more active. Textbooks on preschool pedagogy for pedagogical institutes were published (edited by E. A. Flerina, Sh. I. Ganelina); the department of preschool pedagogy of the A. I. Herzen Pedagogical Institute issued several volumes of "Scientific Notes" devoted to matters of preschool education. The degree of doctor of pedagogical sciences was awarded to I. V. Chuvashov for fundamental works on pedagogy, to A. M. Leushina for work in the arithmetic preparation for school, and to A. P. Usova for work on preschool didactics. The title of professor was conferred on the famous specialist in the field of early childhood, N. M. Aksarina. A number of works on the history of preschool pedagogy were completed (O. A. Frolova, E. I. Volkova, E. A. Grebenshchikova, et al.), and the results of research into the family training of children were published in a book by E. I. Volkova, T. A. Markova, N. P. Eiges, et al.

Psychological research on children of preschool age was conducted in the Moscow Scientific Research Institute of Psychology (A. V. Zaporozhets, D. B. El'konin, Ia. Z. Neverovich, T. V. Endovitskaia, et al.), in the Leningrad Scientific Research Institute of Pedagogy (B. G. Anan'ev, A. A. Liublinskaia, V. A. Gorbacheva), in the Kiev Institute of Psychology (G. S. Kostiuk, P. R. Chamata), and in Tbilisi University (B. I. Khachapuridze). A. N. Leont'ev's Psychic Development [Razvitie psikhiki] appeared in 1959; in particular, it summarized a great deal of research conducted on children of preschool age. This book received a Lenin Prize.

Under the leadership of Professor N. M. Shchelovanov, the USSR Academy of Medicine conducted an intensive investigation of the problems of educating young children. The investigation conclusively showed that the full nervous and psychic development of young children is basically determined by education.

At present the number of institutions investigating matters of preschool pedagogy and psychology has increased even more. In addition to the broader inclusion of the preschool pedagogy departments of pedagogical institutes in this work (RSFSR and other union republics), research is being carried on in the preschool departments of republic scientific research institutes of pedagogy and psychology and in universities (e.g., in the Ukraine, Georgia, Belorussia, and Uzbekistan).

Further development of preschool education requires the theoretical and methodological solution of the problem of preschool teaching (its essence, forms, and methods). Although the struggle against the theory of spontaneous education began in the first years of Soviet power, survivals of this theory were rather firmly retained in the theory and practice of preschool education right up to the end of the 1950's. No one appeared to dispute the need for "required" lessons in kindergarten; but the teacher's role was reduced to presenting tasks which the child was supposed to solve independently, without receiving precise instructions about the correct ways of performing them. Thus teaching was sometimes replaced by self-teaching, which reduced the efficiency of the didactic process, giving it a spontaneous, undirected character.

A decisive role in abolishing this serious defect was played by the department of preschool education in the Institute of the Theory and History of Pedagogy of the RSFSR Academy of Pedagogical Sciences, under the leadership of A. P. Usova (E. I. Radina, V. G. Nechaeva, L. A. Pen'evskaia, R. I. Zhukovskaia). Theoretical research was conducted in depth to give concrete definition to the tenets of Marxism-Leninism about learning as the acquisition of social experience, as they applied to the special features of preschool education. The content and methods of preschool training were worked out experimentally in demonstration kindergartens, on the basis of the theories advanced. The data obtained were refined in the process of experimental work in a number of kindergartens, with the participation of a large group of pedagogue-practitioners. The books containing the results of the investigations — Questions of Kindergarten Instruction [Voprosy obucheniia v detskom sadu] and A. P. Usova's monograph Kindergarten Instruction [Obuchenie v detskom sadu] — were the basis for the creation of Soviet pre-

school didactics.

An essential role in solving the problems of preschool teaching was played by the preschool sectors of other institutes of the academy, as well as by the departments of preschool pedagogy in pedagogical institutes. E. A. Flerina (Moscow) elaborated the elements of teaching in the overall system of kindergarten education work. A. M. Leushina (Leningrad) wrote works on the process of teaching preschoolers elementary mathematical concepts and operations. N. P. Sakulina and N. A. Vetlugina (Moscow) studied the role of teaching in art education. A. I. Bykova (Moscow) developed scientific methods of teaching children basic movements in the action game situation, and M. M. Konina (Moscow) studied child speech development.

The work of the kindergartens in which the experiments were conducted demonstrated the viability of the new ideas and system of teaching preschoolers at lessons (in native language, drawing, construction, counting, etc.).

An important stage in work on problems of teaching was the organization of research (1957), in the course of kindergarten teaching, by scientists in close contact with the Ministry of Education of the RSFSR and the departments of preschool pedagogy in the Leningrad and Rostov Pedagogical Institutes. The need to solve the problem of preparing children for learning in school became apparent; a joint investigation by the sectors of preschool training and primary teaching of the APS RSFSR was devoted to this. The teaching of grammar to six-year-olds was given special investigation by A. I. Voskresenskaia, a corresponding member of the APS RSFSR.

Study of the educational effect of different types of teaching and its influence on the child's cognitive development deepened the content of didactic research. An important step in this direction was taken by A. P. Usova who, along with co-workers (N. P. Sakulin, N. N. Podd'iakov, et al.) from the laboratory of experimental didactics, began an analysis of sensory training [sensornoe vospitanie]. This work was conducted in close collaboration with the laboratory of developmental psychophysiology and the laboratory of preschool psychology in the Institute of Psychology.

The investigations permitted the creation of a new system of sensory training in kindergarten which guaranteed the balanced formation of the child's sensory capacities and gave him a broad orientation in apprehended reality. In the first years of his life, the child begins to process the sensory information he receives, to generalize given impressions by means of words, and to pass from perception to thought. To guide this process requires effective methods of pedagogical supervision of the formation of thinking capacities at the preschool age. Modern psychological and pedagogical research shows that the intellectual capacities of preschool-age children are considerably higher than had formerly been supposed. Our institute's laboratory of educating young children devoted particular attention to increasing the didactic components in solving problems of the mental and speech development of toddlers; it was established that, given a special organization of didactic games and lessons, a high level of development in visual-effective thought can be achieved with two- or three-year-old children.

Studies by the institutes of psychology and preschool education have shown that, given certain methods of teaching, children of six and even five years not only master reading successfully but, what is most interesting, prove more receptive to learning grammar than do children of seven and eight.

A study of intellectual development during the process of learning elementary mathematics conducted at the Moscow University department of psychology, the A. I. Herzen Institute, the V. I. Lenin Institute, and the Institute of Preschool Education revealed that under certain conditions older preschoolers can learn not only counting, but even means of solving fairly complex (e.g., "oblique") problems which until now were considered very difficult even in primary school. The studies of P. Ia. Gal'perin, G. S. Kostiuk, and A. V. Zaporozhets testify that, given a rational organization of the pedagogical process and using different kinds of visual models, preschool children can form complex logi-cal operations (classification, seriation, establishing elementary functional dependencies, etc.) which, in the opinion of leading Western European authorities (J. Piaget), can only develop in adolescence.

Thus we are beginning to accumulate the experimental data necessary for a radical transformation of the content of preschool teaching in order to ease the burden of the primary school curriculum and provide for a considerably higher level of cognitive development in preschool-age children.

Physical training is a basic component in the Soviet system of preschool education. The CPSU Program emphasizes the importance of a correct solution to this aspect of communist education from the child's earliest years, in order to train the new man for life and for the struggle for communism. Prominent Soviet scientists — L. I. Chulitskaia; M. D. Arkin; and E. A. Arkin, Member of the APS RSFSR — who have laid the basis for the system of physical education in children's preschool institutions, have closely related the tasks of physical education to its basic purpose and have shown the organic connection between physical education and the other components in the development of the child's personality.

Soviet pediatrists did a great deal to establish and improve the system of physical education by studying optimum conditions for the physical development of young children and its interdependence with the overall pedagogical process in the children's institution (G. N. Speranskii, A. F. Tur); research in the field of gymnastics and physical exercises in children's institutions were of vital importance (E. G. Levi-Gorinevskaia, A. I. Bykova, M. A. Sorochek, R. G. Uvarova). Research has been stepped up in the fields of children's dietetics, hardening the child's organism, and physical culture (O. P. Molchanova, E. A. Arkin, E. G. Levi-Gorinevskaia, T. I. Osokina). The results of scientific research have become a basic part in the practice of preschool training.

The Institute for Preschool Education, in studying the organization of regimes for preschool children as a factor in their health and correct physical development, has ascertained the relationship of regime features in kindergarten groups and has defined more rational ways of constructing and implementing the regimes recommended in the "Kindergarten Education Curriculum." A study has been started of the major physical characteristics whose timely development is extremely important in the child's physical education. Research in applying new forms of physical exercises in kindergarten and developing methods of using them is planned.

Research is presently being done in the departments of preschool pedagogy in Leningrad (N. A. Leskova et al.), the Lithuanian SSR, and Armenia on a number of problems in physical education.

An important place in the work of the Soviet kindergarten is occupied by training in the arts, which has a fruitful influence not only on the esthetic but on the intellectual and even on the moral development of the child. A tremendous contribution to the development of Soviet preschool esthetic training has been made by outstanding writers (A. M. Gor'ky, V. Mayakovsky, S. Marshak, K. Chukovsky, et al.), theatrical directors (S. Obraztsov, N. Sats), and musicians, who have created genuinely "great art for children," distinguished by high moral intelligence, remarkable artistic skill, and deep understanding of the young child's psychology.

Basic achievements in the theory and practice of Soviet preschool esthetic education included overcoming the spontaneous education theories current in the West and working out new methods of actively developing esthetic perception, artistic skills, and abilities during lessons. One should particularly take note of scientific work on the pedagogical guidance of children's pictorial activity (E. A. Flerina, N. P. Sakulina), in the field of music education (N. A. Vetlugina, N. A. Metlov), and in training children with the help of literature (N. S. Karpinskaia, O. A. Solov'eva, et al.).

The child's active, creative insight into the world of art creates particularly favorable conditions for him to develop an esthetic attitude toward reality and to form various artistic abilities. In their day, people in the arts (G. Roshal', K. Chukovsky) and preschool pedagogues as well (E. A. Flerina and others) raised this problem, but later it was undeservedly forgotten.

Our institute's laboratory of esthetic training has now begun to study the artistic creativity of children. Laboratory workers are studying the ages at which children display creativity in the field of pictorial activity and word usage, and are developing methods of training and stimulating this creativity for pedagogical goals.

Problems of moral training are particularly important in Soviet preschool pedagogy, which has always paid much attention to matters of educating children in the spirit of communist morality. The content and methods of moral training in kindergarten were studied in departments of preschool pedagogy in pedagogical institutes and in the Scientific Research Institute of the Theory and History of Pedagogy in the APS RSFSR. To some extent, these problems were solved while developing methods of teaching children's games. They were also elaborated in the psychological plan.

Kindergarten devotes much attention to general problems of education. However, in preschool education, as in social and family training, there are basic defects and imperfections, as a result of which preschool children sometimes display — along with good behavior — disobedience, rudeness, egoism, laziness, untruthfulness, etc. In young children these negative phenomena usually take mild, harmless forms, but one should not forget that they can lead to the formation of vicious, antisocial personality traits.

The moral upbringing of children is a most difficult problem for preschool pedagogy and child psychology. The process of the formation of moral qualities is considerably more complex and depends on a considerably wider range of conditions than the process of learning any special skills or information.

As is shown by research in our institute's laboratory of preschool education, we must return to a scrutiny of the content of preschool moral upbringing and concentrate our attention on teaching children the simplest forms of morality which govern their attitude toward parents, teachers, and peers. Only on this elementary basis can they really learn the considerably more complicated norms of communist morality.

In teaching the child habits of everyday moral conduct toward the people around him, the simple universal moral qualities, the teacher can inculcate a positive attitude towards peers and adults of other nationalities and lay the basis for genuine patriotism. This does not mean, of course, that fulfillment of this group of tasks can be separated from solution of a more complicated group of problems. The fact is that more complex feelings, attitudes, and personality traits are not formed without those primary norms and moral requirements presented to children of two and three years.

An important factor in moral training is the creation of conditions that will ensure the most effective learning of moral norms. The function of the latter is to regulate children's relations within the collective. Without appropriate social conditions, with only sermons, it is impossible to carry out the child's moral development. Solution of this complex pedagogical problem will require special socio-pedagogical and socio-psychological research into the nature of children's collectives, their different types and levels, the factors determining their progressive development or regression, the mechanism of their positive (or even negative) influence on individual children, and the effective forms and methods of pedagogical guidance of these collectives.

Study of all the factors in effectively teaching moral norms and rules of behavior to preschool children, and successful solution of the problems of children's spontaneous activity, require that investigators pay special attention to developing methods of moral upbringing. Considerably more importance should be given to methods by which young children are provided with a practical, effective mastery of moral norms and rules; for this purpose one must develop definite games, work, and life situations, as well as lessons with a concrete program content of a consistent order. There should also

be more studies of the formation of relations among children during cooperative practical activity, and explanations of moral phenomena in the child.

The staff and graduate students of the laboratory of education in the Institute for Preschool Education are presently conducting a complex psychological investigation of the forming of relations within the collective during the cooperative activity of preschoolers. Psychological study of the conditions and laws of the transfer of moral demands from adults and the children's collective to the internal behavioral motivations of the child, and of the role of various emotions in this process, is of great importance in solving the pedagogical problems of the moral training of preschoolers.

Research in the moral development of preschoolers has broadened noticeably in recent years; young scientists are taking an active part. Scientific research institutes of psychology and pedagogy in the Ukraine are studying the characteristics of moral feelings in small children and the paths of their formation; work has begun on the interrelations between the intellectual, emotional, and volitional development of the child at different age levels; studies are being done on how children learn rules of conduct during activity and on how their relations develop during active play.

The department of preschool pedagogy of the Moscow Pedagogical Institute has conducted a study of individual differences and the individualized approach to children during lessons.

In recent decades Soviet preschool pedagogy has done much to solve the problem of play and pedagogical supervision. Effective methods have been found of using children's play activity as an important means of training (D. V. Mendzheritskaia, R. I. Zhukovskaia, A. P. Usova, A. V. Cherkov, Z. V. Lishtvan, B. I. Khachapuridze, and others).

The psychological studies of L. S. Vygotskii, A. N. Leont'ev, D. B. El'konin, and others have refuted the idealist and biologizing conceptions of creative role play widespread in the West and have shed light on its origin, some laws of its development, and its mechanisms of influencing the development of the child's personality.

Despite certain achievements of Soviet preschool pedagogy in the field of play, one must note that research has not encompassed the problem as a whole. When studying this question, pedagogues concentrated primarily on the subject aspect of play. The subject is an indisputably important side of this children's activity [creative role play], and through the subject the teacher can exert a great influence on the game and on relations among the players. But one must not believe that if the subjects of children's games have positive moral content, if in play the children reproduce human activities that possess positive moral value, then this in itself (with pedagogical direction, of course) must inevitably guarantee the formation of corresponding moral qualities in the child. Does the educational value of play consist only in its subject content, and does the subject content by itself guarantee the child's full-fledged moral development?

The results of a study recently undertaken by the Institute for Preschool Education compel us to answer this question in the negative. Professor A. P. Usova discovered, so to speak, a new layer of processes and relations in children's play, hitherto little known and insufficiently studied. She showed that, in addition to the mutual relations which are played out by the children in accordance with the subject and role assumed, another kind of relations arose during play or as a side effect — and this time not pretended relations, but real ones. Although closely connected, they are not identical and sometimes diverge (in their day, D. V. Mendzheritskaia and V. P. Zalogina turned their attention to this phenomenon when studying children's relations during play).

In children's moral upbringing, it is very important for the adult to know how to direct the subject of play activity. But this problem cannot be solved without close study and conscious direction of the actual relations among the players. It is necessary to organize the children's life with regard to their needs and abilities, and to direct the independent action of the children's collective into the required channel. The solution of problems of play as a form of organizing

the children's life has only begun, and much remains to be done in planned sociological study of the real relations that develop among children of different ages during play and under various forms of pedagogical guidance, as well as in study of the influence of such relations on the formation of moral qualities in the child's personality.

Of great importance in the moral and rounded development of the preschool child is child labor in accessible content and forms. Work according to ability occupies an essential place in the pedagogical process; it is a form of organizing the children's life. And even though this activity is controlled by adults considerably more than creative role play, its character changes from one age to the next: by age six or seven, children's work is considerably independent and self-reliant; they begin to use work as a form of self-organization.

It was shown above that from the first days of the existence of the Soviet kindergarten, labor entered the child's daily life as a new content, without which the tasks of communist upbringing could not be solved. While overcoming the errors of overloading and overcomplexity which marked child labor education until 1936, advanced practice and investigators are beginning to devote increasing attention to combining children's observation of adult labor with their own child-labor activity. However, in community practice of the late 1930's and early 1940's, attention was still centered on organizing the labor milieu, rather than on the content and methods of supervising schoolchildren's labor. The specifics of labor training were not elaborated with sufficient intensity even in the postwar years. This has various explanations, one of them being that child psychology and pedagogy had not sufficiently studied the specific role of labor activity in the child's rounded education and development.

Attention to problems of labor education in the preschool period of childhood increased sharply after the decisions of the 20th and 22nd CPSU Congresses and the appearance of the CPSU Program. Studies appeared, revealing the prerequisites of child labor appearing in the independent action of the young child (primarily in everyday work).

The influence of certain types of labor in forming responsibility in older preschoolers was studied. Child psychology studied the conditions under which labor motivation and love of labor are formed. The decisive influence of the motivational sphere in the child's formation of a positive attitude toward labor and efficiency in labor was revealed.

Publications of the Academy of Pedagogical Sciences analyzed and shed light on the content and methods of labor education of children of different ages, the interconnection between labor and play, and ways of inculcating a positive attitude toward labor. Along with experimental work, advanced pedagogical experience in labor education has been widely studied and analyzed; the basic processes by which preschool children form a love of labor have been revealed.

Further studies in the field of the labor education of young children should be directed even more to the specifics of child labor and to the reciprocal influences of work and play; one must more actively elaborate differential methods of supervising child labor and inculcating children with a labor orientation.

The improvement of preschool educational theory, of its main problems, and the elaboration of curriculum and methods documents for kindergarten, have enriched the advanced experience of teachers. This was also helped by the traditions of close cooperation between scientific workers and teachers when studying the same problem. The result of this cooperative work, and of the pedagogues' own creative thought, was a series of scientific and practical conferences (1940, 1941, 1942, 1948) which had considerable importance for the creative growth of workers in children's preschool institutions, as well as for raising new questions requiring theoretical analysis. Many kindergarten teachers who read papers at these conferences later became scientific workers and famous methodologists (V. A. Gorbacheva, E. Iu. Demurova, E. L. Kossakovskaia, K. P. Smirnova, L. P. Katina).

The rounded development of children and the improvement of their preparedness for school learning require thorough study of the preschool child's potentials for psychic development. At the same time, fulfillment of these tasks requires not so much an increase in the volume and quality of the knowledge and skills acquired by preschool children as the development of their cognitive and creative abilities. Therefore a major problem of research in developmental psychology and physiology is the structure of abilities and ways of directing their development purposefully in early and preschool childhood. A more active study of the development of motivations of action and feelings in preschool children is required in connection with pedagogical tasks in personality formation.

The subsequent development of the system of social preschool education, embracing all children of preschool age, requires that we define specifically the content and methods of family training, its agreement with and reinforcement of social training. This would seem to require complex studies of a sociological nature, to be conducted jointly by pedagogues, psychologists, sociologists, specialists in the field of ethics, and physiologists.

One must raise the scientific level of studies and more actively apply modern experimental methods and mathematical processing of data received.

The directives of the 23rd CPSU Congress on the five-year plan of national economic development of the USSR for 1966-1970 provide for a sharp increase in the number of children in state preschool institutions. A tremendous number of children will enter school from kindergarten. This requires an expansion of scientific research topics in the field of preschool pedagogy and psychology and an improvement in their methods.

* * *

Elementary Education

Nachal'naia shkola, 1966, No. 10

THE DRAFTS OF THE NEW CURRICULA FOR GRADES 1-3

OF THE ELEMENTARY SCHOOL AND THEIR TESTING

According to the information published in No. 8 of our journal, the Minister of Public Education of the RSFSR has issued an order entitled "Experimental Testing of Draft Curricula Covering the Three-Year Period of Instruction." The curricula were formulated by the commission charged with determining the content of school education. The USSR Academy of Pedagogical Sciences has been entrusted with testing the drafts in a comprehensive manner and with directing the experiment.

The experimental testing will take place for a period of three years in the primary grades of all schools of the Tosnensk District of the Leningrad Region, the Beloiarsk District of the Sverdlovsk Region, and the Suzdal'sk District of the Vladimir Region. The order instructs the Presidium of the Academy of Pedagogical Sciences, the Leningrad, Sverdlovsk and Vladimir regional departments of public education, together with the chairs of pedagogy and methodology of the Leningrad and Sverdlovsk pedagogical institutes, to organize training courses for all primary grade teachers of the three districts where the experiment will take place.

The order requests the Presidium of the Academy of Pedagogical Sciences to present a yearly progress report to the board.

Each methodological office of the districts where the experiment is being conducted is being allotted an additional post of a methodologist.

The Editorial Board of Nachal'naia shkola has requested the Sector on Primary Education of the USSR Academy of Pedagogical Sciences' Institute of General and Polytechnical Education to provide it with a brief outline of the draft syllabus for the three-year school. A resume of the draft is presented below. The results of syllabi testing in the mass schools of the districts mentioned above will tell whether the syllabi will fit the educational requirements.

Editorial Board, Nachal'naia shkola

* * *

What then are the drafts of the new curricula and what are their particular features? A brief summary of each syllabus follows.

Russian Language Syllabus for Grades 1-3

In determining the content of primary education in the Russian language, the compilers of the drafts started from the assumption that the main guideposts in the teaching of Russian should be the teaching of standards of literary language, pronunciation, spelling, word formation, morphology, syntax, and narration — that is, of speech development in the broadest sense of the term. This should be adequate preparation for primary grade pupils for a systematic Russian language course at the intermediate level of the secondary school, a course which contains material that children of early school age are able to understand. And since thinking and speech are interconnected and speech cannot be developed without developing the child's thought processes, the authors of the draft wanted to guarantee that the child's thought processes would develop to a maximum degree during language study; this in turn would foster the child's general development, the development of cognitive abilities, and the ability to apply the acquired knowledge in speaking.

The draft of the new syllabus therefore emphasizes the need to develop the child's ability to express thoughts coherently in written and oral language.

The new syllabus, like the one presently in force, sets up an entire system of oral and written exercises in coherent language; the system will be followed with greater consistency, cover a greater variety of exercises, and be allotted more time than the one presently in force. The new syllabus emphasizes the ability of pupils to transmit impressions, opinions, and feelings according to an outline given by the teacher or found in a textbook, or by the pupils collectively under the teacher's guidance or by each pupil independently. Approximately the same amount of time as in the present curriculum is being devoted to so-called business language, i.e., writing letters, advertisements, and notices.

General educational development through study of the native tongue can be accomplished not only by means of practical language instruction but also through the pupils' assimilation of a certain amount of grammatical knowledge. The main criteria for the selection of these knowledge components are as follows: 1) prevalence of conditions under which the children will be able to assimilate interrelated grammatical concepts; 2) stressing knowledge in the system of pupil training in speech and spelling, and in developing their mental abilities.

In terms of topics and terminology, the volume of grammatical knowledge planned for the three-year school differs only slightly from the range covered by the present curriculum for grades

1-4. It covers the same data on phonetics, on word formation and parts of speech, the same types of sentence, parts and component parts of sentences (phrase variants are excluded), the simplest types of direct speech, and the same punctuation signs as in the present curriculum. It is being assumed that within the three-year period the children will have assimilated the case, number, gender, tense, and person modifications, and will know the relevant terminology of these grammatical categories: cases (nominative, genitive, etc.); masculine, feminine, and neuter genders; three declensions of nouns; present, past, and future tenses; the first, second, and third persons; pronouns and verbs; the first and second conjugations, and the modification of parts of speech according to number. The children will be able to reproduce the same spelling patterns as the ones contained in the present curriculum. It is planned to expand slightly the curriculum with respect to compound sentences. While now only sentences with two main clauses joined by the coordinating conjunctions <u>and</u> or <u>but</u> [i, a, no] are being studied, it is proposed to introduce into the new three-year curriculum other coordinating conjunctions such as <u>what</u>, when, in order that, etc.

Since it is being planned to have the children absorb the four-year curriculum within three years, how can excessive study loads be avoided? Will the children be able to assimilate the volume of material they are given?

In an addendum to the draft, the authors state that the following conditions would help prevent excessive study loads. They propose a more rational distribution of study material by years of study. They suggest that language instruction proceed in a ladder-like fashion, that each step fully prepare for the subsequent one, and that each subsequent step be a logical and sequential continuation of the contents of the preceding one so that the principle of sequential teaching may be easily put into practice in the future.

Thus, it is being planned to begin studying, in grade 1, the most difficult spelling assignment: "spelling of stressed and unstressed vowels." This is why the concept of stress is thoroughly assimilated in grade 1; children are introduced to the uniform representation of stressed and un-stressed vowels (<u>slon</u>-<u>slony</u>, <u>travka</u>-<u>trava</u>, <u>les</u>-<u>lesnoi</u>, etc.). However, the assimilation of the spelling rule for unstressed vowels is not envis-aged for grade 1, pupils are not required to check the spelling of unstressed vowels according to the rule, nor is the rule taught at that level.

In the 2nd grade, pupils tackle the topic "Word structure" and thus learn spelling rules for un-stressed vowels in the root. The study continues in grade 3, where the skill is perfected. There is a similar approach to teaching the spelling of voiced and voiceless consonants that are intro-duced in grade 1, the study of which is continued in grade 2 in conjunction with the same topic, "Word structure."

Another section of the syllabus, "Parts of speech," is assimilated in logical sequence in the course of the three-year span of instruction. In grade 1, children learn about three groups of words: words which answer the question who-what, which (masculine and feminine), and what is he, she, it doing, i.e., words which denote the object or indicate action. Upon this foundation the concept "parts of speech" is explained in grade 2. It covers the noun, the adjective, and the verb. Pupils are told about a few basic forms of these parts of speech: gender and number of nouns, noun ending changes according to other words in the sentence, agreement of adjectives in gender and number with words they define, and verb changes according to tense. However, flex-ion of nouns and adjectives according to cases, and verb changes according to person, i.e., de-clensions and conjugations, are not studied in grade 2. The study of parts of speech goes on in grade 3. But here it is no longer necessary to ac-quaint children with parts of speech or with such concepts as gender, number, and tense, material already assimilated in grade 2. In grade 3 chil-dren learn about pronouns (personal), which are required for an understanding of conjugations (change in person), and adverbs, or, more pre-cisely, about a group of words which do not an-swer the same question as nouns, adjectives, and verbs and remain invariable. At the same time children learn the spelling of some adverbs ac-cording to a list.

Prepositions, conjunctions, and particles are studied together with other parts of speech. Thus some notions about prepositions are given the children in grade 1 when they are introduced to nomenclature and terminology; in grade 2 they come back to that category when they study pre-fixes; and in grades 2 and 3 prepositions cannot be omitted in the study of declensions and conju-gations. As at present, the conjunction is taken up during study of the simple sentence, with com-pound subject and compound predicate being cov-ered in the study of the compound sentence. All grammatical terms dealing with word structure (root, prefix, suffix, and ending) and all parts of speech except interjections (noun, adjective, verb, etc.), gender number, case, the 1st, 2nd, and 3rd declensions, the 1st and 2nd conjugations, number and tense are widely used in the new syl-labus. Terms dealing with sentence structure are also widely used: parts of sentence, main clause, subordinate clause, subject, predicate, simple sentence, compound sentence, compound subject and compound predicate, and direct speech. This terminology is assimilated by pu-pils in grades 2 and 3.

The compilers of the new syllabus tried to avoid the need to learn "exceptions." Thus, when establishing the concept of noun declension, the spelling and the declension of nouns ending in -<u>ii</u>, -<u>iia</u>, and -<u>ie</u> will be omitted. Study of these exceptions complicates matters at the very be-ginning to such an extent that children are pre-vented from learning the fundamentals of spelling and declension of the particular part of speech. For this reason the paragraph dealing with these declensions was omitted in the new syllabus.

With respect to the 1st and 2nd conjugations, only the study of the most frequently used verbs is being contemplated in the syllabus. A short list of questions about which children will only be told or will have to study follows: uniform rep-resentation of voiced and voiceless consonants, stressed and unstressed vowels in grade 1; suf-fixes in grade 2; pronouns, adverbs, compound sentences, and direct speech in grade 3.

Some of the more difficult paragraphs of the curriculum were cut down so as to help in learn-ing spelling.

The authors of the syllabus believe that thanks to the way, as stated above, in which study material has been distributed, by years of study, with more precise definitions and the abridgment of grammatical and spelling concepts, the schools will be able to cope with the proposed volume of grammatical knowledge, skills and spelling habits. In this context considerable importance is being attached to the improvement of Russian language teaching methods planned in the syllabus addendum.

In teaching grammar and writing, methods that mobilize the child's cognitive functions are stressed.

The formation of fundamental grammatical concepts and writing habits takes place not through learning by rote, rules and definitions, but through the process of speech activity. Children make up sentences and coherent texts, they tell stories, express thoughts, and at the same time get acquainted with new language and spelling phenomena and perfect the use of their knowledge and skills.

Systematic speech exercises, repetition and generalization at regular intervals of studied material based on the establishment of connections, similarities, and dissimilarities between the various phenomena — this is one of the chief methodological requirements in Russian language instruction. For this reason the draft syllabus has maintained the existing custom of giving information in each grade on all four subdivisions, i.e., sounds and letters, words, sentences, and coherent speech. The application of this method demands constant repetition of material. A discussion of these language aspects takes place at nearly every session. Children do exercises dealing with the sound, letter and morphological word structure, parts of speech, syntax, and coherent speech.

In addition to spelling exercises based on grammatical knowledge, word and spelling exercises based on dictionary use are of the utmost importance in language study.

The teaching of spelling through dictionary use is not less important. Spelling instruction cannot be based entirely on the assimilation of grammatical rules, but it must also make use of the dic-

tionary. Sound-letter and syllable exercises are greatly stressed. These exercises continue for the entire three-year span of instruction; they prevent the making of mistakes in letter omission, substitution and switching, and in letter combining.

The authors of the curricula believe that the methodological premises discussed above will enable the children to assimilate successfully the knowledge and skills envisaged in the three-year syllabus for the Russian language.

Mathematics Curriculum for Grades 1-3

With the exception of the topic "Computation of volumes," the draft syllabus covers most of the study material formerly studied in grades 1-4. In addition to the topics being studied in grades 1-4, the following new topics were introduced: "Operation results changes due to changes in components," elements of algebraic symbols, and a considerably larger volume of knowledge in geometric propaedeutics.

It is being planned to finish the study of the topic "Interdependence between components and operation results" in grade 2 and, on the basis of this knowledge, to begin solving some types of problems with the help of the simplest equations.

And now the question arises: how is it possible to achieve a saving in time that will enable the pupils, according to the authors of the syllabus, to assimilate knowledge that exceeds the volume presently required?

It is assumed that the saving in time will be achieved through some modifications in the actual course of elementary arithmetic by means of converting it into a course of elementary mathematics, the backbone of which will be formed by the arithmetic of natural numbers and of fundamental quantities, and around which elements of geometry and algebraic propaedeutics will converge.

The draft of the new syllabus proposes that:

1. Each question should be examined at a high level of generalization; this would enable "the child to understand the general principles that underlie arithmetical operations and to grasp

the connections and relationships between the various elements of these operations." Thus the role that theory plays in elementary mathematics is being greatly enhanced; this, according to the authors of the syllabus, is a decisive factor for developing the child's mathematical abilities and a means for mobilizing the internal learning resources that are insufficiently utilized at present.

This approach is used not only with respect to a single topic, "Whole numbers," and to the senior 4th grade, as in the present syllabus; on the contrary, it is used with respect to all grades and all topics. Beginning with the first topic in grade 1, the process of forming habits and skills is predicated upon theoretical information deduced from generalizations. According to the syllabus authors, this will permit abridging the topic "Whole numbers," to which over 50 study hours are allotted in grade 4.

2. While maintaining the concentric arrangement of study material in grades 1-3, the authors of the new syllabus have reduced the number of cycles from six to four and have consolidated tens and hundreds from the first and second, respectively, into one cycle and millions and billions into another. Thus it was possible to cut down slightly the time allotted to the study of these concentric cycles. It is being assumed that the study of material in the concentric cycle "One thousand," which, under the present curriculum, is being studied in grade 3 only and takes up over 50 hours, could begin in grade 2.

3. The changes in the syllabus affect not only the content but also the system governing the layout of study material. Study material has been switched around so as to bring closer together in time the examination of interrelated concepts, operations, and problems. In the process of study, the correlation between direct and inverse operations, direct and inverse problems, components and results of operations is revealed, and their similarities and dissimilarities are established. Conditions have been created for a broad application of methods of comparison, contraposition, and opposition. This principle is applied not only with respect to contrasting and reciprocally inverse concepts, but also with respect to related concepts and, in particular, to operations with

abstract and composite concrete numbers. These last items do not form a special concentric cycle in the new syllabus, but are studied jointly and parallel with operations dealing with abstract numbers.

It is assumed that the switching of the study material and the changing of its layout system will greatly improve teaching efficiency and produce a considerable backlog of time. Preliminary tests have shown that the parallel study of operations with abstract and composite concrete numbers, beginning with grade 1, results in a saving of between 15 and 20 hours; the change in the study system of multiplication and division tables releases over 20 hours, etc.

4. The improvement in teaching methods planned for in the syllabus will also further the process of mathematics instruction. "Methods improvement is directed toward a peak mobilization of the cognitive ability of the child in the process of education, a broad use of independent study not only at the stage of consolidating studied material, but also when new material is being presented; toward an all-round development in the process of education, the inculcation of an interest in study, the ability and desire to master knowledge, and the ability to apply it to the solution of various questions and problems."

Thus, according to the syllabus authors, the overhauling of the arithmetic course and the radical changes in its direction, principles, and methodology — all these elements will permit imparting to the child a greater sum of knowledge, skills, and habits within a shorter span of time and achieve better results in the mathematical development of the pupils.

Syllabus in Natural Sciences

The natural sciences syllabus has undergone extensive, fundamental changes.

Beginning with grade 1, it becomes a separate subject of instruction with separate textbooks and separate scheduled hours; it is allotted 60 hours in grade 1 and 70 hours each in grades 2 and 3. An enumeration of syllabus topics for each grade will give some notion about the contents of this school subject.

The section entitled "Mineral, vegetable, and animal kingdom" is studied in grade 1. It is subdivided into the following independent topics: "The world around us," "Land," "Water," "Air," "Animals," and "Plants."

According to the authors' thinking, this section should help mold the child's original integrated concepts of nature based on experiment and observation. General notions about the earth are also discussed in this section so that the cause of the most prevalent natural phenomena may be ascertained. In getting acquainted with the globe, children find out that the earth is a spheroid, that it consists of solid bodies, that water covers three-quarters of its surface, and that it is surrounded by air. Through experimentation children learn about the fundamental physical properties of solids, granite, sand, clay, and chalk, and about the properties of water and air.

Familiarity with water, air, and solids underlies the study of plants and animals.

The section entitled "Seasonal changes in nature and in man's work" is studied in grade 2. Here children learn about useful and harmful plants and animals in the woods, the orchard, and the vegetable garden, and about the work of people in their locality. In conclusion they tackle a very important and difficult question: "Causes of seasonal changes in nature." By means of experiments with the globe and a source of light, it is established that change from day to night is caused by the rotation of the earth on its axis and that seasonal changes are explained by two correlated causes: the revolution of the earth about the sun, and the inclination of the earth's axis to the plane of the ecliptic.

Familiarity with nature in the immediate environment creates premises for learning about the natural kingdom of the earth. A whole section entitled "Nature's diversity on earth" is devoted to this topic. It includes the following subdivisions: "Diversity of the earth's surface," "Land waters," and "The nature of oceans and continents." The syllabus for grade 3 covers three topics: "The nature of our local area," "The diversity of nature in our nation," and "Man and nature."

Nature study of the local area is emphasized, but the main stress in grade 3 is on the study of nature in the USSR. The final section of the natural science course is devoted to the following topics: the structure of the human body, which is linked with health protection, and how man conquers and remakes nature.

An opening section entitled "Observations" is an essential feature of the new syllabus for each grade. Systematic observation of seasonal changes and of changes in human labor takes place in all schools. The syllabus determines what objects are to be observed in each grade. Children should learn observation methods to be used in the study of weather, plants, and animals and of man at work. In the present syllabus nature study is guided by the seasonal principle. In the new syllabus this principle is maintained only with respect to the observation of nature in the USSR. The balance of the material is structured systematically and does not follow the seasonal principle. In the opinion of the authors of the draft, this approach will permit raising the scientific level of the syllabus and bringing it closer in line with the systematic courses in the subsequent grades.

The methods of natural science teaching were also revised. Methods that provide a direct contact between the child and nature occupy a dominant place, i.e., systematic observations, object lessons, experiments and experimentation, excursions, practical sessions in the classroom and outdoors, independent work, and showing of educational movies. Classroom use of the natural science textbook is varied. Some chapters of the textbook can be used at the beginning of the lesson, while illustrative material in the process of forming the various concepts, science reader texts, and articles can be used for home reading. The explanatory notes to the curriculum state that the educational process in its totality should spur the children on to do outside reading, an activity whose aim is to develop an interest in a first-hand investigation of nature. Such is the very essence of the new syllabus in natural sciences, which opens up to the child the world of nature in all its diversity and complexity.

Syllabus in Polytechnical Work Training
of the Pupils

The authors' desire to slant the syllabus in the direction of polytechnical instruction as much as possible is demonstrated by the syllabus' very title. The great influence polytechnical work training exercises upon the upbringing of the child in the spirit of love of work and a communist attitude to work and working people is greatly stressed in the explanatory notes to the curriculum.

"It is highly important to select the objects for work training and to organize the lessons in such a manner," say the explanatory notes, "that the child takes an active part in selecting the articles to be made, drawing up the plan for the execution of the assignment, making the technical drawing and an estimate of the required materials, etc." Under these conditions schoolchildren develop executive as well as creative abilities. "From doing work 'by dictation,' pupils gradually switch over to solving the problem of designing and making an article independently. In this process the level of ability to do independent work, creative ability, and personal initiative increase steadily."

The syllabus makes provision for technical and agricultural work. The section on technical work comprises working with cardboard, fabrics, and various materials, and making working models.

The section entitled "Technical modeling" is included in the syllabus of practical work in each grade, starting with the 1st. At present it is part of the syllabus for grade 4 only. A proper organization of technical modeling at work instruction sessions is of the utmost importance for broadening the concepts of primary grade pupils with respect to polytechnics and for developing their designing abilities. The formation of general work skills, so important in any work activity, is particularly emphasized. A few of these essential skills are: ability to plan work activity, organization of work and work discipline, self-control, appraisal and control of work performed, and ability to work independently.

Elements of graphic expression are being introduced into the syllabus. They include the ability to represent graphically the basic work operations: layout, processing, and assembling; the execution of technical sketches and of the simplest technical drawings. In order to broaden the polytechnical knowledge of the children, the syllabus gives a sample list of technical objects children should get to know and of excursions to production facilities; it also includes a schedule of object lessons.

In conformity with the syllabus, children get acquainted with the uses of electrical power and of various machines in the home and in the communal enterprises of their city, settlement or village.

The syllabus directs the teacher to employ various methods: laboratory and practical sessions in making articles according to sample, making a technical sketch or technical drawing according to an oral description or to one's own idea; talks, showings, excursions, outside reading by children, meetings with workers in plants and at school.

Such is the general outline of the syllabus content for polytechnical work training of schoolchildren.

In addition to the school subjects mentioned above, the following subjects are contained in the draft syllabus for grades 1-3: physical education (2 hours per week for all grades), singing (one hour per week), drawing (one hour per week).

The Russian language syllabus is set up in the following manner: letter study up to December 1 (12 hours a week); this is followed by: a) grammar and speech development (5 hours a week), b) reading and speech development (5 hours a week), c) natural science (2 hours a week).

* * *

It should be noted that the Sector on Elementary Education of the Scientific Research Institute on General and Polytechnical Education has already tested the assimilability and efficiency of the new syllabi in a limited number of schools, i.e., in Nos. 315, 444, and 204 in Moscow, in the "Lenin's Memory" school of the Moscow Region, No. 7 in Kursk, the Kardymov school of the Smolensk Region, and 20 schools in Leningrad. Subsequently a few other schools in the following localities were included: Kuibyshev,

Inta in the Komi ASSR, in Ulan-Ude, and also some schools in the Krasnoiarsk Territory and the Sverdlovsk and Moscow regions.

The testing of the syllabi in the schools of the three regions will be thorough and embrace many facets. The syllabus volume will be checked first. As has been shown, the syllabi are saturated with material. The authors made every effort to fill them with the richest possible content. Test results will determine how the material can be best assimilated without undue pressure, haste, and hurry in each grade and leave free time for exercises that create stable habits and skills so essential in the study of the Russian language and mathematics. Test results will also tell whether the curriculum load is too heavy, whether it could be cut down without impairing the schools' general-education goals, and whether the allocation of subjects by years of study was done in a rational manner. It is essential to check the ability of children to grasp all of the curriculum material, particularly material that is being introduced for the first time in primary grades. Experimental research results over the recent years have shown that children are endowed with greater abilities than those the present syllabi acknowledge. This is why the authors of the new syllabi often introduce new concepts, broader and more intricate (abstract) than the ones that had been considered to be the rule up to now.

Is the main body of schoolchildren capable of understanding these concepts? Should any adjustments be made in the new syllabi, and specifically what kind?

The efficiency of the systems governing the structuring of material in the syllabi is also being checked, particularly with respect to subjects where the system is being drastically revised. This occurs in mathematics, where operations with abstract and composite concrete numbers are studied jointly beginning with grade 1, and in the natural sciences, where the principle of the systematic study of material is being introduced.

There is no doubt that syllabi testing in the mass schools of the three regions will produce material that will make further improvements possible.

Nachal'naia shkola, 1966, No. 2

L. Zankov

OUR DIFFERENCES (Primary Education Today)

The Soviet school must play a large part in fulfilling the task of educating the new man, the roundly and harmoniously developed individual. This is a clear and indisputable truth. Instructional and upbringing work can and should be organized in accordance with this task from the very beginning stage of schooling.

Recognition of these truths produces questions. Which pedagogical methods should be explored so that the school can fulfill its duty in the best possible way? How can they be realized?

A marked improvement in the effectiveness of primary education for the general development of the pupils is an important aim in its reconstruction. Of course, it is not only the school that influences the development of the child's mind, but also the family, children's organizations, books, radio, movies, the theater, etc. However, insofar as the instruction and upbringing in school represent a purposeful system that is based on equipping children with diverse scientific knowledge and habits, the school plays a leading role in their development.

With this aim in view, school activity is primarily concerned with the careful formation of the best personal qualities that are needed now and in the future. This is necessary so as to develop the potential of every pupil, so that he will be attracted by all that is beautiful in human labor, in human actions, in nature, science, literature, and art. And not only attracted, but internally motivated to satisfy his need for knowledge, to communicate with nature and the world of art, and to translate his spiritual wealth into deeds and actions.

One can scarcely overestimate the importance of the general development of the pupils for their future activity after they have left school. The progress of science and technology in our country is too rapid for school education to keep pace with it, however well it may be presented. Of course, it is absolutely necessary to bring the programs, textbooks, and methods of instruction into accord with the present level of science and technology. However, after leaving school a young person will sooner or later come up against some unfamiliar scientific discovery, some new technique. He will be able to orient himself rapidly and successfully absorb this new data only if he possesses the appropriate qualities of intellect, will, and emotion.

Teachers who carefully look after their pupils

introduce various amendments in the normal, traditional method of primary education. When they feel that the potential of the younger pupils is considerably above the requirements of the standard method, they make problems more difficult, cover the program in greater depth, and introduce additional material.

These searchings clearly testify to the shortcomings of the traditional method. In teaching circles there is a growing conviction that the primary grades could give children far more than they do at present.

The teachers' searchings are in accord with the research of the Laboratory of Education and Development in the Institute of the Theory and History of Pedagogy of the Academy of Pedagogical Sciences. The object of its research is to discover the nature of the objective connection between the structure of education and the process of the pupils' general development. Such research is essential: although much has been, and is being, written on the subject of developmental instruction in pedagogical works, we lack reliable data that would show just what instruction really contributes to the development of schoolchildren.

Our laboratory has studied the process of child development under the conditions of the standard, traditional method. But still more important questions must not be left unanswered. Is the level of development reached by younger schoolchildren under the traditional method the limit? Is it impossible to create another didactic system which would be much more effective both in the general development of the children and in their acquisition of knowledge and habits?

In order to answer these questions the laboratory began to construct, as early as 1957, a new system of primary education.

During the first stage of the experiment (1957-1961) a new system was created, and its principles were defined and embodied in a concrete method, for the process of instruction and upbringing throughout the years of primary education. When new programs had been created, and methods, techniques, and teaching material prepared, the laboratory moved on, in 1961, to broad experimentation.

Our experiment was indissolubly linked with the teachers' experience. They evaluated the new system positively and joined the experiment because the system corresponds to the aspirations that arose from teaching experience. In putting the new system into practice, the teachers analyze its methodological realization and simultaneously introduce much that is their own and original.

Some Principles of the New System of Primary Education

The new system of primary education elaborated by the Laboratory of Education and Development of the Academy of Pedagogical Sciences' Institute of the Theory and History of Pedagogy has been discussed in a number of articles (see No. 11 of the journal Nachal'naia shkola for 1964, and Nos. 1, 2, 3, 4, and 5 for 1965). The experiment being conducted by the laboratory is partly elucidated in L. V. Zankov's article "Experiment with a New System of Primary Education" [Eksperiment po novoi sisteme nachal'nogo obucheniia], in Nachal'naia shkola, 1964, No. 10.

Some of the teachers who took part in the discussion had been in the experiment for less than a year: M. F. Zyrianova, T. I. Kirgintseva, N. V. Smirnova, B. P. Syrov, N. V. Iatsuta. They speak of the positive results of the experimental instruction and, at the same time, concretize and generalize its principles.

A number of other articles (by L. N. Skatkin, V. A. Kiriushkin, N. S. Rozhdestvenskii, B. P. Esipov, and M. I. Ivanov) mainly contain arguments against the principles of the new system and criticism of the experiment.

A critical examination of the principles of the experimental instruction is useful insofar as it helps once more to test our basic positions and their realization in school practice, and thereby contributes to the successful completion of our research.

The critical articles devote a great deal of space to the principle of instruction at a high level of difficulty.

N. Rozhdestvenskii considers that "it is not a question of how hard or easy it may be, but whether in the process of instruction the pupils are actually able essentially to master the knowledge" (Nachal'naia shkola, 1965, No. 2, p. 71).

But acquisition of knowledge can take place in such a way that the process produces an insignificant result in the development of the pupils. This is borne out by numerous facts that have been clarified in laboratory publications. (1) Our experiment has also shown that if instruction is conducted at a high level of difficulty, the process of acquiring knowledge and habits becomes a source of intensive development of the pupils. In other words, it is impossible to agree with Rozhdestvenskii when he states that "it is not a question of how hard or easy it may be." We find it impossible to agree that any method is acceptable so long as it achieves the acquisition of knowledge. No, we must adopt that method which is highly effective both for the general development of the pupils and for their acquisition of knowledge and habits.

We included the following topic in the grammar program for the 3rd grade: "Meanings of Noun (Verbal [priglagol'nye]) Cases. Some Basic Meanings." This is difficult work for 3rd graders, but studying grammar in this way helps achieve significant success in the development of their thinking.

Before they reached this topic, the pupils had studied the first, second, and third declensions of nouns. Familiarity with noun endings relating to different types of declension, but belonging to the same case, provided good training in the formation of the mental process of differentiating linguistic material. The children distinguished the endings on the basis of the particular type of declension to which they belonged.

Now the children's thought shifts to another plane: they must abstract themselves from those distinctions which are characteristic of particular types of declensions, but at the same time comprehend the meaning of each case as such, in a generalized form. For example, the instrumental case, depending only on the verb and without a preposition, appears in its fundamental and most typical sense as an instrument or means by which an action is performed (to smooth off with a plane, to draw with a pencil, to write with ink, and so on). This generalization conflicts

with one which was formed earlier: if grammatical phenomena were mentally connected before by the specific type of declension to which they belong, now they are connected irrespective of declension type.

This is not merely and not so much a matter of forming a concept of "case meaning." It is highly important that this concept reflect numerous advances that have been made in the child's thinking. This is a transition from lower to higher forms of thinking, but it is not a smooth and easy one; it is a complex and contradictory process. It is precisely such evolution in the child's thinking that guarantees further intensive development.

A high level of difficulty is distinguished not only by the fact that it exceeds the average norm of difficulty, but primarily because it reveals the intellectual powers of the child and gives them scope and direction.

In rejecting the efficacy of instruction at a high level of difficulty, Rozhdestvenskii writes: "It seems to us that the didactic principle of accessibility or feasibility is much more correct and pedagogically sound" (No. 2, p. 71). What does this principle consist of? "The principle of accessibility expresses the necessity of correspondence between content and method in teaching and the age peculiarities of the pupils, by virtue of which the pupils acquire knowledge, skills and habits with a certain amount of effort" (B. Esipov and M. Danilov, Didactics [Didaktika], RSFSR Academy of Sciences Publishing House, 1957, p. 203).

Thus, this principle demands that instruction correspond to the age peculiarities of the pupils. And, of course, the development of instruction must rely on the scientific data which characterize the given age. However, this reflects only one side of the connection between instruction and age peculiarities: surely the characteristics of particular ages depend, in their conrete expression, on how teaching is structured. Investigations have proved the truth of this proposition.

Thus, the investigations of I. Budnitskaia, M. Zvereva, and I. Tovpinets have shown that during the first two years of instruction in the

experimental classes the pupils undergo qualitative changes in their powers of observation,
abstract thought and practical operations. These
changes bear witness to a transition to higher,
more complex forms of mental activity. No such
changes take place in the pupils of regular
classes (see The Development of Pupils in the
Process of Instruction [Razvitie uchashchikhsia
v protsesse obucheniia], RSFSR Academy of
Pedagogical Sciences Publishing House, 1963).
Thus, the intellectual aspect of children of eight
years of age differs according to the content,
methods, and concrete approach to their instruction.

Representatives of the traditional method make
extensive use of the word "inaccessibility" in
order to justify somehow their objections to a
sharp rise in the requirements of primary education. However, the inference of inaccessibility is not borne out by modern scientific data.

L. Skatkin believes that the principle of instruction at a high level of difficulty "can, in
the case of some pupils who find the work beyond their powers, lead to revulsion and not to
satisfaction in learning" (No. 11, p. 76).

This supposition of Skatkin's is contradicted
by our experimental data. The principle of instruction at a high level of difficulty, like the
other principles of the new system, has been
applied since the 1957/58 school year. Two full
cycles of primary education (1st through 3rd
grades) have already been completed. During
this period the new system was put into practice in more than 500 classes, consisting of
about 20,000 pupils, and revulsion to studies
was not observed in a single class. On the contrary, a pronounced enthusiasm for learning was
noted in all classes.

B. Esipov was highly perplexed by our demand
that a standard of difficulty be adhered to. He
considers that this requirement implies accep-
tance of the principle of accessibility (No. 3,
p. 67). However, Esipov is mistaken. The un-
soundness of the principle of accessibility lies
in its onesidedness, as we have stated earlier,
and not at all in its acknowledgment of the need
for definite limits in making the educational
process more difficult.

We feel that adherence to a standard of difficulty serves to make instruction promote development to the maximum degree. The standard of difficulty emerges as an indispensable
component in the efficacious application of the
principle of a high level of difficulty. This principle, when indissolubly connected with the other principles of the new system, turns out to be
so effective in the pupils' development because
the material that is used in its realization can
be understood by the pupils. If standards of difficulty are not observed, the child, not being in
a position to understand what is presented to
him, is forced to learn mechanically. The high
level of difficulty then changes from a positive
to a negative factor.

Representatives of the traditional method of
elementary education also reject the correctness of another principle of the new system,
namely, that of covering educational material
at a fast pace. Thus, for example, L. Skatkin
writes: "This principle is absolutely harmful:
its application inevitably leads to the isolation
of a group of lagging pupils from among those
who work more slowly" (No. 11, p. 76).

Skatkin has incorrectly made a connection
between the rate of working of individual pupils
and rapid progress in the study of material,
i.e., enrichment of the pupils with more and
more new information and the rejection of marking time. The differences in the pupils' rate of
working make themselves felt in any method.
Traditional methodology has been wrestling with
this problem for decades; much has been written on the subject, but hitherto no satisfactory
solution has been found.

Our approach absolutely excludes the pursuit
of "records" in the sense of the number of tasks
performed by the pupils. We react negatively to
requiring children to solve as many examples
or do as many exercises as possible in the
course of the lesson. Advancing at a fast rate
in studying material does not at all mean rushing through the lesson. We demand that the
teacher and the children work calmly. The teacher should not begrudge the time needed to listen
carefully to the child, to hear his accounts of
observations and impressions that he wants to

share, to hear the doubts and questions that must be answered. The teacher should not begrudge the time needed for heart-to-heart talks with the children. Such a mode of working bears fruit, as the experience of teachers in the experimental classes has shown.

The above-mentioned principle requires that the pupil be given more and more new material in order to move forward as soon as he has mastered what has gone before. The continual enrichment of the pupil's mind with all kinds of information creates favorable conditions for ever greater understanding of the information he receives, provided that it is included in a broadly developed system.

As to the presence in the same class of so-called "strong" and "weak," "lagging" students who work at different speeds, the solution to the corresponding pedagogical problems was determined in our experimental instruction. One of our most important theses is that it is necessary to carry out intensive and systematic work on the development of all students, including the weakest. The experience in experimental instruction accumulated over a number of years has shown that teachers can fulfill this requirement successfully and achieve positive results. Since the weak pupils also cover enormous ground in their development, they manifest increasing possibilities for mastering educational material. This is extremely important, since "weak," "lagging" students particularly need unremitting and purposeful work on their development. Meanwhile, it is usually on just these weak and lagging pupils that the avalanche of coaching exercises falls: after lessons these children remain for supplementary work in an attempt to overcome their lack of progress by increasing the number of assignments. Such a method of working with these pupils retards their development even more and makes them lag even further behind.

Of course, there are and always will be differences between pupils, both as regards development and the mastering of knowledge. There are such differences in our experimental classes, too, although naturally they are different in quality from those in standard classes. In our

experimental instruction the effective means that permits us to make rapid progress with all members of the class is the application of differentiated methodology. We adopted this approach long ago, at the very outset of our experiment. Differentiated methodology has a number of aspects, but perhaps the most essential is that the same questions of the program are not studied with uniform depth. Thanks to this the whole class, the weakest pupils included, can advance at a rapid rate.

Authors of critical articles also consider the principle affirming the prime role of theoretical knowledge to be unacceptable. "Grammatical concepts are abstract," writes N. Rozhdestvenskii, "but a child, according to the psychologists, thinks concretely, although he can grasp some abstractions as well" (No. 2, p. 72). This author's view of the concreteness of the child's thought (more precisely, the young school-age child in question) is incorrect, and referring to psychologists cannot serve as proof, since modern psychology does not provide any grounds for this.

Strictly speaking, ideas that are characterized by the presence of visual images are concrete (in a psychological sense). These ideas can contain elements of generalization. However, in its extended and developed form, a generalization emerges as a concept. Here it is realized in an indissoluble connection with the abstraction, the abstracting of definite aspects from the object.

The investigations of psychologists (G. Kostiuk, E. Kudriavtseva, R. Natadze, V. Praisman, T. Rubtsova, P. Chamat, and others) have shown that abstraction and generalization in verbal form do take place in the thinking of pupils of the primary grades. They are observed in the formation of new concepts, in the general recognition of little-known objects, and in the appreciation of the moral qualities of characters from works of literature. This by no means denies the important role of visual images in the thinking of a young pupil. However, ideas based on visual images cannot be regarded as the primary component of a young pupil's thinking. It is precisely progress in the areas of abstraction and generalization that primarily characterizes the changes that occur in thinking in the course of early school age.

The conception that development of thought in the young pupil takes place in the form of gradual accumulation of verbal abstractions and generalizations is outdated. As early as 1934, in his book Thought and Speech [Myshlenie i rech'], V. Vygotskii noted, on the basis of research into concepts at school age, that the formation of concepts occurs in different ways, including from the abstract to the concrete.

It follows from what has been said that psychology does furnish a basis for the principle affirming the decisive role of theoretical knowledge in elementary education.

The terms "noun," "singular" and "plural" of a noun, which we introduce in the 1st grade, and also other terms help to overcome the onesidedness that is characteristic of the thinking of a young pupil. They make it possible for the child to think of a word in terms of both its semantic sense and its purely grammatical aspect.

These grammatical terms acquire an active meaning thanks to the fact that the pupils employ varied linguistic material to make observations and perform assignments involving the comparison of singular and plural nouns, the distinguishing of noun endings according to changes of preposition, etc.

Operating with terms greatly develops the pupil's capacity for understanding material in Russian language, mathematics, and other subjects.

Furthermore, under the new system theoretical knowledge is by no means confined to terms and definitions. A much greater amount of attention is given to the mastery of relationships and laws (e.g., the combinative rule of addition and multiplication and direct and inverse proportional dependence in the mathematics course; the regularity of seasonal changes in the life of plants and animals in natural science, and many others).

We present a diversity of theoretical knowledge in various school subjects: not only in Russian language, mathematics and natural science, but also in geography, labor training, drawing, and music.

T. Terekhova's article deals with the principle of the scientific character of Russian language instruction in primary grades. Referring to our Russian language program, in particular the sections "Aspects of the Verb" and "Voices of the Verb," she writes: "This extension by itself contradicts the principle of scientific teaching. Is it really necessary to study the aspects of the verb in the primary grades?" (No. 3, p. 70). But what has this to do with the scientific character of instruction? The question of whether or not to introduce these sections in the program cannot be resolved from the viewpoint of the science of language. The solution to this question is determined by the propositions and facts that form the scientific pedagogical foundation of the program.

Our programs are oriented toward the maximum general development of the pupils. The sections "Aspects of the Verb" and "Voices of the Verb" were included in the program with this object in view.

A large portion of this author's article was devoted to analysis of a fragment of a lesson in one of our laboratory's experimental classes. Terekhova writes that the pupils seemed to come to the conclusion that "prepositions were to be found only in secondary parts of the sentence, and prefixes in predicates (and sometimes in secondary parts of the sentence)" and that such a conclusion "is capable of disorienting the pupils: the science of Russian language proves that prefixes can be present both in predicate words and in words expressing secondary parts of a sentence (No. 3, p. 71). But the pupils certainly did not reach a conclusion about the presence of prefixes only in certain parts of the sentence. The same place in the book On Primary Education [O nachal'nom obuchenii], to which Terekhova refers, states: "The pupils made some observations during the sentence analysis. . ." (p. 85). We were talking about some observations, and not about a conclusion at all. The fragment of the lesson cited was not posing the task of linking the presence of prepositions and prefixes with parts of the sentence (see L. V. Zankov, On Primary Education, p. 84). Further on Terekhova writes: ". . .a prefix (part of a word) and a preposition (a link word) are morphological categories, while parts of a sentence are syntactical. They cannot be compared" (p. 71). But in that fragment of the lesson to which she refers, the pupils did not compare prepositions to sentence parts. In addition, as is well known in the science of language, the difference between morphological and syntactical categories does not prevent the existence of definite links, relationships, between them. Thus, for example, complements are expressed in particular in the form of oblique cases with prepositions.

The demand that instruction be scientific is extremely important. It is precisely for this reason that any discussion of the program, of methodological means and devices, in terms of their scientific character must be objective and well founded. Incidental observations made during the lesson, on which Terekhova comments, could have been excluded or differently handled, and this would not change the essence of the matter, since the lesson had a different object. To interpret these incidental observations arbitrarily as Terekhova does, and hurl the charge that the experimental instruction in Russian language contradicts the principle that instruction must be scientific, is improper and in no way serves to reveal the truth.

The Integrity of the New System and Its Effectiveness

In our opponents' articles some didactic principles of the new system are criticized in isolation. We have already replied to their objections. At the same time it must be emphasized that these principles are organically interrelated. Their interdependence has been specially stressed in the laboratory's publications. Thus, instruction at a high level of difficulty is connected with the other principles. Consequently not just any difficulty will do, but only the difficulty that finds its expression in mastering theoretical knowledge or furthers the pupils' understanding of the learning process.

For example, mastery of the concepts of "word-changing" and "word-construction" is work of a high level of difficulty for 2nd-graders, but its difficulty consists not in learning by heart the spelling of twenty words with unstressed vowel roots per day, but in differentiating between concepts that reflect large areas of linguistic phenomena. Thanks to this, knowledge that has been acquired earlier is brought into a more organized and precise entity.

Our experiment affects all elementary education as a whole, and not just separate subjects or parts thereof. It is based not on just any isolated and diverse propositions, but on general principles that are organically interrelated. The new system is not limited to the construction of school work on didactic precepts that differ from the traditional method; it alters the whole tenor of the life and work of the class. Laboratory publications have mentioned this frequently (L. V. Zankov, On Primary Education, 1963; The Development of Pupils in the Process of Instruction [Razvitie uchashchikhsia v protsesse obucheniia], 1963; L. V. Zankov, "Primary Education and Problems of Didactics" [Nachal'noe obuchenie i voprosy didaktiki], Narodnoe obrazovanie, 1964, No. 7, etc.).

Let us recall only one characteristic feature of the new system. Through the realization of its principles, it arouses an inner motivation toward learning in the pupils. Instead of studying for the sake of grades, they study in order to acquire more and more knowledge. The children are captivated by indefatigable progress, by the fulfillment of difficult assignments; they derive satisfaction from intensive mental work. This is one of the signs of the profound educative essence of the new system.

Implementation of its principles evokes the spiritual powers of the child and furthers their formation. The teachers taking part in the experiment see this: they discover an unfamiliar source of the inexhaustible thirst for knowledge in their pupils, the source of achievements in the mastery of complex material that seem so improbable to people accustomed to the traditional method. The teachers participating in the experiment have written about the intense increase in the creative powers and capabilities

of the child under the experimental instruction:
K. Vasil'eva, M. Demidova, Z. Petrova, and A.
Serebrennikova (Narodnoe obrazovanie, No. 3
and No. 10 for 1964; Uchitel'skaia gazeta for
1963-1964).

The intensity of the process of the children's
general development under the conditions of the
experimental instruction and their decisive superiority over pupils taught by the traditional
method are shown by the investigations of I.
Budnitskaia, M. Zvereva, and I. Tovpinets (see
The Development of Pupils in the Process of
Instruction [Razvitie uchashchikhsia v protsesse
obucheniia], edited by L. Zankov, 1963). These
data were later confirmed by Budnitskaia and
Zvereva on the basis of material drawn from
the schools of Tula and Kalinin (1963/64 school
year), and also by A. Krotov in Novosibirsk
(1964).

A high standard of acquiring knowledge and
habits is achieved on the basis of intensive development of the pupils. The book On Elementary Education and other laboratory publications
cite corroborating facts. Subsequent check-ups
gave analogous results. Thus, for example, in
April 1964, on the instructions of the RSFSR
Ministry of Education, a check-up was conducted
in the experimental classes of the schools in
Tula and Kalinin by inspectors of the regional
department of education. The inspectors gave a
dictation and assigned a composition about a
picture, an arithmetic problem, and a labor task.
The check-up involved eighteen classes in all.
For purposes of comparison, the same work
was given to pupils of regular classes with the
best teachers. In all types of work the experimental classes had significantly better results
than the regular classes of the same grade, and
often better results than higher regular classes
(e.g., the 2nd-grade experimental classes as
compared with the 3rd-grade regular classes).

Great successes were achieved, in particular,
by those teachers in Tula and Kalinin who had
taken part in the experiment as early as the
1961/62 school year and who continued to work
hand in hand with the laboratory: S. Budyleva,
K. Vasil'eva, A. Vinogradova, V. Zakaznikova,
M. Zakharova, M. Kosheleva, S. Meshcheriakova,
T. Orlova, and Z. Petrova.

The significant results of our experimental
instruction are confirmed by the teachers who
are participating in the experiment (over 400
last year), by parents, and also by teachers of
other classes and leaders of public education
who visit the experimental classes. Another
indication of the effectiveness of the new system
is the fact that students of the experimental
classes in Kalinin who finished their primary
education in three years were promoted to the
5th grade. They worked successfully in the 5th
grade in the past academic year, and at the end
of the 1964/65 school year they were moved up
to the 6th grade. In the same year the students
of experimental classes in Tula were also promoted to the 5th grade after a three-year primary education.

The rate of expansion of this mass experiment, which is based on the teachers' desire
to work in the new way, also confirms the success of the experimental instruction. In the current (1965/66) school year, 30,000 1st-graders
are working from textbooks compiled by the
Laboratory for Education and Development in
accordance with the principles of the new system
(Z. Romanovskaia and A. Romanovskii, Living
Language. A Reader [Zhivoe slovo. Kniga dlia
chteniia]; A. Poliakova, Russian Language
[Russkii iazyk]; L. Zankov, Mathematics Textbook [Uchebnik matematiki]).

The great effectiveness of the new system of
primary education as compared with the traditional method is indisputable. At the same time,
however, it must be emphasized that the Laboratory for Education and Development does not
limit its activities to a comparative study of
the knowledge and habits of the pupils in experimental and regular classes. A great deal of
attention is given to detailed study of the process of acquiring knowledge and habits throughout the course of primary education in individual children, particularly the weakest ones (the
papers of A. Poliakova, N. Chutko, E. Obozova,
and M. Berkman in the collection The Mastery
of Knowledge and the Development of Young
Pupils [Usvoenie znanii i razvitie mladshikh
shkol'nikov], 1965).

We analyze those cases in which the teachers' work does not produce the results characteristic of the new system. An analysis carried out along these lines by the laboratory shows that a fundamental cause of shortcomings is the teachers' difficulties in reorienting themselves: the new system requires not only a radical reconstruction of teaching methods, but also changes in the general pedagogical approach to the educational-upbringing process in primary grades. As the teachers master the new system, these difficulties are overcome.

But there are other problems. The methods of the experimental instruction have to be refined and made more concrete in certain places. The elaboration of a differentiated methodology is especially necessary; the differentiation should bear in mind the different groups of children in each class and their peculiarities, and primarily the weakest students.

The laboratory has a great deal to do in this and other directions to achieve even better results in the general development of schoolchildren and in their acquisition of knowledge and habits.

What Do the Opponents of the New System Recommend?

Some opponents of the new system suggest combining its principles with those of the traditional method. A. Liublinskaia belongs to this group (Nachal'naia shkola, 1965, No. 4). She gives an account of an experiment in 1st-grade classes that was conducted in the 1963/64 school year by the Department of Pedagogy of the Primary School in the Herzen Teacher Training Institute in Leningrad.

The department's experiment introduced principles that had been worked out earlier by the Laboratory for Education and Development and that had been explicated in its publications as early as 1962-1963: instruction at a high level of difficulty, the study of material at a rapid rate, and an increase in the level of theoretical knowledge.

The principles of the new system of primary education elaborated in the Laboratory for Education and Development are opposed to those of the traditional method. The latter differs in that the process of learning is made too easy. According to the new system, instruction is to be carried out at a high level of difficulty.

In accordance with the recommendations of the traditional method, rather limited academic material is dragged out over a four-year period. The new system demands that the material be studied at a rapid pace.

In its present form, primary education is aimed first and foremost at the inculcation of habits in Russian language and arithmetic, and an insignificant place is assigned to theoretical knowledge. The new system allots a decisive role to theoretical knowledge. Liublinskaia adds other propositions to these principles: the delineation of concepts in the process of numerous exercises, the establishment of interdisciplinary connections, the utilization of the practical experience of the child. These propositions are perfectly acceptable to the old, traditional method, but they do not in any way characterize the new system of primary education.

Combining completely heterogeneous principles and propositions, Liublinskaia presents this combination sometimes as "a verification and refinement of L. Zankov's propositions," and sometimes as the "very own methods" of the department in the Herzen Teacher Training Institute in Leningrad. It is generally accepted that science is called upon to reveal the truth. However, Liublinskaia's article succeeds only in obscuring and confusing what was clear before the appearance of the article.

Liublinskaia's statement represents a unique objection to the new system. The completely improper mingling of principles of the new system with propositions of the old method distorts the new system, emasculating its essence.

B. Esipov, N. Rozhdestvenskii, and L. Skatkin reject the new system of primary education. But do they, then, propose any other system that would be far more effective than the traditional method? No, they have nothing to recommend in exchange for the old method. There remains only one conclusion: these authors

74

think it best to leave the traditional method in effect.

One of our antagonists, Rozhdestvenskii, expresses himself quite clearly on this subject in his article "On the Elementary Grammar Course" [O nachal'nom kurse grammatiki] (Nachal'naia shkola, 1965, Nos. 7 and 8). He suggests more than modest additions to the current program: to give some role to control (however, Rozhdestvenskii specifies that this term is not necessary); to acquaint the pupils with the fact that sentences can also be linked with the help of subordinate conjunctions; and to reintroduce the topic "Numerals," which used to be in the primary school program. Rozhdestvenskii specially emphasizes that "it is inadvisable to teach students the concept of the stem of a word, since the younger pupils constantly confuse the stem with the root" (No. 7, p. 67). But Rozhdestvenskii has not engaged in research into the different techniques and methods by means of which the distinction between root and stem can be taught. And in fact, as our experiment has shown, with the appropriate instruction, the young pupils successfully master these concepts. This is very important, since the distinguishing of stem and root, like other cases of fine distinction, provides favorable material with which much can be achieved in the development of the schoolchild.

In the same article he advances similar arguments on the question of the terms "complex" and "compound" sentences. In the opinion of Rozhdestvenskii, the introduction of these terms into the program would mean "the confusing of something that is already not simple" (No. 8, p. 87).

Many of the propositions in the above-mentioned article are devoid of any substantiation; instead, there is the repetition of formulas: "ought not to be studied," "ought not to be introduced," and the like.

Instead of substantiating his opinions, Rozhdestvenskii writes: "The work under the existing program confirms the overall correctness of its stated principles" (No. 8, p. 89). From this author's point of view it is only pertinent to consider the extension and consolidation of the existing situation, which is characterized by the subordination of theoretical knowledge to the task of inculcating habits. "The question can be one of giving an even greater practical orientation to grammar studies in the elementary Russian course," writes Rozhdestvenskii (No. 7, p. 66).

But our experiment, which has embraced two full cycles of primary-school instruction, has shown, on the basis of extensive factual material, that the enrichment of primary education with theoretical knowledge has entirely justified itself and gives good results, especially in Russian language.

By rejecting the new system and simultaneously defending the traditional method, our opponents confirmed the conflict between the new system and the traditional old method. This is not a simple conflict of individual views, but an acute struggle between the old and the new in primary education.

Footnote

1) A list of the works referred to here and subsequently is given at the end of the article.

Bibliography

Research into the problem of instruction and development, and also the new system of primary education, are clarified in the following books and articles: L. V. Zankov, "Razvitie mladshikh shkol'nikov v protsesse obucheniia," Nachal'naia shkola, 1958, No. 7; I. I. Budnitskaia and N. V. Kuznetsova, "Trudovoe obuchenie i razvitie mladshikh shkol'nikov," Nachal'naia shkola, 1959, No. 9; L. V. Zankov, Nagliadnost' i aktivizatsiia uchashchikhsia v obuchenii, Uchpedgiz, Moscow, 1960; L.V. Zankov, O nachal'nom obuchenii, RSFSR Academy of Pedagogical Sciences Publishing House, Moscow, 1963; L.V. Zankov (ed.), Razvitie uchashchiksia v protsesse obucheniia (I-II klassy), APN RSFSR, Moscow, 1963; K.D. Vasil'eva, "Nuzhna korennaia perestroika nachal'nogo obucheniia," Narodnoe obrazovanie,

1963, No. 3; M.I. Demidova and Z.V. Petrova, "Razvivat' tvorcheskie sily i sposobnosti uchashchikhsia," Narodnoe obrazovanie, 1963, No. 10; L.V. Zankov, "Nachal'noe obuchenie i voprosy didaktiki," Narodnoe obrazovanie, 1964, No. 7; L.V. Zankov and N.V. Kuznetsova, Opyt obucheniia russkomu iazyku v I klasse, APN RSFSR, Moscow, 1961; T.L. Berkman and K.S. Grishchenko, Muzykal'noe razvitie uchashchikhsia v protsesse obucheniia peniiu, APN RSFSR, Moscow, 1961; Usvoenie znanii i razvitie mladshikh shkol'nikov, ed. by L.V. Zankov, "Prosveshchenie" Publishing House, Moscow, 1965; L.V. Zankov, Novoe v obuchenii arifmetike v I klasse, "Prosveshchenie" Publishing House, Moscow, 1964.

Nachal'naia shkola, 1966, No. 2

SUMMARY OF THE DISCUSSION ON L. V. ZANKOV'S "NEW DIDACTIC SYSTEM"

L. V. Zankov's article "Our Differences," published in this issue, concludes the discussion of the "new didactic system" begun by Zankov's article "Experiment with a New System of Primary Education," which appeared in our journal in No. 10 for 1964.*

The journal offered its pages for readers to express their opinions "for" and "against" the concepts advanced by Zankov.

The basic significance of this discussion is that the fundamental tenets of the didactic system promoted by Zankov were subjected to broad and comprehensive discussion for the first time.

Both positive and weak aspects of the system were brought out in the course of the discussion.

The discussion touched upon a broad range of problems and questions related to the system. The participants expressed their attitudes toward the principles which lie at the base of the new system, toward the draft programs worked out on the basis of those principles, toward the instructional methods and techniques reflected in the system, and toward some of the results of work in the schools using the new system.

A number of the responses gave full support to the experiment: some teachers accept its

general direction, its concrete content, the didactic principles underlying the programs and methods, as well as its methodological techniques. They like to work "according to L. V. Zankov's system."

Readers of our journal are already familiar with the favorable evaluation of the experiment given by such teachers as A. V. Plekhanov and N. V. Iatsuta, B. P. Syrov, and M. F. Zyrianova. The authors of other articles sent to us — A. Temrezova, I. Titova, E. Kolas, and N. Kolesnik — are also in favor of the experiment.

Temrezova wrote: "The method of accelerated study of the program evoked cognitive activity in the children such as I have never seen in any class during thirty years of teaching."

The teacher I. Titova wrote: "I would now be unable to work in the old way. And my pupils would also be unable to work at half capacity any longer. I have had particularly good results in arithmetic. The students do their assignments consciously; they reason, make comparisons, and draw conclusions and generalizations. I think that it is necessary to issue [vypustit'] the new program."

Thus, there are aspects of Zankov's experiment which attract the attention of some teachers. In Zankov's statements and proposals they find thoughts that are in accord with their

---

*See Soviet Education, Vol. VII, No. 3 — Editor.

thoughts, that correspond to their requirements and aspirations.

And, indeed, the positive aspect of the experiment of the Zankov laboratory is that it is directed against the underestimation of development in the process of instruction. Zankov is against slowness in the study of programs. He aspires to raise the theoretical level of the pupils' knowledge and wants to fill the programs with more cognitive material. He exhorts teachers to adopt a new style of work and to come closer to their students both in class and in out-of-class work. All these aspects of his experiment quite rightly received a favorable response during the discussion.

But Zankov does not act in the given case merely as an experimenter who is seeking the solution of separate pedagogical problems in order to improve the existing system of instruction and upbringing. Instead, he is in the position of a creator, through his own efforts and those of his laboratory, of an unprecedented and integral didactic system, which he feels should radically change the didactics and methodology of primary education as a whole. It is therefore natural that participants in the discussion should raise many questions related to the "new didactic system" as such. What is this system, and what is its essence? What are its fundamental elements, and how are they conditioned? How are they interconnected and interdependent? Since every system has characteristic relationships of elements, of their dynamics, continuity — what are they in this case? How do the methods correlate with the content, and how do they change at various stages of instruction? Finally, how do the fundamental propositions of the new system find concrete expression in teaching Russian, mathematics, and the other school subjects?

The discussion developed on the level of these questions. Let us examine them.

How the Discussion Participants Evaluated
the Didactic Principles of the "New System"

In order to achieve the general and rounded

development of children, Zankov formulated several didactic principles which he has used as his point of departure in building his system: 1) instruction is to be at a high level of difficulty; 2) the program should be covered at a rapid pace; 3) the volume of theoretical knowledge should be increased, etc.

During the discussion these principles were subjected to thorough consideration. Comrades N. S. Rozhdestvenskii, B. P. Esipov, L. N. Skatkin, V. A. Kiriushkin, and others dealt with them in their articles.

The problem of the development of pupils in the process of instruction occupies a central place in the works of L. V. Zankov and his co-workers. As Zankov correctly remarks, in our times the principle that the "school must construct its academic work so that it not only imparts to the pupils a system of knowledge and habits, but also promotes the development of the children . . . is generally accepted in Soviet pedagogy." (1) As regards the relationship between instruction (upbringing) and development, even here, as Zankov acknowledges, "the proposition concerning the leading role of upbringing in development" has already assumed "an important and firm position in our science." (2)

The conclusions to which L. S. Vygotskii came after having considered this problem are regarded by Soviet pedagogy as having important and serious significance. We refer especially to the idea he expressed in 1934 that instruction should not "drag behind development, but that, on the contrary, it should pave the way for it," that "instruction is only worthwhile when it anticipates development." (3)

Thus, the problem of the development of pupils in the process of instruction is nothing new for Soviet pedagogy. It would be wrong to think that the idea had been undeservedly forgotten and was "reborn" only in the works of Zankov.

It can be said without exaggeration that in recent years the efforts of almost all Soviet didactics specialists, psychologists, and methodologists have been directed toward working out some aspect or other of the questions relating to the problem of the development of pupils in the process of instruction. In the process, naturally, various approaches to the solution of some theoretical questions have emerged (see the material of the special discussion conducted during 1956 and 1957 in the journal Sovetskaia pedagogika) and problems for further investigation in this field have been advanced, particularly the task of revealing the law-governed connections between development and instruction, and, as one of the conditions for the solution of this fundamental task, the elaboration of the criteria (indices) by which one might evaluate progress in children's development.

All these questions must be studied experimentally, and therefore one can only welcome the fact that the laboratory headed by Zankov has undertaken to resolve them.

The advantage that Zankov has over other experimenters is that he removed his investigation from the confines of the laboratory and organized a bold pedagogical experiment, in the course of which there emerged, as a side effect, the highly important conclusion that the cognitive potentialities of children in the lower grades have been underestimated (a conclusion that has since been confirmed by experimental work organized in schools by the laboratories of D. B. El'konin and V. V. Davydov and other groups).

However, it should be noted that the Zankov laboratory, despite the many years it has been investigating the fundamental problem — elucidation of the law-governed connections between the structure of educational-upbringing work and the course of children's development — has not made much progress in solving that problem. Indeed, we cannot find any convincing answers in the works published by the laboratory to the basic questions relating to this problem. What is development? What are its stages and levels? What are the transitions, aspects, and variants that occur in the process of the mental development of children? What regularities of the process of development has the investigation revealed? One must concur with A. A. Liublinskaia when she writes: "It is impossible to take seriously as a picture of development those few tables of figures which show either the state of progress of children in the experimental classes

at various moments of instruction or the change in the number of characteristics of wild ducks [utki-kriachki] given by the pupils at the beginning and end of instruction" (see The Development of Pupils in the Process of Instruction [Razvitie uchashchikhsia v protsesse obucheniia], edited by L. V. Zankov).

The Editorial Board also agrees with Liublinskaia when she asserts that the works of the laboratory "lack theoretical substantiation for those experiments by which development is 'located.'"

Indeed, Zankov's laboratory, having failed to resolve one of the most important questions concerning the objective criteria for evaluating development, has proceeded to use extraordinarily dubious means and methods to check the results of the experimental instruction with respect to its value for the pupils' general development.

Let us examine, however, what the laboratory has actually done. Zankov claims that he and the colleagues working under his direction have created "a new and integral system of primary education" that is different in principle from the one which has evolved historically in the Soviet school and is currently in use. The changes introduced concern the curriculum, programs, the methods of instruction, and the methods of upbringing (see the above-cited article in Nachal'naia shkola). Zankov considers his proposed reconstruction of the didactic and methodological system of primary education as an "entirely appropriate and justified" process. But the only reason he gives in favor of a radical break with the system of primary education that has been worked out comes down to this: "We do not live in a time to bolster and patch up, without touching the very foundations of the didactics and methodology of primary education." One would have thought that the necessity for a break with the foundations of the didactics and methodology of primary education in our country and in our time would have required serious scientific substantiation! Indeed, let us turn to history and try to explain what prompted Zankov and his colleagues to raise the question of creating a new system of primary education to replace the old one.

In his book On the Subject Matter and Methods of Didactic Research [O predmete i metodakh didakticheskikh issledovanii], Zankov uses as an example the methods employed by his laboratory in studying the problem of the relationship between instruction and development. He says: "To find the laws governing the relationship between instruction and development, the methodological system now used in the primary grades must be compared with another system. But which other system is it to be?" (p. 32). Evidently this question was the starting point for the creation of Zankov's "new system." He goes on to explain that the comparison must be made with a system "which contributes considerably more to the general development of the pupils." And the efforts of the laboratory were directed toward elaborating such a system.

However, in solving this task Zankov and his colleagues found themselves in a vicious circle: to explain the relationship between instruction and development it is necessary to create a system of instruction that will give the maximum effect as regards development, but such a scientifically substantiated system cannot be created without first revealing the nature of the law-governed connection between instruction and development. Under these circumstances, the elaboration of a "new" system of primary education could not but lead to the scientifically unsubstantiated introduction of changes into various aspects of the process of instruction, to this or that change for the sake of change. And the subsequent "experimental verification" and "proof" of the effectiveness of the system developed with respect to the children's development were conducted without the objective criteria of development needed for this purpose, so that the whole of the investigation and the conclusions derived from it were left in mid-air.

A great many criticisms have been leveled at the principle of "teaching children at a high level of difficulty." When explaining the principle, Zankov added the concept of "adhering to a measure of difficulty." But this addition changes nothing in the principle as such, for a high level of difficulty is also a measure of

difficulty. The measure of difficulty can be either high or low or average. But given a high level of difficulty the measure cannot be average, and certainly not low. It has to be high or you will not have a high level. If Zankov allows that the degree of difficulty that is accessible to the children can act as the measure of the high level of difficulty, he must then necessarily acknowledge the principle of accessibility, as B. P. Esipov rightly remarked. But Zankov does not agree with this and asserts that the given requirement does not signify the principle of accessibility. He is quite afraid of the principle of accessibility and strives to prove how profitable the principle of a "high level of difficulty" is as compared with that of accessibility. Actually, to say that one must be aware of the "measure of difficulty" is tantamount to saying that one must adhere to the principle of accessibility. Accessibility and adherence to a measure of difficulty are very similar. T. G. Terekhova rightly comments: "The idea of conducting instruction on a high level of difficulty . . . as a general assertion and without a detailed examination of the criteria of various levels of difficulty (e.g., a low level, an average one, an above average level, and a high one) is not much of a practical guide."

In any labor, whether it be physical or mental, people have always attempted somehow or other to lighten the burden and have never set themselves the goal of making the work process more difficult. But in learning, it turns out, the child's labor must be complicated, made more difficult, and raised to a high level of difficulty, as if only under this condition can children's development be achieved. This assertion must be considered unproven and lacking in substantiation, and L. N. Skatkin is right when he asserts that the proposed introduction of difficulties into the process of instruction could evoke from some children a revulsion toward learning.

The principle of instruction at a fast rate also evoked objections. Skatkin had grounds for calling this principle pernicious, since its application would inevitably lead to the isolation of a group of lagging pupils from among those who work more slowly. How does Zankov reply to this valid remark by Skatkin? It seems that he is against any chasing after records in the sense of the quantity of assignments performed by the pupils; he is against the children solving as many examples as possible, doing as many exercises as possible, etc., during the lesson. Given this explanation, the question of the fast rate of instruction disappears.

According to Zankov, the given principle must be understood in the sense that it "requires that the pupil be given more and more new material in order to move forward as soon as he has mastered what has gone before." But a thorough "mastery of the previous material" can also lead to reduced rates. Besides, more and more new knowledge does not necessarily mean that such knowledge is either perfected or lasting. It must not be forgotten that in addition to knowledge, the pupils must also acquire skills and habits and that time is necessary for their formation. There must be heterogeneous and varied exercises; the very fact that the material of a topic is divided into parts means that the process of covering it is divided into stages, each of which has its own problems and exercises.

V. A. Kiriushkin also objected to the fast rates. "The rate of instruction," he states, "cannot be considered as an essential index of how effective the instruction has been." Just as one ought not to mark time or "chew over" the material, so, too, one ought not to hurry. Besides, a "fast rate" and a "slow rate" are relative concepts. Some of the lessons in reading that are cited in the works of Zankov are clear examples of marking time, although they are presented in the materials of the system as models of "energetic progress." Thus, the principle of "covering the course material at a rapid rate" does not correspond to the basic goal of the experiment — to link instruction with development.

As a fundamental inadequacy of the principle of teaching children at a rapid rate, O. I. Malinovskaia pointed to the fact that Zankov never even mentions the necessity of constant review and consolidation of previous material.

Zankov is wrong in thinking that all his opponents are against the extension of theoretical knowledge in grammar, mathematics, and other subjects, that they are against an earlier introduction of grammatical and mathematical terminology, or that they are in general ill-disposed to the idea of the important role of theoretical knowledge. The Editorial Board does not have the impression, for instance, that N. S. Rozhdestvenskii is opposed to the study of grammar in primary education. But, after all, this is precisely a matter of primary education and the first steps in the theoretical study of the native language. It is impossible to make the same demands on this period of school instruction as we make on later periods of schooling.

In his second article, Zankov asserts: ". . . abstraction and generalization, abstractions in verbal form, do exist in pupils of the primary grades. . . . This by no means denies the significant role of visual images in the thinking of a young pupil." To be sure, Zankov makes a qualification here, too: "However, ideas based on visual images cannot be regarded as the primary component of a young pupil's thinking. It is precisely progress in the areas of abstraction and generalization that primarily characterizes the changes which occur in thinking in the course of early school age." No one has yet calculated the percentage relationship between the concrete and the abstract in a child's thinking, and therefore it would be fruitless to argue about which of them is primary or decisive. One thing is beyond question: the relationship gradually evolves toward the development of abstract thinking, but it does so gradually. Rozhdestvenskii therefore says: "Abstract thinking must be developed in the child, but by adhering to the principle of gradualness, taking the children's capabilities into account. Only under this condition will the child develop normally and consciously master the grammatical material. . . ." It would be difficult not to agree with this assertion, but keeping in mind that the children's capabilities also gradually grow.

How the Discussion Participants Evaluated the Progress Based on the Above-Mentioned Principles

Zankov's laboratory worked out draft programs for Russian language and mathematics and drew up outlines of the contents of other school subjects. (4)

During the discussion these programs were thoroughly considered. T. G. Terekhova, V. A. Kiriushkin, A. M. Chernysh, L. N. Skatkin, M. I. Ivanov, P. M. Erdniev, and others dwelt on them.

Let us look at the program for Russian language.

If one considers the content of instruction in Russian as presented by Zankov, it is, in comparison with the present program for the four-year course of instruction, an expanded course in grammar plus spelling that is intended to be covered in three years of primary school. In these three years the students are expected to learn many things that are now studied not only in the 4th grade, but partly in subsequent grades as well. In this 3rd grade we find not only personal, but also possessive and indicative pronouns. The topic "The Verb" has been expanded by the inclusion of such items as "Aspects of the Verb" and "Voices of the Verb" (active and passive). The section on "The Sentence" includes the item "Complex and Compound Sentences (Some Aspects)."

In connection with the expansion of the 3rd-grade program, those of the 1st and 2nd grades have also been changed, incorporating material that is now taught in the 3rd and 4th grades. In the 1st grade, for instance, it is proposed to study the roots of words with only one root and unstressed vowels in the roots of words; the 1st grade is also introduced to nouns (animate and inanimate, proper and common, singular and plural, and gender), to adjectives (gender and number), and to verbs (present, past and future tense). There is a corresponding expansion in the 2nd-grade program, which, in addition to the material of the present program, contains word structure (prefix, suffix, endings, stems and compound words), noun declensions, case meanings, the main, secondary and homogeneous parts of sentences, simple and complex sentences, and the corresponding rules of spelling.

It can and should be said that, given our country's compulsory eight-year education, primary education could be confined to three years. But this does not mean that the three-year program of education should be excessively expanded.

The comrades participating in the discussion noted in their articles the great overloading of the given programs. The Editorial Board completely agrees with the critical comments on this question.

The 1st grade is obviously overloaded. From the standpoint of both child psychology and pedagogy, it seems completely improbable to propose such a program for the 1st grade.

Let us remember the wise words of K. D. Ushinskii: "Why," he asked, "wear yourself out in premature explanations to children of some point, why torture both yourself and the child to no purpose, when he does not understand you now but will, perhaps, see it clearly in six months simply because he has lived these six months" (Collected Works [Sobranie sochinenii], Vol. VI, 1949, p. 245). Perhaps a child will understand and memorize something (in the main he will memorize it), but that is not enough for the child to master what he has studied, for him to be able to use it for practical purposes, or for him to receive the necessary development on the basis of this material.

Prematurely "inflating" pupils with such a volume of abstract grammatical concepts and terms can be not merely useless but even harmful to their development. Perhaps the present 1st-grade program should be supplemented somewhat, but it certainly should not be overloaded, because grammatical concepts are abstract and the children are not sufficiently prepared to master them properly.

The other grades are overloaded, too. Participants in the discussion pointed this out. The inclusion in the program for the primary grades of such concepts as "perfective and imperfective aspects" and verb voice (active and passive) evoked objections. For instance, Comrade Terekhova expressed surprise at the inclusion in the program of aspects and voices of the verb. Differences in aspect are connected with the formation of tenses, and if you discuss aspects you should also discuss how the perfective verbs form two tenses, and the imperfective — three; unless this is done it is impossible to understand why it is necessary to give 3rd-grade pupils the concept of aspect. "It is even harder to understand why the voices of the verb were included in the program for the 3rd grade. . . . At the price of considerable effort, pupils of the primary grades can be taught to master the terms 'active' and 'passive' voice. . .but what is the point of such efforts? Will it raise the general development of the pupil?" And we can only give a negative answer to these puzzling questions: the concept of "voice" is a very complicated one, and there is good reason for the failure of the science of language to achieve unanimity on its meaning; the terms "active" and "passive" cannot be made clear without the concepts of the transitive and intransitive. Why should we oversimplify and thereby confuse the matter? As Terekhova correctly remarks, "Even if it happens that pupils do memorize the concepts, such knowledge would probably be formal. . . ." Incorrectly mastered concepts bring neither knowledge nor development. This proposition seems so elementary that it hardly requires demonstration.

Or take the topic "Case Meanings (Adjectives; Some Basic Meanings)." In practice children master the case meanings that they use in their speech. As the children's general speech develops, case meanings become richer. Naturally, the process of enrichment occurs in a practical way. To be sure, theoretical knowledge about case meanings can improve the level of speech cultivation, but it will not expand the linguistic capabilities of children. Zankov's program is concerned, of course, with theoretical study and not with the practical mastery of case meanings because, as he puts it, instruction should be at a high theoretical level. But is such instruction possible in the matter of case meanings? As we know, case meanings are numerous, and in addition they are not so easily understood theoretically that they can be lightheartedly included in

the program of secondary education, let alone in the program of the primary school.

The program is also overloaded in <u>mathematics.</u>

The majority of the responses to Zankov's article expressed alarm at the unusual expansion of this program by including sections and problems in the 1st to 3rd grades that are reserved for the systematic courses in mathematics and that children of seven to nine are inadequately prepared to study. The principles of instruction at a high level of difficulty and at a rapid rate have led to the inclusion in the 3rd-grade program of positive and negative numbers, directly and inversely proportional dependence, the drawing of graphs of directly proportional dependence, different positional systems of numeration, and the five-digit system and its comparison with the decimal system.

P. M. Erdniev and many other people think that the inclusion of such questions in the program for primary grades is pointless. "These questions," Erdniev says, "cannot be studied in detail in the younger classes; it is impossible to construct any sort of meaningful exercises around them. In other words, knowledge of these questions at that stage cannot act as seeds of the self-development of thought, and such knowledge remains as mere islands of information."

The Zankov program shouts "at the top of its voice" about the laws of arithmetic operations, which apparently are to be taught without any limitation and without making any concessions to the age or mathematical development of schoolchildren of seven to nine years of age. From the 1st grade the program is filled with mathematical definitions and abundant mathematical terminology.

The only thing missing in this program is problems, that is, the heart of any course in arithmetic.

It is not surprising that such a program has confused a great many teachers. Is all this not too difficult for children who come to school when they are seven years of age? Teachers Z. L. Pugacheva, K. S. Evdokimova, A. S. Sadchikova, and others asked that question.

There is a great deal that is remote and

abstract in the program. It is enough to read the article of teachers A. V. Plekhanova and N. V. Iatsuta (1965, No. 4, p. 77) to be convinced of this. They present extracts from their 1st-grade lessons. Here are the extracts:

"On the blackboard are $\underline{a} + \underline{b}$ and $\underline{a} + \underline{c}$.

"Can they be compared in magnitude? (Not yet, because we do not know the value of $\underline{c}$ and $\underline{b}$.)

"But if $\underline{c} > \underline{b}$? (Then the sum of $\underline{a} + \underline{c} > \underline{a} + \underline{b}$.)

"Why? (The first items are identical, but the second item in the first sum is larger, which means $\underline{a} + \underline{c} > \underline{a} + \underline{b}$.)

"The letters are then replaced by numbers and the correctness of the reasoning is demonstrated.

"Here is another example: $\underline{a} - \underline{c} > \underline{a} - \underline{b}$.

"What can be said about the numbers $\underline{c}$ and $\underline{b}$? ($\underline{c} < \underline{b}$.)

"Why? (The difference between $\underline{a} - \underline{c}$ is greater than that between $\underline{a} - \underline{b}$.)

"What is being subtracted from in the inequalities is the same; consequently the subtrahends are unequal ($\underline{c} < \underline{b}$)."

These examples show the jungle of abstractions into which the given program leads 1st-grade pupils. Children who have just come to understand "that 10 is one ten" are obliged to operate with the sum and difference as mathematical expressions, with changes in the sum and the difference expressed in a general and abstract form, and with the concepts "magnitude," "value of the magnitude," "inequality," etc.

Such abstractionism in the 1st-grade course in arithmetic evokes in some of our comrades a feeling of tender emotion about the alleged unbounded capacity of children. But a great many teachers are alarmed by such an orientation in work with 1st-graders.

"Yes, I am in favor of three years of instruction," writes the teacher E. P. Kolas. "One might even study this program in three years. But nonetheless L. V. Zankov's program is not the thing. It seems to me that what we need is the golden mean, which both teachers and students have long been awaiting."

Of course, the arithmetic programs must be revised, the level of the pupils' theoretical knowledge must be raised, and the program

must not only ensure the communication of knowledge and the inculcation of habits, but also the mathematical development of pupils. But all this must be done with a sense of proportion, taking into account the powers and capabilities of the children from seven to nine who study in the first three grades.

Thus, the volume of grammatical and mathematical theory included in Zankov's programs for the primary school evokes serious doubts as to whether it corresponds to the aims and tasks of the development of children, and also to the real possibilities of three-year primary education.

When considering the question of introductory nature studies, Zankov quite rightly criticizes the existing curriculum and points to its impoverished content.

Zankov proposes that we return to the positive experience of past years, when the undivided sway of explanatory reading did not exist in the school curriculums. The 1st and subsequent grades then had two independent subjects, geography and natural science, which Zankov wishes to revive with some modifications in their programs. But he has not succeeded in comprehending all that was done before; he has not compared all the main ideas and tendencies, nor has he evaluated them objectively and selected that which most corresponds to the spirit of our times.

Thus, he rejects the notion of creating a new school subject — nature studies — on the grounds that such a science, which would be called "Nature Studies" and would combine natural science and geography, does not exist.

Zankov is right about there being no single science today which would correspond to the school subject.

But it is no secret that any school subject rests not on a single science, but on a whole system of them. Nor can this be otherwise, for the contemporary sciences themselves are undergoing an intensive process of ramification. "Geography, the description of the earth, is a complex of closely connected sciences embracing physical and economic geography." (5)

"Natural science is the totality of sciences

about nature. . . . Two opposite processes are organically interwoven in natural science: the continual differentiation of natural science into increasingly narrow fields and the integration of these separated sciences." (6)

However, a school subject, while resting on definite sciences and taking from them its methodology and, to a certain extent, its content, structures all this in logic that is more appropriate pedagogically.

The question of which subjects should be used to introduce education in natural science has a long history. An objective analysis of this history leads to the conclusion that, from every point of view, the most justified approach is precisely to have a course on nature studies and not two — natural science and geography — because they do not enable the pupil to acquire the only correct, integral view of nature. I. Ia. Gerd spoke very sharply on this matter; he emphasized frequently that there is no room at the primary stage of instruction for separate natural sciences and that a single course is necessary in order to form a materialist view of nature. Many methodologists, geographers, natural scientists, didactics specialists, and psychologists held the same view.

While advancing the proposition that the fundamentals of the sciences must be studied, Zankov departs from it to a considerable extent when he begins to work out the contents of the programs for geography and natural science. We will cite only one of many possible examples. From the point of view of geography as a science, it is completely unacceptable to give the concept of climate at the beginning and to go on to the question of the shape and movement of the earth a year later. It is perfectly evident that, given such an approach, one cannot speak of the children understanding the causes of the phenomena and their connections. And since that is the case, it is impossible to suppose that this system directs the development of the children's thinking along the correct path.

The elaboration of the contents (especially for the 1st and 2nd grades) is very reminiscent of the unrelated raggedness of the programs for explanatory reading.

The Presentation of Teaching Methods in the "New System"

The methodological aspect of the "new system" was also subjected to serious discussion. V. A. Kiriushkin, T. G. Terekhova, M. I. Ivanov, P. M. Erdniev, P. I. Sorokin, L. N. Skatkin, and others turned their attention to the methods of instruction. There were also comments on individual questions of methodology in the responses of teachers.

These writers noted a rather considerable number of inadequacies and mistakes, both of a general and specific nature.

"The most depressing thing in Zankov's books and articles," says Kiriushkin, "is that when proclaiming a 'new system of instruction,' he indiscriminately consigns the current methods and techniques of teaching to the category of 'useless.'" He sees no achievements in the methodological theory and practice of the Soviet school. To be sure, under the influence of the discussion, Zankov declared in his last article: "Our experiment is indissolubly connected with the teachers' experience." But in saying that he has in mind only the teaching experience of that comparatively small group of educators who are "realizing his new system in practice."

Having thoroughly familiarized himself with Zankov's methodological precepts and having analyzed the transcript of lessons given in accordance with the "new system," Comrade Kiriushkin came to the conclusion that Zankov's methodological recommendations are contradictory and inconsistent. Calling for "energetic forward progress," he publishes lessons that are a clear example of "marking time"; fighting for theory, he opposes all theory when it is a matter of teaching children composition; struggling for an acceleration of the pace, he is for the kind of development of habits of observation which artificially separates old knowledge from new and slows down the rate of acquiring new knowledge.

Zankov is in general sharply opposed to everything that would prepare the child to overcome the difficulties facing him. Thus, he decisively rejects the demand for complete answers although the teacher must often extract well-composed, precise and complete answers from the children in the form of sentences; he decisively rejects teaching children how to form sentences from given questions and words in the hope that the ability to connect words and to construct sentences will appear all by itself. There are many other unfounded, unverified, and contradictory suggestions in Zankov's methodological recommendations.

But the major fault of Zankov's methodological views is their absolute and categorical preference for one method, type, and mode of work. This is to be observed both in teaching Russian and mathematics, to the detriment of other methods which have justified themselves in practice and have been substantiated theoretically.

Terekhova (in Russian) and Sorokin (in mathematics) have revealed mistakes of an elementary nature in Zankov's methodological publications (e.g., his book On Primary Education).

Terekhova's article cites a fragment of a lesson devoted to the distinction between prepositions and prefixes in which "the difference between prefixes and prepositions is connected with the syntactical analysis of the sentence." Under the guidance of the teacher, the children only made the observation that "prepositions appear only in secondary parts of the sentence, and prefixes in the predicates (and sometimes in secondary parts). An observation like that, of course, leads the pupils to a corresponding false conclusion. The fact is that prefixes can be in words expressing the predicate as well as in words expressing secondary parts of the sentence; the secondary parts can be expressed by words with prefixes or by words without them (vyshel iz shkoly, zhdal vykhoda); the predicate can also be expressed with or without a prefix (iabloni tsvetut — iabloni v tsvetakh). Thus, it is impossible to connect the difference between prefixes and prepositions with snytactical analysis: prefixes are morphological phenomena, and sentence parts are syntactical. To violate this rule is a crass mistake. Skatkin also noted this mistake: "It hardly needs to be explained that a word with a prefix can be any part of a sentence."

Zankov disagrees with Terekhova's comments on the grounds that: 1) the children did not draw a conclusion but only made an observation (can this be a serious argument?); 2) the students allegedly did not contrast prepositions to parts of a sentence (but they obviously did in the sentences "Okhotnik nastrelial mnogo utok" and "Tetradi lezhot na stole"); 3) there are "definite connections and relations" between morphological and syntactical categories (of course there are, but they are not the ones established during the lesson). Complements are expressed by the case forms, but not, of course, of parts of the sentence but of parts of speech: nouns, pronouns, etc. Terekhova is right and Zankov is wrong. To be sure, the given mistake by the teacher was a particular case that may not be characteristic of the "new system," but it is difficult to understand why Zankov should defend an obvious mistake.

A series of shortcomings in the methods and techniques of work in arithmetic were noted in the replies of comrades Ivanov, Skatkin, Erdniev, and Sorokin (the articles of the latter two were not published due to lack of space).

Erdniev disagrees with some of the statements of Zankov on the solving of problems. For instance, Zankov proposes to present 1st-graders with "such problems, and in such a sequence, that each one is new to them." Understood literally, this means that all the problems should be different as regards subject and numerical values. We all know that such is the case in the existing system of instruction.

"But," says Comrade Erdniev, "one must recognize as one of the results of our investigation the elucidation of the following important circumstance: as a rule, the problem solved cannot be dropped once the answer is given; it is necessary to seek another solution of the problem, to attempt immediately to reconstruct the problem in reverse, and to solve thereby a group of mutually inverse problems through comparison and opposition."

Erdniev also objects to Zankov's assertion that the 1st-grade pupils generally need not practice making up problems.

Erdniev writes that this conclusion is based

on the argument that problems composed by 1st-graders "will inevitably be very primitive." Zankov cites an example of such an "unsuccessful" problem: "Misha met 9 bears in the woods. He killed 5. How many were left?"

Yet we know that in such cases the teacher can easily bring the child back to reality. It is enough to point out that one man cannot meet so many bears at once and kill them.

Sorokin and Ivanov made a series of critical remarks on the methodological techniques recommended in Zankov's article and on the book by him and N. V. Kuznetsova, From the Experience of Teaching Arithmetic in the 1st Grade [Iz opyta obucheniia arifmetike v I klasse]. "Many lessons are given in this book," writes Ivanov, "but active methods are not used; all the lessons consist of questions from the teacher and answers by the pupils. This monotony in the lessons cannot stimulate the pupils."

Both Sorokin and Skatkin have noted that the book contains an irrational method of counting and a mathematical mistake: the addition of units to tens. Units and tens are different magnitudes, and it would be as impossible to perform operations with them as it would be, for instance, to add 2 kilograms to 5 meters. One might not attach great significance to this mistake if Zankov did not publicize it as his great methodological achievement.

Sorokin writes: "In the book From the Experience of Teaching Arithmetic in the 1st Grade there is talk on dozens of pages about various methodological techniques and methods as if they were new while, as it happens, they have long been known to everybody and are employed in every school as quite ordinary." "You read," he goes on, "endless lesson transcripts and you wonder why all this has been printed and duplicated in 100,000 copies."

Thus, the methodology of instruction according to the new system has not been worked out. The vague, confused methodological principles proposed by the "new system" have put their stamp not only on the programs, but also on its methods; they do not open the way for the construction of a new, "non-traditional" methodology.

Some Results of Work Under the "New System"

Zankov attributes to his system an exceptionally important role in the speedy and successful progress of the pupils. And in fact a number of teachers, in their comments on Zankov's article, have reported that they are achieving excellent results in their work.

But is it only those teachers who work under the leadership of Zankov who are achieving great advances in the children's progress at the present time? Does not the experience of the teachers of Lipetsk, Rostov, Leningrad and Voronezh demonstrate that rationalization of instruction can be reached by other means than the principle of speed in Zankov's "new didactic system"? Have not thousands of teachers in other regions had some success in the fight against the repeating of grades?

Therefore, the cause of the success of teachers working with Zankov's system requires analysis. It can be determined not so much by the virtues of the new system as by the great role of the teacher's personality. School administrations and departments of public education usually assign the best teachers, the enthusiasts, to work in the experimental classes, and they will have good results in other conditions as well.

But there are also some definitely shady aspects to those methods which are used in some classes to effectuate the principles of accelerated study of the program and instruction at a high level of difficulty. Let us hear what those comrades who have been in close contact with the work of the experimental classes have to say on this question.

M. I. Ivanov, a methodologist from the city of Tula, is familiar with the work of the experimental classes. He writes: "It is certainly true that some experimental classes have had the achievements that have been written about. But other facts must be taken into account here. These classes are given enormous attention. And students who lag in their rate of work are sometimes transferred to regular classes." Facts of this sort, even if they are not widespread, do not testify to the advantages of the new system.

And here is what V. S. Sergeeva, the mother of a girl who is studying in the 1st grade under the "new system" in Stavropol', has written to the editors: "It seems to me that the authors of the new program have overdone it and have put the teacher in a difficult position. The teachers who have written in the journal have given their approval to this method; they have rejoiced and shared their successes, but they have spoken very timidly about the difficulties involved and have completely ignored the woes and despair and the price they paid to get out of the difficulties. We parents have had to suffer and endure a great deal, and in some instances we have not only taken away from some children their childhood, as M. I. Ivanov puts it, but we have alienated the children from themselves." She went on to relate how parents have helped their children at home to grasp what they did not master in class. "The teachers are well aware of this work at home, but for some inexplicable reason they keep it a secret. L. V. Zankov's laboratory must study this work at home and realistically define the possible volume of the 1st-grade program. . . ." "My daughter," continues Sergeeva, "entered school from kindergarten when she was seven years and four months old. She did not know how to work independently, and I could work with her only in the evening. Having only a minimum of time, it was necessary to intensify the pace at home as well, and this 'high speed' completion of lessons led to mutual nervousness and reached the point that I was forced to hand over the homework to my sister, a teacher in the primary grades." In conclusion, Comrade Sergeeva wrote: "A parents' meeting instructed our teacher to appeal to all the teachers of the experimental classes to boast less of their results and to talk more about the inadequacies and difficulties of the work, to relate the extreme strain which the children and their parents have experienced during the year."

These excerpts from a mother's letter are alarming. It is quite natural that the accelerated study of an overloaded program, and one that is at a high level of difficulty, must create for the children, the teachers, and the parents the extreme strain that Sergeeva's letter warns of.

Zankov is inclined to attribute all the successes in instruction, development, and upbringing to the miraculous influence of the "new system," which created the conditions, in his words, for the "outstanding progress in the general development of the pupils in the experimental classes." He speaks repeatedly about the outstanding progress. To what results in mastering knowledge and habits has this "outstanding progress in development" led?

Zankov cites some numerical indices obtained from a survey of the quality of knowledge and habits of pupils in the experimental classes of Tula and Kalinin.

Here are the figures: 79% of the pupils in the experimental 2nd-grade classes gave correct or partially correct answers to the problem. There was an average of 1.3 mistakes per pupil in the dictation in the 2nd grade. Sixty-one percent of the pupils of the experimental 1st-grade classes correctly planned all the operations."

Some of the participants in the discussion were puzzled by these figures. For instance, teacher A. M. Chernysh is in a state of confusion; here we have "the most effective new system," " outstanding progress in development," "eloquent results," and only . . .79% of the students gave correct and partially correct (which means wrong) answers to the solution of a problem! And what will happen to this percentage when the "new system" falls into the hands of an average teacher? Does it not "guarantee" that at least 25% of the pupils will fall behind in arithmetic? And 61% of the pupils were able to cope with planning labor operations! It would be hard to appear at any pedagogical council with such a percentage; it would be impossible to look any principal in the eye, let alone a district inspector.

The number of mistakes made in the dictation (1.3 per pupil) is not bad. But such a result does not require high-speed methods of instruction at a high level of difficulty; good teachers get such success with the usual method.

In order to have these quite modest figures produce a great impact on the reader, Zankov creates for them a dismal background in the form of the poor results achieved in the same work in the regular school. This is the old, fallacious style, long since condemned, of going into a regular school, working with another system, with materials which even in the experimental classes only 61% to 79% could handle.

The Editorial Board believes that the data presented do not indicate that the "new system" is exceptionally effective.

That Which Is Best and Rational in the "New System" Is Not the Creative Achievement of Zankov and His Laboratory Alone

We have already said that in the course of the discussion many of the contributions emphasized the positive elements of the system which have attracted progressive teachers. Many teachers stated in their articles, as has already been indicated, that the system forced them to work in a new manner and to achieve good results. And indeed, if you discard some of the far-fetched, artificial, and largely fallacious principles in the "new system," if you discard the huckstering tone of its propaganda (which is so unnecessary in such a serious matter), if you free Zankov's books, articles and speeches from their peculiar methodological nihilism toward the achievements and gains of many generations of people in pedagogical science and practice, then, as was noted at the beginning, one can find in the "system" a number of propositions which deserve our close attention.

But it would be a mistake to attribute everything that is worthwhile solely to the creativity of Zankov and his laboratory. Much of what is worthwhile in the didactic "system" of Zankov was born and is being born now in the searchings and numerous experiments conducted by various groups of scientists and by individual investigators. Mention should be made, first of all, of the work of the Leningrad Institute of Pedagogy, which, under the direction of B. G.

Anan'ev, collected and published from 1949 to 1959 a considerable body of valuable material on the problem of the connection between instruction and development. Furthermore, there has been, and is today, the intensive experimental work of the Institute of Psychology (the experiment of D. B. El'konin and V. V. Davydov, the investigations of N. A. Menchinskaia), of the Institute of General and Polytechnical Education (the experimental work of N. Rozhdestvenskii, K. Neshkov, M. Moro, etc.), of the Herzen Teacher Training Institute in Leningrad (A. A. Liublinskaia and M. Bantova), of the Institute of Theory and History of the Academy of Pedagogical Sciences (the investigations of M. Danilov and B. Esipov), the investigations of P. Erdniev (in Elista), N. Skripchenko (in Kiev), and so forth.

The experimental work of these groups tested and verified a number of propositions which were later reflected in the "new didactic system" (such as letter symbolism, improved techniques for teaching mathematics, etc.).

The draft programs of Zankov were also formed under the influence of ideas which were developed in various groups; it is enough to say that his programs were formulated and published in 1963, after the outline programs of the El'konin and Davydov laboratory were published in 1962.

In recent years, as we all know, the problem of a differentiated methodology has been strenuously debated; it is employed in the schools of Moscow, Rostov and the Rostov region and is being popularized in the press. Nor has Zankov been indifferent to this idea. He included it in his experiment, as is evident from his concluding article, in which he writes: "The application of a differentiated methodology. . . is an active element of our experimental instruction." (We note parenthetically that Zankov did not mention this methodology in a single one of his previous works.)

A number of the ideas about the study of nature which Zankov shares were ardently defended earlier by Herzen, Pisarev, Gerd, Shimkevich, Rudnev, Polovinkin, and many other people. The proposition that children should be given a notion of our planet and that their knowledge should not be confined to their immediate environment has frequently been incorporated in the programs and textbooks (thus, before 1959 the 4th-grade program, and earlier even the 3rd-grade program, included such sections as "The Shape of the Earth" and "Tropical Zones").

The ideas concerning the connection between animate and inanimate nature, flowing from the materialist view of nature, have also been incorporated in many methodological works and textbooks created in different periods since the time of Zuev, and later of Gerd and others. The proposition that "the historical aspect must be included in the study of nature" is extensively used in the system of natural sciences and was successfully realized in the first textbooks of M. N. Skatkin.

What do all these facts indicate? They indicate that whatever is new in pedagogy or in particular methods is created and developed not by one person, and not even by the efforts of one laboratory, but rather by the protracted and persistent work of many creative groups, relying on the experience of progressive teachers.

Insofar as the advances of collective methodological thought and the achievements of progressive experience find reflection in Zankov's proposals, they can be used to some extent in the improvement of our system of primary education. But Zankov took the wrong path of sharply opposing his system to the broad experience of developing our schools; he tries to break the connection and violate the continuity of the "new system" with the existing one, and he subordinates the content and methods of this "system" to principles which are of dubious pedagogical value.

All this introduces internal contradictions into Zankov's system, deprives it of unity, and reduces its scientific and practical significance.

Finishing this survey of the results of the discussion, the Editorial Board considers it necessary to note the fact that Zankov's concluding article, "Our Differences," is written on the plane of a complete rejection of the critical comments of all opponents who participated in the discussion.

Zankov has accepted nothing from all the critical material. He rejects it all. Yet the discussion materials contain many valuable and correct ideas both on general and specific questions. And Zankov did not respond at all to the interesting article of V. A. Kiriushkin, a Candidate of Pedagogical Sciences.

Such a careless attitude toward the statements of comrades who have different opinions is not seemly to Soviet criticism and the traditions accepted in it. And it is now absolutely impermissible to pin the label of conservative in principle and opponent of innovation on those who came forward with critical remarks on serious questions and express their opinions.

There can be no doubt that all of Zankov's opponents were guided in their contributions by the sincere desire to inquire profoundly into the truth.

One must not, when struggling with the inadequacies of present experience and of theoretical works on pedagogy and methodology, react intolerantly to criticism of new experience. Soviet criticism must be one of collaboration and mutual help, directed in this case toward improvement of the system of instructing and rearing our children.

In conclusion, the Editorial Board would like to express its gratitude to all those who took part in this discussion.

Footnotes

1) L. V. Zankov, "Eksperiment po novoi sisteme nachal'nogo obucheniia," Nachal'naia shkola, 1964, No. 10.

2) L. V. Zankov, ed., Razvitie uchashchikhsia v protsesse obucheniia, RSFSR Academy of Pedagogical Sciences Publishing House, Moscow, 1963.

3) L. S. Vygotskii, Izbrannye psikhologicheskie issledovaniia, RSFSR Academy of Pedagogical Sciences Publishing House, 1956, p. 499.

4) See Zankov's book O nachal'nom obuchenii, pp. 99-101 and 130-134.

5) MSE, Vol. II, p. 946.

6) MSE, Vol. III, pp. 824-825.

Narodnoe obrazovanie, 1963, No. 9

O. Petukhova

THE EMERGING CONTOURS OF THE FUTURE SCHOOL

(On One Experiment)

Educational Miracles

"Today we are going to work on a statement of equality and turn inequality into equality," said Aleksandra Aleksandrovna.

On the blackboard she wrote:

$$K > G$$
$$K = \ldots$$
$$\ldots = G$$

"This inequality can be turned into equality in two ways. Try to find them by yourself."

The class immersed itself in the work, and the teacher wrote another assignment on the blackboard:

$$n < v$$
$$\cdots\cdots\cdots$$
$$\cdots\cdots\cdots$$

"That inequality can also be turned into equality in two ways. When you have solved the task, we'll check it."

These problems would cause no surprise if they were assigned during an algebra lesson in, say, the 6th or 7th grade. But one must experience shock on learning that they are being solved by 1st graders! And when? At the end of November, when they have been in school less than three months, and when, according to the syllabus for the 1st grade, children are supposed to learn digits up to ten and to master operations with them. The children have not learned a single figure, and they have heard nothing about numbers or arithmetical operations, and suddenly they are confronted with algebra!

But let us return to the lesson.

The children have coped with the assignment quickly and the check-up has begun. What have they done with the right-hand member of the first inequality (G)? They have added an "x" to it. Why? Because it is less than the member on the left (K). And the member on the left has been diminished by "x." Then they analyze the second problem. The material on the blackboard was set down as follows in the children's notebooks:

$$K > G \qquad N < B$$
$$K = G + x \qquad N + x = B$$
$$K - x = G \qquad N = B - x$$

All this is so unusual and so incompatible with our accepted notion of seven-year-olds as completely unthinking that we do not believe our own eyes and ears. Doubts take hold: do the children really understand what they are doing? Do they understand the letter symbols? Isn't this simply a case of rote training?

The further course of the lesson gradually dissipates our doubts. The teacher shows the children two wooden sticks. "How can they be compared?" she asks. "By their length," the children answer. "And what does the comparison show?" "It shows that one of the sticks is shorter than the other." "How can the difference be stated?" They designate the length of the shorter stick by the letter A, and that of the other stick by the letter B.

This statement appears on the blackboard, and then in the children's notebooks: $A < B$. "What must we do to equate A and B?" And a little girl, whom we would hardly expect to be able to pronounce such words, firmly states:

"For A to be equated to B, we must add an x to A. The larger A will equal B."

No, this is not like rote training. From their lively countenances, from the eagerness with which they raise their hands to answer, and from the clearly formulated definitions of the operations, it is clear that the children fully understand what they are doing.

And here is another surprise.

"Let us solve a problem...."

A problem? Without knowing arithmetical operations?

"A gardener had several flower pots (we'll designate them with the letter A) and also several sprouts of flowers he wanted to plant in those pots (B stands for the number of plants). When the gardener compared the number of pots and the number of plants, he found that $A > B$. What had he discovered? What could he do?"

The children analyzed the problem at once, and defined two ways of solving it: either the number of pots had to be reduced to bring them into accord with the number of sprouts, or the number of sprouts had to be increased so that all the pots could be used. The second course was discussed. The children wrote the formula: $A = B + x$. When the teacher checked their answers, it appeared that Vova had written: $A - x = B$. This was judged by the class to be a mistake, because he had not "solved the problem as given."

There were other tasks after that. The children analyzed them and reasoned like "grown-ups."

When the lesson came to an end, the visitors left the classroom exclaiming:

"It's a miracle, there's no other word for it!"

But many such "miracles" could be observed in other classrooms. I should like briefly to describe a Russian language lesson for 2nd-graders.

The subject of the lesson was the spelling of unstressed vowels. The teacher, Varvara Titovna, dictated a series of words: zvezda, osen', snezhinka, zvonok, sadovnik, kosilka, zveno, glaza, stoiat', sestra, litso, nosy, vragi, stena, skripit. Why were all the unstressed vowels (a, o, e, i) presented at once? Was this a review of ground already covered? No, the 2nd-graders were only beginning their study of the unstressed vowels simultaneously.

The children wrote down the words and underlined the root of each word in red pencil (they already knew the composition of the word!). Every child could immediately see his mistakes. "Oh, I wrote it wrong: it should be 'zvon,' and not 'zvan,'" exclaimed my little neighbor, who had just underscored the root of the word "zvonok."

Then came "work with words." Each row of children was assigned a word: the first row — "boroda," the second — "ozera," the third — "polianka." The teacher asked the children to follow the rules they had already learned and written down in their notebooks. There were four such rules: first, isolate that part of the word whose spelling is doubtful; then find different forms of the original word (in this case, change the word endings according to cases) and also related words (find as many as you can think of by yourself, and then use the dictionary); next, find the words in the series that are obviously written with unstressed vowels; and finally, find this part in all the words and make sure that the spelling of the orthogram studied is everywhere the same and correct.

It was an unusual spectacle to see 2nd-graders, each with the Ozhegov dictionary in his hand (the books seemed very big in the little hands of the children), quickly find the right word and begin to perform the task according to rules that had been written down. The development of these children was striking when compared with that of other 2nd-graders. They knew many things that are included in the syllabuses for the upper grades.

And who could suppress a feeling of wonder at seeing 3rd-graders solving problems by both arithmetical and algebraic methods? The teacher, Elena Semenovna, dictated a problem: "Two workmen made chairs. The first made N chairs, the second — P chairs. How much money did they collect in all, if their pay for one chair was C rubles? The solution was expressed by the formula: (C rubles · N) + (C rubles · P) = ... To the teacher's question as to how many operations would be required if the letters were replaced by figures, the children correctly replied: two or three.

The next problem ran as follows: "The distance between two cities is 600 kilometers. Two trains left them, heading toward each other, at exactly the same time. The speed of the first train was 30 km. per hour, that of the second — 70 km. per hour...."

"What question follows from this task?" the teacher asked the children.

"How long will it take the trains to meet?" the pupils answered. They wrote down the answer as a numerical formula: 600 km.: (30 km. + 70 km.) = ...

To anticipate matters a little, we might say that the 3rd-graders in Elena Semenovna's class got through the whole Berezanskaia problem book for the 5th grade before the school year ended!

And now a word about the 4th grade, where there is also much that is extraordinary. Suf-

fice it to say that the 4th-graders were studying the structure of compound sentences, were manipulating difficult concepts and terms, and were discussing intonation, logical stress, the origin of written and oral speech.

How is one to explain such unusual phenomena in the primary school? Is there an "educational miracle" at work?

There Is No Miracle

We need hardly say that science is at work here. A highly interesting experiment is under way to adapt the content of primary school instruction to the mental possibilities of children, an experiment that is exposing many educational prejudices and old-fashioned ideas.

It is being conducted by the Laboratory of the Psychology of Young Schoolchildren at the Institute of Psychological Research under the RSFSR Academy of Pedagogical Sciences. The work is being directed by Candidate of Pedagogical Sciences Daniil Borisovich El'konin.

Everything about the experiment, beginning with the way it has been organized, is unusual. The laboratory personnel do not believe in the usefulness of isolated psychological inquiries into separate mental processes (memory, attention, perception, etc.), such inquiries, moreover, that involve individual laboratory experiments. It is their opinion that the children's educational activity as a whole must be investigated, and that systematic observations must be made of their mental development in normal classroom conditions throughout the years of schooling. The present experiment is one of the few cases in which psychological research has been conducted in the school, in the classroom, day after day, throughout the entire school year, and on a sufficient scale.

The experiment was started in 1959 in a 1st grade of Moscow Secondary School No. 91. It now takes in four grades there, the 1st to the 4th. In addition, there are three experimental classes at Tula Secondary School No. 11, (one 1st-grade and two 2nd-grade classes) and three classes (two 1st grades and one 2nd) in schools situated in the village of Mednoe and the town of Torzhok, Kalinin Region.

In the initial phase of its work, the laboratory did not have such far-reaching goals as it does now. At that time it set out only to study the development of the learning activity of the younger schoolchildren in order to ascertain, if only approximately, the structure and basic elements of that activity. But the experimenters soon found that the learning process was not successful in developing the children, chiefly because of the poor content of primary instruction. Thus, the psychologists, on going deeper into the concrete work of the schools, found themselves compelled by the very logic of their inquiry to deal with the most pressing problems of the school reorganization involving the contents and methods of instruction. Although their investigations take in only three subjects so far — Russian, mathematics, and labor — they needed a wider framework and varied conditions in which to pursue them. That is why the laboratory organized experimental classes in Moscow, in a regional city, a district center, and a village. All the experimental classes have been functioning under the direct guidance of the laboratory's associates, in accordance with syllabuses, lesson plans and methods instructions worked out by them.

The organizers of the experiment, interested in obtaining really objective results, have avoided extraordinary features as regards the make-up of the classes or the conditions of work. Above all, they have not made a special selection of the best prepared children for the experimental classes. In fact, one of the experimental 1st grades in Moscow last year accepted only children who did not know how to read or count at all. As for the village school, there was no chance of any sort of selection, for it has only one 1st grade with 35 children.

The teachers in the experimental classes are also ordinary teachers. Some of them have considerable experience, while others are young or have just started teaching. All of them become ardent supporters of the laboratory. In their reports on the results of work with the experimental program in their classes, they all stress the great successes achieved and the children's marked development. "I was amazed when my children, after learning all the vowels, suddenly began to 'read,' even before we had studied all the consonants," stated a 1st-grade teacher at Tula School No. 11 in describing her impressions to a meeting of teachers of the experimental classes at the end of the first semester.

Naturally, the teachers in the experimental classes bring much ardor and zeal to their work. The experiment has led them beyond their customary notions about the primitive nature of primary education and the limitations on the children's intellectual possibilities. It has opened up new perspectives, enthralling "educational horizons," for them.

Abstract Thinking by 1st-Graders? Yes!

For many years it has been considered a fundamental premise of primary education that young schoolchildren are capable of concrete thinking only, and that they can acquire knowledge only in a graphic, visual form. That premise is repeated in the textbooks on education and psychology, in the methods literature, in lectures and articles; it has become the alpha and omega of educational doctrine. Syllabuses, textbooks and visual aids for the primary grades were all "adapted" to the concrete thinking of children, while methodologists and teachers based their work on it. The chief concern of everyone was the "accessibility" of the material for the children, the conformity of the content and methods of teaching to the "age peculiarities" of the pupils, although hardly anyone has taken the trouble to find out exactly what young children can or cannot understand at one or another stage of the learning process, or when and how they are to be led from concrete to abstract thought.

In the practice of the schools, this concern that the material be "accessible" has often had a rather doubtful attribute. Even many good teachers have so sheltered their concrete-minded pupils up to the 4th grade as to make it impossible for the latter to learn to think or act for themselves or to surmount the difficulties they encounter in learning, with the result that their development has been artificially retarded. And in the 5th grade, the teacher is distressed by the fact that the graduates of the primary schools are not able to think logically or to work independently.

It is true that the educational process must be based on the actual level of the children's development. It is also true that young children think in concrete terms. But it is precisely the task of schooling to stimulate the development of the child, to expand his mental powers. When it merely adapts itself to the children's level, education can hardly fulfill its development role. Although this seems perfectly obvious, the schools have not changed their practices. So many "problems" have emerged: the problem of the continuity of instruction, the problem of the "5th grade." Many school faculties have been grappling unsuccessfully with these problems for a long time. Heads of schools and public education departments, as well as methodologists, are again remarking, on examining the results of the work of the primary grades, that the children are not able to think logically, to express their thoughts, to solve problems, to apply rules when doing practical tasks. Incidentally, upper-grade pupils of the eight-year schools suffer from the same deficiencies.

There is a paradox here: studies are the main form of the child's mental activity, and they do not properly promote his intellectual development! The correct didactic and psychological principles upon which primary education is based unexpectedly lead to negative results. What is the matter? What methods must be employed in order to develop the child's thinking from the 1st grade on, and mainly in the process of instruction and upbringing based on school material? That is the question the Laboratory of the Psychology of Young Schoolchildren set out to answer in its experiment. The associates of the laboratory have begun a radical reorganization of the content of instruction, an elaboration of new syllabuses, in the course of the search.

We should like to point out before we go any further that the experiment is far from complete, and that it does not yet take in all the subjects in the primary school course. It is often difficult for the small laboratory staff to sum up the results of what it has initiated; gaps are revealed in the results of its work, as well as in the work itself. But what has been accomplished and demonstrated is enough to overthrow our customary notions about the mental activity of young schoolchildren and the content and methods of primary education.

By radically reorganizing the courses in mathematics and the Russian language from the 1st grade on, the experimenters were able to show quite convincingly that the mental development of seven-year-olds (and, even more so, that of eight-, nine-, and ten-year-olds) presents no inherent barriers to abstract thought, but that special paths to the latter must be sought. And the experimenters found methods of instilling abstract ideas in children.

Before 1st-graders begin to study numbers, they are acquainted with the relation between magnitudes. This work is based on operations with material objects. The children compare various objects in terms of length, width, height, weight, volume, area, force of sound, and so on. They reach independent conclusions about the variability of the properties of objects and the comparability of these properties, and they learn to distinguish quantitative relationships — "equal," "more," and "less." They learn the mathematical symbols for those relationships and how to put down the results of their comparisons. Gradually they break away from the concrete, and go from the thing and its representation to the designation of magnitudes by circles, squares, and then lines. For a time all relations of magnitude continue to be indicated by lines. But finally the pure abstraction — the letter symbols and formulas — are introduced.

Vasilii V. Davydov, Candidate of Pedagogical Sciences and head of the laboratory, is in charge of the mathematics aspect of the experiment. He has found a definite line of mathematical development in young schoolchildren. Further along we shall briefly sketch the original version of the experimental syllabus for the mathematics course from the 1st to the 4th grades. But first we shall give an example of how abstract ideas are formed in the minds of children.

Let us return to the class of Aleksandra Kiriushkina at Moscow School No. 91. Shortly before the end of the first semester, her pupils were given a test in mathematics. The problem was a difficult one: to find "x" in this type of equation: $K > G$; $K = G + x$; $x = K - G$. The test revealed that it was not clear to some of the pupils that "x" was not any random quantity, but the particular quantity that expressed the difference between the sides of the equation. That is a very fine point to grasp; the children must understand the conventionality [uslovnost'] of such a quantity. There is no factual diminution of K, and the minus sign denotes a conventional rather than a real operation.

In order to give the children a clear idea about a conventional subtraction, Davydov worked out, and Kiriushkina practiced, a number of special exercises with the class. Here is one of them.

Two paper squares were placed on each pupil's desk. The orange-colored square was larger than the blue square. The teacher held the same kind of squares in her hands. It was agreed that the orange square was to be denoted by the letter M, and the blue square by the letter N.

"Show me with your squares what I am writing," said Aleksandra Kiriushkina, as she wrote $M > N$ on the blackboard.

Without a word, all the children raised the orange square.

"I am transforming this inequality into the equation: $M = N + x$," the teacher explained. "Now what should you do?"

All went well at first. The children replied that the blue square had to be increased by "an unknown quantity" and that the unknown quantity could be found by placing the smaller square on top of the larger one, after which the difference in the areas of the two could be seen and cut away. But when that was done, the children were disappointed to discover that in cutting away the "difference" from M and adding it to N, they had made N larger than M, so that the two squares were not equal now either. What could be done? Having thought about it, the children hit upon the correct answer: the difference would have to be cut away from a third square that was the size of M and added on to N; then M and N would be equal.

Each child was given a piece of cardboard, which he cut out to the size of M. Then he trimmed away the difference, marking it by an "x." The "x" was added to N, and the problem was solved. By this practical exercise the children were prepared for the explanation by the teacher to the effect that the difference they had found could be expressed in two ways: by means of "x," and also by M−N: $M = N + (M − N)$.

After several such exercises, the children clearly understood the abstract dependence of magnitudes. All the 1st-graders learned to state the equation for the problem, to find "x," to substitute, and to explain the meaning of the formula. Thus, on the basis of material drawn from life and proceeding from the concrete mental processes of the children, the experimenters instilled general, abstract concepts, and the children's development proceeded rapidly.

We want to remind the reader that the 1st-graders grasped all this without having studied numbers and without knowing a single digit. That is what particularly surprises the observer when he first enters this experimental 1st-grade class, and also what arouses the stormiest protests from those who, without attempting to think about the profound content of this experiment, argue against it.

The system of teaching mathematics in the experimental classes is based on an understanding of magnitudes and the quantitative relations between magnitudes. Why have the experimenters rejected the usual method of teaching arithmetic, a process that begins with the mastery of numbers — first the number 1, then 2, 3, and so on up to 10? Because the number is only one kind of relationship between magnitudes; it is a measure of magnitude but not magnitude as such. The psychologists conducting the experiment consider it to be one of the gross errors of the present didactical and methodological system of the primary-level mathematics course that it instills the incorrect and unscientific idea, from the very beginning, that the number is a magnitude in itself, thereby creating a barrier to the development of the child's mathematical thinking.

A System of Scientific Knowledge — from the Early Years!

The relationship between instruction and development is the basic problem of the primary school. That problem must be solved if the school is to meet the requirements of today and, especially, of tomorrow, and properly prepare its charges for life and work, for mastery of the ever growing volume of modern scientific and technical knowledge. The primary school has just as large, if not a larger, role to play in the training of the scientific, technical, economic and cultural personnel of the future communist society as the other levels of the school system. The first years of education are the most favorable for the formation of the individual's mental powers. It is no accident that the problem of instruction and development has received greater attention in recent years from scholars, psychologists, didactics specialists, methodologists, teachers, and the public. We all know, for example, that the Laboratory of Education and Development (headed by Academician L. Zankov) of the Institute of the Theory and History of Pedagogy under the RSFSR Academy of Pedagogical Sciences has been conducting experiments on that problem for many years. Its work has been described quite fully in the educational press.

The experiment described in the present article is also intended to further the solution of this basic problem. It will probably take many more such inquiries to resolve it fully, that is, to reorganize primary education fundamentally so that it will fully meet our present-day objectives.

The primary school cannot go on being the kind of school it was for many decades or, for that matter, the kind of school it still is, a school that does not meet the growing demands of our society, of extraordinarily rapid scientific progress, of the increasing significance of physics and mathematics for people in the most diverse professions.

Even in the preschool age, "from two to five," children are eager to learn. They want to know everything. Their favorite question is "why?". Unfortunately, their questions are often left unanswered or are answered incorrectly; adults rarely know how to talk clearly and simply to little children about big and complicated things and phenomena.

The child comes to school eager to know everything, but even there his curiosity is not properly encouraged. Instruction in the primary grades chiefly seeks to impart certain practical skills and habits. The systematic teaching of the fundamentals of the sciences begins in the 5th grade. Even the simplest theoretical knowledge is presented dogmatically. Definitions and rules are so oversimplified that later, in the 5th and subsequent grades, the children have to relearn many concepts in broader and more correct terms. This applies, for instance, to many of the rules of grammar and arithmetic.

Since practical skills are developed in the primary grades without a firm scientific foundation under them, they disintegrate quickly, and are forgotten. That is why teachers of the primary grades are reproached so often for failing to arm their charges with really lasting knowledge and habits. This is not so much the fault of the teacher, however, as of the way in which primary-grade instruction is organized.

In its experimental work, El'konin's research group has proceeded from two basic premises. The first is that the closed-circle aspect of the primary school must be liquidated as a historically obsolete phenomenon; the primary grades must be treated as the first stage of a single school course that provides the fundamentals of present-day knowledge and instills scientific habits of thought in the pupils. The transition to compulsory, universal eight-year education and the prospect of universal eleven-year education make this imperative. The second premise is that we must get rid of the notion common among educators that the mental powers of young schoolchildren are limited and that they are incapable of assimilating systematic courses in the sciences. The aims of the experiment are to find out whether children of seven or eight can be taught the fundamentals of the sciences, to determine the content of the elementary courses in the sciences, and to work out methods and forms of conducting them.

The ultimate goal of the investigators is to elucidate the prospects of primary education. They have already proved that there are huge untapped reserves for the intellectual development of young schoolchildren, and that the latter can reach a much higher level than that envisaged in the present primary school syllabuses. Pupils in the experimental classes have shown themselves to be quite capable of abstract thought. It follows that children can and must be fed not baby food from their first days at school, but a systematic course of knowledge, and that they must be equipped, step by step, with truly scientific ideas and concepts.

It may take years of experimental research, testing, effort, on the part not only of psychologists, but of didactics specialists, methodologists, and specialists in the individual subjects before we know exactly what the system of scientific knowledge in the primary grades should be. But even now the pupils of the experimental classes are being given knowledge in mathematics and grammar in accordance with a definite system.

Take the teaching of reading and writing. El'-konin's experimental ABC book and his method of teaching reading and writing are based on analysis of the sound forms of language and the sound structure of words, on the development of the children's phonemic ear. Someone may ask: what is so new about that? We have long been practicing the analytical-sound method of teaching reading and writing. But the method in use now, as the experimental work of the laboratory has demonstrated, does not fully acquaint children with the sound aspect of language. All it does is bring out the sound value of one or another letter studied. The child does not analyze the sound form of the word as a whole, and for that reason he does not perceive it well.

In the experimental class, the child is immediately acquainted with the sound form of the whole word. In addition to a picture of the object represented by the word, the child is given a diagram of the sound structure of that word. For instance, he is shown a picture of a poppy [mak] and, under it, a diagram divided into three boxes corresponding to the three sounds that form the word. The children say the word, distinguish the three sounds of which it is composed, and fill in the boxes with the chips that stand for these sounds. That is the first, very important stage in the teaching of reading and writing, during which the child, without having learned the letters of the alphabet, materially fixes their sounds and, as it were, writes down the word. It should be noted that at this stage the children analyze the sound form of not only one-syllable, but also of two- and three-syllable words.

The next stage in the study of reading and writing is acquaintance with all the vowels and word change. By replacing one vowel by another in the diagram of the sound structure of a word, the children form new words: stul — stol, kot — kit, and so on. Later on they change the words orally by replacing the consonants at the beginning and the end of the word. In this way they acquire the technique of reading even before they have studied the consonants.

The next stage involves learning the consonant letters and developing syllable reading.

Several years of experimental work have shown that this method of teaching reading and writing, which has been presented very schematically, exercises a tremendous influence on the children's mental development and eases the process of learning to read and, later, to spell and to handle grammar. The children finish their ABC book by the end of the first quarter of the year and can usually read quite well.

Last year Aleksandra Kiriushkina's pupils finished the ABC book a little later, at the end of November, but that was because the experiment was deliberately made more complicated in her class. The laboratory personnel wanted to find out whether it was possible, simultaneously with the instruction in reading and writing, to give the children elements of grammar information concerning vowels, the hard, soft, voiced and voiceless consonants, stress, and stressed and unstressed vowels. A supplement to the ABC book was supplied. It was established that this material was completely feasible for the 1st-graders.

Study of the systematic program of Russian grammar begins in the 2nd grade. The 2nd-graders work mainly on the theme: "The Foundations of the Grammatical Theory of the Word. The Morphological Structure of the Word." The word is presented to them as a complex entity expressing, first, a system of morphemes, and, second, a system of information (the root meaning and the meanings added to the word by its formal elements). In other words, as soon as they begin to study grammar, the children are taught to recognize the formal and semantic aspects of language phenomena. They learn, for instance, that suffixes add a value description to the word (greater, lesser, endearing, contemptuous) and also suggest occupation, etc.; that word endings are used to indicate the number and case, to vary the form of one and the same word, and to effect different connections with other words in the sentence.

The children acquire a correct, scientific understanding of the form of the word and its morphological structure. This helps them to distinguish the different categories of words with different potentials of information (nouns, adjectives, verbs) as well as different forms of one and the same word. This broad orientation in the morphological structure of the word facilitates the formation of spelling habits.

In the 3rd grade, the pupils learn the declensions of nouns, the significance of the cases, and case forms as a category of syntax, and also the basic types of simple sentences.

In the 4th grade, they study the verb and its significance, the basic types of compound sentences, and such aspects of syntax as intonation and word order.

In mathematics, as we have already noted, the pupils' attention is focused on the general mathematical concept of magnitude. By comparing physical magnitudes and fixing the results of the comparison in equality-inequality statements (first concretely and then symbolically), the children distinguish the mathematical characteristics of objects in a general way and master the kind of abstraction that reveals to them peculiarly mathematical relations (reflection, transitiveness, symmetry, association, etc.). The transformation of inequality into equality and vice versa makes it possible, in the first quarter of the 1st grade, to introduce addition and subtraction as the special means of describing changes in magnitude, to present the functional relation between the members of the equality and the method of expressing the unknown with the help of the symbol "x." Even in this period 1st-graders can be taught to solve problems by building equations that contain a single unknown. In the second semester of the 1st grade, the children are given an idea of the numerical expression of relations of magnitude. In their study of the natural sequence of numbers, pupils of the experimental classes are guided by different laws than those followed in the present syllabuses, and they seem to do better as regards quality of knowledge and general orientation in magnitudes and numbers.

In the existing curriculum, study of the general laws of arithmetical operations does not begin until the 5th grade. The experimenters consider such programming incorrect psychologically as regards the development of arithmetical skills. These skills can be more quickly and lastingly acquired if they are based on knowledge of the permutative, combinative and distributive laws of addition as applied to all magnitudes. The introduction of that subject in the 1st grade enables the children to arrive consciously at the rules of addition and subtraction of numbers and to use them for rapid and exact calculations.

In the 2nd grade it is necessary to acquaint pupils with identical transformations as a means of simplifying symbolical and numerical formulas. This creates the psychological conditions for the introduction, in the 2nd and 3rd grades, of "complex" equations with one unknown and systems of equations with two unknowns.

The brief syllabus outlines presented above must not be regarded as the final syllabuses for Russian and mathematics adopted by the laboratory. There is continuous experimental verification of the actual volume of intellectual data acquired by the children. Every year new problems confront the experimenters. For example, three years ago they set out to ascertain whether 1st-graders could learn to count up to 100. Now they have no doubts on this point, and the task has arisen of giving 1st-graders an idea of functions and of broadening that idea in the 2nd grade so as to introduce, in the 3rd grade, the concept and method of using functions in solving suitable problems. The concept of functions runs through the whole of contemporary mathematics. But it is neglected in the primary grades, although the children come up against the functional relations of magnitudes at every step of the way.

Another idea that is maturing in the minds of the experimenters involves reorganizing the whole elementary course in physics and mathematics so that it will take in arithmetic and elements of algebra, geometry and physics. Then the school can really lead the pupils into the study of modern physics and mathematics from the 1st grade on. In the second half of the past school year, a laboratory researcher, Evgenii Shuleshko, conducted a number of special assignments and exercises during the drawing lessons of a 1st-grade class in order to introduce elementary geometry concepts. In the new school year, these assignments will be given right from the beginning in the 1st and 2nd grades.

The laboratory deliberately introduces difficult material during the early stage of instruction. Despite this, the children do not have to cram, they are not overloaded with school work, and they do not have extensive homework or extra classes. Definite psychological laws are in operation here — in particular, that difficult material can be more readily and quickly assimilated and become more firmly fixed in the mind if the children are given an adequate idea of the object to be learned, some general method of working with it, and a form of symbolization that does not conceal from them the proper-

ties of the object itself.

Activation: Real and False

The new content of education calls for new methods and a new approach to the organization of classroom work. We can see this for ourselves in the widespread creative work on methods engaged in by teachers since the adoption of the law on the schools. The activation of instruction has become the main goal and topic of the teachers' work on methods. The practical work of the schools and teachers has been enriched by various new methods and devices for conducting the lesson. But the innovations must be analyzed. It is not unusual for teachers to pass off as innovations methods that contribute nothing to making the learning process more profound or to developing the children's mental activity. It is false activation when the teacher "interests" the pupils with a display of visual aids that convey nothing, or introduces "independent work" which does not add to the pupil's fund of knowledge, or tries to vary the forms of classroom work without knowing what the pupils will gain by performing the new tasks.

The authors of the experiment under consideration have worked out certain basic principles with respect to instruction. The foremost one is that the pupil must do something with the material being studied before he can learn anything about it; without action by the child himself on the material whose properties must be revealed, there can be no process of assimilation, there can be no learning. The theoretical work of the psychologists was aimed at defining the mental operations by which the pupil gains knowledge.

Laboratory personnel have defined and experimentally checked the actions that are required to assimilate the syllabuses created for the Russian language and mathematics. With regard to sound analysis of words, the action is the material modeling of the sound form of the word; in developing morphological concepts, the action is concrete comparison of the different forms of one and the same word in order to elucidate its grammatical forms. In mathematics the action is the commensuration of magnitudes and quantitative relations. The child assumes the attitude of an explorer. He himself discovers the properties of the material he is studying, of the new phenomena and concepts. As a result, the children learn complicated material without special effort, without straining the memory, without tedious cramming, and they learn it well and firmly. Successful mental development, as the work of the laboratory proves, is only possible when definite actions on objects (including mental operations) have to be performed. That is the meaning and essence of genuine activation of instruction.

Another important factor is the didactical material that is given to the pupils in work on a given theme. We are not talking about the usual kind of "visual" material that gives the child a picture of an object or phenomenon in its finished form. The laboratory personnel are very much opposed to such visual material because they believe that it impedes the child's mental development rather than promoting it. The new didactical material is intended to help the child in his mental operations.

The material may take the form of the paper squares with whose help the 1st-graders found the concrete value of "x," or various yardsticks for measuring magnitudes, or a diagram or line to indicate the relation between the magnitudes or numbers given in the problem; it may be the schemes according to which 4th-graders make up definite types of complex sentences. On drawing up the outlines of the lessons, the experimenters not only plan their content, but establish what mental operations the children will have to perform in order to master one or another concept and what kind of didactical material should be used.

It is of interest that during the experimental lessons the children are very active and eager to learn, even when the subject matter is not very "interesting" in itself. What is so interesting for children about unstressed vowels, roots and suffixes? We all know that children are often bored at their grammar lessons, and become much more interested when reading or retelling stories from their readers. But strange as it may seem, the pupils of the experimental classes, who study the "dull" grammar material with great interest, become inattentive, listless and noisy during reading lessons conducted in the usual way. Why? Because they are accustomed to meeting serious challenges, to working independently with their minds and hands. They find it tiring to have everything predigested for them, to mark time, as is so often the case in the primary grades by and large. The lessons conducted according to the usual syllabuses and methods do not satisfy them. They are far ahead of their peers as regards mental development and factual knowledge.

What About Practical Habits?

This is a perfectly legitimate question, for the primary grades are indeed supposed to give the children the basic educational habits and skills. But how are they to be developed so as to ensure correct and lasting practical skills? As a result of its investigations, the Laboratory of the Psychology of Young Schoolchildren has arrived at entirely new conclusions in this area as well.

We are accustomed to thinking that practical habits are "built up" gradually, and that their acquisition involves prolonged training. The present syllabuses, textbooks and methodological aids orient the teacher to think in these terms. But in the experimental classes run by the laboratory, many things that cause 1st- to 4th-graders a great deal of trouble are mastered simply and easily.

Take one of the most agonizing sections of the syllabuses — the multiplication table. How many tears have been shed over it by all generations of pupils! They crammed it, memorized it, worked on it for months or even years. No wonder it has been given such unpleasant nicknames. Yet poor command of the multiplication table is still singled out as a typical shortcoming of the primary grades.

The pupils of the experimental 1st grades learn the multiplication table in two weeks!

We pointed out earlier that, using El'konin's experimental reader, children learn to read (and to read well!) in about two months, or twice as fast as in the ordinary schools.

In the past school year, the 1st-graders under teacher Kiriushkina studied "mathematics without numbers" during all of the first semester. They only began to study numbers in January. By the 1st of February they knew all the digits, could do operations with numbers up to ten, and by the end of the year had learned to count up to a hundred. Many of the children even learned to work with larger numbers — up to 200, and some mastered numbers up to 300 and even 1,000.

What "secret" had the psychologists conducting the experiment uncovered? They formulate that "secret" approximately as follows: in organizing the pupils' work on objects in studying the material, they must be taught the general property of the object, and it must be fixed in their minds by acquainting them with individual manifestations of the object. A "broader zone of learning" must be created, and the children must be given not isolated concepts divorced from each other, but a system of concepts based on the common initial concept. We saw this, for example, in the 2nd grade, when the children studied unstressed vowels not in isolation, one after the other, but all of them at once on the basis of a general idea of their properties, i. e., in a system.

The same applies to the study of numbers in the 1st grade. Numbers are not presented in a "ready-made" form; the children are led up to them by exercises in measuring and counting. This helps them to grasp the main thing, that the number depends on the object being measured and the unit of measure used: where the number is smaller, the measure is larger.

The children grasp the essence of multiplication in the same way: it takes too long to work with a small measure, so let us replace it by a large one. For instance, how many apples are there in the orchard? It would take too long

simply to count them. The thing to do is to take a large measure — to count not the trees, but the rows of trees. There are five rows. How many small measures (trees) are there in the larger measure (the row)? Seven. Applying the law of multiplication, it turns out that there are 35 trees in the orchard. That is the method by which the multiplication table is mastered in the experimental classes.

The "columns" of the table were not memorized as such, but throughout the lessons the children had to find out how many 3's there are in the number 12, or how many times the number 2 has to be increased to get the number 16. Or the children were given problems of this kind: what is the unknown number by which 3 must be multiplied to get 6; given the number 3, how many 3's must be added to it to produce the number 21, and so on. In this way, "imperceptibly," as the teacher put it, the pupils learned the multiplication table.

Now we can evidently supply a general answer to the question of practical habits: they are more quickly and lastingly acquired if the children's thinking powers are developed and they understand the meaning of the technical operations they have performed.

The Pedagogical Experiment and Broad School Practice

We repeat: the experiment we are describing is by no means completed. The laboratory's associates are highly critical of their work and have not shown the least inclination to overestimate it. Here is their own appraisal of what has been accomplished so far: "Study of the psychological bases for the construction of school syllabuses is only beginning, and the results achieved so far are limited, but the achievements of our experimental classes warrant certain conclusions of both a theoretical and a practical nature."

The teachers of the experimental classes have been less cautious in their appraisals, however. There are no more enthusiastic champions of the experimental syllabuses and methods than

Aleksandra Kiriushkina, Elena Orlova, and Tat'iana Pil'schikova of Moscow School No. 91, Tamara Pustinskaia (Torzhok), Tamara Frolova (Tula), Antonina Pavlova (village of Mednoe), and other teachers of the experimental classes. The creators of the experiment still entertain many doubts, are still repeating and checking up on many points, accumulating scientific facts, and advancing new ideas. But the teachers, having evaluated the practical results of the new system of instruction in the experimental classes, have endorsed it without reservations. This is true not only of the teachers in the experimental classes, but also of their colleagues in the ordinary schools and classes. In Kalinin Region, for instance, ten schools used El'konin's new ABC book last year. The same holds for Moscow.

Their practical participation in the experiment has also had a noticeable effect on the teachers. As Elena Orlova expressed it, she could no longer work with children in the old way. This means that the teacher now also needs more than the usual "mental load," and has acquired a more scientific approach to teaching. Daily work under the guidance of psychologists has led to marked growth on the part of the teachers. This is confirmed by the fact that many teachers of the experimental classes presented reports at the central "Pedagogical Readings" that took place this year at the Institute of Psychology in Moscow. The very titles of their papers point to the teachers' invasion of this scientific field: "The Psychological Role of Equations in Solving Problems in the 1st Grade" (A. Kiriushkina); "On the Possibility of Systematic Study of Word Morphology in the 2nd Grade of the Village School" (A. Pavlova); "Psychological Analysis of the Learning Process in Mastering Syntax in the 4th Grade" (T. Pil'schikova); etc. Teachers of the experimental classes at Moscow School No. 91 also gave talks at the district scientific and practical conference held in the spring.

The Board of the Ministry of Education and the Presidium of the RSFSR Academy of Pedagogical Sciences held a meeting in School No. 91 before the end of the past school year. The participants attended lessons in the experimental classes and then heard and discussed a report by El'konin entitled "Investigation of the Psychological Premises for the Construction of New Syllabuses." There was much justified criticism of the work of the laboratory, but it did not alter the generally favorable appraisal of the experiment and its prospects.

What do educators like about this experiment, for all its defects and incompleteness? The main attraction, I think, is its humanistic basis, which expresses itself primarily in faith in the child and the spiritual potentialities of the growing man, and in the desire to create conditions of learning that will ensure the rational expenditure of his mental energies and continual enrichment of his mind in the process of learning. "There are no children incapable of learning mathematics." "The child can understand any difficult concept, provided we find the correct practical action to help him learn that concept." Such assertions of the psychologists conducting the experiment speak for themselves. And year after year the results of the work of the experimental classes add confirmation of the correctness of their educational "credo." Suffice it to say that in four years, despite the double load (the children are required to cover both the experimental and the regular syllabuses), only one child was left behind for a second year, and his case was not indicative since, according to medical findings, he should have been placed in a special school.

So far only the outlines of a new system of instruction are visible. But the experiment is making us view the prospects of the whole system of education and upbringing for children and young people in a new light. The creation of new systematic courses in each of the subjects taught in the primary grades will make it necessary to revise the courses in these and other subjects in the 5th to 8th grades, and then in the 9th to 11th grades. Children who have received systematic knowledge and extensive mental development in the first phase of education will be better able to understand the fundamentals of modern science in the intermediate and, especially, the upper grades. They will be able to encompass the vast fund of scientific information that keeps growing as all branches of knowledge progress. They will be more soundly prepared for serious scientific pursuits in the higher schools or for the mastery of complicated vocations in production.

The new opportunities for reorganizing preschool education also come to mind. Certain elements of primary education will have to be "sent down" to the preschool institutions if we want the mental development of the children to be speeded up. We are losing a great deal by starting the real intellectual development of our children at the age of seven. It has been fully proved that instruction in reading and writing can and, in fact, should begin at the preschool age, and that correct elementary spatial concepts and an understanding of the relations between magnitudes, etc., can also be communicated to them at that level.

What forms, methods, syllabuses, didactical material and textbooks shall we use for this? The answer to this question will come only if we organize a broad program of experimental work that has the participation of psychologists, methodologists, didacticians, specialists in the scientific subjects, heads of the public education departments, teachers, preschool workers, in short, all those who are concerned with children and the youth, with science and the school.

The new system of education and upbringing will not appear ready-made when we arrive at communism. It must be created, organized, built today, and only by organizing broad educational experiments.

By the very nature of her work, the teacher is an experimenter. Finding a special approach to each pupil, presenting the lesson differently today than yesterday, organizing the study of a topic in a new way — what boundless opportunities exist here for creativity! Good teachers have always worked in this manner.

But the need now is for this creativity of the teacher to be directed into the educational experiment that is based on the latest findings of psychologists, physiologists and educators and on closer study of the mental capacity of the child. Accordingly, the scientific organization in the field of education, the Ministry of Education, the local education bodies, and the school principals have more extensive tasks — to organize the experimental, creative work of the teachers and school faculties, and to activate the scientific research of the departments of the teacher training institutes, whose direct guidance can ensure broader scope and greater clarity of purpose in this creative work.

Each and every one of us must think more about the future of our school and experiment more daringly in education and upbringing. That is the way to create the genuinely new school system of the communist society.

Secondary Education

Uchitel'skaia gazeta, November 19, 1966

MEASURES FOR FURTHER IMPROVEMENT OF THE WORK OF THE

GENERAL EDUCATION SECONDARY SCHOOL

(In the CPSU Central Committee and the USSR Council of Ministers)

Recently the Central Committee of the CPSU and the Council of Ministers of the USSR examined questions relating to further improvement of the work of the general education secondary school and adopted a corresponding resolution.

In the resolution it is noted that under the leadership of the Communist Party a cultural revolution took place in our country that is unprecedented in depth and scope. The Soviet school played a prominent role in the accomplishment of this great task. For the first time in the history of mankind a genuinely democratic system of education was created, a system that provides citizens with a real possibility to obtain a secondary and higher education. All peoples in the Soviet Union have schools in their native language. Universal obligatory eight-year education has been introduced everywhere. The number of young workers and collective farmers who are studying without leaving their production work is growing.

All the same, the level of instruction and upbringing in the general education school still does not correspond to the increasing demands of life.

The ministries of education (or public education) of the union republics are not undertaking the measures needed to overcome the disparity developing between the curriculums and programs and the contemporary level of scientific knowledge, and to eliminate the overloading of pupils with schoolwork. There are serious inadequacies in upbringing work, as well as in the matter of training and raising the qualifications of teachers and other personnel in the field of education.

Pedagogical science must have a most important role in solving the problems involved in the education and communist upbringing of young people. However, the scientific-research pedagogical institutions of the country are slow in working out the key, vitally important problems of public education. The enormous and multifaceted experience accumulated by the Soviet school system is not analyzed in good time and it is not subjected to profound generalization.

The educational and material facilities of the school system are in need of serious strengthening. Meanwhile, the resources allocated for this purpose are not fully or opportunely put to use in a number of republics, territories and regions.

The party, soviet, Komsomol, and trade union organizations still render insufficient aid to the public education bodies in the instruction and upbringing of children, in the improvement of the joint work of the school, family and public, and in the dissemination of pedagogical knowledge among the population.

The Central Committee of the CPSU and the Council of Ministers of the USSR direct the attention of the party, soviet, Komsomol, and trade union organizations to the fact that under the condition of rapid scientific-technical and social progress, the role of the school is growing as never before; the school must secure the rounded development of the rising generations, of worthy builders of a communist society. The interests of further growth of the culture of the people and the development of the productive forces insistently demand a considerable increase in the quality of the students' knowledge and the best training of them for socially useful labor.

In accordance with the decisions of the 23rd Congress of the CPSU in the field of the education and communist upbringing of the youth, the CPSU Central Committee and the Council of Ministers of the USSR worked out a series of measures for further improvement of the work of the general education secondary school.

It is emphasized in the resolution that the Soviet school must continue to develop as a general education, labor, polytechnical school. Its chief tasks are to give the pupils a firm knowledge of the fundamentals of the sciences, to develop in them a lofty communist consciousness, and to prepare them for life and for a conscious choice of profession.

In linking all upbringing work with life, the school must equip the pupils with an understanding of the laws of social development; educate schoolchildren in the revolutionary and labor traditions of the Soviet people; develop in them a lofty feeling of Soviet patriotism; inculcate a readiness to defend the socialist Motherland; reveal the meaning of the fraternal unity of all peoples of the Soviet Union, and of their friendship with the working people of the socialist countries; educate the students in the spirit of

solidarity with all peoples waging a struggle against colonialism and the power of capital, and for freedom and national independence; struggle resolutely against the penetration of bourgeois ideology into the minds of the students, and against manifestation of an alien morality.

The school is called upon to realize esthetic training and also to concern itself with the physical development and improved health of the students.

In the resolution it is pointed out that the most important task of party and soviet bodies in the area of public education is to basically complete, by 1970, the introduction in the country of universal secondary education for the rising generation.

It is proposed to the councils of ministers of the union republics, the Ministry of Education of the USSR, and branch ministries and departments that they ensure, in accordance with the assignments of the national economic plan for 1966-1970, the development of the network of general education schools and the growth of the contingent of pupils studying in them during each year of the Five-Year Plan, and also complete fulfillment of the plan targets for the construction of schools and for the strengthening of their educational and material facilities.

In order to further improve secondary education, create the necessary stability in the work of the school, and consistently effectuate the principles of polytechnical instruction and labor education, the Central Committee of the CPSU and the Council of Ministers of the USSR have made it incumbent upon the Ministry of Education of the USSR and the ministries of education (or public education) of the union republics to introduce scientifically substantiated curriculums and programs. Here it is necessary to bring the content of education into accord with the requirements for the development of science, technology and culture; it is necessary to provide continuity in the study of the fundamentals of the sciences and a more rational distribution of study materials over the years of instruction. It is also necessary to have systematic instruction in the fundamentals of the sciences begin in the fourth year of study and to eliminate the overloading of pupils with schoolwork.

The planned and organized conversion of the secondary school to new curriculums and programs was begun in the current academic year and it must be essentially completed no later than the 1970/71 academic year. The recommendations on curriculums and programs that were prepared by the Academy of Sciences of the USSR and the Academy of Pedagogical Sciences were accepted as a basis. The standard school curriculum must have the following maximal number of obligatory hours, including lessons on labor, physical culture, and art: for the 1st through the 4th grades — 24 hours per week; for the 5th through the 10th (11th) grades — 30 hours per week. With respect to the national schools of the RSFSR and the schools of the other union republics, it was decided to permit an increase in the study load, as against the above-mentioned norms, of up to 2-3 hours per week in each grade.

In order to deepen the knowledge of the natural sciences, including the physical-mathematical sciences and the humanities, and also to develop the varied interests and abilities of the pupils, the schools have been granted the right to conduct elective courses beginning with the 7th grade. The following maximal class sizes in the general education schools have been established: 1st-8th grades — 40 pupils; 9th-10th (11th) grades — 35 pupils. Moreover, it was decided that for the study of the Russian language in the 4th to 10th (11th) grades of the rural national schools, where the number of pupils in a class exceeds 25, the class should be divided into two subgroups.

With a view toward improving the polytechnical instruction of pupils and their preparation for socially useful work, the resolution obligates party, soviet, Komsomol and trade union organizations, and the leaders of industrial enterprises, construction sites, collective farms and state farms to render all possible assistance to the schools in the organization of labor training for pupils, the creation of the educational and material facilities necessary for this, and the apportionment of specialists. It has also been suggested that systematic vocational orientation be given to the pupils by acquainting them with the various branches of the national economy and culture, enterprises, collective farms, state farms and institutions, and the most widespread vocations.

Taking into account the positive experience accumulated by the schools, it has been decided to have a certain number of secondary schools and classes provide more intensive theoretical and practical study, in the 9th-10th (11th) grades, of mathematics and computer technology, physics and radioelectronics, chemistry and chemical technology, biology and agrobiology, and the humanities.

The Ministry of Education of the USSR and the Academy of Pedagogical Sciences of the USSR, jointly with the ministries of education (or public education) of the union republics, have been charged with working out measures to improve the instruction and upbringing of pupils and to enhance the responsibility of school leaders and teachers for the quality of knowledge acquired by the pupils, and also with drafting new regulations on the awarding of medals to those completing secondary general education schools; the new regulations should provide for the introduction of honor certificates as a reward for graduates of secondary schools who have shown special progress in particular subjects.

The resolution directs the attention of party and soviet bodies to a practice that has become widespread of late, namely, the diversion of pupils in school time to agricultural and other work that is not directly related to the educational process. It has been proposed not to permit the diversion of pupils, or teachers and school leaders, from their direct responsibilities.

The Ministry of Education of the USSR, the ministries of education (or public education) of the union republics, the Academy of Sciences of the USSR, the Academy of Pedagogical Sciences of the USSR, the Ministry of Higher and Secondary Specialized Education of the USSR, and the Press Committee attached to the Council of Ministers of the USSR must adopt measures for the creation of standard high-quality school textbooks, study aids for pupils, and methods guides for teachers. Prominent scholars and experienced teachers should be involved in writing these works.

It is necessary to pay special attention to the development of study aids on questions of inculcating communist morality and international friendship and solidarity among the peoples of the world.

It has been proposed to the public education bodies that they improve the work of the schools in instilling conscious discipline and cultural behavior on the part of the pupils. Each school must become an organizing center for upbringing work with the children in its district.

The post of organizer of out-of-class and out-of-school upbringing work with children (with the rights of an assistant principal of the school) is being introduced into the staff of the secondary school.

The Central Committee of the CPSU and the Council of Ministers of the USSR have made it incumbent upon party and soviet bodies to demand more of the departments of public education, the principals of schools, the physical culture and Komsomol organizations, and the organizations of the Voluntary Society for Assisting the Army, the Air Force and the Navy with respect to the state and quality of physical training and defense-and-sports work with pupils.

The Ministry of Education of the USSR, the Ministry of Culture of the USSR, the Cinematography Committee attached to the Council of Ministers of the USSR, the Press Committee attached to the Council of Ministers of the USSR, and the unions of creative workers have been charged with working out measures to improve the esthetic training of pupils. In this area the following are envisaged: the release of films, the preparation of new performances for schoolchildren; an increase in the number of performances and film showings for children on days off and during school vacations; the publication of a school series of the classics and the best works of Soviet and foreign writers; the issuing of phonology readers [fonokhrestonatii] and reproductions of the best artistic works; the organization of special concerts for pupils; the involvement of specialists and creative people in the field of art in school and out-of-class work with children.

Measures have been outlined for a fundamental improvement of the printed and oral dissemination of pedagogical knowledge among parents and the population.

It is pointed out in the resolution that the most important task of the Central Committee of the Komsomol is a significant improvement in the leadership of school Komsomol and Young Pioneer organizations and a rise in the level of their work. It is necessary to concentrate the attention of Komsomol and Young Pioneer organizations on instilling in the pupils ideological conviction and a love for knowledge and work, and on developing initiative and independence. They must work out measures for the organization of work with children at their place of residence. They must adopt measures to provide the schools with senior Pioneer leaders. They must organize, jointly with the Ministry of Education of the USSR, the training of Pioneer workers.

It has been proposed that the party, trade union, and Komsomol organizations of industrial enterprises, construction sites, collective farms, and state farms maintain constant contact with the schools where the children of their workers study, and that they interest themselves in the conditions in the family for the upbringing of schoolchildren. They must engage in the practice of discussing questions pertaining to the upbringing of children at party, trade union, and Komsomol meetings. They must more actively help the family and the school and exert influence on parents who are negligent with respect to the upbringing of their children. It has been recommended that there be commissions or councils for assisting the family and school in the matter of rearing the rising generation at industrial enterprises, construction sites, institutions, collective farms and state farms.

Proceeding from the fact that the further improvement of public education depends above all on the teacher, on his scholarly and methodological qualifications and his ideological-political and cultural outlook, the Central Committee of the CPSU and the Council of Ministers of the USSR direct attention to the necessity of creating proper conditions for the successful work of the teachers, raising their qualifications systematically, and achieving unconditional fulfillment of the laws for labor protection, benefits and advantages for personnel in the field of education. Constant concern for the authority of the teacher, for the most correct utilization of his labor for the instruction and upbringing of young people, must be a matter for all party, soviet, Komsomol, and trade union bodies.

The Ministry of Higher and Secondary Specialized Education of the USSR and the Ministry of Education of the USSR, together with the State Planning Committee of the USSR and the ministries of education (or public education) of the union republics, are obligated, in working out the annual national economic plans, to determine for each union republic the number of applicants to be admitted to the teacher training institutions, with the aim of satisfying the actual need for teachers.

Provision must be made for training the necessary number of teachers of music and singing, the fine arts, physical education, drawing, and labor in the teacher training schools [uchilishchakh], the corresponding departments of teacher training institutes, and in specialized secondary and higher educational institutions.

The resolution points to the need for strengthening boarding schools and schoolchildren's homes. It is planned to expand the network of forest sanitorium schools and special boarding schools.

For the purpose of creating more favorable material and technical conditions for the work of the schools, it has been suggested to the State Planning Committee of the USSR, the State Construction Committee of the USSR, ministries and departments of the USSR, and the councils of ministers of the union republics that provision be made in the summary estimates for new industrial enterprises and agency residential developments for the construction of general education schools, to be financed by capital investments of the corresponding branch.

It has been established that the construction of schools in rural areas must be in the form of a complex, with apartments for teachers and the building of eight-year schools and secondary schools, as a rule, and with dormitories for pupils living in distant population centers. The means for the construction of dormitories and homes for teachers are to be allocated as a special assignment from the general appropriations for housing construction.

The resolution determined that the school housing fund belongs to the public education bodies and is not available for residence by persons who are not working in the schools.

Taking into account the broad scope of school construction initiated by collective farms and other organizations, the State Planning Committee of the USSR and the State Committee of the Council of Ministers of the USSR for Material and Technical Supply are obligated to assign funds to these construction sites for materials and equipment, doing so on the same basis as with schools erected at the expense of state capital investments. All school buildings in the process of being constructed must be ready for use by the beginning of the school year.

The party, soviet, Komsomol and trade union organizations and economic executives are called upon to do everything possible to promote patronage — on the part of industrial enterprises, construction sites, collective farms, state farms, institutions, educational establishments, scientific research institutes, and civic organizations — over the schools for the purpose of rendering them aid in strengthening their material facilities and in educating the pupils.

Industrial, agricultural, and other enterprises and organizations are permitted to give equipment and materials to schools free of charge, and also to expend funds for the construction, repair and equipping of schools out of above-plan accumulations.

Measures have been outlined for the more extensive use in the educational process of technical means, films and television.

The resolution points out that the contemporary stage of development of the general education school insistently demands that the scientific level of leadership of the schools be raised and that the inspection staff of the public education bodies, especially of the district departments, be strengthened. In connection with this, the Ministry of Education of the USSR, the Ministry of Finance of the USSR, and the State Committee of the Council of Ministers of the USSR on Questions of Labor and Wages have been charged with developing proposals for the number of inspectors in public education bodies and the terms of their remuneration.

It has been proposed to the local party agencies that they render assistance to the departments of public education in promoting authoritative school leaders, teachers and specialists, who are well acquainted with school affairs and who know how to disseminate positive experience, to inspection work.

The Ministry of Education of the USSR has been charged with elaborating a draft charter for the general education secondary schools.

The Central Committee of the CPSU and the Council of Ministers of the USSR have called on all party, soviet, Komsomol, and trade union organizations to devote tireless attention and concern to the schools, remembering that the communist upbringing of the young generation and the further development of education in our country are a matter for the entire party, for all of the Soviet people.

* * *

Sovetskaia pedagogika, 1965, No. 7

IN THE COMMISSION TO DETERMINE THE VOLUME

AND NATURE OF EDUCATION IN THE SECONDARY SCHOOL

I

In October 1964 the Presidium of the Academy of Pedagogical Sciences of the RSFSR and the Presidium of the Academy of Sciences of the USSR formed a commission for the determination of the volume and nature of the knowledge, skills and habits in each school subject studied in the secondary school. A central commission was created to coordinate the work of the subject commissions and to solve problems of a general character. The commissions are composed of members and corresponding members of the Academy of Pedagogical Sciences, thirty members and corresponding members of the Academy of Sciences of the USSR, leaders of sectors and laboratories, senior scientific workers of the institutes of the Academy of Pedagogical Sciences, more than one hundred doctors of science, professors of the Moscow, Leningrad and Novosibirsk universities and of the Moscow, Leningrad, Kuibyshev, Gorky, and other teacher training institutes, and more than sixty teachers of the secondary schools.

The commissions were entrusted with determining the volume and nature of education in the secondary school, having in view:

a) the results of the reorganization of the school on the basis of the Law on Strengthening the Ties of the School with Life and Further Developing the System of Public Education in the USSR;

b) the need to reflect the modern achievements of science, technology and culture more fully in the content, organization and methods of school education; the elimination of outdated and secondary material from the school syllabuses and textbooks;

c) the results of comparative research into the curriculums, syllabuses and textbooks used in other countries – socialist and capitalist;

d) the prospect of the transfer to universal compulsory secondary education;

e) the results of pedagogical and psychological research and the achievements of the advanced schools and teachers in making the mastery of the foundations of the sciences more firm and conscious, and in forming the students' world outlook and their all-round development;

f) putting an end to the overloading of students with compulsory school tasks and expanding the opportunities for independent work in accordance with the wishes and abilities of the students.

The commissions have basically completed

this stage of the work on determining the content of education in the secondary school. The conclusions and proposals concerning each subject were discussed with the most active teachers of Moscow, Leningrad, Gorky, and Sverdlovsk, in a number of regions and territories in the RSFSR, in specially created commissions and groups on the problems of school education in the institutes of the Academy of Sciences of the USSR, and in the scientific societies for mathematics, botany, pedagogy, and other disciplines. The central commission examined the proposals of all fifteen subject commissions and drew its conclusions.

The subject commissions have now proceeded to the compilation of the syllabuses for each subject. The institutes of the Academy of Pedagogical Sciences of the RSFSR and the departments of a number of teacher training institutes and universities are testing many of the proposals in experimental teaching.

II

The commissions examined the data of the experimental research and the experience of the advanced schools in enhancing the effectiveness of instruction, and they came to the conclusion that the developmental level of children of younger and intermediate ages and their cognitive capacities are significantly richer than had been assumed during the compilation of the current curriculums and syllabuses. The course of the primary school is unnecessarily prolix; the programs of the 5th-8th grades are impoverished in their ideological and scientific aspect and, along with that, are overloaded with material requiring memorization. Theoretical material on the foundations of the sciences is given chiefly in the upper grades of the secondary school, which results in a cursory and often even superficial study of it.

Therefore, a resolution has been adopted on a three-year course of primary instruction and the teaching of systematic courses on the foundations of the sciences beginning with the 4th grade. It has also been suggested that some of the school material be transferred from the extremely overloaded upper grades to the eight-

year school.

According to the draft of the curriculum, the number of obligatory lessons, in comparison with the 1st to 10th grades of the eleven-year school, is reduced by 26 hours per week. This testifies to a diminution of the students' load of class lessons. Additional measures to overcome the overloading of students will be adopted during the compilation of syllabuses; outdated and secondary material will be excluded and the organization and methods of instruction will be determined so as to reduce the volume of homework required. In order to prevent the overloading of students during out-of-class time, definite limits will be established as regards its utilization.

In the primary grades, just as now, there will be lessons on the Russian language (in the national schools – on the native and Russian languages), mathematics, drawing, music and singing, physical culture, and labor instruction. It is proposed to diminish the number of lessons on the Russian language in the 1st to 3rd grades and to isolate excursions, subject lessons and observations from the reading lessons, making them an independent school subject – natural history. This measure is unanimously supported by teachers and scientific personnel. The character of lessons in the primary grades has been defined in closer correspondence with the children's level of development at the ages of 7 to 10.

The study of systematic courses in the Russian language, mathematics, foreign language and biology (botany) from the 4th grade does not cause special difficulties. Students in the 4th grade manifest a great interest in the study of Russian and foreign languages and achieve better results than students who begin the study of these courses in the 5th grade. Certain difficulties with the study of systematic courses on the foundations of the sciences in the 4th grade arise in the rural small-unit schools, whose students cannot be transferred to the eight-year and secondary schools. The teaching in these classes of all school subjects, except foreign language, can be entrusted to the teacher of the primary school. But the latter, as a rule, is not prepared to teach foreign languages. In such cases, this school subject will not be taught in the 4th grade. When the students transfer into the 5th grade of the eight-year and secondary schools, individual groups will be established and the number of their lessons will be increased, so that in the 5th grade the knowledge of these students in foreign language will be brought up to that of the rest of the students.

Beginning the study of systematic courses on the foundations of the sciences in the 4th grade permits us to move a significant amount of school material from the upper to the intermediate grades and, thereby, to enrich the scientific aspect of the content of education in the 5th-8th grades and lessen the overloading of students in the 9th and 10th grades. As regards mathematics, inequalities will be studied in the eight-year school, and the students will become acquainted with logarithms. In physics, hydrostatics and aerostatics, heat phenomena and geometrical optics will be studied, and information on electricity and the structure of the atom will be given in significantly greater volume. In chemistry, the study of the periodic law and D. I. Mendeleev's periodic system and of the structure of matter will begin earlier. A systematic course on the history of the USSR will begin in the 7th grade and will be completed in the 10th, and a course on the modern and contemporary history of foreign countries will be taught in the 8th-10th grades. It is also intended to give part of the systematic course on the history of literature – from ancient Russian literature to the literature of the second period of the liberation movement in Russia – in the 8th grade. The entire volume of school material shifted from the upper grades to the eight-year school amounts to approximately 500 school hours, which comprises roughly half the school year.

As a result of all these changes, the content of education in the secondary school assumes the following form.

The Russian language is studied in the 1st-8th grades, but most intensively in the 1st-6th grades. An examination on the Russian language is given upon completion of the 8th grade.

Literature is studied from the 4th to the 10th grades, inclusively. The children are acquainted with accessible works, arranged in accordance with the ideological-thematic and genre principles. The basic tasks of instruction in this course are the ideological-esthetic and moral upbringing of the students and their literary development. A course on the history of literature will be studied in the upper grades: in the 9th grade – literature of the second period of the Russian liberation movement; in the 10th – literature of the third period of the Russian liberation movement and Soviet literature. The time allotted for the literature of past centuries is being reduced, while it is being increased for contemporary Soviet literature of the peoples of the USSR and contemporary foreign literature.

In mathematics, physics and chemistry, the intention is to maintain the same number of school lessons in the ten-year school as was determined for the eleven-year school. However, the students' acquaintance with elements of modern natural and mathematical scientific theories will be significantly broadened by means of curtailing the descriptive material.

Important changes are being made in the content of the biology course. In attempting to improve this course, the commission on biology treated the following principles as basic:

elimination of the current school syllabuses and textbooks that contain distortions of biological science;

restoration of the foundations of the Darwinian doctrine of evolution in its present-day development;

restoration of the foundations of classical genetics and the introduction of the indisputable achievements of modern genetics;

the evolutionary principle in the construction of all biological school subjects;

utilization, as far as possible, of the achievements of physical, chemical and mathematical biology;

the "physiologizing" and "ecologizing" of botany and zoology; extensive utilization of the study of biology in accomplishing the general educational and upbringing tasks of the school (in particular, the labor upbringing and polytechnical education of the children and youths).

Physical geography is to be studied in

approximately the same volume as before. Owing to a significant curtailment of the number of geographical objects studied, the students' acquaintance with contemporary scientific views in the fields of geology, geomorphology, hydrology, climatology, and others will be broadened. Economic geography will be studied for one year – in the 9th grade – instead of two. Part of the material will be shifted into the 8th grade and part into the social science and contemporary history course.

The number of lessons allotted for the study of a foreign language will be the same as the number determined for the eleven-year school. The program for this subject is oriented, to an even greater degree than the current one, toward the development of the spoken language and reading in a foreign language. Nevertheless, we must acknowledge that our secondary school does not have enough time for the majority of its graduates to master a foreign language (mastery of a foreign language requires 1,500 to 1,600 hours; our school has less than half of this amount). The secondary schools of the capitalist countries secure the students' knowledge of two and even three foreign languages by allotting to their study 3,000 to 3,500 school hours. Under the conditions of public and, all the more, of universal compulsory secondary education, such a volume of training in foreign languages is impossible and even unnecessary for all boys and girls. But expansion of the training of part of the students, if only up to the minimum necessary for mastery of one foreign language, is completely necessary. The schools in which some of the subjects are taught in a foreign language solve this task well, but there are not enough of them, and the organization of new schools runs up against the difficulty of finding teachers of the foundations of the sciences who have knowledge of a foreign language. The solution may be in the organization of specialized classes of students who have shown progress, with an additional allotment for these classes, at the expense of elective and optional lessons, of 500 to 600 school hours for the study of a foreign language according to an expanded program.

The number of lessons in drawing, designing, music, singing and physical culture was determined within the volume of the ten-year school (1958); we will achieve an enhancement of their role in the instruction and upbringing of the rising generations by means of out-of-class lessons and a more persistent inculcation of acquired knowledge, skills and habits in the students' daily lives.

Instruction in the secondary school should continue to be directed toward preparing the students for practical activities and the continuation of education. In contrast to the practices of the Soviet school during the past six years, it is necessary to give much greater attention to the quality of the students' knowledge. In particular, the preparation for practical activities should be based to a greater extent on a lasting mastery of the foundations of the sciences and the formation of abilities to apply knowledge in life. In accordance with this, the students' preparation for practical activities is realized in the process of labor instruction and upbringing and polytechnical education, in the process of studying general educational polytechnical subjects, at special lessons (theoretical and practical), which are united in a school subject entitled "Labor." The participation of students in various clubs and in socially useful labor during out-of-class time will also play a large role. Professional training for work in one of the branches of the national economy or culture is unsuitable in the secondary school.

Practical lessons in workshops and on experimental agricultural plots will continue in the 1st-8th grades, but their program has been reworked for the purposes of achieving an enrichment of its technical and technological information, a closer tie with general education subjects, a broader utilization of electrical installation work, and the development of the children's technical creativity and of the movement of young naturalists.

Depending on the conditions of the school's work, labor instruction in the 9th and 10th grades is to be realized in terms of the work of the branch of the national economy predominant in the district or of the patron enterprise. In the classes that work according to expanded programs and are filled with students who are making faster progress in learning mathematics, physics, chemistry, biology, foreign languages or humanities subjects, labor instruction is constructed in accordance with scientific and technical fields: computational mathematics, mechanics, electrotechnology and radiotechnology, applied chemistry, biology, foreign languages, and others.

In the schools that do not have a production base, labor instruction can be realized by means of the study, according to the students' choice, of subjects of a scientific and practical nature from a list approved by the Ministry of Education. Depending upon the local conditions, such subjects could be: mechanical drawing, assembly and repair of radiotechnical equipment, the foundations of electrotechnology, stenography and typing, bookkeeping and accounting, elements of pedagogy, foreign language, selected sections of mathematics, physics, chemistry, biology, and others.

III

One of the most important tasks in the perfection of education in the secondary school is a fuller and more organic reflection of the modern achievements of science, technology and culture. The practice of "adding" information about the latest achievements of science to the traditional school courses has not solved this task satisfactorily. It has led to an overloading of school syllabuses and textbooks and to contradictions in the interpretation of the same material at different stages of its study. The aim should be to bring the foundations of the sciences studied in the school closer to the main trends in the development of science, technology, and culture.

The basic way to enhance the quality of the students' knowledge of the cycle of the natural and mathematical school subjects and to get a fuller reflection of the modern achievements of science, technology, and culture in school education is to raise the theoretical level of these subjects. An understanding of the laws of nature and society, of the limitless possibilities for

human cognition and creativity on the basis of these laws, is achieved according to the degree of mastery of theoretical knowledge and the skills to apply it in practice.

Raising the theoretical level of the courses of mathematics, physics, chemistry, biology and other subjects will make it possible to show the role of scientific knowledge in modern production not in individual, often rather accidental, examples of the practical application of science, but as the true basis of modern production, which is what the physical, chemical and biological sciences are.

The descriptive character of the school courses of mathematics, physics, chemistry, and biology is in contradiction with the trend of development of these sciences, which is characterized by penetration into the cognition of increasingly profound regularities. The development of the students' cognitive abilities especially suffers from the prevalence of descriptive material in the foundations of the sciences. Abundant factual material, intended only for memorization, is meager food for the student's thought. Intensification of the theoretical element in instruction will permit a broader utilization of induction and deduction, analysis and synthesis, the drawing of comparisons, conclusions, and so forth. All this, in combination with appropriate changes in the methods of instruction, will do more to further the development of the students' logical thinking and habits of independent work and will deepen their interest in science.

In physics, the gap between the school course and the science is characterized by the existing contradiction between classical physics and modern scientific views. The chemistry program is filled with descriptions of the properties of individual substances, the methods of obtaining them and chemical transformations, while their theoretical elucidation and the penetration into the mechanism of chemical reactions is completely inadequate. A significant part of the physical geography course is reduced to a description of "what is where." The commissions on these subjects correctly determined that the basic way to bring the school courses closer to modern science is to raise the theoretical level of instruction.

In mathematics this is to be achieved by eliminating the gap between arithmetic and algebra, by consistently realizing a functional approach to the study of material, and by forming theoretical-plural [teoretiko-mnozhestvennaia], algorithmic, and structural conceptions. The mathematics course in the upper grades is to be completed with the study of elements of analytical geometry, differential and integral calculus and the elements of probability theory, and this will bring the school and higher mathematics much closer together.

The basic ideas that form the school course of physics are the laws of conservation (of mass, energy, momentum, electric charge, and others), molecular and atomic structure of matter, molecular-kinetic and electronic theories, radio-electronics, wave and quantum theories of light, basic theories of relativity, atomic and nuclear physics, and the physics of elementary particles and antiparticles.

The theoretical level of the chemistry course is being raised by moving up (from the 9th to the 8th grade) the study of the periodic law and the periodic system of elements, the structure of matter, and the theory of electrolytic dissociation, as well as by deepening, with due regard for modern ideas, the examination of the problems of chemical ties and the dependency of the properties of substances on their structure, and by acquainting the students with the most important regularities in the course of chemical processes (speed of reaction, shift of chemical equations, and others). The sections on the properties and structure of proteins, the chemical nature of nucleic acids, and their role in the organism are being intensified.

Education in mathematics, physics, chemistry, biology, and geography will include acquainting the students with the methods of science – with the methods of theoretical research and with experimental methods (in physics, chemistry, and biology) – by means of expanding the demonstration of experiments, laboratory work, and systematic practical lessons. Raising the theoretical level of teaching does not entail the necessity of enlarging the programs. On the

contrary, if the indicated conditions are observed, it can serve to lessen the overloading of students with school tasks.

IV

The need to raise the theoretical level of knowledge also applies to such subjects as history, social science, literature, and economic geography. An abundance of hurriedly mastered descriptions, features, characteristics, and situations leads to sketchiness, to the memorization of purely external ties between phenomena and their evaluations, and to a weakening of interest and confidence in the conclusions of science. It diminishes the upbringing influence of these subjects on the students. Therefore, with respect to this group of subjects, it is especially important to select a minimum of phenomena and facts for study, to describe them fully in combination with an esthetic and moral appraisal, and to give them as deep a scientific elucidation as possible.

As regards such subjects as native and foreign languages, drawing, fine arts, singing and music, physical culture and labor instruction, their content was determined with an eye to strengthening their upbringing and developmental significance. Considering the significantly greater relative weight of practical information, skills and habits in these subjects, the commission attempted, in determining the volume and nature of this education, to limit strictly the memorization of rules and definitions, and to concentrate attention on the organization of the students' individual practical activities in school and out-of-school time and on the development of their abilities.

The volume of knowledge on the Russian language was determined from the same viewpoint. The orientation of study in this subject – development of the students' speech and practical mastery of the literary language – was retained. In contrast to the current syllabuses and textbooks, emphasis was placed on solving broad educational and upbringing tasks in the Russian language lessons. Sections of theory connected with the students' speech culture (vocabulary, style) were strengthened, and better defined limitations on the memorization of rules and definitions were provided.

In order to ensure a fuller reflection of the modern achievements of science, technology, and culture in the content and nature of school education, the commission also advocated further expansion of the students' independent work. It should not only be utilized for enhancing the quality of the students' knowledge, but should also be developed into a system that assures a natural transition of young people from a school regimen of education to self-education and the continuation of education upon completing secondary school (with or without leave from production).

For the purpose of creating optimal conditions for the development of the abilities of students who have had marked success in the study of various school subjects, it is recommended that the eight-year school engage more extensively in the individualization of instruction within the bounds of class work and out-of-class and out-of-school forms of educational work (clubs). Moreover, in the upper grades of the secondary school, it is considered advisable to have additional time for the study of individual school subjects or their cycles, while maintaining all-round education in the volume determined for the secondary school. In certain schools that have several parallel 9th- and 10th-grade classes, and also in populated points that have several secondary schools, it is recommended that classes be created in which one of the subjects – mathematics, physics, chemistry, biology, humanities, foreign languages – is studied on an expanded scale. The curriculum for such classes would provide an additional allotment of 3 or 4 hours per week for the special subjects, at the expense of optional lessons. The training for practical activities (hours for labor instruction) also corresponds to the specialization of the class. The conditions for the organization of such classes should be determined by special instructions from the RSFSR Ministry of Education.

In connection with the inclusion of ever greater numbers of children and youths in different types of secondary educational institutions (general educational school, secondary specialized educational institutions, evening secondary school, vocational and technical educational institutions) and the prospect of universal compulsory secondary education for school-age children, the shift to a linear construction of programs for the secondary school is acknowledged as possible. This will permit the elimination of unnecessary repetitions of educational material at various stages of instruction. There is also a need to coordinate the volume and nature of general education in the educational institutions in which graduates of the eight-year school continue their education. The solution of the second of these tasks should be entrusted to the appropriate departments.

A. M. Arsen'ev, Vice-Chairman of the Central Commission and Director of the Scientific Research Institute of General and Polytechnical Education of the RSFSR Academy of Pedagogical Sciences, gave a report on the preliminary results of work on the determination of the volume and nature of secondary education. The report was discussed by the Presidium of the RSFSR Academy of Pedagogical Sciences, and it approved the basic directions for the improvement of the content of school education.

As a result of the work of the commissions on the school subjects of primary instruction, history, mathematics, physics, chemistry, astronomy, drawing, foreign languages and physical culture, the volume of knowledge, skills and habits has been determined with sufficiently complete consideration of the modern achievements of science, technology and culture, the data of pedagogical science, and advanced pedagogical methods.

In the Russian language, literature, geography, singing and music, the present volume of the students' knowledge, skills, and habits has been changed with account of the same data. In biology and labor instruction, we have as yet succeeded in determining only the direction and basic ideas for radical changes in the content of instruction and in compiling the initial variants of programs.

The Presidium of the academy gave detailed instructions on the further work of the program commissions. They are to concentrate their efforts on unsolved problems and the compilation of draft programs. The intention is to publish the prepared programs for general discussion among teachers, scientific workers, and parents.

The commissions will offer brief conclusions on the current textbooks and elaborate recommendations concerning the nature of textbooks in each subject. Decisions with respect to the authorship of textbooks will be made jointly with the RSFSR Ministry of Education and the "Prosveshchenie" Publishing House.

The academy is preparing proposals on school equipment for new course themes, on the utilization of films, radio, television and sound recordings, and also on the training of teachers to work with the new curriculum and syllabuses.

* * *

Sovetskaia pedagogika, 1965, No. 6

A. V. Zosimovskii

AN INTERESTING EXPERIMENT

(Experience in Instruction in a Specialized School)

A specialized physics and mathematics boarding school, under Moscow University, has been operating for two school years. It is one of four schools organized as an experiment to find a rational system of preparing scientific cadres in the field of the exact sciences.

The task of the schools is to give the students, along with a full-valued general education, advanced training in physics and mathematics and professional skills in the specialties of physics laboratory worker, mathematics laboratory worker, and computer mathematician.

There are now three 9th, three 10th, and four 11th grade classes in the physics and mathematics school; 357 students study in them. They came to the school from 48 regions, territories and autonomous republics of the Russian Federation and from Belorussia. A large proportion of the children are winners of

---

The author is associated with the Scientific Research Institute of the Theory and History of Pedagogy of the RSFSR Academy of Pedagogical Sciences.

physics and mathematics Olympiads. The rest had appropriate recommendations from the school pedagogical councils. Enrollment in the boarding school was finally decided by competitive examinations on the major subjects and individual interviews, which were conducted with the entering students.

In the classes specializing in mathematics, the curriculum for the 1964/65 school year looks like this: mathematics with drawing in the 9th, 10th and 11th grades occupies, respectively, 12, 11 and 12 hours per week; physics with astronomy — 7, 6 and 6 hours; literature and foreign language are allotted 3 hours per week; history — 3, 3 and 2 hours; chemistry — 3, 2 and 2 hours. Two hours per week are allotted to the study of biology in the 9th grade, geography in the 10th grade, and social science in the 11th. In each class 3 hours are provided for physical culture and from 2 to 5 hours for elective studies.

In the classes specializing in physics, 2 to 3 hours less time are allotted to mathematics and correspondingly more hours are set aside for physics. But the main distinction between this school and the ordinary ones, of course, lies not in the increase of time for the disciplines of physics and mathematics, but in the fact that they are taught much more intensively and seriously here. The instruction pursues a completely defined aim: to introduce the students to great science as early as possible and, thereby, to help them as early as their student years, at the ages of 18 to 20, to enter into independent scientific work. This enables future mathematicians and physicists to take advantage of a period that is most propitious for scientific activities. The indicated aim also determines the nature of the lessons in the school. What can be said about their content?

In the syllabuses, elementary mathematics is combined with higher mathematics, and the classical sections of mathematics with the most modern, such as discrete mathematics, set theory and the theory of differential equations. The students are thoroughly acquainted with such concepts of higher mathematics as derivative, integral, probability, vector space, groups, and others. As a result, even many facts from elementary mathematics are presented to them in an entirely different light.

The physics course relies on higher mathematics and is constructed on the basis of the newest ideas and theories in physics. It includes, for example, a concept of relativity theory, of elements of the quantum theory of matter, of the structure of the atomic nucleus, and of elementary particles and other sections of physics. The students study statistical physics and elements of thermodynamics. The program differs little from the usual school program as far as the nomenclature of the sections is concerned. However, the level of exposition of these sections approaches that of the university.

When speaking of the volume of the physics and mathematics courses, it is interesting to note that they include, according to calculations of the teachers, no less than half the volume of the university courses on general physics and mathematical analysis. In addition, the students master all the material contained in the program of the general education school during their stay at the boarding school.

It would be premature at this point to assert that precisely this volume of special subjects is optimal for the students. Work on the creation of new mathematics and physics courses for the physics and mathematics school is still not completed. Difficulties arise not only in selecting scientific material for study, but also in solving the problem of intersubject ties, and this means that there is also a problem with respect to the system for distributing, in time, the most important sections of the course. In the current school year, for example, mathematicians had to reorganize the earlier plan for covering the school program in the 9th grade, since the physics teachers demanded that the students have the appropriate mathematical basis for an illumination of certain sections of mechanics.

Thus, the programs in use at the present time are approximations; much of their content is still not determined.

The organizational and methodological aspect of instruction is also in an experimental stage. In the main, forms of organization of school work used in the higher educational institutions are applied in the school, especially in the special subjects. The school year in the boarding school is divided into two semesters, which coincide in time with the higher school semesters. The boarding school and higher school holidays also are completely coincident. Examinations are conducted upon completion of the large program topics and at the end of the school semesters. In the boarding school schedule, lectures on special subjects are alternated with practical lessons. (1) In the lectures for various groups of students, the leading pivotal ideas of the course are revealed. The lectures are conducted once or twice a week. As a rule, each lecture takes 90 minutes, with a ten minute break. The theoretical mathematics course is given by Academician A. N. Kolmogorov and docents V. M. Alekseev and V. A. Skvortsov, and the physics course is presented by Academician I. K. Kikoin and Doctor of Physical and Mathematical Sciences

Ia. A. Smorodinskii. Before the lecture, a short synopsis of it, occupying two small typed pages, is put up in the classes. Preliminary acquaintance with it facilitates listening to the lecture and permits the students to assimilate it better and to make a more complete abstract of it.

"Doubled" and even "tripled" hours are allotted in the schedule for practical lessons (adjoining the lectures). They are conducted two or three times a week by experienced school teachers, postgraduate students, and students of the upper courses of the university. At the lessons, the teachers make the content of the lectures concrete, explain what the students did not understand, and solve problems in mathematics and physics with them. In order to achieve the unity of the theoretical lectures and practical lessons, the leaders of the practical work attend each lecture and exchange opinions with the lecturers on the content of the lecture as well as the content of the forthcoming seminars. The methods of these lessons also are essentially those of the higher educational institutions, but there is quite a bit in them that is characteristic of the usual school lessons. While applying the system of examinations, for example, the teachers do not reject individual assignments or current checks on the students' knowledge and skills. Such checking is done by oral questioning and by conducting various types of written work.

In the specialized school, just as in the ordinary one, the cognitive capabilities of the students vary. Taking this into consideration, the teachers differentiate the tasks for independent work: they present the students with a required minimum and additional educational literature and tasks.

As regards laboratory work in physics, the experience accumulated in conducting it is still insignificant. The equipping of physics laboratories was begun recently. At present, three laboratories have been equipped — for mechanics, electricity, and electromagnetic fluctuations. Two more laboratories will be completely equipped by the time the new school year begins: laboratories for molecular physics and optics. In all, 12 specialized laboratories are

to be created so that students can participate in real scientific experiments.

At present the school does not have any special textbooks or manuals. Besides their synopses, the students use university courses, in the main, for their studies. Many children use the following as reference books: A Short Course of Analytical Geometry [Kratkii kurs analiticheskoi geometrii] by N. V. Efimov, Mathematical Analysis [Matematicheskii analiz] by P. P. Korovkin, A Short Course of Higher Mathematics [Kratkii kurs vysshei matematiki] by I. P. Natanson, Mechanics [Mekhanika] by S. P. Strelkov, A Physics Course [Kurs fiziki] by S. E. Frish and A. V. Timoreva, A Physics Course [Kurs fiziki] by K. A. Putilov, Molecular Physics [Molekuliarnaia fizika] by I. K. Kikoin, and a number of others. Textbooks on narrow individual sections of mathematics and physics, such as Functions and Graphs [Funktsii i grafiki] by I. M. Gel'fand, E. G. Glagoleva and E. E. Shnol', are widely used, as are numerous collections of problems from competitions and Olympiads. Of the school textbooks, Geometry [Geometriia] by A. I. Fetisov and collections of problems may be named. Besides that, the students use the Elementary Textbook of Physics [Elementarnyi uchebnik fiziki], edited by G. S. Landsberg.

As in all the schools of the country, examinations in the physics and mathematics school are conducted only in the 11th grade. The children take a special, more complicated examination in algebra than is given in the regular schools; the rest of the examinations are typical, but the practical part is more complicated. Besides that, an additional examination in mathematical analysis was introduced for the boarding school students. In order to avoid overloading the students in the current school year, it has been decided to give them two examinations (in algebra and analysis) in January and the rest in June.

The whole system of teaching in the physics and mathematics disciplines is designed to develop the students' powers of observation, the ability to think strictly and demonstratively, and the inclination to distrust that which seems evident at first glance. A great deal of attention is given to the development of creative thinking and the training of future physicists and mathematicians for scientific discoveries. "In unravelling the secrets of nature," the teachers impress upon their students, "you must learn to pose questions. Nature gives answers only to skillfully and correctly stated questions." In this connection, indeed, the whole lecture course bears a problem, research character. The teachers acquaint the students both with solved scientific problems and with those that have as yet only been posed by science; they introduce them to the circle of their own scientific research and interests. An attempt is made to organize the instruction in physics experimentation in such a way that each student essentially helps the scientist. The conducting of experiments thought up by the students themselves is encouraged in every way possible. At the practical lessons the teachers present the students with original problems in the main, problems which require a creative approach.

The general leadership of the school's educational work is realized by a council of trustees, whose membership is approved by the chancellor of the university. Together with the school administration (the principal and two directors of studies), this council, headed by Academician A. N. Kolmogorov, organizes the admission of students into the boarding school, selects the teachers, and directs and coordinates their activities. The appropriate methodological councils solve the basic problems of current school work that have to do with the content and methods of teaching.

Being acquainted with the activities of the teachers and the organization of studies in the school, we strove to learn more about the boarding school students themselves. We tried to find out, in particular, what brought them to the special school and how instruction there was reflected in their intellectual and spiritual development. The students' enthusiasm for science and their exceedingly serious attitude toward it probably made the strongest impression. No one here has to be coerced to do his school work. On the contrary, the teachers

sometimes must even distract the students from it a little, advising them in hours intended for rest to tear themselves away from their books once again and to go out into the street, to take part in sports.

In their compositions and answers to questions on a questionnaire, the children relate in detail when and how their interest in studying the exact sciences emerged. "As early as my childhood," writes 10th-grader Zakhar M., "my father gave me various simple puzzles, which I solved with great pleasure. When I went to school, I also clearly preferred mathematics, perhaps because my mother is a mathematics teacher. In the 5th grade I was even presented with a little book with the inscription 'To the best mathematician in the class.' But all this was only one of my passions, since I was attracted to a great many things — from dancing to bee-keeping. I felt a real interest in mathematics in the 7th grade, after I had been to the municipal Olympiad in mathematics." The enthusiasm of another 10th-grader, Taras L., for the exact sciences also began when he was 14 or 15 years old, under the influence of lectures for schoolchildren and studies in a study circle at the radio institute. Vladimir Ia. developed an interest in mathematics at approximately the same age. "Before this," notes the youth, "I was merely able to solve tasks rather quickly and had a grade of excellent in mathematics. The birth of my interest was promoted by my friendship with a person employed at Kazan University, who gave me a book on mathematics and, mainly, was able to show me its strict beauty." An inclination for the exact sciences was conceived by many students in the 9th and even the 10th grade, i.e., when they had already begun studying in the physics and mathematics school.

We looked over about 80 written statements by the students and talked with many children. Only a few individuals noted that a stable, sharply expressed interest in mathematics or physics had emerged in them before the age of 14. That is why we believe that some specialization in physics and mathematics is possible and advisable precisely from this age on. Of course, it must be very carefully thought out, and pedagogical considerations must be taken into account.

As one might expect, an inclination toward the exact sciences was not conceived by any of the students by himself: with some, its source was participation in mathematics Olympiads, with others — studies in school circles under the higher educational institutions, and so forth.

It is necessary to note especially that the bulk of the students had studied under experienced, thoughtful teachers before coming to Moscow, and these teachers awakened their first interest in physics and mathematics. However, not a few of those questioned (and this is a serious symptom!) recalled their previous schools with regret: they noted a low level of studies, lack of erudition on the part of the teachers and their isolation from present-day science. "Were I to study any further in the ordinary school," the student Aleksandr Z. remarked, "I would most likely look upon mathematics from the viewpoint of a naive 3rd-grader up to the very end."

It is characteristic that some children see the cause of the notorious "school tedium" in the inadequacies of the school programs. For example, boarding school student Sergei Iu. declares in his questionnaire: "The school program comparatively quickly ceases to satisfy those who are attracted to mathematics. Indeed, the most interesting parts of mathematics lie beyond the limits of this program. Anyone who is acquainted with current solved and unsolved problems in mathematics, I believe, can no longer study any others with great enthusiasm. Unfortunately, this already happened to me personally in this school. Thus, I discovered mathematics for myself later on."

In speaking about school instruction in physics, the children point to the poor organization of laboratory lessons and the shortage of materials and equipment which could be used for constructions, experiments, and the performance of simple computations. Some express alarm about the fact that the study circles and Olympiads for physics are less popular with us than those for mathematics. Incidentally, let us note that the students entering the physics and mathematics school generally know mathematics better than physics, although the majority of them also feel that the latter is "more fascinating, more romantic, and much more important for people" than mathematics.

And, finally, a great number of children complain of the absence of the necessary individualization of studies in their former schools. The teachers of these schools were oriented in their tempos and methods of instruction toward some "average" student, thereby hampering the development of students who were not "average." That is why, for example, the student Sergei M. writes: "I wanted to find a school in which it would be possible really to learn, and one would not have to sit half a year over three theorems." Along with that, the students recalled with gratitude the teachers who thoughtfully combined collective forms of teaching with individual ones, differentiating, for example, individual forms of school tasks and recommending additional literature and more complex physics and mathematics problems to the strong students.

The students at the Moscow Physics and Mathematics Boarding School unanimously declare that they have, in the main, found what they were seeking. They are pleased that the teaching of the physics and mathematics disciplines here is in step with the development of modern science and that mathematics and physics are presented to the students as the scientists, for whom science is a world of very difficult but captivating research, see them. The students value the lectures given by the scientists most of all for their demonstrativeness and theoretical depth. These lectures arouse in them an aspiration "to know the unknown," and they serve as a source for a lively exchange of opinions and as the basis of theoretical debates.

The students are pleased that the teaching in the school provides broad scope for their intellectual independence and that it is realized on a high level of difficulty. "The method of teaching in the Physics and Mathematics School," writes 11th-grader Iakob P., "does not limit the opportunities for independent studies connected with the lecture course: in preparing for tests, usually you read not one, but several books; at the lessons the teacher not only recounts and demonstrates, but also compels the students to solve problems and even to demonstrate some theorems independently. In a word, you are not presented with a finished product, already chewed over, but are taught to think independently. And this is healthy!" The children are pleased that in the boarding school, as a rule, they are given only difficult problems, about which "it is possible to think and wrack one's brain, and not the kind that can be solved easily, a full dozen in 30 minutes." Indeed, the more difficult the problem, the students declare in one voice, the more interesting it is to solve. The children experience a special satisfaction when the solutions they have found are "elegant, beautiful, and original."

There is one more feature of the specialized school, for which the students value it: this is the great intensity of the school lessons, the intolerance of the teachers toward aimless expenditures of time, and their aspiration to teach the students to work selflessly and, along with that, rationally. We were present at a talk between the students and Academician Kikoin. Alluding to facts from the lives of famous scientists and to his own experience in scientific activity, he invariably emphasized that without the most persistent, maximally purposeful work, it is impossible to become a true specialist in any field. And the teachers not only enunciate this thesis, but also realize it practically in their daily demands and in the whole organization of school work.

As the students' knowledge in the fields of physics and mathematics deepens, their cognitive interests become differentiated: against a background of general interest in the exact sciences, there appears a heightened interest in individual sections of these sciences. The 11th-grader Vania A., for example, is especially attracted to differential geometry, Iasha P. — to the mathematical foundations of the theory of gravitation, Sveta R. — to wave phenomena, and so forth. This, of course, is one

more step along the path which leads the young man or woman to the selection of a topic for the first independent research.

The well organized dissemination of literature on physics and mathematics in the school and a system of study circles and elective courses further the development of special interests. For example, an elective course on "Differential Equations" is given in the school, and there are circles concerned with topology, set theory, the theory of numbers, mathematical logic, theoretical and experimental physics, and many others. Besides that, lectures on cybernetics, bionics, nuclear physics, and other sections of modern science are conducted regularly for the boarding school students. The school scientific library, a significant part of which consists of books given to the school by scientists, also helps satisfy the students' special interests. In addition, many students have their personal physics and mathematics libraries.

We asked Academician Kikoin: "Are you confident that good specialists will come from the boarding school students?" "I am firmly convinced that they will come," the scholar answered. "You know, they work very hard and with enthusiasm!"

We were interested in more than the specialized training of the students. We also attempted to establish whether it harmed their general education, the more so since, in comparison with the regular school, the number of school hours for the humanities is somewhat less here. As we saw above, 3 hours per week are allotted to literature in the 9th, 10th and 11 grades (in the ordinary school — 5/4, 3, and 3 respectively); 3, 3, and 2 hours are given to history (in the ordinary school — 3/4, 4, and 2/4 respectively).

First of all, let us speak about the students' attitude toward the problem of general and specialized education. Not one of them denies the necessity of a broad general education for physics and mathematics. It is notable that almost all the boarding school students (about 95 percent of those questioned) have their "nonspecialized" interests and passions beyond the limits of mathematics and physics. Mark B., a 9th-grader, takes a great interest in tennis and chess and plays the piano. Mikhail B. (10th grade) is enthusiastic about choreography, photography and filming, and his classmate, Gennadii G., is interested in model airplanes and sports and plays the violin and mandolin.

The ideal of a highly erudite specialist in the field of mathematics or physics, for whom, however, "nothing human is alien," is cultivated in the students by the entire pedagogical collective. The leading teachers of special subjects, who, naturally, enjoy the greatest authority among the students, play an especially important role in this. Thus, Academicians Kolmogorov and Kikoin, Professor Smorodinskii, and other teachers constantly orient their students toward not being locked within the narrow boundaries of their specialty, and toward aspiring to be broadly educated and spiritually enriched people, who love and understand creative literature and art and who are patriots of their socialist motherland and active participants in its social life. Kolmogorov once invited a group of new students to be guests at his dacha. The students thought that this very eminent mathematician would only talk with them about mathematics. But their forecast did not prove true: the main topics of conversation turned out to be questions of music, art, architecture.... The children recounted to us afterward that they were embarrassed by their lack of learning in these matters, but, mainly, they told how very sharply they felt the power of art and its great role in human life. Andrei Nikolaevich is a frequent participant in the students' walking and skiing trips. To set off on a trip with him means, for the children, not only to get physical exercise for the school week, but also to enter a beautiful world and to learn many new things about architectural and historical sights in the districts around Moscow. Kolmogorov's lectures in the assembly hall of the boarding school are not always devoted to mathematics either. One day, for example, he gave an interesting, richly illustrated lecture on Michelangelo Buonarroti. In the last school year he gave the student collective his record player and collection of classical music. Naturally,

such an attitude on the part of the venerable mathematicians and physicists toward art and the humanities is transferred to the students.

In their turn, the literature and history teachers try not to allow a gap to develop in the level of teaching of the humanities and special subjects. G. N. Nagaitseva, a literature teacher, gives a great deal of attention to an analysis of the views and vital interrelations of literary heros and of the motives and principles of their conduct. During the lessons she poses problematic questions of an ethical and philosophical nature for the students to discuss. Time and again, for example, long conversations took place at her lessons about the meaning of life, personal happiness and social duty, "physics and lyricism," science and morality. The literature teachers, like the teachers of the special subjects, cultivate the spirit of creativity and independence of thought at their lessons. They persistently root out mere compilations and clichés from the students' compositions on literature. The written and oral questioning of students at the literature lessons is not conducted in a stereotyped way either; those whose answers are distinguished by great depth and independence receive the highest marks. The students of the boarding school do not endure marking time in literature instruction any more than they do in the teaching of special subjects. "If the lessons are effortless," remarks Nagaitseva, "the children lose their enthusiasm. Therefore, I do not 'belabor' literary standards with them, but, in accordance with their high work capacity and intellectual activity, I condense the school course and often go beyond the limits of the program. In the 11th grade, during the study of the creativity of V. V. Mayakovsky, the students became acquainted with the texts of, for example, such 'unprogrammed' works by the poet as the poems 'War and Peace' [Voina i mir] and 'The Cloud in Trousers' [Oblako v shtanakh]. In the 10th grade, the 'unprogrammed' novels by I. A. Goncharov, The Same Old Story [Obyknovennaia istoriia] and The Precipice [Obryv] were treated."

The teaching of history is realized just as

creatively, and through broader material than is used in the regular school. The teachers of this subject, N. A. Ampleev, G. Z. Reznikov and L. N. Fainshtein, teach the students to work independently with original sources and to utilize synopses, theses, and additional literature.

As we see, the broadening of the course with fewer weekly hours is achieved through a well thought-out intensification of lessons. Moreover, the reduction in school time for the humanities is compensated at the boarding school by diverse and pithy out-of-class work. Lectures, reports and evenings devoted to sociopolitical and literary themes and to various questions of art are conducted regularly. The students often go to the movies, theaters, museums, and various types of exhibitions; they watch television broadcasts.

A check conducted in the current school year showed that the knowledge of the boarding school students about humanities subjects is characterized by thoroughness and depth.

We asked the children whether they were satisfied with everything in the content and methods of their humanities education. Not with everything, it turned out. Their most pointed remarks were addressed to the school literature course. Not a few students suggested, for example, that our classics be "squeezed" significantly in the course and that a number of modern Soviet and foreign works be included. The students also maintain that the volume of historical and literary facts in literature instruction should be reduced, to the point of giving up the unnecessarily scrupulous "analysis of models" of literary heros.

As regards foreign languages, their teaching is organized at the Physics and Mathematics School with consideration of the students' specialization. Besides the general literary texts in foreign languages, the children read, for example, unadapted texts on physics and mathematics, and many work on the mastery of special terminology. They do this work willingly, going beyond the teacher's assignments, since they see its practical usefulness distinctly. It is also worth noting that a part of the study material on mathematics is pre-

sented in the English language. These lessons are conducted by young specialists from Moscow State University (mathematicians), who know English perfectly. Besides that, young scholars from England and some other countries, whose specialization is mathematics and who are working temporarily at Moscow State University, are drawn into educational work with the students. Thus, by the time the students complete school, all of them can independently obtain any scientific information that interests them from foreign sources. (2)

The teaching of such subjects as biology and chemistry in the Physics and Mathematics School also takes into account the students' specialization. In particular, the teachers tell the students about the ties of these sciences with mathematics and physics and about the development of biocybernetics, biophysics, physical chemistry, and other "transitional" sections of knowledge.

A question must occur to anyone who learns of the volume and intensity of the students' cognitive activity at the boarding school: does this not lead to excessive strain on their intellects? But, as we were convinced, the problem of excessive intellectual work is not especially acute here. More than that, individual students declare that they became more tired in the ordinary school than they do in the specialized one, and they attribute this to those features of teaching which we have mentioned. In this school, they assert, although learning is "difficult, it is interesting and, therefore, not tiring." Along with that, the pedagogical collective in the school struggles against everything that interferes with concentration and lowers the productivity of intellectual work. After lessons, all the school premises are at the disposal of the students. Each student, at his own discretion, selects a place for extracurricular pursuits. The boarding school teachers do not pester the children with importunate tutelage; they do not distract them from their pursuits without special need to, and they maintain complete quiet in places of self-instruction.

Physical training occupies an important

126

place in the prevention of intellectual overloading and in the strengthening of the students' health. The teachers of the boarding school and university (Department of Physical Training) strive to assure that each student combines intellectual work with physical occupations and labor in the most rational way. The boarding school curriculum allots three hours per week to physical culture, instead of the two hours per week in the 9th-10th grades and the one hour in the 11th grade in the ordinary school. There are various sports sections in the boarding school, and a "health hour" is conducted three to four times per week. What is valuable in this is that the work on physical training involves all the students and is differentiated in accordance with the state of their health. The weaker students engage in medical gymnastics, according to individual programs. The teachers set themselves the task of wholly eliminating, during the course of the students' two-year sojourn in the boarding school, the defects in physical development that were detected at the initial health examinations.

Nevertheless, some of the students are evidently overloaded, and here, it seems to us, are the reasons for it.

Many students (especially 9th-graders), not wishing to lag behind the other, more knowledgeable students, must "overwork" in order to fill in the gaps in their previous preparation in physics and mathematics. Thus, a serious, very complex problem arises concerning the continuity of instruction in the physics and mathematics disciplines in the ordinary eight-year school and the secondary specialized school.

At the present time, as we noted above, the students of the Physics and Mathematics School do not have special textbooks, designed for them, in the subjects of specialization, and this undoubtedly also makes their school work more difficult. In addition, the volume of the students' preparation in nonspecialized disciplines, for example, in economic geography (foreign countries), seems clearly exaggerated to us. Some teachers believe that the entire school geography course should be substantially

compressed, and that its study should be completed not in the secondary school, but in the eight-year school. Besides that, it is suggested that the compilation, which is carried out in the boarding school, of vocabulary cards on foreign languages be given up. As the students declare, this compilation "takes a great deal of time and is of little use."

The experience of the Physics and Mathematics School testifies to the great upbringing force of a young people's collective that is united by common cognitive interests. The singleness of purpose and closeness of the student collective has a positive effect on all their behavior too. In the school, for example, there are no serious disturbances of order, and, therefore, there are no people on duty especially to maintain it. The children characteristically strive to dress and conduct themselves modestly and simply. The relations between boys and girls here are also truly comradely. What we have said does not mean, of course, that there are no deficiencies at all in the boarding school collective. It is possible to attribute to it, for example, insufficient militancy and initiative on the part of its Komsomol organization, a certain isolation of the students from the social life of the district in which they live, and some other things. On the whole, however, the student collective of the school is a friendly and hard-working collective, acting in close unity with the teachers.

It is already possible to say that, in the main, the system of selecting students for the Physics and Mathematics School makes it possible to fill it with capable and inquisitive children. The overwhelming majority of those accepted are making great progress in their studies. In the past school year only four students did not cope with the complex course of special subjects and were transferred to the regular schools. As yet, however, neither the physics and mathematics Olympiads nor individual interviews with graduating students allow the members of the admissions committee to arrive at a sufficiently firm judgment about the extent of the student's abilities, not confusing this with the level of his physics and mathematics training. This is clearly indicated merely by the fact that among those entering the school (which does not accept students from Moscow, Kiev or Leningrad) there are very few children from rural localities. Thus, of 192 students in the current school year, 141 are from cities and only 51 are from rural localities. And it is not a question, of course, of talent being scarce in the villages; it is simply that there are better conditions for training in physics and mathematics in the cities.

One cannot but recall, in this connection, the suggestions by Academicians A. Berg and B. Konstantinov (Izvestia, April 14, 1963) about the elaboration of objective criteria for the preliminary evaluation of the abilities of young people. With the rapid development of special types of schools, the availability of such criteria becomes especially necessary. They would help us in more confidently recommending to the students the type of further instruction that would be best for them and for society and would permit us to remove more successfully the contradictions, which are frequently encountered, between the children's inclinations and their abilities. Along with that, the fact that there are only 38 girls among the 357 students now enrolled at the Physics and Mathematics School compels us to ponder the causes for such a severe lag in their physics and mathematics training in our regular schools.

The apprehension is frequently expressed in the press that selection for a special school and instruction in it could develop conceit in the students and a consciousness of their exclusiveness. In the Moscow special school we did not observe manifestations of such traits, nor did we encounter factors which would give rise to them. The teachers demand a great deal of their students and do not nourish youthful pride with terms like "gifted" or "talented." The boarding school students have learned sufficiently well for themselves that talent is work and that the evaluation of talent is based on the results of man's creative activity.

In the organization of the students' daily lives and in interrelations with them, the pedagogical collective strictly follows the principle: attract them to science with science and not with privileges. As regards the latter, there is nothing here that would distinguish the Physics and Mathematics School from the boarding school of the usual type. The students do not enjoy any advantages in the payment of their upkeep, and they take examinations in the higher educational institutions on the same basis as everyone else. "The only advantage that we offer them," says the school principal P. A. Kuznetsov, "is the opportunity for persevering school work under the guidance of teachers who know their work." That is why the students do not consider themselves some kind of "Soviet wunderkinder." In addition, the danger of such arrogance arising becomes ever more ephemeral as the number of specialized schools and special classes in our regular schools increases.

It is completely evident that there are still many unresolved problems in the activities of the Physics and Mathematics School, which has been in existence only two years. The content of its school program is not completely finished; for example, the base for its experimental work in physics is narrow, and the theoretical lessons in special subjects (the lectures) are not always in step with the practical lessons. As was already noted, there are also weak points in the upbringing work with students. On the whole, however, the school has achieved substantial pedagogical results. The children studying there receive good specialized and general educational training. Despite the stiff demands on the students' knowledge and the complexity of the school program, only a few students are unable to cope with it; about half the students received grades of "4" and "5." It is also notable that 4 students of the school were members of the USSR's team at the Sixth International Mathematics Olympiad (the entire team consisted of 8 persons); two of them (Gennadii Arkhipov and Iurii Matiiasevich) received first prizes, and two others (Valerii Alekseev and Boris Ivlev) received second and third prizes. Through general examinations, all 19 of the school's first graduates in 1964 entered: the Mechanics and Mathematics Department and the Physics Department of Moscow University (14 persons), the Moscow Institute of Physics and Technology (3 persons), the Moscow Physics and Engineering Institute (1 person), and the Moscow Institute of Energetics (1 person), where they are doing very well. At the physics and mathematics Olympiads conducted at the Moscow Institute of Physics and Technology and Moscow University in 1965, the boarding school's students received significantly more diplomas, certificates, and encouraging comments than the graduates of other Moscow schools.

The experience acquired in teaching in a specialized school poses a number of important and urgent tasks for pedagogical theory and practice. We refer, above all, to such tasks as the elaboration of the problem of the optimal correlation of general and specialized education for various specializations in the differentiated school, the creation of textbooks and methodological guides for specialized schools, the elaboration of criteria for preliminary evaluation of the abilities and inclinations of students, as well as of the methods for revealing abilities and inclinations, and the improvement of the scientific-theoretical training of the teachers.

In conclusion, we would like to emphasize that the work experience of the specialized Physics and Mathematics School under Moscow University has general pedagogical significance. It indicates strikingly how far boys and girls between 15 and 17 years of age can advance in narrow specialized and general development if we work with them creatively and purposefully. Much of this experience can be taken into consideration and used with success in our regular schools.

Footnotes

1) Teaching of nonspecialized subjects in the boarding school is carried out in the form of ordinary lessons.

2) The scientific and methodological guidance of foreign language teaching in the Physics and Mathematics School is carried out by Professor O. S. Akhmanov (Moscow State University, Department of Foreign Languages), Doctor of Philological Sciences.

* * *

Narodnoe obrazovanie, 1967, No. 7

N. Balov

PROBLEMS OF THE EVENING AND CORRESPONDENCE SCHOOLS

From October to December 1966, the Ministry of Education of the RSFSR conducted zonal conferences in the cities of Ulan-Ude, Rostov, and Leningrad; they were attended by officials of public education agencies, evening schools, and correspondence schools. Officials of the Communist Youth League [Komsomol] also participated. They discussed the condition of and measures for improving the evening and correspondence education of working youth and made plans regarding the fulfillment of the decree of the CPSU Central Committee and the Council of Ministers of the USSR "On Measures for the Further Improvement of the Work of the Secondary General Education School."

These conferences took place on the eve of the fiftieth anniversary of the Soviet state; and for this reason it is appropriate to recall here the history of the development of the general education of working youth and adults in the Russian Federation. Such an excursion will enable us to evaluate more correctly the state of this work

_____

The author is Chief of the Administration of Evening Schools, Ministry of Education of the RSFSR.

at the present moment.

From the first years of the existence of Soviet power, the party and government devoted great attention to raising the cultural level of the population. Along with solving the main problem — the liquidation of mass illiteracy — measures were taken to raise the general educational level of the people.

The Party Program adopted by the Eighth Congress of the Russian Communist (Bolshevik) Party in March 1919 set the task of comprehensive governmental aid for the self-education and self-development of the workers and peasants, and for the creation of a network of institutions of out-of-school education for these purposes: libraries, schools for adults, people's homes and universities, courses, movie theaters, studios, etc.

In accordance with the decisions of the Eighth Party Congress, the first All-Russian Congress on Out-of-School Education, in May 1919, adopted resolutions in which out-of-school work was regarded as the communist education of the population organized by the state. The congress also elaborated a decree on the organization of out-of-school education in the RSFSR, as well as "Principles of Organizing a Network of State Institutions of Out-of-School Education."

On November 12, 1920, the Council of People's Commissars organized a Central Political and Educational Committee (Glavpolitprosvet) under the People's Commissariat of Education, headed by N. K. Krupskaya.

All organizational work in the field of the out-of-school education of the population was determined by the fact that the building of the new socialist society was blocked by the illiteracy of the broad masses which had been permitted under tsarism. The need was obvious for an unprecedently high tempo of educational work, which had to be strictly planned, and the results obtained systematically evaluated.

Institutions concerned with the general education of adults had great importance in the system of cultural and educational institutions. They included illiteracy liquidation points [punkty likbeza], schools and courses for the semiliterate, a higher type of schools for adults, soviet party schools, and Communist universities.

Workers' faculties (rabfaks) had an important place in the general education of adults; their task was to prepare persons from the ranks of the laboring class and the working peasantry for study in higher educational institutions. The rabfaks were both day schools and night schools. In the latter, workers studied without leaving production. The creation of rabfaks was conclusively formalized by the Decree of the Council of People's Commissars of September 17, 1920, which was signed by V. I. Lenin. The rabfaks had prepared over 41,000 workers and peasants for higher educational institutions by the tenth anniversary of the October Socialist Revolution.

The higher type of schools for adults [shkoly vzroslykh povyshennogo tipa] played a special role among all the cultural and educational institutions in the general educational preparation of the population. Arising during the first years of Soviet power, they continued to exist right up to the beginning of World War II, and can with full justification be considered the precursors of modern evening (session) secondary general schools, since their aim was to provide workers

who could not leave production with systematic academic knowledge equal in volume to the incomplete secondary and secondary school course. While all the other institutions concerned with adult education in time ceased to exist, the schools for adults proved viable; and despite various difficulties, their number increased every year and ever more students entered them.

In the 1925/26 academic year, 55,000 people studied in the higher type of schools for adults; the following year, the number was 76,400; ten years later, it was 326,600.

Until 1937 these schools did not give their graduates a secondary school diploma. From 1937 on, they began to be called incomplete secondary and secondary schools for adults, and their students were granted the right to enter higher educational institutions and technical schools.

Beginning on October 1, 1926, when the Bureau of Correspondence Study was organized under the Glavpolitprosvet, correspondence study began developing. It was possible to cover the curriculum of both first- and second-level schools by correspondence. Students were accepted throughout the entire year. In 1926 there were 3,940 persons enrolled as correspondence students in first-level schools. In 1927, 1,836 correspondence students were enrolled in second-level schools.

In March 1937, the Council of People's Commissars of the RSFSR adopted a decree "On Organizing General Correspondence Education for Adults in the System of the People's Commissariat of Education." In accordance with this decree, general secondary correspondence schools began to be created under the people's commissariats of education in the autonomous republics and in the territorial and regional departments of public education. These schools prepared students to take the examinations for incomplete and complete secondary school as external students, but did not have the right to issue diplomas of secondary or seven-year education.

The attack of the German fascist aggressors on our country in June 1941 forced an end to lessons in the schools for adults; but two years later, when the war was going full blast, on July 15, 1943, the Council of People's Commissars [Sovnarkom] adopted a decree "On the Education of Adolescents Working at Enterprises"; this dealt with those who had left children's schools and come to the factories and plants in order to replace their fathers, brothers, and sisters who had left for the front.

In accordance with this decree, schools for the education of young workers were established. In 1944, they were renamed schools of working youth. At the same time, by a decree of the Sovnarkom of the USSR on June 6, 1944, evening schools for rural youth were created; until 1956, these were only seven-year schools.

As early as 1945, the government provided privileges for the students of schools for working and rural youth: during the final examinations, they were permitted a leave from work with retention of wages (15 working days in grade 7 and 20 days in grade 10).

In 1944, a decree of February 4 by the People's Commissariat of Education reestablished the city, regional, territorial, and republic correspondence secondary schools that had been closed during the war.

When the war ended, many people decided to continue their study in school. In the very first postwar academic year, 402,800 persons were studying in schools for working and rural youth in the RSFSR. Ten years later, up to 1,500,000 persons were studying in evening schools and in the growing number of correspondence schools.

At present, evening and correspondence schools of general education enjoy the very same rights as day schools. The best graduates are awarded gold and silver medals and, as production workers, enjoy an advantage in entrance competition for higher educational institutions and technical schools. About 2,500,000 persons are studying in evening and correspondence schools today.

From 1959 to 1965, over 3 million persons received eight-year and secondary education in evening and correspondence schools of general education (of which secondary education accounted for 1,650,000). From these data it is obvious what a great contribution evening and correspondence schools have made to the implementation of the cultural revolution.

Now let us turn to the zonal conferences of public education officials which took place in 1966. Representatives of the ministries of education of the autonomous republics, territorial and regional departments of public education, officials of institutes of teacher improvement, city and district departments of public education, teachers, managers of enterprises and of collective and state farms, and officials of the regional and district committees of the Komsomol Central Committee participated. Representatives of the Central Committees of the CPSU and the Komsomol took part in the work of the conferences.

The following reports were read at the conventions: "Tasks of Public Education Agencies, Evening and Correspondence Schools in Carrying Out the November 10, 1966, Decree of the Central Committee of the CPSU and the Council of Ministers of the USSR 'On Measures for Further Improving the Work of the General Secondary School' " — the Ministry of Education of the RSFSR; "Ways of Improving the Content and Methods of Teaching the Students of Evening and Correspondence Schools" — the Scientific Research Institute of Evening (Shift) and Correspondence Secondary Schools, the Academy of Pedagogical Sciences of the USSR; "The Work of the Ministry of Education in Carrying Out the National Economic Plan and Maintaining the Quotas of Evening and Correspondence Schools" — the Ministry of Education of the Buriat ASSR; "The State of and Measures for Improving the Evening and Correspondence Education of Working Youth in the Rostov Region" — the head of the Rostov regional department of public education [oblono]; "Supervision of the Work of Evening and Correspondence Schools" — the assistant director of the Leningrad city department of public education [gorono].

Joint reports were read by the directors of evening schools: No. 1 in Ulan-Ude, No. 3 in Rostov-on-Don, No. 93 in Leningrad. They told about the experience of academic and training work in their schools. The representatives of plants, factories, and state farms spoke about joint efforts by schools and enterprises in the field of educating young people.

Participants in the conferences visited a number of city, rural, and correspondence schools, became acquainted with their work, visited the classes of the best teachers, and exchanged opinions.

Participants in the Leningrad conference visited the Scientific Research Institute of Evening and Correspondence Schools of the Academy of Pedagogical Sciences of the USSR, where they were informed of the problems on which the institute was working and became acquainted with the work of the sectors, as well as of Experimental School No. 83.

Other reports investigated the basic problems of the organization and content of education for working youth.

During the past seven years, significant advances have been made in improving the system of evening and correspondence education. For working adults with a primary education, classes have been organized which cover the eight-year school course in 2-1/2 to 3 years instead of 4. Classes and schools for master workers [mastera-praktiki] have been established, in which highly qualified workers and master workers with incomplete secondary education receive secondary education along with an increase in their professional qualifications and level of technical knowledge. For the same purpose, training centers [uchebnye kombinaty] are being organized on collective and state farms.

The length of the academic year has been increased in schools for rural youth. In addition to the previously existing regional, territorial, and republic correspondence schools, correspondence divisions have been created in secondary schools, and regional schools with peripheral classes [in outlying districts] have been created for the education of blind and deaf adults. Entrance to evening schools is forbidden in January.

As a result, the system of evening and correspondence education has become more flexible and adapted to the labor circumstances of the students.

There are special programs and textbooks for grades 5-8 of evening and correspondence schools. A skillful use of different forms of education, taking account of local conditions, always leads to positive results. In this case, matters of staffing the schools, maintaining the quota, improving the material base and, most important, the quality of the students' knowledge are being solved successfully.

Another prerequisite for success is joint work by teaching staffs and civic organizations, managers of enterprises, state farms, collective farms, and institutions. Success is guaranteed wherever this is fully carried out. This is one of the main special features which must be taken into account in organizing the teaching of working youth, since the pupil is the member of two collectives simultaneously: the school and the enterprise.

In the Petrov District of Stavropol' Territory, the creation of training centers was dictated by necessity. The collective farms and state farms had turned into large multisectored enterprises equipped with advanced technology and a powerful energy base. The tractor and auto fleet expanded sharply, the economy of the district strengthened considerably, and a need appeared for cadres of machine operators and other technical specialists.

In his report, Sotnikov, the head of the district department of public education, announced that during the past three years 323 tractor operators, 598 second- and third-class drivers, 104 builders, 44 electric repairmen, 20 sanitary engineers, and 134 accountants had been trained in the district training centers.

More than 4,000 people increased their general education during this time, including 963 who received an eight-year education.

At present, 1,181 persons study in training centers, 382 are in the correspondence division, and 282 in the school for working youth. Students in the training centers combine general education and professional training.

This district is successfully completing universal eight-year education among working youth.

The chairman of the "Dawn" collective farm in the Peschankopskii District, B. Kuchma, discussed the education of rural youth in a training center.

In order to perform the tasks set by the CPSU Program in the field of developing the education of working youth, the party committee, collective farm management, and school administration worked out a long-range plan (till 1970) of education for young collective farm workers who lack eight-year and secondary education. At the general meeting of the collective farm workers, the indices of this plan were included in the financial and production plan of the collective farm.

During the past three years, 230 collective farm workers have increased their education, including 61 who received eight-year and secondary education.

The collective farm is a multisectored enterprise with a great need for qualified cadres in different specialties.

The need arose to combine the general education and professional training of collective farm workers. And thus the training center appeared.

During the past three years, 106 tractor operators, 15 drivers, 15 vegetable-growers, 15 irrigators [polival'shchiki], and 112 cattle-breeders have been trained in the training center. In the current academic year, 38 tractor operators and 15 drivers are being trained; machine operators, irrigators, and cattle-breeders are raising their qualifications. One hundred thirty-nine collective farm workers are receiving general education in the school; in addition, 59 study by correspondence in higher educational institutions and technical schools. Those who wish to become tractor operators and drivers must have an eight-year education.

This is how the problem of training literate cadres for the collective farm was solved.

At present, all responsible posts in this collective farm are held by persons who have completed secondary school or are studying in institutes by correspondence. Comrade Buchma [sic] showed convincingly, by a number of specific examples, that collective farm workers who raise their general educational level and their professional know-how make better use of equipment and achieve higher labor productivity. Furthermore, competent leaders understand the farm's economy better and apply more efficient methods for improving the collective farm economy.

Material incentives have been set on the collective farm for those who study successfully and perform production tasks. They receive 10% above the average salary; those who complete eight grades are paid a bonus of 30 rubles, and those with secondary education are paid a bonus of 50 rubles.

The participants in the conference were able to observe personally similar work in a training center when they visited the "Kalinin" collective farm in the Zelenograd District (Rostov Region).

Some comrades suppose that training centers are possible only in areas of large population. The conferences showed that such a belief does not correspond to reality, since there are examples of good work by training centers in other districts as well. For example, the Torei (skii) training center in the Dzidiansk District of the Buriat ASSR carries on good work. So does the training center on the "Friendship" collective farm in the Iakut ASSR, where conditions are completely different from those in the Rostov Region or Stavropol' Territory.

The Luzhskaia correspondence school in the Leningrad Region presents an interesting example of organizing the teaching of rural youth. In this district the rural population lives in small population settlements that are concentrated around comparatively larger villages, in which collective farm centers are usually located.

Not all the villages have children's schools. A unique form of teaching has taken shape under these conditions. The Luzhskaia school has 24 study-and-consultative points and 15 correspondence groups in the territory of the district. Thirty permanent teachers and over 120 substitutes work in the school. The far-flung network of consultation points guarantees that each student will be helped. The entire staff of permanent teachers is divided into small brigades of two or three. Every day the teachers ride out to the consultation points. At 18 of these points, general education is also successfully combined with professional training. Again, this was necessitated by the training and retraining of cadres of workers in different agricultural professions, since a mechanization of agricultural production is being successfully carried out in the Luzhskii District. There, industrial technology is being applied to vegetable-growing, cattle-raising farms are being mechanized, as is the production of potatoes, grain, etc. As an experiment, instructors of professional disciplines were added to the school staff. The results were encouraging. It became easier to maintain an interrelation between general education and professional training.

The combination of professional training and general education promotes the development of an interest in study and a sound, intelligent mastery of information.

The students attend consultations twice a week; on the other days they work independently. Professional training takes place on days specially set aside for it. The beginning and end of lessons are adjusted to the schedule of the students at a given consultation point.

As a result, the contingent of students in the school grows from year to year. While there were only 400 students in the school in 1960, at present there are 1,600. Grades 5-8 account for 72% of the students. Out of 60 who received diplomas, 39 entered higher educational institutions and technical schools. A small number of students drop out of school for insufficient reasons. Systematic explanatory work conducted by both teachers and the party and Komsomol organizations of the farms helps to maintain student enrollment. The teaching of workers in the Gorno-Altai correspondence school is also well organized.

Thus, the success of the student body depends on the correct organization of teaching and its correspondence to the living and working conditions of the students. Let us take Evening School No. 1 in the city of Ulan-Ude (O. Stepanova, principal). This school annually fulfills the national economic plan and maintains its enrollment of students. In the beginning of the 1965/66 academic year, 414 students enrolled. During the year, 29 dropped out, including 2 for insufficient reasons; 49 new students arrived, mainly during January registration.

Preparing the school for a new academic year begins well ahead of time. A count is made at enterprises in the subdistrict and in the housing development administrations of persons who lack eight-year and secondary education. The teachers and the commissions of aid to the school carry on joint explanatory work right in the shops, on plots, and in brigades. The school serves a great number of small enterprises. Together with the management of these enterprises, it draws up long-range plans for raising the education of workers and achieves fulfillment of these plans. Workers with much production experience who lack an eight-year education are enrolled in accelerated classes. The students of the school play an important part in this work. Since the classes are organized long before lessons begin, the class leaders know what sort of group they will have to work with in the new academic year. They study the aptitudes and interests of the future students, and thereby are able to carry out an individualized approach in the process of teaching and training.

The accelerated classes for the eight-year school course help to bring education to a great number of people who have much experience in production and in life. Such classes have become widespread and have fully justified themselves. Thus, in School No. 12 in the city of Irkutsk, workers from the "Kuibyshev" plant study in these classes. The directors and the Komsomol committee of the plant devote particular attention to recruiting students for accelerated classes. Workers from age 25 to 50 who express a great desire to do so, study in them. Here is what one worker said: "I work at the Kuibyshev plant, I'm a Communist, I've had four years of school. Each year the equipment in the shop becomes more advanced. Study has greatly helped me to master the new equipment, and I understand it well. I will finish my eight-year education and then study in a technical school."

The teachers of School No. 12 work hard to improve the teaching methods in these classes. They organize lessons in such a way that students receive the basic information during the lesson and the study material has a practical orientation. Good students invariably receive incentives from the directors of the plant and the school.

The desire of adult students both to obtain general education and to increase their professional qualifications is fully satisfied in the masters' classes. They have received the approval of workers at enterprises in the Cheliabinsk, Sverdlovsk, Rostov regions, in Moscow, etc.

Unfortunately, here and there some enterprises and offices still have a negative attitude toward such a form of education for workers; they see in it extra trouble for themselves and believe that the training of master workers should take place through technical schools. Here we encounter an obvious lack of understanding of the tasks of the masters' schools and classes set up by a decree of the Council of Ministers of the USSR. By no means can every master worker study in a technical school, nor does every qualified worker set himself the aim of attaining a technical school diploma, since he is satisfied with a certificate of secondary education and with valuable knowledge about his specialty. Therefore it is unwise to oppose one form of education to the other; they can and should exist simultaneously. Let the worker himself choose that form of study which is best for him.

Many evening schools have accumulated valuable experience in maintaining student enrollment and eliminating the practice of dropping out. Filling the school in time is only half the battle; dropping out must be prevented. The teaching staff of School No. 2 in the city of Kursk copes well with this matter, regarding it as a genuine pedagogical task. The most important requirement for keeping students in school appears to be the readiness of students to study in one grade or another. Therefore the teachers help entering students to fill in gaps in their knowledge (by supplementary group and individual lessons).

The correct composition of classes is of great importance in maintaining enrollment. Each class in this school has a nucleus of students who studied in the school before. The presence of this nucleus has a great influence on the newcomers because the "old" students have already learned the operations of the school, have had experience in combining work with study, and have developed a school spirit.

The link between the school and the enterprise is extremely important. It is proving successful when the enterprise directs workers to study, since this increases the students' responsibility to the collective. Great importance is attributed to working with parents and to home visits by class leaders. The influence of the students' collective on the individual student is utilized.

As a result, during the past three years, there were only seven dropouts in School No. 2.

In the past academic year, 112 persons graduated from the school, of whom 14 were awarded medals and all entered higher educational institutions.

The practical work of evening and correspondence schools convinces us that the student body cannot be separated from the educational process; these two matters are closely intertwined. However, for convenience, we will separate the problem of fulfilling the national economic plan in evening and correspondence education in discussing it from the organizational standpoint.

The Program of the CPSU sets the task of giving, by 1970, an eight-year education to all young people who are employed in the national economy and do not yet have such an education.

The directives of the 23rd Congress regarding the five-year plan for national economic development in the USSR require that by 1970 the number of students in schools for working and rural youth must be increased by more than 1.4 times.

In their research, Soviet economists and sociologists have proven that technical progress and the educational level of the workers influence one another. All other things being equal, educated workers fulfill a task considerably more quickly than workers with low education; for the majority of workers, the percentage of their fulfillment of the production norm increases in proportion to the increase in their general education. Unfortunately, many economic executives pay little attention to this fact, often failing to see this correlation, and hence have a careless attitude toward raising the general education of the workers.

Yet it must again be mentioned that the government, which attributes the greatest importance to this matter, has issued a number of decrees in recent years: the establishment of a shortened workday or work-week for good students in evening and correspondence schools, salary increases for teachers in evening and correspondence schools, the organization of masters' schools and classes, etc.

It is the task of public education agencies and the schools to make full use of the opportunities offered by the government for the education of working youth. However, for the past two years, the student quota set forth in the national economic plan has not been fulfilled. In the 1965/66 academic year it was fulfilled for all types of schools by 95.7%, and in 1966/67 — by 86.5%. In the current year the plan for evening and correspondence schools has been especially poorly fulfilled in the Altai Territory, the Arkhangel, Kemerov, Tiumen, and Kamchat regions, and in the Bashkir, Checheno-Ingush, Karelian, and Komi autonomous republics.

This occurred mainly because the public education agencies, school principals, and faculty did not reorganize the work of recruiting young people for school by taking into account the new difficulties which arose in 1965. In that year the transition of evening and correspondence schools to an eleven-year term of study was completed (in children's schools, ten-year study was introduced), the privileges for college applicants with production experience were abolished, and the group composition of persons lacking an eight-year education changed qualitatively (for the most part they are people who display no particular desire to study, and it is essential to carry on serious explanatory work with them).

At the same time the national economic plans for student quotas increase every year. All these circumstances required that public education agencies and the schools decisively increase organizational work during the period of preparation for the new academic year, actively enlist civic organizations, and radically improve the work of the commissions of assistance to schools. However, none of this was done in many re-

gions, territories, and ASSRs, and the enrollment in evening and correspondence schools was left to chance.

But where proper attention was devoted to this matter, the national economic plans were fulfilled. At the meetings the successful work of public education agencies in the Buriat and Severo-Ossete autonomous republics and the Saratov and Iaroslavl' regions was noted.

Particular attention was paid to the unsatisfactory state of the teaching of rural youth. In the rural areas there are considerably more difficulties than in the cities, and the organizational work is much weaker. Quotas in the national economic plans for schools for rural youth have been fulfilled almost nowhere for a number of years.

The successful experiment of the work of training centers, as well as the recommendations of the Ministry of Education of the RSFSR, the Ministry of Rural Economy, and the All-Union Society, "Sel'khoztekhnika," and the data in the Approximate Situation in Training Centers and other documents, are being poorly applied. The number of training centers is decreasing rather than increasing. This is explained by the fact that a number of collective and state farms have not come to a decision about the wages of teachers of special disciplines and/or have not created a material base. Despite the existence of a great number of young collective and state farm workers who lack an eight-year education, only 41.3% of the places in grades 5-8 of evening schools are now filled. For example, on the "Friendship" collective farm (Staro-Iur'ev District, Tambov Region), there are 291 workers up to 30 years of age with only a primary education and 270 who have an incomplete secondary education; but there are literally only occasional students in the school for rural youth. According to incomplete data, in the Liven District of the Orlov Region, 108 machine operators with a five- or six-year education work on collective farms; there are about 50 milkmaids and other workers on cattle-raising farms with a primary education; more than 200 collective farm workers lack an eight-year education — and none of them are studying.

On the collective and state farms in the Bogoroditskii District (Tula Region) there are 1,125 workers aged 16-30 who lack an eight-year education, of whom 339 are studying; among 209 brigade leaders and farm directors in this district, 74 have an incomplete secondary education and 85 have only a primary education.

There is an analogous situation is the Tambov Region, where only 96 out of 924 farm directors have specialized training, while the remaining 828 have incomplete secondary and primary education. In the Urich District (Orlov Region), 111 out of 118 middle-level supervisors lack an eight-year education, and none of them are studying.

Local work in teaching deaf workers on collective and state farms is poorly organized; there are particularly many deaf workers in the villages of Altai and Krasnodar territories, Perm, Penzensk, and other regions.

Evening school students often do not make use of the privileges established for them by the government, either because of the fault of collective and state farm supervisors or because of their own desire not to "lose wages."

The main reason for the poor organization of the teaching of rural youth is the fact that in rural areas the general education of young people is conducted by the same people who have regular teaching jobs, and these teachers and principals are generally already overburdened. The reason for this is that the small staffs of schools for rural youth, the presence of different grades, and the great number of small consultation points do not permit the creation of separate staffs for schools and correspondence divisions. Out of 117,000 teachers in schools for rural youth and correspondence schools, 108,000 are holding two jobs, i.e., only 7.8% of all rural teachers work exclusively in evening or correspondence school.

Under these circumstances, district schools for rural youth ought to be established, and they must have all forms of teaching, thereby making it possible to staff these schools with permanent teachers and principals. Relying on this collective, the district offices of public education for rural youth will be better able to organize the teaching of working youth.

The method of paying wages to the heads of consultation points, to school principals for supervising a correspondence division, and to teachers for classroom supervision needs to be changed. The material incentives to persons involved in the teaching of rural youth must be increased.

A number of districts still lack a rationally organized and continuously operating network of schools, classes, consultation points; in some cases the teaching of rural youth has not been organized at all. There are no inspectors of evening and correspondence education in the majority of district offices of public education.

Owing to a lack of teachers, certain subjects are not taught in rural areas or are taught by nonspecialists. In the current academic year, 10th grade lessons were stopped in the Rechich school (Liven District, Orlov Region) due to a lack of teachers of physics, literature, and chemistry. The principals of the Rechich school and the Maloarkhangel school (Glazunov District), the methodologist of the correspondence division in the Shablykin District, and certain teachers in the Stanovokolodez' school are all persons who lack appropriate education or have been dismissed from children's schools for "ineligibility." Sixteen thousand teachers (42% of the total) of grades 5-11 in schools for rural youth lack higher education, and methodological aid to them is poorly organized.

As a result of all this, the quality of educational work in many evening and correspondence schools and divisions remains unsatisfactory.

The students in schools for rural youth and correspondence students are completely inadequately provided with textbooks and visual aids. Only 20% of the schools for rural youth have access to physics classrooms and 12% have access to chemistry classrooms; 95% of these schools lack biology classrooms.

The majority of schools cannot organize sessions for workers on cattle-raising farms who work evenings.

There are few students in the accelerated eight-year school course in a number of regions, territories, and autonomous republics.

A considerable number of students drop out

because of the poor organization of educational work and the lack of necessary working conditions. While recognizing the defects in the organizational work of the public education agencies and the schools, the participants in the conferences pointed to a number of objective difficulties that hinder the school enrollment of working youth: excessively large plans, lack of aid to public education agencies and to schools under industrial sponsorship, neglect of this matter by ministries and departments, lack of material incentives to industrial and agricultural workers to study, etc.

In connection with these difficulties the following suggestions were made: to establish a general educational minimum for the basic fields of specialization in industry and agriculture, and also to take account of educational qualifications when raising job categories; to include orders for the education of workers in the production orders of enterprises and collective and state farms, to impose responsibility for their fulfillment on the managers; to establish the material responsibility of students who leave school without valid reasons, to set the date of October 1 as the deadline for schools to present their accounts, which will make it possible to show the permanent quota of students.

In analyzing these suggestions, it should be noted that some of them are entirely unacceptable while others warrant close study. The proposal to make a student who leaves school without valid reason materially responsible is unacceptable, since one cannot drive people into school by force. The suggestion about establishing a general educational minimum for the basic fields of specialization in industry and agriculture deserves attention. Of course, this is not such a simple matter. In the opinion of education officials, implementation of this proposal would be a serious incentive to study for working youth. But it must also be investigated from the productive and economic point of view. Therefore it is important to hear the opinion of economists, sociologists, enterprise managers and officials in ministries and departments.

A comprehensive discussion would yield the correct answer to this question.

It is indisputable that the responsibility of ministries, departments, managers, and civic organizations of enterprises for the implementation, above all, of eight-year education for working youth must be increased.

The Central Statistical Administration of the RSFSR would have to concur with the proposal that evening schools present their accounts on October 1. During September, the schools could plan a more stable enrollment of students. It is precisely in September that many are sent to agricultural jobs, after which they often fail to return to school.

The question of the quality of knowledge of evening and correspondence school students was investigated at the conferences in depth and from all sides. In their decree concerning the schools, the CPSU Central Committee and the Council of Ministers of the USSR point out that the school's chief task is to provide students with sound academic knowledge, high communist consciousness, and preparation for life.

The specific nature of evening and correspondence education for working youth demands that the faculty constantly improve teaching methods. In recent years the practice of leading teachers has contributed much that is new to the organization of lessons: they have begun to make more extensive and more skillful use of the students' experience in production and life, introduce heterogeneous forms of independent work, apply technical teaching aids, conduct outings and lessons directly on the production site, and skillfully concentrate the students' attention on the chief, basic problematic topics of the syllabus during lessons and in group and individual consultations.

The best teachers have convincingly shown the advisability of rejecting the traditional structure of the lesson, which amounts to testing the performance of homework, explaining new material, and assigning it for further home study. It is being replaced by an organization of the lesson which begins, as a rule, not with testing homework or an oral quiz, but with enlisting the student in active independent work that guarantees fruitful educational work by each student throughout the entire lesson.

When explaining new material, the best teachers show, in a profound, dramatic and accessible way, the inevitability of processes, phenomena, their causes and effects, by making use of facts from the actual surroundings, from the students' industrial activity, and by utilizing all possible visual aids.

One of the guiding principles of teaching in evening school is the principle of increasing the active and independent participation of students in the educational process. Various types of independent work are organized in such a way that they require intense mental work, analysis, generalizations, and a search for the most rational solutions to intellectual problems by the student. Problems prepared for each student ahead of time play a great role in attaining this aim.

The methods of repeating and reinforcing information are of extremely great importance in the struggle for a high quality of student knowledge. In these schools the teacher must find out during each lesson which students have understood the new material; for this reason reinforcement is essential here.

A variety of teaching methods result in activating the students' cognition, holding their attention, and maintaining an individual approach, taking account of gaps in the knowledge of each student.

The methods of evaluating knowledge are of particular importance in teaching sound and conscious knowledge to evening school students. Obviously, here one cannot rely on the usual routine questioning during lessons, since there is not sufficient time for that; besides, a considerable number of students attend classes irregularly, and one cannot repeat the questions several times. Some students receive a final evaluation for half a year from only two grades or even one grade, which, of course, in no way defines their knowledge. The most effective method of evaluating knowledge is an examination system which makes an objective test possible.

"A test for every topic" is the best method of evaluating knowledge.

Recently many schools have gained interesting experience in using technical aids. For example, in School No. 1 in Tambov (Comrade Zavadskii, principal) it was correctly decided that at present

it is impossible to solve the problem of the quality of knowledge by relying only on the old, though tried and tested, means. For three years the school staff has worked consistently on methods of using technical aids. This refers both to the quantitative and qualitative side of the matter. Last year, 1,200 out of 13,600 lessons were conducted by technical means; these were lessons in the most varied disciplines. For this very reason each teacher had to be taught to use a film projector, epidiascope, film strip projector, and tape recorder. The school has 3 film projectors, 4 epidiascopes, 7 film strip projectors, 1 LETI apparatus [possibly, a projector produced by the Leningrad Electrotechnical Institute — Editors, Soviet Education], 2 universal projectors, and 4 tape recorders. The school has film strips and reels, microfilms, and its own phono-library [fonoteka]. The tape recorder is used to record talks about social science, radio broadcasts, and lectures. The school has a huge arsenal of visual aids. Thus the technical aids are supplemented by didactic material. Eleven classrooms have been equipped for showing films and slides. The introduction of technical media into the educational process has given good results. Students' work has improved, the number of dropouts has decreased significantly, and attendance has improved.

In School No. 1 in the city of Novokuznetsk (Kemerov Region), excellent special rooms [kabinety] have been equipped for every subject with the help of [enterprise] patrons, and now lessons are conducted by the cabinet system [kabinetnaia sistema]. The school is adequately supplied with technical aids. It has two automated classrooms with testing and teaching machines. These technical devices make it possible to direct the learning process and increase students' cognition.

The physics teacher, Comrade Ostrovskii, together with Blokhin, a student, constructed an "Ekzamenator" machine; an 11th grade student, V. Korneev, constructed an automatic testing machine. This device is used to check performance on independent test papers, as well as on examinations in mathematics, physics, and chemistry. Machines are being built in this school which will communicate scientific and technical information. Yes, we are referring to programmed teaching. Similar experience has been accumulated in schools No. 82 in Leningrad, No. 29 in Sverdlovsk, and No. 6 in Ulan-Ude. These experiments must be studied closely and methodological recommendations made for the further improvement of programmed teaching.

The materials of inspection checkups, tests, and higher school entrance exams indicate that the task of providing students with sound and thorough knowledge is not being performed satisfactorily in many evening and correspondence schools. Many students do not understand the essence of the processes occurring in nature and social life, the main theoretical tenets, the basic concepts. Many students cannot apply knowledge in practice.

There are various reasons for this state of affairs: poor preparation, a long break in studying, little time for homework. But the main reason lies in defects of the teaching process. Inspection tests show that a great many lessons are conducted on a low theoretical and methodological level. Many teachers do not fulfill elementary didactic and methodological requirements, do not conduct practical and laboratory work, make little use of visual aids, etc.

Here is an example: a history teacher, the principal of School No. 8 in Tula, devoted all 45 minutes of an 11th grade lesson to material expounded during the previous lesson. Discussion was conducted only with one student called to the board, while the rest were given no assignment and distracted themselves as well as they could. They read the magazine Crocodile [Krokodil'], talked among themselves, etc.

Questioning revealed that the students did not know the topic "The United States in the Late Nineteenth and Early Twentieth Century," and the teacher again assigned the very same material for homework.

Another example: a woman teacher of Russian language and literature at School No. 3 in Makhachkala came to a 6th grade lesson with a lesson plan which contained only one word: "Exposition." It turned out that the exposition

had not been planned ahead of time, but that the teacher gave it only because the inspector had come to the school. The students spent two hours writing an exposition of Turgenev's short story "Mumu." And this is at a time when all the workers of Dagestan were preparing to celebrate the 23rd Congress of the CPSU, and when much was being said in the newspapers and magazines about the labor feats of the Soviet people.

One more example: the mathematics teacher of School No. 1 in Derbent came to a 10th grade lesson with this plan: "Theme of lesson — solving problems. Plan of lesson — checking homework, solving problems (numbers indicated), assigning homework (numbers indicated)." The homework assignment was checked formally. The teacher ignored the fact that some of the students did not do the assignment. Then 36 minutes were spent solving one problem. It turned out that the teacher himself had not solved it beforehand, and when a student made an error in computation, the teacher did not notice it. The solution to the problem was not obtained. The teacher himself could not make out why, and was rescued by the principal, who was present at the lesson.

These are examples of flagrantly bad lessons. But how many mediocre, dull lessons there are, which do more harm than good!

Will anyone acquire thorough, sound knowledge this way?

Often, in order to conceal their own poor work, teachers resort to raising marks. This results in rumors among young people about the extraordinary "kindness" of evening school teachers.

At the conferences, the absence of proper inner-school control over the work of teachers was noted; some school principals essentially neglect to supervise the teaching process, do not study each teacher's work thoroughly, seldom visit lessons, do not issue warnings, and do not organize methods of work in the school.

Also discussed was the fact that the public education agencies do not systematically inspect the work of evening schools. For example, in the Slaviansk and Temriuk districts of Krasnodar Territory, not one evening school has been inspected for a year.

Matters of evening and correspondence education are rarely discussed at councils on public education by the regional (territorial) departments of public education and the ministries of education of the autonomous republics.

Institutes of teacher improvement neglect to study and theorize on the best experience of evening and correspondence schools. Work to increase the qualifications of teachers is not always organized differentially.

A successful solution to the problem of improving the quality of education in evening schools is possible if the creative work of the faculty is supplemented by a conscientious attitude toward learning on the part of the students.

Of course, a conscientious attitude toward learning does not come of itself. It must be inculcated both at lessons and in out-of-class work. Out-of-class work is now acquiring ever greater importance in evening school. Many participants in the conferences shared their experience in this work.

In evening school this educational problem (out-of-class work) can be successfully resolved only by relying on the student body and promoting the development of its independence. Both independent activity and initiative should appear first of all in out-of-class work.

Many evening school students have sufficient experience in life and production; they have the habits of social work, can cope with vitally important problems, and conduct themselves properly in public places and at home. As a rule, these students are the nucleus of the student collective on which school supervisors and teachers rely in all their work.

Various forms of out-of-class work with students have developed in evening schools, with good results. They include lectures, debates, discussions, outings to historical sites, visiting museums, subject evenings [tematicheskie vechera], and "interesting meetings" clubs.

The experience of leading schools (No. 1 in Iaroslavl', the Severodvinskaia school in Arkhangel Region, No. 10 in Kalinin, the Zelenodol'skii School in the Tatar ASSR, Nos. 1 and 7 in Ulan-Ude, etc.) shows that correctly organized out-of-

class character-training has a beneficial influence on students' attitude toward study.

Thus, the teacher's attitude toward his work, his skill, and the level of leadership on the part of school supervisors are the most important factors in raising the quality of teaching.

At the same time one cannot ignore the importance of the quality of curricula and textbooks.

The Commission of the Academy of Sciences of the USSR and the Academy of Pedagogical Sciences of the USSR have now largely completed work on the curricula for children's secondary general schools. It remains for the Ministry of Education of the RSFSR and the Scientific Research Institute on Evening and Correspondence Schools to work out new curricula for evening schools. The existing curricula for grades 5-8 must be revised and new curricula created for grades 9-11.

Currently, the "Prosveshchenie" Publishing House is preparing to issue a series of textbooks for the upper grades aimed primarily at correspondence school students. These textbooks will be provided with a methodological apparatus that will enable students to study subjects on their own. At the same time these textbooks may be used successfully by evening school students as well.

The participants in the conference proposed a reduction in the length of study in evening school (to teach the upper grades in two instead of three years). However, experimental work with the two-year program of study in individual classes did not fully justify itself. This is why the proposal, tempting at first sight, was overwhelmingly rejected. A reduction in the length of study can inflict irreparable damage on the quality of education.

At the same time, interest was shown in the experimental work of the Scientific Research Institute for Evening Schools with differentiated teaching in the upper grades. The researchers believe that evening school students cannot obtain sufficiently sound knowledge on all subjects because of the existing "critical" lack of time.

Therefore upper grade students should choose some definite area [profil']: in the humanities, physics-mathematics, etc. This choice would be based on aptitude. In the curriculum of the given area or "profile," a greater number of hours are devoted to the specialized subject. This enables teacher and students to study certain subjects more thoroughly during lessons. As for the non-specialized subjects, the teacher's task essentially will be to expound new material during the lesson, while the students must prepare for exams in these subjects by independent work based on the textbook.

Raising the quality of educational work depends a great deal on the school's material base. It was noted at the conferences that in recent years the number of evening (shift) schools has increased because the accommodations of children's schools have been freed. The evening schools acquired buildings and patrons. Sometimes new school buildings were constructed (extremely rarely). At present, in the RSFSR, 1,954 schools have their own buildings, and 1,074 are quartered in buildings made available by enterprises.

It should be noted that many of the buildings were not planned for holding lessons. For the time being, more than half the schools for working youth do not have their own buildings and are therefore obliged to carry on during the third shift in children's schools. [Regular school classes are carried on in the first two shifts — Editors.]

Yet it sometimes happens that the best evening school buildings are transferred to other organizations. And, alas, public education agencies are reconciled to such facts and do not turn for help to the Ministry of Education of the RSFSR.

There must be a radical improvement in pro-

viding evening schools with equipment, visual aids, and textbooks. In many schools there are either no specialized classrooms at all, or they are very poorly equipped; students are ill provided with textbooks.

Right now the whole country is preparing to celebrate the glorious fiftieth anniversary of the Great October Socialist Revolution. Officials of schools and public education agencies are also taking an active part in this exciting creative work. The schools will begin the new academic year on the threshold of the Great Holiday!

The Decree of the Presidium of the All-Union Central Council of Trade Unions, the Central Committee of the Leninist Komsomol Organization, and the Ministry of Education of the USSR, dated April 27, 1967, "Regarding the Work of Trade Union and Komsomol Organizations and Education Agencies in Raising the General Educational Level of Young People Employed in the National Economy," will be of tremendous help to public education agencies and schools in solving the complex problems of evening and correspondence education for working youth.

The decree efficiently coordinates the efforts of trade unions, the Komsomol, and education officials in improving the teaching and training of working youth.

The regional and territorial divisions of public education and the ministries of education of the autonomous republics should take measures for the practical fulfillment of the decree and complete the preparation of the schools for the new academic year.

* * *

Higher Education

Izvestia, September 10, 1966

MEASURES TO IMPROVE THE TRAINING OF SPECIALISTS AND TO

PERFECT THE GUIDANCE OF HIGHER AND SECONDARY SPECIALIZED

EDUCATION IN THE COUNTRY

(In the CPSU Central Committee and the USSR Council of Ministers)

The Central Committee of the CPSU and the Council of Ministers of the USSR considered the questions involved in improving the training of specialists and perfecting the guidance of higher and secondary specialized education in the country and adopted a resolution.

This resolution notes that considerable success has been achieved in training specialists for the national economy. The higher and secondary educational institutions are training personnel in all the specialties required by our national economy.

However, the tasks set forth by the 23rd Congress of the CPSU regarding the further development of the socialist economy and culture call for considerable improvement of the work of the higher and secondary specialized educational institutions and enhancement of the quality of training given to specialists.

At the present stage of development of socialist society, which is characterized by the deep penetration of science in all spheres of material production, cultural development and social life, specialists who graduate from higher and secondary specialized educational institutions should be well equipped with Marxist-Leninist theory, be familiar with the latest scientific and technological knowledge, and be able to competently solve problems of economic development, of the scientific organization of work, and of the management of production. However, the higher and secondary specialized educational institutions do not always cope with these tasks, and there are substantial shortcomings in their work.

The Ministry of Higher and Secondary Specialized Education of the USSR, as well as other ministries and departments that have jurisdiction over educational institutions, are making inadequate use of the rights granted them with respect to guiding the educational-methodological, scientific-research, and ideological-upbringing work in those institutions, and they are exercising inadequate control over the quality of the training given to specialists. The Ministry does not carry out systematic work to

144

raise the qualifications of teachers in educational institutions; it does not ensure the preparation and publication, in the necessary quantities, of worthwhile standard textbooks for higher educational institutions and secondary technical schools [tekhnikumy]; and it gives insufficient attention to the elaboration of questions concerning the long-term development of higher and secondary specialized education in the USSR, problems relating to the economics of education, and questions of the scientific organization of the educational process. There are serious shortcomings in the planning of specialist training. The most desirable relationship has not been established between the training of personnel with higher educations and the training of personnel with secondary education.

The educational and material facilities of a considerable number of educational institutions do not fully meet the present-day requirements of the educational process and the organization of scientific research. Not enough is done to involve the higher educational institutions, which have highly qualified scientific personnel, in the elaboration of problems of national economic significance.

The party agencies of some republics and regions have reduced the amount of attention they give to ideological-upbringing work among the students and pupils, and they have become less exacting with respect to the agencies responsible for guiding educational institutions and with respect to the party and Komsomol organizations of the higher and secondary specialized educational institutions.

The Central Committee of the CPSU and the Council of Ministers of the USSR have worked out a series of measures to improve the training of specialists and to strengthen scientific research in higher educational institutions.

The resolution emphasizes that the most important task in the area of higher and secondary specialized education is further improvement of the quality of specialist training with due regard for the demands of modern production, science, technology and culture and their future development. Graduates of higher and secondary specialized educational institutions should be trained in the spirit of high communist consciousness; they should know Marxist-Leninist theory and possess the skills required to organize mass political and educational work.

The central committees of the communist parties of the union republics and the territorial and regional committees of the party have been asked to intensify their control over the activities of the party, Komsomol and trade union organizations of higher and secondary specialized educational institutions, to concentrate their attention on fulfilling the tasks aimed at raising the quality of instruction and improving the ideological and political education of students and pupils, to devote particular attention to raising the level of teaching of the social sciences, and to strengthen the departments of social sciences by the appointment of highly qualified teachers.

The Ministry of Higher and Secondary Specialized Education of the USSR has been authorized to organize institutes for raising the qualifications of teachers of the social sciences at the Leningrad, Urals, Rostov-on-Don, and Tashkent state universities.

A number of higher educational institutions have been placed under the direct jurisdiction of the Ministry of Higher and Secondary Specialized Education of the USSR. These higher schools will serve as a base for generalizing and developing educational and methodological materials, compiling textbooks and study aids, and providing training and additional training for scientific and teaching personnel for all higher educational institutions.

It has been decided that the creation and liquidation of secondary specialized educational institutions, branches and educational-consultation centers of higher educational institutions, as well as the approval of the list of new specialties in which specialists should be trained in each higher school, will be effectuated by the ministries and departments that have educational institutions, with the agreement of the Ministry of Higher and Secondary Specialized Education of the USSR.

With a view to strengthening control over the quality of the training given to specialists, the

Ministry of Higher and Secondary Specialized Education of the USSR has been charged with carrying out the state inspection of all higher educational institutions in the country.

As has been shown in practice, the training of specialists in day instruction has fundamental advantages both in terms of the quality of the training and in terms of economic considerations. It has therefore been proposed that in the formulation of plans for training specialists, provision should be made for the further priority development of day instruction in higher and secondary specialized educational institutions. At the same time, it is necessary to draw up a list of specialties in which specialists will receive training through the system of evening and correspondence instruction. With regard to enrollment in higher and secondary specialized educational institutions in order to study while continuing to work in production, it has been decided that persons who have been sent by enterprises, collective farms, state farms, institutions and organizations to receive instruction in specialities corresponding to the nature of their work and who have passed the entrance examinations will be given priority consideration.

In order to improve the practical training of future specialists, a system has been worked out for assigning institutions and enterprises to higher educational institutions and secondary technical schools as permanent bases where students and pupils can receive practical training.

Faculties for raising the qualifications of teachers at higher schools will be set up in universities and other higher educational institutions that have the most qualified teaching personnel and modern laboratory facilities.

For the purpose of raising the qualifications of teachers of educational disciplines at universities and teacher training institutes, higher educational courses will be organized on a permanent basis in 1967 under the auspices of the Academy of Pedagogical Sciences of the USSR.

Beginning in 1967, teachers of specialized disciplines of higher educational institutions will go through a training course at outstanding industrial and agricultural enterprises and

leading higher schools and scientific research organizations; they may continue or temporarily discontinue their work in higher educational institutions while attending these courses.

The heads of enterprises, higher educational institutions and scientific research organizations are obliged to accept teachers from higher educational institutions for the period of training and to create the necessary conditions for them to become acquainted with technology, modern equipment, and the economics and organization of production.

The Ministry of Higher and Secondary Specialized Education of the USSR has been authorized to set up, at major day higher educational institutions, faculties for raising the qualifications of teachers from secondary specialized educational institutions.

The Ministry of Higher and Secondary Specialized Education of the USSR, together with the councils of ministers of the union republics, the Academy of Sciences of the USSR, and the ministries and departments of the USSR, has been asked to take measures designed to attract larger numbers of prominent specialists of the establishments of the Academy of Sciences, branch scientific research institutes, design and construction organizations and industrial enterprises to scientific and pedagogical work in the higher educational institutions as staff or part-time employees.

The central committees of the communist parties of the union republics and the regional and territorial committees of the party have been called upon to provide the Ministry of Higher and Secondary Specialized Education of the USSR with the necessary assistance in this matter.

The Ministry of Higher and Secondary Specialized Education of the USSR has been granted the right to allow, by way of exception, major higher educational institutions to publish scientific and educational-methodological literature and to set up their own presses for this purpose.

The Ministry of Higher and Secondary Specialized Education of the USSR, ministries and departments, and the State Committee of the USSR Council of Ministers on Science and Technology have been instructed to provide, in planning scientific and research activities, for the participation of higher educational institutions in carrying out scientific research under contracts with enterprises and establishments and to allocate the necessary material, technical and financial means for that purpose.

The Ministry of Higher and Secondary Specialized Education of the USSR is to provide additional professors and instructors and auxiliary teaching personnel to twenty-five of the country's higher educational institutions engaged in scientific research of important national economic significance, the number of additional personnel to depend on the volume of the research carried out. The intention here is to partially reduce the teaching load of scholars participating in scientific research.

It is also planned to award bonuses from the resources of the centralized fund of ministries and departments to professors and instructors of higher educational institutions for the creation and introduction of new technology, irrespective of the agencies to which the institutions are subordinated. With a view to the further development of scientific research activity and the improvement of the educational process, sectors of higher educational institutions have been granted the right to use 75 percent of the net income derived from scientific research carried out under contracts for the purpose of expanding and strengthening the material and technical facilities of those institutions. This is to be over and above the allocations provided in the capital investment plans.

The ministries and departments of the USSR, with the agreement of the State Planning Committee of the USSR, and the ministries and departments of the republics, with the agreement of the state planning committees of the union republics, have been granted the right to allocate capital investments up to an amount of 2.5 million rubles per year for each ministry and department to higher educational institutions

for the construction of buildings and the acquisition of educational and scientific equipment. The Ministry of Higher and Secondary Specialized Education of the USSR has been asked to develop and implement measures to involve large numbers of students in scientific research activity under the guidance of professors and instructors of higher educational institutions and scientific personnel of scientific research institutes, factory laboratories, and experimental agricultural stations.

Up to 300 medals will be awarded yearly to students for achievements in scientific research work.

It has been decided that secondary specialized educational institutions will be built and equipped through capital investments allocated for production construction to the ministries and departments for which specialists are being trained in these educational institutions.

A number of measures have been outlined to improve the planning of the training and distribution of young specialists, as well as to provide higher educational institutions with special educational and scientific equipment and to enhance the role of the Ministry of Higher and Secondary Specialized Education in this matter.

The Ministry of Higher and Secondary Specialized Education of the USSR has been entrusted with the task of formulating draft regulations on the higher and secondary specialized educational institutions that will provide for a further democratization of the activities of such institutions, increased rights for their directors, and greater independence in deciding educational, scientific and economic questions, as well as greater initiative and increased participation on the part of civic organizations of students and pupils in the work of improving the educational process, ideological and political upbringing, and the provision of cultural and everyday services for students and pupils.

* * *

Izvestia, August 14, 1966

M. Anuchin

IS TUTELAGE NEEDED IN MATURITY?

The new system for managing the economy, as developed by the party, has also met with the liveliest response in the higher educational institutions. They are advancing proposals to improve the administration of higher education with increasing persistence. There are good grounds for this. The higher educational institutions presently do not have the right to make independent decisions on numerous matters pertaining to education, research, economic management. For example, they cannot invite a prominent specialist or scientist from industry to one of their departments while he holds another position. They cannot independently reinstate a student who, by good work in production or excellent service in the Soviet Army, has won the right to continue his education in a higher school. Many similar examples might be cited. Professor Iu. A. Zhdanov, Rector of Rostov University, has specifically written on this, and with full justice, in his article "The Higher Educational Institution: Responsibilities and Rights" [Vysshaia shkola: otvetstvennost' i prava] (Izvestia,

1966, No. 56).

Excessive limitation of the rights of universities and institutes overloads the staffs of the agencies administering them with numerous and often petty questions and creates annoying procrastination in resolving these questions. For example, the head of one of the main administrations in the ministry of the Russian Federation, Professor V. G. Shorin, instead of dealing with truly major problems of fundamental importance, is compelled to give the bulk of his time to questions that could be handled successfully by the rectors themselves, and to going over thousands of papers, 90 percent of which could be handled locally in all their aspects.

The insufficient independence of the higher educational institutions has a negative effect upon the quality of the training of specialists. The curriculums and syllabuses of the higher educational institutions are, as a rule, overly standardized. The point is that the staff of the Ministry of Higher and Secondary Specialized Education of the USSR cannot, no matter how much they wish to, take account of the distinctive features of the numerous specialties, not to speak of the special features of the individual

---

The author is Chief of the Bureau of Science and Culture, USSR Committee for Popular Control.

higher school and, in some cases, even of departments. Naturally, it would be wrong to deny the need for model curriculums and syllabuses. However, we must not permit them to prevent higher educational institutions from manifesting individuality in the training of specialists. After all, we often speak of the scientific "school" that a particular scholar has founded. The training of personnel is also a creative matter, and there can be no doubt that the collectives of scholar-teachers have the right to create their own schools for the preparation of specialists.

Production and science can only benefit from the fact that young engineers of the same specialty but from different higher schools will, while having the necessary range of knowledge, show distinctive differences. The head of one design bureau has said, for example, that he hires young specialists in radio engineering not only from the Moscow Institute of Energetics but also from the Moscow (Bauman) Higher School of Technology. The former are distinguished for their basic knowledge in the electrical engineering disciplines, while the latter traditionally have good training in design. And when they work together, they supplement each other and resolve more intelligently the problems confronting them, and they themselves grow more rapidly.

It should also be borne in mind that the higher educational institutions most often provide personnel primarily for a small number of branches of the economy, and in many cases they regularly send their graduates to particular large enterprises. As a consequence, firm ties are established that are strengthened by joint scientific investigations and the participation of production personnel in the educational process. These ties enable the enterprises to arrive at informed judgments with respect to the level of specialist training at particular higher institutions. However, under the existing state of things, it is rather difficult for the institutes to carry out proposals from enterprises for improving the training of personnel.

It should be stated that a number of large higher educational institutions have been granted the right to work in accordance with individual curriculums. But in reality this is only a formal right, since the majority of disciplines in these curriculums are regulated by the Ministry of Higher and Secondary Specialized Education of the USSR. It seems to us that there is nothing to fear in transferring, even if at first only to our leading higher schools, the drafting of the basic documents defining the educational process. Many of them have decades, and some have centuries, of experience in training highly qualified specialists. The personnel of these institutions jealously protect the honor of their "trademark" and seek unceasingly to improve the quality of their "product." Such institutions might be given state certificates testifying to their right to train specialists on an independent basis. Naturally, this right should not be granted in perpetuity. If a higher educational institution loses its good traditions, it should also lose the rights it has been granted.

It may be objected that there is no need for this, and that the ministry, by involving a large number of prominent scholars in the work of the scientific-methods councils, has provided the opportunity for solving, in the best possible way, the questions involved in drafting syllabuses and curriculums. But it must be borne in mind that these councils are advisory bodies. Moreover, they by no means always take into consideration the need for the entire range of disciplines and they fail to consider the special characteristics of the higher school scientific collectives. Consider, for example, the scientific-methods councils for the individual disciplines. As a rule, they concern themselves with improving the training of students only in "their own" fields of knowledge. It is no accident that most of them demand an increase in the volume of "their own" courses. Essentially, they are not very disturbed about how this will affect the training of the specialist in another field of science.

These problems would be resolved differently by a meeting of all the scholars responsible for training a specialist. I have in mind the academic council of the higher institution. It has no interest in expanding certain courses at the expense of others. There is no need to fear, for example, that the academic council of a technical institute will thoughtlessly make a sharp cut in the number of hours given to mathematics or physics. However, it would not under any circumstances permit the classical engineering disciplines underlying the training of mechanical engineers for machine building to become the general-engineering basis for the training, say, of technologists for the public catering industry. But this was literally the situation until very recently.

The scientific-methods councils of the USSR-wide ministry are needed; there is much work for them to do, but chiefly in another direction. For example, people have been discussing for many years — and not in our country alone — the need to revise the content of the cycle of general-scientific disciplines in the higher technical schools (physics, chemistry, mathematics, theoretical mechanics, etc.). It is unanimously agreed that they are inadequately related to the special disciplines, and that the data presented require serious updating. The scientific-methods councils could do much, particularly, to improve the methods of instruction in these disciplines, as well as the content and quality of the textbooks. One might name numerous other basic questions with which they should concern themselves.

A serious expansion of the rights of the professors and other faculty members would require a reorganization of the system of higher school administration. In order to create conditions under which scholars can participate most actively in determining the direction of development of a higher educational institution, it would seem necessary to limit somewhat the undivided authority [edinonachalie] of the rector. The academic council should be given the right to choose a rector for a fixed term and to approve the principal indices for the functioning of the institution. The rector should be required to report to the council on the fulfillment of these indices.

The elimination of unnecessary limitations upon the rights of the higher educational institutions will compel them to do a great deal of intensive work on matters that the ministry now handles, and it will increase the responsibility borne by the higher schools for the quality of the training of specialists. This criterion is now becoming the most important one in evaluating the work of the educational institution. The higher school must understand clearly that enterprises will not go on forever accepting their graduates indiscriminately, as they do today because of the shortage of specialists with diplomas. It is appropriate to say that this shortage is today an artificial product in many cases, inasmuch as the staff schedules of enterprises and organizations usually specify an excessively large number of engineering positions. Much has already been said about the reasons for this, and everyone knows them. Under the new economic conditions for the operation of enterprises, these causes will be eliminated. Then the higher educational institutions that have not grown accustomed to making decisions on their own will find themselves in a very difficult position in the competition to graduate highly qualified personnel.

Naturally, the granting of broad rights to the higher educational institutions in the training of specialists is not a simple matter; it must be effectuated gradually, starting with the most qualified higher school collectives. At first this should take the form of an experiment, and this will clear up all the things that it is impossible to anticipate beforehand. The sooner we proceed to the solution of this problem, the less painful will be the shift to more rational methods of administering the higher school.

Enlargement of the rights of the higher educational institutions will not at all signify that the role of the USSR Ministry of Higher and Secondary Specialized Education will be denigrated. The elaboration of proposals to develop the network of higher schools, the planning of the training of specialists, financing, capital investment, the organization of supplies of materials and equipment, the elaboration of the principal USSR-wide statutes and rules on the functioning of the higher educational institutions — all these questions will have to be settled by a state agency. The ministry should become something on the order of an academic council for the country's higher educational institutions; it should decide the fundamental questions of instruction, research, and character-building in the higher schools. It is very important to establish, as an adjunct to it, a highly competent inspection system that would make a systematic and thorough analysis of the functioning of the higher educational institutions and would monitor the execution of party and state directives.

I should like to pose one more question related to improving the system of guidance to the country's higher educational institutions. As a consequence of the reorganization carried out in 1959, the USSR-wide ministry found itself isolated from the higher institutions and removed from the resolution of a number of the most important questions in higher education. Its work was limited essentially to questions of methodology.

The agencies established at that time in the union republics to administer the higher schools in most cases manage a small number of institutions, often of the most diverse nature. Consider the Armenian SSR, for example. There are only nine institutions under the Ministry of Higher and Secondary Specialized Education of that republic, among them the university, the polytechnical institute, the conservatory, the arts and theater institute, the physical education institute, and four teacher training institutes.

Prior to the reorganization, only the first two in this list fell within the system of the USSR Ministry of Higher and Secondary Specialized Education. To establish a republic-wide ministry just to direct these two institutions was inconvenient. And therefore another seven were "thrown in" from other ministries. But even this step produces little of value. For in so small a group of highly diverse institutions it is virtually impossible for there to be a creative exchange of experience in the realms of teaching and character-building. And the Armenian case is no exception.

In a number of cases the republic-wide agencies resolve problems of higher school life not from the standpoint of the interests of the country as a whole, but in terms of "their own" local interests. As a consequence, the organization of the training of specialists is greatly complicated, as is cooperation in this work among the republics, the exchange of experience, the exchange of scholars, the training of teaching and research personnel, etc. Moreover, the reorganization roughly doubled the number of people employed in the agencies guiding the higher schools, and the cost of maintaining the apparatus has more than doubled.

The training of specialists in our higher educational institutions is a matter of importance to the entire state. Therefore, in our opinion, the continued existence of the majority of republic-wide agencies for the management of the higher educational institutions is not justified in any way. It only exacerbates the shortcomings in the organization and quality of specialist training. Reestablishment of direct connections between the USSR-wide Ministry of Higher and Secondary Specialized Education and the higher schools is dictated by the interests of further improvement in the training of specialists for the national economy.

* * *

Vestnik vysshei shkoly, 1965, No. 7

M. N. Rutkevich

WHY A STUDENT DOES NOT ARRIVE AT THE "FINISH"

In recent years a significant increase in student dropouts has been observed in the higher school. The causes of this phenomenon should be studied, and such a study has already been initiated: last year the RSFSR Ministry of Higher and Secondary Specialized Education instructed the sociological laboratories of the Moscow, Leningrad, and Urals universities to investigate this problem.

We in Sverdlovsk began with Urals University and then, having elaborated a definite methodology, studied dropouts and the reasons for them in all the higher educational institutions of this city, which is one of the most important higher educational centers of the nation. The statistical reports of the higher schools from the 1958/59 to the 1963/64 school year were subjected to analysis; the chancellors' orders on the dismissal of students and their transfer to other higher educational institutions and from one form of instruction to another, the summary records on student progress, and the data of the admission committees on the composition of the

students enrolled in the first year were analyzed; and, where it was possible, the personal affairs of the dismissed students were also studied. Personnel from the sociological laboratory talked with vice-chancellors, deans, and other workers at the higher educational institutions. In June the research results were discussed in the bureau of the Sverdlovsk City Committee of the CPSU, which recommended to the higher schools that they discuss the problem of dropouts at council meetings. General recommendations were also given on how to correct the situation which had developed.

Before relating the results of our research, let us make several preliminary remarks. The information obtained by us suffers from very substantial shortcomings and problems, for if the number of students leaving the higher educational institutions is recorded exactly, the actual reasons for dropouts are, for the most part, not established. The causes for dismissal indicated in the orders ("at their own request," "failure to attend the sessions," and so forth) are secondary in relation to the true causes compelling the students to leave the higher school. "The percentage of dropouts," mentioned further on, represents the ratio of the

---

The author is a Doctor of Philosophical Sciences and a Professor at the Urals (M. Gorky) State University.

152

number of students dismissed during the school year to the number being taught on September 1. In the case of a number of higher schools, we were able to compare the number of students who had completed instruction with the number of those who had been admitted to the school a corresponding number of years before. Naturally, only a small part of the statistical data obtained is cited in the article.

The Growth of Dropouts

The total number of students who have dropped out of the day divisions of the Sverdlovsk higher educational institutions during the six years constitutes a very impressive figure — 8,319. This is almost as many as are now studying in the day division of the city's largest higher school — the Polytechnical Institute. If one compares the percentage of dropouts by years, one observes an upward tendency: in the 1958/59 school year it was 4.6%, and in the 1962/63 year it was already 7.4%. Only in the 1963/64 school year did the dropouts decrease a little — to 7%. The largest percentage of dropouts is observed in the technical higher schools — the Institute of Railway Transport Engineers (9.8%), the Forestry Technical Institute (10.2%), the Mining Institute (6.3%) — and also in the natural science departments of the University and the Teacher Training Institute and in the Agricultural Institute (7.5%).

The average over the six years is 5.3% per year. This means that over five years (the average term of instruction) it will be 26.5%, i.e., more than a fourth of the students admitted. If the dropouts remain at the level of the last two years (7.0-7.5%), this means that over five years, 35-37% of all the students, i.e., more than a third of those admitted, will drop out. And if the present level of dropouts among future forestry and railway transport personnel is maintained, half of the students will drop out over a five-year period!

The correctness of these conclusions can be corroborated if one applies another method of calculation — a comparison of the indices con-

cerning graduates and students admitted. A comparison of the lists of students in the present fifth-year class of the University with lists of persons who were admitted five years ago revealed that, of the number admitted to the day division in the autumn of 1960, more than half (253 students of 483) have left at the present time. There is no question that some of those who have left are receiving a higher education either in the evening or correspondence divisions or in other higher educational institutions. But each of these cases almost always means certain additional difficulties, prolongation of the term of instruction, and so forth. Roughly speaking, of 10 students who entered the University to study full time five years ago, 8 persons are receiving diplomas, but only 5 are completing the whole course of instruction on time, and 3 are added "along the way" — students who have entered from evening and correspondence divisions and from other higher schools, and also students who have prolonged the term of instruction. And in some technical higher schools in the city, there are half as many graduates as there were students admitted.

The Basic Reasons for Dropouts

What are the reasons for such a significant number of dropouts and — mainly — for the upward tendency in recent years?

In all the city's higher schools (except the Medical Institute), lack of proficiency [neuspevaemost'] occupies first place among the reasons for dismissal (on an average, 36.6% of those dismissed). In fact, however, the role of "lack of proficiency" is significantly higher than the records indicate. For example, such reasons as "failure to attend sessions" and "omission of lessons" are essentially very close to "lack of proficiency." If we combine all these three columns (in the tables we compiled), we get a group of students who were unable (for one reason or another of a deeper nature) to cope with the difficulties of mastering a science in a higher school. Over the course of six years, these students constituted about half of all those who were dismissed from Sverdlovsk's higher educational institutions. And the more "difficult" the higher school, the more significant was the role of these factors. In the technical higher schools, 55% of all the students who left were obliged to abandon their studies for these reasons.

But "lack of proficiency" itself demands explanation. The collected data indicate that inadequate preparation on the part of students entering the higher schools is the main cause of dropouts due to "lack of proficiency" and, thereby, of dropouts in general. More than that, the results of the entrance examinations and lessons in the first year testify that this preparation has deteriorated in recent years.

What produced the deterioration? We will indicate two causes. In the first place, the changes in the system of admissions, whereby privileges were granted to all persons who have done two years of production work. For the so-called "stazhniks," i.e., yesterday's students who have worked in production, these two years simply mean a break in the time between completing school and entering a higher educational institution. Much is effaced in two years, and the mind loses the habit of daily training. Another variation of "stazhniks" are the young people who left the 8th and 9th grades, began working and, at the same time, studied in the schools for working youth. These conditions are not easy, and the knowledge acquired in these schools is generally not on as high a level as that given in the regular school.

As an illustration, let us cite the results of the entrance examinations in mathematics at the Polytechnical Institute in 1963 and 1964. The percentage of unsatisfactory grades received in 1963 on the written examination in this subject constituted 23.5% among the graduates of the secondary schools, and 43.9% among the graduates of the schools for working youth; in the oral examinations, the percentages were 8.9% and 31.3%, respectively. The next year the respective figures were: 28.9% - 60.2% and 6.6% - 14.9%. However, for many "production workers" who received even a "3" on the examination, their level of knowledge turned out

to be sufficient for them to be admitted to a higher educational institution, under preferential conditions, but not sufficient for them to hold their own in the school later on.

From 1958, up to 80% of "production workers" were enrolled in the Sverdlovsk higher educational institutions, when a "3" was sufficient (in almost all specialties) for admission. It is true that in subsequent years, when it became evident that the level of knowledge of the entering students was becoming lower in the higher schools, the proportion of "production workers" accepted for full-time study declined somewhat, but even in 1964 it amounted to 52.8%.

Meanwhile, it is possible to judge the differences in the level of preparation of the two basic categories of people admitted — "production workers" and "students" — just by the following facts. Of those who entered the University in 1964, 45.6% of the "production workers" and 22.7% of the "students" received unsatisfactory marks on the entrance examinations in mathematics; of the number of persons sent to the Forestry Technical Institute by the enterprises in 1963, only 48.3% passed the entrance examinations. The difference in preparation of persons in these two categories is usually compounded by a number of "age factors" (for example, the presence of a family), which increase the dropouts among student-"production-workers." For example, of the 513 persons accepted into the University in 1962 (300 "production workers" and 213 "students"), 330 persons, among whom 171 were former "production workers" and 159 were former "students," studied in the third-year class in 1965. Thus, in just two and a half years, 129 of the 300 (43%) "production workers" left; the dropouts are also significant among the "students," but still they are far less — 25%.

Work in accordance with one's future specialty for two or more years helps the future engineer and agronomist, and this should have an effect on the entrance examinations and be taken into consideration in admitting students. But it is well known that it is rare for there to be a correspondence between a specialty acquired before entry into the higher educational

154

institution and the profile of the department (when the student enters into full-time studies), and that production service, in the majority of cases, has turned out not to be a supplementary means of mastering the future specialty, but a means of studying in a higher school under reduced demands. The corrections introduced into the rules for admission in 1965 repaired the situation to a certain extent; it seems to us that they should be still further improved next year.

The second cause is defects in the reorganization of the secondary school, which attempted to give the students, simultaneously, full-valued knowledge of the basic sciences and vocational and technical training.

It appears that production training in the upper grades of the secondary school should not be vocational in nature, for polytechnicalization and professionalization of the school are not one and the same thing. A survey of schools in one of the Sverdlovsk districts — Ordzhonikidzevskii — showed that approximately 10% of those who finished the 11th grade in these schools went to work in the specialty acquired in school. Consequently, for 90% of the students the vocational training turned out to be a useless waste of time and, in addition, it had a negative effect on the students' knowledge of mathematics, physics, languages, and so forth.

The first two years are the most difficult of all. Three out of four students who drop out of the University, the Mining Institute, and the Forestry Technical Institute do so in the course of the first two years of study. In the railway institute, this index is still more striking: 9 out of 10. There is no doubt that the higher school should share the responsibility for these figures with the secondary school, which was unable to prepare the youths for instruction in the higher educational institution.

The physics and mathematics disciplines cause the most "unpleasantness." For the physicists at the University, the mathematics disciplines give 41% of the unsatisfactory marks; for chemists — 36%, and for mathematicians themselves — 95.5%. As regards philologists, language and literature "are guilty" of more than half the "unsatisfactory marks."

This testifies, in our view, to an inadequately motivated choice of department and, consequently, to the fact that, upon entering an institution of higher education, many young persons do not succeed in developing an interest precisely in their given field of knowledge. We suggest that specialization in the 9th and 10th grades of the secondary school according to three basic profiles — engineering, physics and mathematics; biology, medicine and agriculture; and the humanities — would accelerate the formation of interests and would help us to select, for the higher schools, people who have some erudition in a given field. The advisability of such specialization is clearly evident in the example of the Urals Conservatory, which admits a significant portion of the graduates of music schools; the graduates of the music schools do not figure among the students who are dismissed from the Conservatory because of lack of proficiency.

It is especially necessary to speak about the persons sent by the enterprises. The number of such students grows with each year. In the Polytechnical Institute they comprise almost a fifth of those admitted, and in the railway institute — up to a third. The higher schools are very interested in this category of students, since the nature of their work generally corresponds to the profile of the departments. However, at the plants, unfortunately, the selection of candidates to send to the higher educational institutions is far from always approached in a thoughtful way. The admission requirements for this category of persons entering the higher schools are made easier: it is enough to pass the examinations even with a "3." The rules for distributing stipends do not stimulate high achievement either: it is possible to fail a certain subject in the examination, but as soon as one retakes it the stipend is restored.

Living conditions are an important factor in determining dropouts. According to our calculations, this factor, in its so-called direct form, accounts for approximately 12% of the total number of abandoned student desks in Sverdlovsk. One must take into consideration that living conditions often are also the cause of "lack of proficiency," "failure to attend sessions," and so forth, so that the total significance of this factor is somewhat greater. Housing conditions have a negative influence on the material aspect of student life. On March 1, 1965, the places in student hostels provided for the Sverdlovsk institutions of higher education constituted, on the average, 77.8% of the number of applications made for permission to live in a hostel. Approximately one-fourth of the out-of-town students found accommodations in private apartments, where the living conditions, as a rule, were worse than in the hostels.

A rather large proportion of the dropouts are students transferring to other higher schools: in the schools of our city, over the past six years, this proportion has constituted 12.9%. In addition to cases in which the family moves to another city, there are other reasons for transfers. Quite a number of youths try to get into any higher educational institution at all, regardless of its type (just as long as they pass the entrance examinations), in the hope of transferring subsequently. Precisely this cause "operates" to a large extent in the Teacher Training Institute (its share among the reasons for dropouts is 23.3%), since there is usually less competition here. In the Medical Institute, 35% of the "dropouts" move to another city. In particular, many students from the southern and western districts, where it is more difficult to enter the medical institutes of higher education, move from their previous place of residence.

The so-called extension-correspondence system of instruction for persons who entered the higher school without a period of production work played a large role in the increase of dropouts in the technical institutes. Work in a plant, mine or timber industry enterprise for the first-year student who experienced difficulty in mastering the institute's school material, especially in physics, mathematics or chemistry, had the result that many were compelled to leave the institute either because of "lack of proficiency" or "at their own request."

In all of Sverdlovsk's institutions of higher education, with the exception of the railway

institute, the general causes of dropouts are compounded by a lag in the development of material facilities: shortage of school buildings, student hostels, and housing for teachers. All this worsens the students' study conditions and does not permit the schools to create stable staffs of qualified teachers; the latter often move to other cities where they are given comfortable quarters. As a result, the extent to which qualified cadres are provided for the city's institutions of higher education is below the average for the RSFSR.

That is how matters stand with dropouts among students who are studying on a full-time basis, i.e., among those who are in the most favorable conditions for receiving a higher education. But there are still more dropouts among those studying while continuing their production work.

Correspondence and Evening Students

In the 1963/64 school year, 5,024 and 27,299 persons, respectively, studied in the evening and correspondence divisions of Sverdlovsk's institutions of higher education, i.e., a larger total than in the day divisions. Whereas in the 1958/59 school year 62.6% of the students studied in the day divisions and 37.4% were enrolled in the divisions for employed students (evening and correspondence together), in the 1963/64 school year the ratio had become 44.6% and 55.4%. Approximately the same situation exists in the country as a whole. As is known, the numerical relationship between those studying in the higher school on a full-time basis and those studying while they work in production has continuously changed in recent years in favor of the latter. An especially great leap occurred in the last two years.

Evening divisions now exist in almost all the city's institutions of higher education, but these divisions either have only begun to graduate students or else have not graduated any as yet. Dropouts among evening students are great — they constitute an average of 14.3% per year — and show no tendency to decrease. Such a yearly dropout, under a six-year term of instruction, means that approximately 40% of the students entering a higher school will complete their studies. Here is an example. In 1958, 33 persons entered the evening division of the Mechanics and Mathematics Department of the University. Eighteen persons left during the first year and 7 in the second; there were no dropouts in the third, 3 in the fourth, and 1 in the fifth. Four persons out of 33, i.e., 12%, completed the university course within the prescribed term in 1964. A total of 7 evening students received diplomas in 1964 in this department, inasmuch as 3 students who had transferred to the evening division or who had prolonged the term of instruction were "added" to the 4. Of 38 physics students who were admitted in 1958, 4 received diplomas in 1964; of 41 history students, 5 received diplomas. In all the evening departments of the University, except the Economics Department, the picture is approximately the same: one student in 8 or even 10 who enter completes his education in the prescribed term. In the final year, in which specialization occurs, it is often the case that lessons are conducted with 3 to 5 students.

Distinctions between the higher educational institutions with respect to the size of the dropout of evening students are great, but the reasons for the distinctions here are different than in the day divisions. The situation is better in those institutions where, in the main, the persons accepted work in the given or a related specialty. In this respect the University turns out to be in the most unfavorable position (the percentage of dropouts is 18.7), excluding the Chemistry Department: more than half the students in this department work in scientific research institutes and in enterprises of the chemical industry. And the large dropout in the evening division of the Mechanics and Mathematics Department is conditioned not only by the difficulties involved in studying disciplines of the mathematics cycle, but also by the fact that almost none of the evening students are working in the field.

The colossal "losses" among evening students in the technical institutes of higher educa-

tion (from 11.9 to 15.6% a year) are explained by the difficulties encountered in combining studies with work in a plant, factory, or on a railroad. In addition, the poor preparation in the schools with respect to the physics and mathematics disciplines, which are basic in the higher technical schools, has its effect here.

One cannot fail to note yet another factor which substantially influences the departure of evening students from the higher school — the state of school discipline. For example, in the evening division of the University in the second semester of the past year, almost half the lessons were skipped by the students. As a rule, the public organizations of the enterprises and institutions exercise poor control over their workers' studies.

Correspondence divisions exist in all the city's institutions of higher education, except the Medical Institute. The number of correspondence students has doubled during the six-year period. There are almost as many dropouts in the correspondence divisions as in the evening divisions (12.7% per year, on the average). Less than half the correspondence students who enter a higher educational institution complete their studies, and many of those take an extra year or two or more to do so. In the University almost half of the correspondence students prolong their terms of instruction, and some of them study for a period of nine years.

The reasons for this phenomenon among those studying while remaining on their jobs are very diverse. The main ones (according to the formulations of the orders) are these: "lack of proficiency," "skipping lessons" and "transfer to another institution of higher education." Thus, the reasons for evening-student dropouts in all the city's higher schools during the six-year period are distributed in the following way: lack of proficiency — 44.9%, failure to attend sessions and discontinuance of lessons — 17.5%, transfer to another higher educational institution — 9.2%, and other reasons — 28.4%. Among the correspondence students, the respective figures are: 45.3, 15.9, 19.9, and 18.9%.

Consequently, lack of proficiency and the causes directly related to it (failure to attend sessions, discontinuance of lessons) account for 70% of the dropouts in the evening division and more than 60% in the correspondence division.

What are the factors which compel those studying without leave from production to capitulate before the difficulties of combining work with studies?

The first such factor is the absence of a genuine competition for admission to the higher educational institution. At first glance there is competition, since there are generally many more applications than openings. But after the entrance examinations it is revealed that the number of persons who passed them, even with a "3," is equal to the number of openings or surpasses it very insignificantly. When, for example, the entrance examinations were completed in 1964 in the evening division of the University, there was no longer any competition. The situation was the same in the evening and correspondence divisions of the Institute of Railway Transport Engineers, although initially 425 applications were received for the 120 openings.

The second factor is the difficulties involved in combining studies with work, which are well known. Not all the students who undertake to study without giving up their production work clearly visualize the difficulties which await them.

Finally, these basic difficulties are aggravated by a number of circumstances, in particular, by shortcomings in the educational and methodological literature. We believe that the provision of such literature to the correspondence students has worsened since the centralization of its publication.

Cases of dismissal because of lack of proficiency and non-attendance at sessions could have been significantly less if the enterprises always gave the correspondence students time to get to sessions. The existence of a discrepancy between the work the student does and the profile of his department also plays a negative role here: the enterprises show more concern for those who raise their qualifications in accordance with the nature of their work in production. For example, about 40% of the correspondence students in the Mining Institute are persons who are working in mining enterprises, and the dropouts among them are fewer than in the other higher educational institutions in the city: over the six years, an average of 6.3% of the students in the division left.

The frequent alteration of curriculums also has a negative effect on the progress of evening and correspondence students: for students lagging behind in their studies (and there are quite a few of them here), this means passing additional examinations and tests; they are obligated to complete their instruction according to the curriculum of the group with which they approach the completion of their higher education.

One should speak separately of the "mobility" of students. It is great. Here are three figures: during the period under consideration, in all the city's institutions of higher education, 1.8% of the students transferred from the regular form of instruction to other forms, 4.3% transferred from evening divisions, and 0.7% shifted from correspondence divisions.

The evening students are the most "mobile." The indices of transfers here fluctuate from 8.0% in the University to 0.7% in the Mining Institute. And if we proceed from the average figure, 4.3%, it turns out that 20% of the evening students will transfer to another form of instruction in the course of 5 to 6 years.

Analysis shows that the students who transfer from the day to the correspondence division are, in the main, either lagging behind or experiencing material difficulties; the students who transfer from the evening and correspondence divisions to the available places in the day division entered these divisions "willy-nilly," not having been able to enter the day division immediately; transfer from the evening to the correspondence division is most often connected with a transfer to work in a specialty.

It seems to us that serious changes are generally needed in the system of correspondence and evening instruction. One of these suggests itself: the evening and correspondence divisions should instruct those students, in the main, whose work is related to the specialization of the department. This one change will substantially reduce the turnover of persons who are studying without giving up their work in production.

Conclusions and Recommendations

Many considerations have already been expressed in the course of the article. However, in our view, it is advisable to formulate more systematically the conclusions and recommendations arrived at on the basis of a study of dropouts, since the phenomenon of mass dropouts expresses, in a concentrated way, the basic shortcomings both of the system of admissions and of the system of instruction in the higher school. Let us attempt to do this.

1. A lowering of the level of knowledge of graduates of secondary schools and the presentation of inadequately justified privileges in admissions to all persons with a record of production service negatively affected the composition of students accepted into the higher educational institutions.

The 1965 rules of admission somewhat corrected the situation: separate competitions for production workers and for graduates of the schools are retained, but the number of places for each of these categories of students entering the higher schools will be proportional to the number of applications submitted. In our view, however, the new admission rules do not settle the matter, since even under these conditions the level of knowledge is not the only criterion for the selection of future students. It is evident that it will be necessary to perfect these rules even further.

2. The basic cause for dropouts is the students' lack of proficiency, which, in turn, is explained first of all by the poor preparation of the entering students. The school, especially the evening school, does not always give its graduates knowledge that is sufficient for successful instruction in the higher educational institution. In our view, aside from the already

resolved question of restoring the ten-year term of instruction, it is necessary in the secondary school:

a) to abolish vocational training, which does not have anything in common with polytechnicalization, and thereby to create the conditions for the mastery of knowledge in the fundamentals of the sciences;

b) to authorize (primarily in the large cities, which have greater opportunities for this) specialized [profilirovannoe] instruction in the 9th and 10th grades in accordance with the three basic cycles that were named above. This will promote the formation of definite interests and abilities in students of 15 to 17 years of age and will enable the youth, when entering a higher school, to make a sounder choice of the department in which they will study. Such specialized instruction in the mathematics, music, and language schools is already yielding positive results;

c) to elaborate measures for strengthening the ties between the higher school and the secondary school, in particular, by means of more actively involving professors in the compilation of school curriculums, methods of instruction, and textbooks. (The RSFSR Academy of Pedagogical Sciences has done little in this regard up to the present time.)

3. In 1964, 820,000 persons were accepted into higher educational institutions in the USSR. This is approximately 2.5 times less than the number of persons who completed the general education school and the secondary specialized educational institutions in that year. This disproportion will increase in the future, since an ever greater portion of the youth will receive a full secondary education at the same time as the growth of admissions in the higher educational institutions, which is determined by the country's need for specialists with higher qualifications, will be slowing down. This means that the higher schools can conduct the competition on a broader base and actually select the most capable persons among the youth. At the moment, the actual competition (after passing the examinations) is insignificant. In 1964, for example, it involved on the average

1.3 persons per place in the Sverdlovsk institutions of higher education. In order for the competitive examinations to fulfill their purpose, it is advisable, in our view, to introduce these changes in the system of admissions:

a) to eliminate advantages for production workers in the matter of admission to day divisions if they are not working in their chosen specialty; the additional knowledge acquired by them should, in our view, be expressed in the entrance examinations, but for this it is necessary to assign a greater role in these examinations to the specialization disciplines;

b) to authorize the higher schools to plan for a somewhat larger number of admissions than graduates, including among those accepted "candidates for student status." This will help to some degree to make up for the dropouts and, along with that, will compel all the students to study better and not be lulled by salutary "3's."

4. It is necessary to make more exacting demands on the students' knowledge, especially that of the evening and correspondence students, for only a low level of demands from deans and chancellors can explain the frequent absences from lessons — and not only lectures, but laboratory and seminar sessions as well. Of course, raising the demands will produce a definite rise in dropouts, but if the students are presented with full demands from the first year on, and the measures enumerated above for improving the selection of students are combined with this, then the "loss" can be compensated as early as the end of the first year of instruction and reduced to a minimum in the subsequent years.

5. The absence of stability in the curriculums negatively affects the quality of training of specialists. Despite all the shortcomings of the existing curriculums, it is necessary to give the higher educational institutions the opportunity to work with them for at least a few years, permitting them at times to make reasonable corrections of a more or less partial nature.

Higher education, like any other area of life, demands a certain stability of organizational forms.

6. It appears to be extremely necessary to improve the material and technical facilities of the higher educational institutions, for example, our facilities in Sverdlovsk. From this point of view, the opening of new higher schools is scarcely justified in all cases: it is inadvisable if smaller expenditures will be required to build up the capacities of already existing higher educational institutions of a given type, which have strong cadres.

The problem of the student hostels is especially acute. This problem has not yet been resolved in 8 out of 10 Sverdlovsk institutions of higher education, even though over the last ten years 300,000-400,000 square meters of dwelling space have been constructed in Sverdlovsk each year. The students are prepared to work on the construction of their hostels without compensation. It is completely possible and necessary to construct them in a year or two.

It is also urgent that we solve the problem of expanding the school premises of the Sverdlovsk higher schools: overcrowding has a harmful effect not only on school work, but also on scientific work; lack of space makes it impossible in a number of cases to equip laboratories with modern apparatus.

7. Finally, a heightening of the level of upbringing work with the students should play a most important role in reducing dropouts. When the basic causes of mass dropouts have been removed, the deans and student organizations will be able in real earnest to attend to each student who is thinking of dropping out of the higher school or who is experiencing some sort of difficulty. Naturally, a small percentage of dropouts due to personal reasons is unavoidable, and no one should and no one will keep lazy people, blockheads or morally unscrupulous persons in the higher educational institutions just for the sake of maintaining the contingent of students.

We suggest that the regulations of the higher educational institutions be changed so as to provide for greater participation by student public organizations in the admission of new students, in the establishment of stipends, in the assignment [napravlenie] of graduates to work, in the solution of the problem of dismissal from the higher school, and so forth. Mobilization of the community of the higher educational institution in the struggle to maintain the contingent of students (those who are capable of completing the instruction) is absolutely necessary.

Grade Repeating

Narodnoe obrazovanie, 1965, No. 8

M. Kashin

THE PROBLEM OF GRADE REPEATING

The Third International Polytechnical Seminar of the Socialist Countries was held in the People's Republic of Bulgaria in April of this year. At this seminar, along with the problems of polytechnical education, the problem of the repeating of grades by schoolchildren was discussed.

The exchange of opinions showed that lack of proficiency and the repeating of grades constitute one of the biggest and most complex problems of concern to all the countries participating in the seminar.

Basic attention was given to an examination of the reasons for the repeating of grades and of ways of overcoming it. All the participants in the seminar unanimously expressed the desire to return once more to the given problem at the fourth seminar.

The repeating of grades, as is known, has its roots in the distant past. At one time it was considered a usual, completely natural, and even unavoidable companion of the work of the general education school.

The author is the Deputy Minister of Education of the RSFSR.

In prerevolutionary Tsarist Russia, for example, the repeating of grades attained colossal dimensions; in many school districts it involved 27, 30, and even 40 percent of the students. Actually, a third of the students were left behind each year. And this occurred at a time when there was no universal compulsory instruction in Russia and school dropouts constituted 25 to 30 percent of the students!

Progressive educators of that time understood the perniciousness of the repeating of grades and attempted to raise the question of its curtailment. In practice, however, little was done.

There was also massive repeating of grades in the first period of the development of the Soviet school. The new school acquired, along with the old teachers, the false conviction that the repeating of grades was unavoidable. In 1925, one of the Moscow conferences of school leaders adopted an official resolution on the permissibility of grade repeating within the limit of 25 percent. This percentage was a generally accepted norm in those years.

But the further the Soviet state developed and the more perfected our school became, all the more persistently and sharply was posed the

162

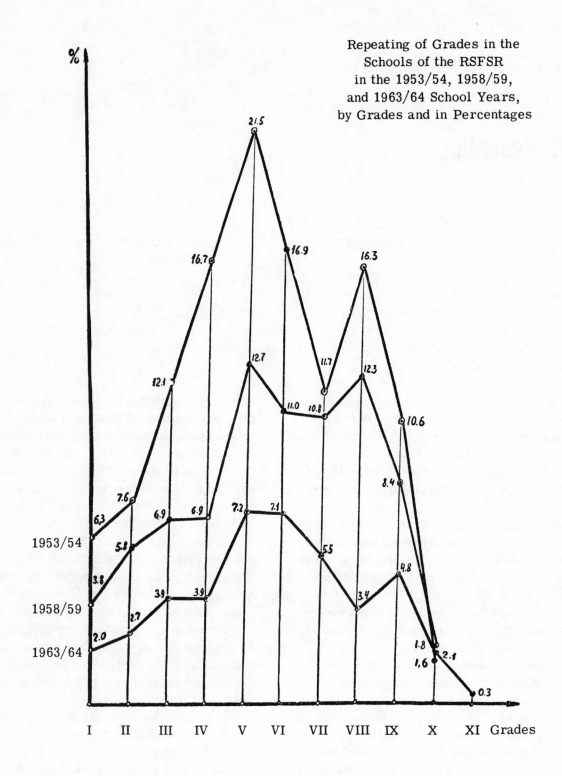

Repeating of Grades in the
Schools of the RSFSR
in the 1953/54, 1958/59,
and 1963/64 School Years,
by Grades and in Percentages

question of the need to overcome the mass-scale repeating of grades. By the end of the thirties it had diminished to 12 percent. However, the Second World War, with all its burdens and misfortunes, had an extremely grave impact on the school. For understandable reasons the quality of instruction declined and, along with this, the repeating of grades increased. In the 1945/46 school year it constituted about 20 percent, i.e., almost every fifth student was left behind for a second year.

As the wounds of the war were healed, along with the strengthening of the material facilities of the schools and the improvement of the pedagogical staffs, the students' progress mounted steadily and the repeating of grades diminished. Here are the indices: in the 1952/53 school year the number of students repeating grades in the RSFSR constituted 14.5 percent, in the 1958/59 school year — 7.6 percent, and in the 1963/64 school year the number of students repeating grades in the schools of the RSFSR amounted to 4.3 percent. Such are the dynamics of the process.

In citing these data, we consider it necessary to emphasize that we do not consider them absolute indices of the state of our students' progress. The percentages of students passing the courses successfully are formed from the evaluations made by the teachers, and, as is known, the subjective factor has no small significance in this. Often different teachers evaluate the same answer from a student in different ways. Moreover, even the same teacher sometimes evaluates essentially identical answers from students in different ways. And the question here is not only of the teacher's sympathies and antipathies; giving a mark is a complex pedagogical act that depends on a whole series of circumstances, of which the teacher's standards probably have the greatest significance. Therefore, great prudence should also be manifested in evaluating the teacher's activity: and in no case is it possible to proceed here solely on the basis of the percentage of students passing.

At the same time, it would be incorrect to nullify the significance of the data on the repeating of grades, to ignore them and not draw

definite conclusions from them. The percentages are easily translated into concrete magnitudes — behind them stand the students and their future.

At first glance, 4.3 percent of repeating students in the RSFSR (for the past year) may not seem such a significant magnitude. But, you know, this is 924,000 (i.e., almost a million!) students. They had to go through the very same grades again.

The repeating of grades causes serious alarm among the personnel in public education and the community. And one can understand why this is so. It inflicts serious moral traumas on many students, engenders in them a lack of confidence in their efforts, and often causes feelings of inferiority and a passive attitude toward life. It inflicts definite economic damage on the state and the family and delays the involvement of young people in the sphere of material production.

It has been firmly established that it is precisely the unsuccessful and repeating students, especially those in the 5th-7th grades, who often cease to study diligently and sometimes even simply give up their studies. Lack of progress and the repeating of grades are the main factors in students dropping out of school. The repeating of grades is a very serious obstacle in the realization of universal eight-year education and, even more so, of secondary education.

It is evident from the data cited that the repeating of grades has been declining gradually in recent years. The question may arise: but is this not due to a lowering of standards with respect to the students' knowledge and a diminution of the quality of instruction? This is a very important question. It constantly agitates us, the more so since in the school's practical work there are quite a few facts testifying to understated demands. Only extensive and systematic observation can give the correct answer.

In recent years the Ministry of Education has annually conducted examinations in the Russian language and mathematics in all 4th-10th grades of 20 to 25 regions. The results of hundreds of thousands of examinations also give us the opportunity to determine not only the quality of knowledge in these two basic school subjects and the nature of the mistakes made by the students, but also the general tendencies toward greater progress which are developing.

The materials obtained from the testing indicate that the diminution of grade repeating does not stem from a lowering of standards with respect to the students' knowledge, but rather that a heightening of the quality of the school's educational and upbringing work lies at the basis of this phenomenon. In those regions in which there is less grade repeating (Lipetsk, Rostov, and others), the quality of the students' examination work is higher. Besides that, the marks for the examination work in many schools turned out to be even somewhat higher than the grades given in the current evaluation of progress.

The examination work and many check-ups give reason to believe that the decline of grade repeating is a natural result of greater skill on the part of the teachers and of the great work conducted by the school together with the family. It is a result of the ever growing attention of the community to the school and of the general upsurge in the well-being and culture of the Soviet people.

Attention to the problem of grade repeating increased markedly after the All-Russian Teachers Congress of 1960. At this congress the remarks of the teachers from Rostov Secondary School No. 1, which had not had repeaters for many years, made a strong impression. After the congress the experience of this school was elucidated in the press, and there began, literally, a pilgrimage of teachers and leaders of schools and public education bodies to School No. 1. They all wanted to be convinced of the possibility of working without grade repeating. This possibility was confirmed simultaneously by the Lipetsk experience, which received wide popularity.

Now thousands of schools — not only primary, but eight-year and secondary schools also — are working with practically no grade repeating. In the Rostov Region, for example, 941 schools (of this number, 70 secondary and 100 eight-year schools) ended their work last year without any students left behind. Now we do not have a single region, territory or autonomous republic in which there are not schools working without repeating students.

Many schools of the union republics have achieved tangible results in overcoming the repeating of grades. This is especially true of the schools in the Ukraine, where the number of students left behind constituted 1.6 percent in the last school year.

While noting the presence of positive results in the work of a great number of schools and, in particular, the lowering of grade repeating in general, one cannot be satisfied with what has been achieved.

The quality of work in many schools is not up to present-day standards. The substantial demands made on the school by the higher and secondary specialized educational institutions are completely just. They oblige us to take more decisive measures to raise the level of the students' preparation.

The problem of lack of proficiency and grade repeating is not only a topical one for our country — it is essentially a universal problem.

At the International Seminar, the representatives of the socialist countries cited convincing data to the effect that in recent years there has been a marked tendency toward the reduction of grade repeating in their countries. In the 1st-8th grades of schools in the Hungarian People's Republic, for example, the repeating of grades in the 1962/63 school year amount to 4.1 percent, and in the secondary schools [gimnazii] — only 1.5 percent in all. In the Czechoslovak Socialist Republic in the same year, the number of students left behind was reduced to 3.4 percent.

This is a completely natural result. It testifies to the great concern that is manifested in the socialist countries for man, for the well-being of the people and its cultural growth, and it shows how much attention is given to the rising generation in countries that are building a new society. Positive results are being derived from the enormous expenditure of funds and effort on the strengthening of the material facilities of the schools, on the preparation of highly qualified staffs, and on the creation of other favorable conditions that contribute to a heightening of the quality of the students' instruction and upbringing.

Methods of Approaching the Problem

It is known that a correct analysis of any complex phenomenon is possible only when it is based on correct methodological positions. A definite ideology always stands behind every scientific theory. This Marxist-Leninist position finds complete confirmation in the treatment of the problem of lack of proficiency and the repeating of grades.

Bourgeois educators, when analyzing the causes of grade repeating, proceed mainly from the "intellectual inferiority" of those students who have to repeat grades, from the presence in them of a supposedly innate inability to master knowledge according to the school program. This invariant hereditary "nature" of man also predetermines, in their opinion, the students' lag in instruction.

Developing this position, many bourgeois psychologists and educators believe that a significant proportion of the children are allotted, by nature, an "average" intellect, while other children are gifted with a "high intellect" or, on the contrary, suffer from intellectual inferiority. Attempts are made to determine a constant proportionality for these three parts. Thus, Louis Cros, in his book School Explosion [Shkol'nyi vzryv] (which was published in 1962 in a 2nd, Paris edition), maintains that among 100 children there are 3-4 very gifted ones and 6-7 deficient [debilov] (intellectually backward) children. The remaining 90 percent are average. Thus, a certain constant ratio between the strong, average, and weak students is established.

In the American schools, at one time, an attempt was even made to establish a norm of excellent, good, average and poor marks in the class, by which the teacher had to be guided. He was directed to maintain the following "scale of symmetrically distributed marks": "5" — 8%, "4" — 21%, "3" — 43%, "2" — 20%, "1" — 8%.

The vicious practice of selecting children with the help of "psychological examinations" and tests is based on this reactionary conception. In the modern English school, all the children, upon completing elementary school at the age of 11, undergo a testing process for the purpose of selection. As a result of this process, 15 percent of the children are directed to privileged "grammar" schools and all the rest go to the so-called "modern secondary school," instruction in which does not give one the right to enter a university. It is characteristic that, as a rule, the children of well-to-do parents fall into the 15 percent category.

Methods based on particularly superficial indices of the type of various tests, and the application of other artificial "psychological" tests without conducting lengthy observations and a comprehensive study of the child's personality, give a very large percentage of mistaken conclusions. It is no accident that some scholars, advanced teachers, writers, and public figures in bourgeois countries severely censure the practice, based on an antiscientific method of determining the children's intellectual worth, of separating students into various types of schools or courses.

The editor of the education section of The New York Times, Dr. Benjamin Fine, on the basis of a six-month study of schools in the USA, wrote a book entitled Our Children Are Cheated [Nashikh detei obmanyvaiut]. In it he says: "The movement for the application of tests to determine intellectual gifts, which is based on an incorrect theory and which leads to the lag of a great number of children, must be assessed as a great fraud. . . . This theory led the methodologists applying it into error; they were stupefied by their own pseudoscientific terminology and methods. It deceived the teachers, who were hypnotized by its false demands and unproven assumptions. It deceived the parents, whose children were offered a second-rate education, adorned with fine phrases about the adaptation of education to the child's abilities. It deluded the entire nation, which received in return for its school taxes a worthless education" [all quotations from non-Russian sources have been retranslated from the Russian — Ed.]. One could cite a large number of such opinions.

In December 1964 a statement made in Parliament by England's Minister of Education, Michael Stuart, was printed in the magazine Educational

Supplement to the Times. He subjected the school system existing in England to criticism and censure. He pointed out that the old system was guided by the theory of innate gifts; as a result of its application the children were divided into fixed groups according to their abilities and sent to different types of schools. "The system of division," he said, "is in error, because it is based on an old view of endowments and proceeds from the idea that intellectual abilities are something innate, something which cannot be enlarged by means of subsequent efforts, and also from the idea that they are sparingly distributed among the population. Neither one of these positions, as we now know, is correct. . . ." Thus spoke the Minister. But he did not introduce any practical proposals.

The selection of students according to testing methods in England gives up to 10 percent of intellectually retarded children from the total child population, which is far higher than the 3 percent provisionally accepted by UNESCO for intellectually retarded of all ages among the population.

Thus, the bankruptcy of the "theory" of innate inabilities, as an explanation of the mass-scale repeating of grades, becomes ever more evident.

Many bourgeois educators believe that the decisive factor in determining proficiency in studies is the social environment in which the student lives.

A work by Walter was published in West Germany in 1959. He asserts that the presence in children of the capabilities for instruction is directly dependent on the social position of their parents. He attempts to prove that 94.6 percent of the children from the higher strata and only 13.6 percent of workers' children are unconditionally and conditionally capable of being instructed in the upper grades of the secondary school. Proceeding from the "theory of the influence of the living standard," the repeating of grades becomes directly dependent on the parents' profession, the material conditions of the family, and the composition of the family. The position was formulated in the Federal Republic of Germany that "the falling social level is proportional to school success."

The antiscientific "theory of two factors" — invariable heredity and social environment — that has been developed by individual bourgeois scholars has a clearly expressed class character and is basically bankrupt. It not only does not reveal the true causes of lack of proficiency and the repeating of grades, but actually confuses the problem and leads one away from correct paths to its solution.

At the end of the twenties and the beginning of the thirties, analogous, deeply fallacious views on lack of proficiency and grade repeating were also widespread in the Soviet Union. It was in these years that the so-called pedology was developed. Proponents of pedology, who uncritically adopted bourgeois views in the West on the "nature" of the child and the methods of its study, inflicted great harm in the matter of the instruction and upbringing of the rising generation, in general, and in the solution of the problem of grade repeating, in particular. With their pseudoscientific research and conclusions, they disarmed the teachers and public education personnel in their struggle against the serious vestiges of the past — against the repeating of grades.

The resolution of the Central Committee of our party, "On Pedologic Distortions in the System of the People's Commissariat of Education" (1936), revealed the reactionary essence of the pseudoscience of pedology and demonstrated the bankruptcy of its conclusions. However, great efforts were required to overcome the harmful consequences of its application.

Are we denying the significance of heredity and the influence of the surrounding environment on the formation of man? No, we are not.

There are many children who from birth suffer from various defects, both physical and intellectual. We have created a network of special schools for children with such types of defects.

Deaf children are placed in certain schools, the hard of hearing in others. There are also schools for blind children and those with poor vision. Special schools are also created for children with serious speech disturbances. Specially trained teachers work in all these schools; with the help of various means, including technical ones, they achieve a great deal in instruction and upbringing. After completing these schools, many young people enter higher educational institutions.

We also have a network of auxiliary schools for mentally retarded children. However, in distinction from the bourgeois countries, we manifest great caution in determining children's intellectual inferiority. A lengthy pedagogical and medical observation of children with symptoms of mental retardation is required.

To establish the degree of mental retardation is a far from simple matter. There are also mistakes made, when children who are completely normal mentally but are weakly developed, or children with serious speech disturbances, are included in this category. The opposite also occurs: a committee will overestimate the capabilities of a child and leave him in a regular school, even though he should be in an auxiliary school. Such mistakes, of course, are undesirable. Therefore, the question of an improved diagnosis of mental retardation is very important, and our defectologists must give it proper attention.

The number of mentally retarded children in our country fluctuates in the various regions of the republic from 0.6 percent to 0.9 percent. The overwhelming majority of them are instructed in special schools, rather than in the regular ones. Therefore, there is no foundation for explaining the mass-scale repeating of grades by the alleged presence of a large number of intellectually inferior children. This is already disproved by the fact that there are thousands of teachers who have been working successfully for many years with the usual composition of students, without keeping any children for a second year.

Advanced teachers are deeply convinced that the absolute majority of children who remain for a second year do not necessarily have to be repeaters. Faith in the child's capacities and in the rich potentialities for his spiritual development is one of the main conditions for overcoming the repeating of grades.

While recognizing the definite significance of innate factors, we believe that instruction and upbringing have decisive significance for the all-round development of students. This is precisely the point of departure for us.

The Causes of Grade Repeating

Data on the repeating of grades in the schools of the RSFSR were cited above. It is not clear from them, however, how the repeaters are distributed among the grades, what the ratio is between repeaters in the city and rural schools, and whether there is a difference in progress between boys and girls. Meanwhile, all these questions are of definite interest.

The number of students remaining a second year is rather different at various stages of school instruction. We have fewer repeaters in the lowest and highest grades. Most of them are in the 5th-7th grades.

The number of repeating students grows beginning with the 1st grade, and reaches its greatest dimensions in the 5th grade. Then its level falls again.

This "curve" is characteristic for all the preceding years. (See the table on p. 19.) In our country, as well as in other countries, the 5th grade attracts attention: it is precisely here that the number of students left behind is especially great. This is apparently due to a number of factors.

In the first place, the child has a shift of teachers. Up to this time the children have studied with one teacher, and now they have several.

In the second place, there is a change in the very content of the material studied — the material is more complex than in the lower grades. Further, the methods of instruction are greatly changed. The inadequate preparation of students by some teachers of the primary grades has its effect. In addition, there are still 5th-grade teachers who manifest, at the very first lessons, excessive strictness and make pedagogically unsubstantiated demands, attempting by this to compel the students to study the given subject diligently (however, they most often achieve the opposite result).

There are also a great number of other causes, among which the teachers' insufficient knowledge of 5th-graders, of their developmental and psychological peculiarities, has great significance.

168

And this, you know, is the initial period of adolescence, which is an especially complicated period in the life of every person!

The pedagogical collectives of schools that have been functioning without failing students correctly give special attention to the 5th grade. It has become the rule in these schools for teachers who will be working in the 5th grade to become acquainted with their future students long before they enter the 5th grade. The teachers attend the lessons in the 4th-grade classes, study the peculiarities of each child, and ascertain his preparedness, studiousness, ability to learn, and much else. It is no accident that the acuteness of the "problem of the 5th grade" is significantly lessened in these schools.

Some of the reasons cited for students falling behind in the 5th grade can also be attributed to the 9th grade (in the past — to the 8th grade, with which the upper stage of the secondary school began). Here the volume and complexity of the material studied acquire still greater significance. In these grades the dependence of subsequent study on the quality of knowledge received earlier is especially strong. And those who did not receive the proper preparation in the 5th-8th grades and, moreover, did not truly master the ability to work independently find themselves in a very difficult situation.

In the better schools all this is taken into consideration by the teachers; and they, least of all, strive "to prove" that the preparation of the students accepted is inadequate, but concentrate their efforts on rendering aid to such students. As a result, they achieve positive results.

All the other grades have their own peculiarities, in particular, the 6th grade, which in our schools also has a large number of repeating students.

The ministry revealed the ratio of grade repeating in the city and rural schools. In all these schools the students study in accordance with common curriculums, syllabuses, and textbooks. Consequently, the volume of material studied is identical. And what are the results?

Study indicates that there is no great difference in the number of students left behind in the schools of the city and the countryside, although the following fact attracts attention: in the lower grades of the rural schools the number of students left behind is somewhat higher than in the city. The somewhat better general development of city children is evidently being expressed; a significantly greater number of them attend kindergartens. Besides that, in the countryside there are still many one- and two-unit primary schools, with a small number of students. In these schools the teacher must handle two and even four grades, and this, of course, makes his work more difficult. As check-ups have shown, the students of these schools are somewhat less prepared. But there are also many rural primary schools in which the students receive very good preparation. The Ministry made a special study of the experience of a number of such schools and gave it a high evaluation.

The question of the ratio of boys and girls among repeating students was also studied. Statistics are not maintained on this question, but the materials obtained from a large number of schools indicate that the proportion of boys among the students left behind for a second year comes to about 70 percent (but this percentage is not the same in different grades). In the 1st and 2nd grades there are no differences — the number of repeating students among boys and girls is generally the same. Beginning with the 3rd grade, however, the predominance of boys among the students having to repeat grades becomes ever more marked. This is particularly manifested in the 5th and 6th grades. In the upper grades there is practically no difference.

Objective data show that there is lack of proficiency in all the school subjects. But the greatest number of student failures, both in our schools and in other countries, are in the native language and mathematics. This can scarcely be explained by any special complexity or difficulty in the curriculum material on these subjects. The explanation is more likely to be that shortcomings or gaps in the students' knowledge become more obvious here than in the other subjects.

Of course, the general data cited are insufficient for an exhaustive definition of the nature and basic causes of grade repeating.

It is necessary to have specific knowledge of the student who is left behind to repeat a grade; we must know the large and small, the obvious and the hardly noticeable conditions and causes which led him to this.

The study conducted by ministry personnel of a large number of repeating students confirms the correctness of the assertion that lack of proficiency is an individual phenomenon as regards its causes.

Some children had to repeat grades because of illnesses that led to a lengthy absence from school lessons. For a part of the students, the reason for failure was the presence of defects in speech, hearing, sight, and intellect. The teachers and parents did not give this the proper attention in time, did not render the student the necessary aid, and did not send him to a special school. The result was that he was left behind for a second year.

When students change schools because their families move to a new place of residence, this has a negative effect on their progress.

Nevertheless, the study showed that these are not the causes of the mass-scale repeating of grades. The main cause is the level of educational and upbringing work in the school. There is convincing proof for this in the fact that many thousands of schools and hundred of thousands of teachers have functioned for a number of years without having to leave students behind for a second year. There are many students in schools where the proper attention is not given to each student, where there is no contact between the school and the family, and where the teachers and leaders of the school continue to assume that the repeating of grades is unavoidable.

We would like to quote the remarkable words of L. N. Tolstoi, concerning the teachers of the school at Yasnaya Polyana: "The teacher never permitted himself to think that the students were to blame for failing — their laziness, playfulness, obtuseness, deafness, being tongue-tied; he knew full well that only he was to blame for the failure, and the teacher attempted to find the remedy for every shortcoming of the student or students. The consequences for the students were that they studied willingly."

It does not follow at all from this that we deny certain objective circumstances, which sometimes lead the student to repeat a grade, or that we underestimate the significance of the conditions under which the school works. One cannot reduce a complex phenomenon, which the repeating of grades is, to a "subjective factor" only. However, the quality of the teacher's work, his skill and his attitude toward his work, and his deep conviction that grade repeating can be eliminated and that any healthy, normal child can study successfully are, nevertheless, of primary significance.

Some Ways of Eliminating the Repeating of Grades

Study shows that the repeating of grades can be prevented not by some one means, but by the whole system of educational and upbringing work of the school and the purposeful and coordinated work of the entire collective of teachers, school leaders, student organizations, and the family.

At the all-Russian scientific and practical conferences of primary-grade teachers held this year (in Rostov-on-Don), the Russian language teachers (in Lipetsk) and the mathematics teachers (in Kazan) comprehensively discussed the means of preventing grade repeating, as applicable to the different grades and school subjects. The materials of these conferences are being published widely in the press, and therefore we can confine ourselves to an examination of only certain of the general ways of eliminating the repeating of grades.

The experience of many schools that are functioning without repeaters convincingly shows that this problem cannot be solved without raising the level of work in the primary grades. The efforts of many public education bodies and schools are therefore aimed at improving the quality of instruction in the primary, lower grades. And definite successes have been achieved in a number of places.

A study of students who were left behind in the primary grades convinces one that the majority of them are children with weak general development. This is precisely what hampers the success of instruction, especially in the 1st grade.

The research of the RSFSR Academy of Pedagogical Sciences, in particular, that conducted by the laboratories of professors L. Zankov and D. El'konin, and also check-ups of the schools testify that many teachers of the primary grades do not give the proper attention to the students' development. A great proportion of the time at lessons is expended on various types of training work and the fulfillment of exercises which do not help to develop the children's powers of observation, speech, or thinking.

Zankov's experimental work, which in recent years has become widely known, shows that if more attention is given precisely to the students' general development in the primary grades, the success of their instruction grows immeasurably. Having reconstructed the system of instruction in the primary grades on this basis, Professor Zankov achieved the result that the students readily mastered the four-year programs of the primary school in three years. At the end of the school year the RSFSR Ministry of Education decided to transfer the students of the experimental 3rd-grade classes in Kalinin directly into the 5th grade. All these 5th-graders successfully advanced to the 6th grade.

This bears witness to the great cognitive potentialities of children. The task is to find the correct approaches to a realization of these potentialities.

In the primary grades, and especially in the upper grades, the timely discovery of gaps in the students' knowledge has great significance in preventing grade repeating. The appearance of a gap is the beginning of falling behind. And if the teacher does not notice it in time, the lag can lead to failure. Gaps in the study of such subjects as mathematics and languages — both native and foreign — have an especially perceptible effect.

Gaps arise for various reasons: absence from lessons, the students' inattentiveness at lessons, superficial fulfillment of homework, inadequate ability to work independently, and so forth.

A rich arsenal of means for discovering gaps in the students' knowledge in time has been accumulated in the course of the schools' work. As is known, the system of oral and written check-ups on the students' knowledge is of paramount importance among them. Their methods have been elaborated in detail.

However, the ordinary, traditional oral questioning of the students and the written work, which take a great deal of time at the lesson, nevertheless do not always give the teacher full assurance that he knows how each student understood and mastered all the problems studied. The feedback, as one says nowadays, is not sufficiently reliable here. Therefore, a search has been going on for some time already for means which, in addition to the existing ones, would help the teacher to determine the students' knowledge quickly and reliably.

Among these means, teaching machines of the different types of "examiners" and "controllers" occupy a definite place. The experiments that we have conducted have yielded rather interesting results. The teachers and the students themselves — which is also very important — quickly determine who has learned the material studied and how. While it is still too early to draw final conclusions, there is no doubt that technical means can play an important role in the teacher's work.

The rationalization and individualization of instruction, with the help of diverse didactic material, acquire ever greater significance in the elimination of gaps and in work with students who are falling behind.

In Moscow, in the Tatar ASSR (Kazan), in Rostov, Lipetsk and a number of other regions, various card-tasks have been employed extensively at lessons, especially in the Russian language and mathematics. Their application makes it possible for the teacher to organize independent work at the lesson so that it is within the grasp of the weak students, helps them to eliminate gaps and, at the same time, cultivates interest in studies and stimulates the development of the strong students, not permitting them to be idle.

This method is highly appraised by teachers and is becoming ever more widespread.

The so-called "Tiumen workbooks" are

receiving broad recognition. The creation of such workbooks is not a simple matter. The ministry organized a special laboratory in Tiumen, which was entrusted with this task. The production of the "Tiumen workbooks" has begun, and they are being tested in many regions of the RSFSR and of other union republics. These workbooks have many merits. They permit us to organize help for the lagging students more effectively. They are also significant in that they free the teacher, in large measure, from the extremely wearisome task of checking the students' work.

But there are also unique "reefs" in the application of the "Tiumen workbooks." The main danger is banality, work according to a stereotyped pattern (since the basis of pedagogical work is creativity). Work is now being conducted in the direction of ensuring that the "Tiumen workbooks" not only do not interfere with the creative principle, but, on the contrary, push the teachers toward conducting different types of creative work.

In recent years we have given especially great attention to the application of technical means in instruction. This task is emphasized in the CPSU Program adopted at the 22nd Party Congress. Educational television and radio programs are given in various cities. Experience in this new field is accumulating. Recently the Board of the Ministry of Education discussed and approved Leningrad's experimental work on this problem.

The educational film and the tape-recorder occupy an ever greater place at the lessons. Linguaphone laboratories are being created for a better study of foreign languages. They significantly increase the students' interest in their studies, save time, permit the teacher to conduct individual work with the students and, consequently, help to raise the effectiveness of the educational process in general and of work with lagging students in particular.

Recently, a great deal of experimental work on the problems of programmed instruction in the school has been developed in a number of places. Much is still unclear and disputable in this area. There was a great deal of hubbub about this supposedly universal method of instruction, and this naturally engendered, along with enthusiasm, a certain distrust and even negative attitudes.

The RSFSR Ministry of Education conducted an all-Russian conference on the problems of programmed instruction in the city of Sverdlovsk. The results achieved so far were summed up at the conference, and the paths for the future elaboration of this problem were defined.

By introducing essential changes in the educational process, programmed instruction permits the students' independent work to be organized more perfectly, greatly individualizes the process of instruction and, with the help of various types of training, achieves greater soundness in the knowledge of all the students and prevents them from falling behind.

It is generally known that the higher the grade, the more strongly expressed is the differentiation of the students' interests, inclinations and cognitive enthusiasms: some of them begin to show a preference for the exact, natural and mathematical subjects; others are attracted by the problems of history, literature, and art. Young people enter a period of independent searching; they want "to find themselves." Unfortunately, these completely natural, psychologically normal phenomena are not always taken into consideration and directed by the teachers, and at times this leads to undesirable phenomena.

At one time the so-called "problem of the physicists and the lyric poets" caused quite a stir among us. To what does the contrasting of the two types sometimes lead? Among some physicists, i.e., those who manifested a special interest in the exact sciences, it came to be considered a sign of "good form" to have a supercilious attitude toward everything related to the humanities. In their turn, "the lyric poets" at times flaunt their "inability" and their lack of desire to study "dry formulas," calculations, and diagrams. These attitudes are also carried over to the corresponding school subjects. As a result, the business ends rather sadly for some of the students: they become numbered among those showing a lack of proficiency and even have to repeat grades.

A strange situation has been created when enthusiasm, this remarkable motive force in the development of man and of his capabilities, becomes an obstacle for the young person in attempting to study successfully in school. Is it possible to avoid this? The experience of the advanced schools shows that it is possible. More than that, a clearly expressed enthusiasm for one or another field of knowledge not only does not lead to one-sided development but, under skillful pedagogical guidance, broadens the interest of the "physicists" in "lyric poetry," and vice versa.

The problem of enthusiasm, of interest in instruction, has the greatest significance in general, and for the prevention of failure in particular. How, but as a loss of interest in education, can one explain one of the causes of grade repeating that is often alluded to by teachers and school leaders — the "unwillingness" of the students to study. It is precisely dry, dull teaching which gives rise to the students' boredom and passivity at the lesson and takes away their willingness to study. That is why the question of the teacher's mastery has now become so important.

When we speak of the teacher's mastery, we necessarily include in this concept his erudition, his knowledge of the subject and of the modern achievements of the science whose foundations he teaches. The children are very sensitive to this; they place a high value on the teacher's knowledge and are proud of the fact that their teacher easily handles the material at the lesson. If the teacher himself is enthusiastic about the science, he can interest and involve his pupils in it. During the training of new teachers and the retraining of those already working, it is necessary to give as much attention as possible to this aspect of the question.

However, the teacher's erudition alone is not enough; his mastery depends to a great extent on how well prepared he is with respect to questions of general pedagogy and psychology. No matter what the teacher's school subject is, he always has to do with a growing, developing personality, and therefore he should know the laws of its development. And these are given

in psychology and pedagogy. As a rule, certain pedagogical mistakes by the teacher lie at the basis of those conflicts which arise at times between the teacher and the students. These mistakes often also engender in the students a hostile attitude toward the teacher, which is transferred to the subject; this can become the cause of failure. A good teacher, in essence, should be a practical psychologist.

But even this is not enough to become an expert teacher. It is necessary to master to perfection the methods of teaching one's subject. Teaching is an art of its own. Can every teacher master it? Some say that teachers must be born, that this is "a gift of nature." One can hardly deny the significance of a person's inclination for pedagogical work, but it is important that every man can learn the art of instructing and educating, if he displays the desire and persistence and if he applies effort and work. We must speak of this seemingly indisputable proposition because the role of methods of instruction and upbringing is sometimes disparaged among us. We consider such nihilism in regard to methods, their underestimation, to be deeply mistaken.

The concept of the "teacher's mastery" is many-faceted. It includes a creative attitude toward one's work, the personal virtues of the teacher, his qualities of will, and many other things. The teacher should work daily on the perfection of all his qualities. This is precisely what constitutes a guarantee that the level of instruction and upbringing will be raised and that there will be success in preventing student failures.

The Teacher's Assistants

While assigning great significance to the role of the teacher in preventing the repeating of grades, one must not underestimate to any extent the role of the student collective either. This proposition has great and fundamental importance.

Learning is not a personal matter for our students; it has social significance. Such an understanding of learning is cultivated from the first days of the children's sojourn in the school. Therefore, when some students experience a lack of success and fall behind in their studies, this is not a matter of indifference to their comrades; it disturbs, and should disturb, the Young Pioneer and Komsomol organizations.

The experience of the advanced schools, working without repeaters, indicates quite clearly how much the students themselves can do in the struggle for proficiency in studies. The students' struggle for a conscientious attitude toward studies on the part of their classmates usually bears a concrete nature: those displaying laziness, indifference, or negligence in their studies are subjected to social censure; if necessary, help is organized for the lagging classmate.

A broad movement has unfolded in the Young Pioneer organization "to study according to one's conscience." This Pioneer appeal does a great deal to instill a responsible attitude toward school lessons, the habit of diligently fulfilling tasks, the ability to save time, accuracy in work, and many other things which promote an upsurge in the students' progress.

The development of curiosity and a thirst for knowledge in the children has enormous significance. Many schools have developed a system for conducting various Olympiads, "competitions of the keen-witted," "tournaments of the inquisitive," and evening and morning gatherings devoted to the lives and activities of prominent scientists and to the modern achievements of science and technology.

Much more attention is now being given to the organization of the students' out-of-school time and to various forms of out-of-class work. In the past, those who participated in this work were mainly the better and, in any case, the successful students; the lagging and unsuccessful ones were shut off from this path (as if out-of-class work detracts from the lessons and interferes with the enhancement of progress). A great many aspects of this question are now being reconsidered. The lagging student often becomes such because nothing is of interest to him, because he is an unorganized and, sometimes, simply undisciplined student. Instead of his being drawn into interesting out-of-class work, he is not admitted to it and the attempt is made to

educate him with reproaches and importunate exhortations. Of course it is easier to work with disciplined, dutiful boys and girls than with "difficult" children, but then how will we put the "difficult" children on the correct path? And, indeed, all our people should enter into communism, all without exception, and the school and the teacher must answer for this to a great extent.

It is increasingly important to organize mutual assistance among the students and to get upper-grade students to work with students in the lower grades, especially with those who are lagging behind. The role of public opinion, this most important means by which students can influence their negligent classmates, is increasing.

The improvement of all aspects of upbringing work is one of the most important conditions for overcoming the repeating of grades. The teachers and leaders of the schools must seek the means to involve the students themselves, from the first days of the school year, in an active struggle to raise the quality of instruction and to prevent lagging in studies.

Community participation in the matter of bringing up the rising generation has grown tremendously in recent years.

Several years ago a council to assist the schools made its appearance in the Moscow plant "Aremkuz." Representatives of the party, trade union and Komsomol organizations in the plant, active pensioners, and housewives became members of the council. The council decided to investigate how the children of parents working at the plant study and behave and how the family looks after the children's upbringing. This required the establishment of ties with the schools in which the children study; there turned out to be 45 such schools, and at different ends of Moscow besides. "Reaching" each child and each family with the help of the most active members, the council got a clear picture of how upbringing was going and saw what help was necessary, and for whom. Constantly maintaining ties with the teachers, the council did much to improve the students' upbringing and to increase their progress in their studies.

The work of the community at the place of the students' residence has exceptional significance. In their own yards the active members of the community organize the children for socially useful activities, conduct morning exercises, athletic games and competitions, see to it that the children attend their lessons in school and do their homework, and organize the students' mutual assistance. As a result, in many homes there are little red stars, signifying that there are no students repeating grades in that home. Thus, the "street" — a source of bad influence on the children — is transformed, with the help of the community, into an assistant to the school.

Many new features have entered into the work of the school parent committees in recent years. The parent committees are giving especially great attention to families in difficult situations. In rendering aid, the committees are simultaneously heightening the parents' responsibility for the behavior and studies of the children.

Along with the teachers, the parent committees are exerting efforts toward the organization of groups and schools with a prolonged day, which have received recognition in the nation. Many children are put on their own and become neglected because their parents are busy at work. Schools and groups with a prolonged day, which have over a million students in Russia, are achieving good results in instruction and upbringing, especially in overcoming the repeating of grades.

The task of the public education bodies and of the pedagogical collectives is to enlist the forces of the community to an even greater extent in helping the schools. It is necessary to improve the work with the family, to help it, and to teach the parents the proper upbringing of children. Success in the solution of the problem of grade repeating will hinge in large measure on this.

* * *

The search that has developed for ways of preventing the repeating of grades in school has advanced a whole series of questions which demand serious examination.

Teachers and personnel in the public education bodies are introducing suggestions for a reexamination of the existing norms for evaluating the students' knowledge, which they consider to be largely outdated. These suggestions are now being studied by the ministry and the Academy of Pedagogical Sciences, and it is evident that some changes will be made in the norms of evaluation. However, it would be incorrect to move in the direction of reducing the standards with respect to the students' knowledge. In our view, the goal should be a different one — the pedagogically judicious applications of the established norms. As check-ups indicate, there are many cases in which the teachers take a quite formal approach in giving current and yearly grades; the nature of the mistakes made and the students' peculiarities are not always taken into consideration. Meanwhile, there are many stipulations in the instructions set forth for the existing norms which give the teacher the right to take the concrete situations into account.

There are also proposals to change the rules for promoting students from one grade to another. In particular, some colleagues suggest that the pedagogical councils be given the right to make conditional promotions, so that, let us say, a student who is unsuccessful in one subject can eliminate the gap during the first two months and study further in this grade (or be returned to the previous one).

The absence of such a right, these colleagues assert, sometimes induces the teachers to overstate an evaluation (in order not to doom the student to being left behind). The given suggestion is a very serious one and demands the most thorough study by all those "for" and "against."

There are also other such suggestions. However, the basic way to solve the problem of grade repeating does not lie in this direction. The main way is to heighten the quality of the students' instruction and upbringing and to improve the whole system of work in the school.

The phenomenon of grade repeating is a complex one, and not every path to the solution of this problem is acceptable. It is no accident at all that, along with a strengthening of attention to the task of eliminating the repeating of grades,

175

the question of excessive concern with percentages [protsentomaniia] also becomes more acute. The point is that some teachers and leaders of the schools attempt to replace the extremely labor-consuming process of improving instruction, which demands efforts and a proper arrangement of the whole system of educational and upbringing work, by a simple lowering of demands on the students' knowledge and an overstating of marks. Such a pursuit after percentages of progress arouses justified indignation.

Inflicting serious harm on the matter of instruction and upbringing in general, the excessive concern with percentages also inflicts a blow on the very idea of the possibility of overcoming the repeating of grades and places it in doubt. It is precisely the pursuit of percentages of progress that is, perhaps, the greatest obstacle to actually preventing the repeating of grades. That is why the control exercised by the public education bodies over the quality of the students' knowledge should now be strengthened and the responsibility of the leaders of the schools for the level of demands on the students' knowledge should be raised. The lowering of

standards and the attempts to employ administrative pressure on the teachers to raise the percentage of progress has nothing in common with a genuine struggle for the prevention and elimination of the repeating of grades. We again repeat: the main path to this is the improvement of the whole system of educational and upbringing work.

A new school year is coming. Each pedagogical collective should thoroughly analyze the reasons for the students' lack of progress and outline a single, clear-cut system of measures and actions to raise the level of the educational and upbringing process and the quality of the students' knowledge. The most important pedagogical task of the teachers and leaders of the schools is to prevent the students from falling behind in their studies from the first days of lessons.

The elimination of grade repeating is a matter of great importance to the state. The responsibility of all teachers, school leaders, and public education bodies is to exert maximum efforts to see that this ancient defect of the school becomes a thing of the past forever.

Mathematics Education

Matematika v shkole, 1967, No. 2

DRAFT OF THE MATHEMATICS PROGRAM FOR GRADES 1-3*

Explanatory Note

The continually growing demands made on the mathematical preparation of students necessitate a revision of the content, system, and methods of mathematics teaching in the primary grades.

The organic unity of teaching and upbringing, of mastering knowledge and developing the students' intelligence, of raising the theoretical level of education, instilling the ability to apply

_____

*The draft of the mathematics program for grades 1-3 is published to provide fuller information about the volume of mathematical knowledge received by primary school pupils, and to establish the necessary continuity in the study of mathematics from grades 3 to 4.

The program was drawn up by a commission for determining the content of mathematics teaching in grades 1-3. It consisted of I. K. Andronov (chairman), M. A. Bantova, Iu. M. Koliagin, N. A. Menchinskaia, M. I. Moro, A. S. Pchelko and L. N. Skatkin. The program is based on plans presented by the Institute of General and Polytechnical Education, the Institute of Psychology of the Academy of Pedagogical Sciences, and the A. I. Herzen Pedagogical Institute in Leningrad.

knowledge in practice and developing the necessary skills for this — these are the principles that should guide the revision of mathematics teaching in the lower grades.

The proposed program preserves a certain continuity with the one now in effect, insofar as the latter reflects the positive experience of teachers of the lower grades. However, the new program solves a whole series of problems in a radically new way.

The mathematics course provided by the program for grades 1-3 represents an organic part of the secondary school mathematics course.

The pivot of this course is the arithmetic of natural numbers and basic magnitudes. Around this pivot are united elements of geometry and algebraic propaedeutics which organically enter the system of arithmetic knowledge, furthering a higher level in the mastery of concepts about numbers, arithmetic operations, and mathematical relationships.

Although the program gives considerable attention, as before, to teaching the pupils sound automatic skills in calculation, it also requires a reasonable increase in the theoretical level of study material, an understanding of the general principles and laws on which the mathematical facts studied are based, and a realization of the connections between the phenomena studied.

Raising the role of theory represents a determining factor in the pupils' mathematical development. This is one of the most important ways of mobilizing the inner resources that have been underutilized until now, since such an approach greatly facilitates intelligent mastery of study material and establishment of connections between what is new and what was studied earlier.

In order to create the most favorable conditions for forming the necessary generalizations, certain changes have been introduced not only in the content but in the system of exposition of the material.

A constant theme in the program is the idea of revealing the correlation between direct and inverse operations, between the components and results of operations. The greatest importance is given to the constant use of comparison and to the juxtaposition of related concepts, operations, and problems, and to distinguishing similarities and differences in the facts investigated.

Consistent implementation of this principle extends not only to reciprocal concepts, operations, and problems, but to similar ones as well. Therefore the material has been rearranged so that the study of related concepts, operations, and problems has been made closer in time.

One of the essential principles on which the new program is based is the requirement that each new topic be studied on a high theoretical level, but within limits accessible to pupils of the given age level.

Grade 1

The Integers

Numeration and elementary shapes (24 hrs.)
Counting objects. Naming, sequence, and value of the first ten natural numbers. Comparison of numbers (equal, unequal, more, less). The signs $=$, $>$, and $<$.

Concepts of point and line (straight and curved).

Segment of a line and a broken line; closed and open lines. Polygons. Counting the ele-

ments of a polygon (altitudes, sides, angles). Depicting a point, a line (straight and curved) and a polygon (on graph paper).

Comparing segments and measuring them with a centimeter ruler and a measuring tape. Introduction to currencies and their components and exchange.

Addition and subtraction (38 hrs.)
Addition and subtraction. Signs of operations. Names of given and unknown numbers in addition and subtraction. The connection between addition and subtraction. Techniques in calculation: a) in addition — rearranging items (property of commutation) and adding one summand by its parts (associative property); b) in subtraction — conceiving the minuend as the sum of two summands, one of which is equal to the subtrahend, and subtracting the given number by its parts.

The number zero and its meaning. The series of natural numbers and zero. Addition and subtraction with zero.

Reading, writing, and comparing expressions of the type: "$5+4$ and $6+4$"; "$7+2$ and $7-2$"; "$3+0$ and $3-0$."

Simple problems in addition and subtraction (direct and inverse). The numerical formula of their solution (with the value of the unknown). Putting verbal problems into numerical formulas.

Numbers Up to 100

Numeration (18 hrs.)
Two-place numbers; their names and notation. The decimal composition of numbers. Ten as a new unit of counting.

Addition and subtraction. Geometric shapes. Magnitudes (94 hrs.)
General formulation of the properties of adding a number to a sum and a sum to a number, and of subtracting a number from a sum and a sum from a number.

Techniques of adding and subtracting within limits of 100, based on these properties. The parenthetical sign for indicating the order of operations. The addition table up to 20 as a basis of adding and subtracting numbers.

The right angle; the set-square. Acute and obtuse angles. The rectangle (square) and its depiction on plain and on graph paper.

Centimeter, decimeter, meter. Breaking up and converting simple and composite, concrete numbers of the type: 2 dm; 13 cm; 4 dm 3 cm; 3 m; 2 m 3 dm.

The increase and decrease of segments by a given segment; finding the difference between two segments.

The kilogram and its everyday application. The liter and its everyday application.

Simple composite problems. The numerical formula of solution.

Multiplication and division (24 hrs.)

The concept of multiplication (like finding the sum of equal items) and of division (by concrete examples).

The signs of multiplication (a dot) and division ($\div$). Comparison of expressions of the type: $5 \cdot 3$ and $5 \cdot 3 + 5$; $6 \cdot 2$ and $6 \cdot 3$.

Simple problems in multiplication (finding the sum of not more than 10 identical items) and division (by equal parts and by content).

Grade 2

Numbers Up to 100

Addition and subtraction (generalization) (24 hrs.)

The general formulation and algebraic expression of adding a number to a sum, a sum to a number, and of subtracting a number from a sum, a sum from a number. The commutative and associative properties of a sum in algebraic transcription. Exercises in calculations using the properties studied.

Multiplication and division. Geometric shapes. Magnitudes (110 hrs.)

Multiplication and division by table and without tables. The names of the given and unknown numbers in multiplication and division. The

connection between multiplication and division. Generalization of two types of division (by equal parts and by content) into a single operation of division as inverse multiplication. The commutative property of multiplication, its general formulation, algebraic transcription, and use in calculations.

General formulation of the properties of multiplication and division of a sum by a number, their algebraic transcription and use in calculation. Multiplication by one and by zero. Division of equal numbers, division by one, division of zero by a natural number. Comparing expressions of the type: $x \cdot 9$ and $9 \cdot x$; $7 \cdot 8$ and $7 \cdot 9$; $10 \cdot 5 + 7 \cdot 5$ and $17 \cdot 5$; $12 \cdot 0$ and $12 \cdot 1$; $14 \cdot 1$ and $14 \div 1$.

Division with a remainder. Simple problems in multiplication and division, direct and inverse, including problems in increasing and decreasing numbers by several times and finding common multiples of numbers. More complex verbal problems than in grade 1 about all four operations. The numerical formulas of their solution.

Increasing and decreasing segments by several times, finding common multiples of two segments (only for selected segments whose length is a multiple of the divisor). Division of segments into equal parts: 2, 4, 8, 3, 6, 12, etc.

Elementary linear diagrams. The rectangle; the equality of its opposite sides. Straightening a broken line and the perimeter of a polygon. The circle; the compass. Center and radius of a circle. Division of a circle into equal parts: 2, 4, 8, 6, 3.

Fractions of a unit with denominators up to 10; their value and comparison. Finding a fraction of a number, and a number by its fraction.

Time and its measurement: year, month, day, hour, minute. The definition of time by hours. Solving problems in calculating time.

Numbers Up to 1,000

Numeration. Addition and subtraction (30 hrs.)

Numeration (oral and written). (At this point an acquaintance with the abacus may also begin.)

Measures of length (meter, kilometer, millimeter). Measures of weight (kilogram, gram). Breaking up and converting simple and composite concrete numbers with not more than two denominations.

Addition and subtraction (oral and written). Finding the unknown component in operations of the first degree (summand, minuend, subtrahend). Finding the numerical value of expressions of the type: $a+2$; $k-3$; $a+b$; $a-b$ for given numerical values of the letters (in problems and examples). Finding the possible numerical values of letters in expressions of the type: $a+3 < 7$; $b-2 > 7$, etc.

Multiplication and division. Geometric shapes (34 hrs.)

Multiplication and division (without a remainder) of round two- and three-place numbers by a one-place number (orally). Finding the unknown in operations of the second degree (factor, dividend, divisor). Finding the numerical value of expressions of the type: $a \cdot 4$; $b \div 3$; $a \div b$; $a \cdot b$; $(a+b) \cdot c$; $(a-b) \cdot c$; $(m+n) \div k$; $(m-n) \div k$ for given numerical values of the letters (in problems and examples). The order of operations in expressions containing operations of the first and second degree.

Triangles, their types: equilateral, isosceles, scalene; right, acute, obtuse. Problem in dividing a given polygon into its parts and the inverse of this problem.

Simple problems (direct and inverse) with numerical and algebraic data. Complex problems in all four operations; numerical formulas of their solution (with and without unknowns), e.g.; $x = 3 \cdot 6 + 2 \cdot 4$; $x + 3 \cdot 10 = 64$; $3 \cdot x - 6 = 36$.

Grade 3

Many-placed Numbers

The numeration of many-placed numbers (oral, written, on the abacus). The metric system of measures of length and weight (20 hrs.)

Operations of the first degree with abstract and concrete numbers (orally, written, on the abacus) (38 hrs.)

Written addition and subtraction of many-placed numbers; commutative and associative properties of a sum; basic properties of a difference and their application in rationalizing calculations. Particular instances of addition and subtraction and their transcription in the general form: $a+0$; $0+a$; $0+0$; $a-a$; $a-0$; $0-0$.

Finding the numerical value of expressions of the type: $1373+a$; $b-4725$ for given numerical values of the letters (in problems and examples).

Finding the possible numerical values of letters in expressions of the type: $1378+x = 1546$; $1278 - x = 924$; $1532+a = a+1532$. Change in the results of addition and subtraction caused by a change in one of the components of these operations; solution of the corresponding problems and examples; rounding off numbers. Estimating and checking the results of addition and subtraction.

Techniques of rapid calculation.

Simple problems with numerical and algebraic data illustrating different cases of applying operations of the first degree (generalization). Complex problems in addition and subtraction; the formulas of their solution.

Operations of the first degree with abstract and concrete numbers (oral and written) (100 hrs.)

The written multiplication and division of many-placed numbers by one-, two-, and three-digit numbers: the commutative and associative properties of a product, their algebraic transcription. The distributive property of a product and a quotient relative to a sum and its algebraic transcription. Using these properties to rationalize calculations.

Particular cases of multiplication and division and their transcription in the general form:

1) $0 \cdot a = 0$; $a \cdot 0 = 0$; $a \cdot 1 = a$;

2) $a \div a = 1$; $a \div 1 = a$; $0 \div a = 0$ (for a divisor not equal to zero).

Finding the numerical value of expressions of the type: $16 \cdot a + 12 \cdot b$ for given values of the letters.

Finding the numerical values of the letters in

the expressions: a · 78 = 78 · a; 18 · x = 1080;
x ÷ 45 = 720; (x · 9) ÷ 24 = 3; 8 · a = 0; b ÷ 8 = 1;
7 · c = 7.

Change in the results of multiplication and division resulting from a change in one of the components of these operations; solving the corresponding problems and examples.

Estimating and checking the results of multiplication and division.

Techniques of rapid calculation (e.g., multiplication and division by 5, 25, 50; multiplication by 9, 11).

Problems with numerical and algebraic data illustrating different cases of applying multiplication and division (generalization).

Fractions with small denominators. Finding several fractions of a number. Breaking down fractions into smaller ones and the reverse transformation, illustrated by circles, rectangles and segments.

Combined operations of the first and second degree. Magnitudes (24 hrs.)

Complex problems in all four operations ("reduced" [terms] [privedennye], without a limit on the number of operations, and "unreduced" [terms], with a limited number of operations). Formulas of solving them.

Particular cases of joint operations of the type: a · 0 + (0 · b) or a · 1 + a · 0 + 0.

Time and its measurement. Table of measures of time. Breakdown and transformation of concrete numbers related to time measurements. Addition and subtraction. Solving problems in calculating time.

Examples of different dependencies among magnitudes (the price of a unit of produce, the number of units and their cost; velocity, time, and distance in uniform motion, etc.). Drawing up tables and formulas illustrating these dependencies.

Polygons and finding their areas (16 hrs.)

The area of a polygon placed on graph paper and on unlined paper. Template. Area of a rectangle (finding it directly, by template, and indirectly, by formula). Table of square measures. Problems in finding the area of a rectangle and inverse problems.

Surveying work on location: marking a direction and measuring straight line segments; constructing a right angle and a rectangle (cross-staff). Calculating the area of a rectangular plot of land. Are, hectare.

Oral calculations using the properties of the four operations studied are carried on throughout the year.

Nachal'naia shkola, 1967, No. 5

A. S. Pchelko and M. I. Moro

THE NEW MATHEMATICS PROGRAM FOR GRADES 1-3

The draft for the new mathematics program was published in the first issue of our journal so that it could be broadly discussed and necessary corrections made on the basis of this discussion, after which the program will be introduced into all schools in the course of the next few years.

Introduction of the new program requires a major reform of mathematics education in our country. The aims of this reform are:

to raise the theoretical level of mathematical knowledge in the primary grades and establish a correct relationship between theory and practice in mathematics teaching;

to increase concern for the development of students' mathematical thinking and to inculcate in them a lasting interest in the study of mathematics;

to bring the content and methods of teaching the mathematics course of the primary grades closer to the basic mathematics courses of grades 4 - 10.

The authors are affiliated with the Sector of Primary Education in the Institute of General and Polytechnical Education, USSR Academy of Pedagogical Sciences.

All this should ultimately ensure that the children receive a level of mathematical training that will correspond to the ever increasing demands of life.

The transition of the schools to the new programs should be preceded by a great deal of preparatory work to raise the teacher's scientific qualifications and, above all, to clarify the essence of what is new in the impending reform planned in the new program.

A clear conception of the program's major principles and a profound understanding of the ideas on which it is based are an important prerequisite for its successful implementation in practice.

The new program reflects the progressive ideas under the banner of which the movement to reform mathematics teaching in secondary school has developed in recent years, namely:

a drive to bring the school mathematics course closer to contemporary mathematical science and its practical applications;

a struggle to organize a single mathematics course in which arithmetic would be organically united with elements of algebra and geometry;

increased concern with the theoretical side of

the school mathematics course, while strictly observing its practical orientation — viz., a connection with life, especially in the lower grades — and increased concern for students' skills [kul'tura] in calculation;

a certain improvement in presentation of subject matter in the lower grades made possible by modernizing its content, by perfecting the system and methods of its exposition and, above all, by making full use of children's cognitive capacities in the teaching process; experiments have shown that these capacities were clearly underestimated until now.

Only if these major principles are noted and correctly seen as effective factors in the further development of our schools can the spirit and orientation of the new program, and the sense behind the reorientation, be fully understood.

What then are the content, range, and system of the new program?

The subject "Arithmetic" will henceforth be called "Mathematics." Such a change is not fortuitous. It reflects a change in the content and structure of the subject.

The pivot of the new mathematics program is the arithmetic of natural numbers and basic measures, around which the elements of algebra and geometry are joined; the latter form an organic part of the system of arithmetic knowledge and are aimed chiefly at raising the level of assimilation of concepts of number, arithmetic operations, and elementary mathematical relations. Thus, the primary mathematics course has a triunal structure, in which an arithmetic, an algebraic, and a geometric component are to be distinguished.

Let us examine each component separately, although in practice they represent a single whole.

As before, in the arithmetic part of the program considerable attention is devoted to teaching the children sound skills in computation (in this respect there is continuity with the present program). But from now on these skills will be developed from two directions: 1) by work with concrete quantities; 2) on the basis of a knowledge of the commutative and associative properties of addition, the commutative, associative, and distributive properties of multiplication, and the properties of difference and quotient. A knowledge of these properties is used as the basis for explaining various techniques of computation; it guarantees an intelligent, sound mastery of computation skills.

As early as the 1st grade, when studying addition and subtraction within the limits of 10, children become acquainted with the commutative property of addition, its standard formulation, and its application in solving examples and problems. At the same time they also become acquainted with using the combinative property of addition.

Let us point out that this method of teaching computation skills is a substantial innovation for our schools. Until now, skills in computation were taught without reference to the properties of operations. An acquaintance with these properties was given only at the end of primary education, when they could no longer be of real help in explaining methods of calculation. Now the situation is reversed: an introduction to the properties of operations is given first, and then techniques of calculation are explained on that basis. This sequence raises the effectiveness of teaching these techniques. But it requires theoretical preparation on the part of the teacher and improved teaching methods. (For a more detailed discussion, see the article by M. I. Moro, "Raising the Theoretical Level of Mathematics Teaching" [O povyshenii teoreticheskogo urovnia obucheniia matematike], in issue No. 1 of our journal.)

From the very first steps of teaching arithmetic according to the new program, the children's attention is directed to the correlation between the arithmetic operations of addition and subtraction, and then to that of multiplication and division. In grade 3, this correlation is plainly expressed in the definitions of the operations: subtraction — the reverse operation to addition, by which the second of two items in a given sum is found; division — the reverse operation to multiplication, etc.

Early study of the properties of operations, and of the relation between them (studied in grade 4 in the present program), not only raises the theoretical level of all arithmetic work and reveals more fully the meaning of each operation, but makes it considerably easier for students to learn the addition and multiplication tables. For example, when experimental classes began to study multiplication and division tables on the basis of the reversibility of these operations, and began to find the results of division from the multiplication table, the time required for learning this subject was cut in half.

Study of the correlation between the components and results of addition and subtraction also begins in grade 1, and later, in grade 2, of multiplication and division. By the end of the second year, the study of this subject is completed, and in grade 3 this knowledge is reinforced thanks to its constant use in solving elementary equations and problems.

In the present program this subject is studied only in grade 4, and receives a particularly formal treatment: the dependency between the components and results of operations is used only in solving "examples with x." The new program greatly increases the importance of knowing the relationship between the components and results of operations: it becomes the basis for solving elementary equations; in turn, equations are often used in solving problems.

Thus, this subject has acquired new importance and a wider sphere of application in the new program. It has been changed from formal knowledge into an intelligent and effective means of facilitating the mastery of a number of other mathematical subjects.

In addition to the already existing topics in the present program, the program plan also includes one new topic: "Dependency Between Changes in the Results of Operations and Changes in the Components." This topic had been in the primary school program in the past, but when the program became overloaded it was transferred to grade 5. Now it has been returned to the primary grades, but with a completely different approach to studying it.

In studying addition and subtraction within the limits of 10 as early as grade 1, exercises of the type

$$6 + 1 = 7 \qquad 8 - 1 = 7$$
$$6 + 2 = 8 \qquad 8 - 2 = 6$$
$$6 + 3 = 9 \qquad 8 - 3 = 5$$
$$6 + 4 = 10 \qquad 8 - 4 = 4$$

can usefully be accompanied by such instructions as: "Solve the examples. Recite the answers to the examples in the first column. What do you notice? Why do the numbers in the answers gradually increase by one? Look at the summands [slagaemye] — first and second. What do you notice?" After a number of such observations, an attempt at generalization can be made: "What is the connection between the summands and the sum?"

Next, similar examples can be accompanied by the instructions: "Without calculating, say which example will have the biggest answer and why. Check your answers by calculations."

In grades 2 and 3, a knowledge about changing results is used in comparing expressions. For example: "Compare the following expressions and place the necessary signs between them (=, >, or <):

$$75 - 19 \ldots 55 - 34,$$
$$84 - 26 \ldots 95 - 26."$$

A change in result depending on a change in components is conveniently shown by drawing up and completing tables. For example: "Complete this table: in column one, the first summand is 15, the second is 8. Find their sum. In the remaining columns, leave the first item unchanged, but increase the second by 3, by 5, and by 8. Compare the sums obtained with the first sum. By how much did each sum increase?"

First summand	15			
Second summand	8			
Sum				

Next, a similar table is to be completed, but this time the second item (8) is left unchanged, and the first item is increased by 5, 20, and 25.

How much does the sum increase each time?

After this, the conclusion is drawn: if one summand is increased by so many units, the sum will increase by the same amount.

In the same way, by means of a series of observations, the children are gradually led to understand the change in a remainder resulting from a change in the minuend or subtrahend, the change in a product resulting from a change in factors, etc. Herein lies the chief value of this topic. It reveals to some extent the functional principle on which the new program is based. By studying this topic, the children realize how one variable depends on another, how a change in the value of one magnitude entails a change in the value of another magnitude connected with it.

In other words, by studying this topic the children become better prepared to perceive and understand the idea of functional dependency. At this point, by the way, school mathematics comes closer to mathematical science, where the theory of functions occupies a leading role.

In addition, it is very important to note that functional propaedeutics does not require introducing any special supplementary material into the program: children easily understand it from the ordinary arithmetic material of the primary grades.

* * *

The program's arithmetic content also includes an introduction to measurements of length, weight, time, area, cost and velocity (only volume remains in the 4th grade program, as before). The children become acquainted with units of measurement and with the instruments used in measuring these quantities.

The study of measures has been rationalized in the new program. In grade 1, children learn about the meter, decimeter, and centimeter, with the centimeter being taught at the very beginning, when the children are forming a concept about the first numbers in the natural series. This enables the children to perform practical exercises in measuring small segments, and enables the teacher to acquaint them

with: a) the concept of a number resulting not only from counting, but from measurement; and b) compound concrete numbers (2 dm. 5 cm., 3 m. 6 dm., etc.).

The advantage to subsequent study of measures is that, in the course of three years beginning with grade 1, the children learn to convert and simplify measurements and practice operations with both simple and compound concrete numbers. As a result, they acquire sound knowledge of the unitary relations of measures, transformations of measures, and sound skills of computation with concrete numbers. This eliminates the need to study concrete numbers as a separate topic. Operations with compound concrete numbers are studied together with operations on abstract numbers, since both are based on the decimal system.

Transformations and operations with concrete numbers connected with time measurements are studied separately.

An analysis of the program's arithmetic content reveals its continuity with the present program. In fact, we find a great deal of familiar and little unfamiliar program material. But one cannot help noticing the program's great saturation, its abundance of material: almost the entire four-year program has been structured into three years of primary education. The questions arise as to whether the program is not overloaded, whether it can be carried out, and on what its authors base their assurance that the material proposed can be thoroughly mastered in a shorter period of time.

For a correct answer to these questions, one must understand and consider the changes made in the system of arranging the program material. The result of revising the program has been a change not only, and even not so much, in its content as in its system.

A radical change in system is what chiefly distinguishes the new program from the old one. As we observed earlier, the relationship between theory and practice has been solved in an entirely new way. The close connection between theory and practice will give the teaching process a new coloration. The nature of teaching, and the quality of the pupils' knowledge, will change.

New connections, broader and sounder associations, are formed in a system of theoretically validated knowledge. As a result, the pupil's thinking will change, his cognitive capacities will develop and strengthen.

Next, the material in the new program is grouped so as to provide broad opportunities for the constant use of the comparative method in the teaching process. Everything close, similar or related in content (e.g., division into equal parts and division by content, comparison of differences and increasing a number by so many units, operations with abstract and concrete numbers, etc.) is brought closer in time, as a result of which extensive use can be made of the comparative method: isolating common features, making generalizations, and teaching information of a general nature in a shorter space of time.

Reciprocally converse concepts, transformations, and operations have likewise been brought closer together, so that they can be studied from all sides and juxtaposed, isolating their differences along with certain common features (e.g., reduction and conversion, problems connected with the increase and decrease of a number, problems in finding a fraction of a number and a number by its fraction, etc.). Such a presentation of material shortens the time required to learn it.

In general, material in the new program is presented in bigger methodological units. Thus, the new program has not two concenters for millions and billions, but one concenter of many-placed numbers; not two concenters for the numbers 11-20 and for 100, but a single concenter for the first 100 numbers, including 11-20; no special concenter for compound concrete numbers, as we mentioned above, since operations on them are studied together with operations on abstract numbers; finally, not four tables of multiplication and division, but a single multiplication table, from which the answers to division are easily found.

Thanks to this concentration of material, it becomes possible to give children a large amount of generalized and sound knowledge in a shorter space of time. In this way the system of grouping arithmetic material has undergone a basic change. It is mainly this which enables it to be covered in a shorter space of time.

* * *

Let us examine the content of the program's second component, algebraic propaedeutics.

The new program announces the principle: the study of each topic and each new concept is to be brought up to a high level of generalization, since only generalized knowledge reveals the broad opportunities for independent application of this knowledge under new circumstances. Our primary means of generalization is the word, i.e., verbal formulations. For example, after explaining the commutative property of addition — first by visual aids and then by performing a series of exercises in solving examples and problems with numerical data — we generalize: "The sum does not change when the position of the summands is changed."

Verbal generalizations made on the basis of work with numerical data represent a perfectly natural and necessary form of generalization, especially in the first stage of teaching young children. This form of generalization will always remain in school practice. But it is inexpedient to confine oneself to this type of generalization in mathematics. The language of mathematics is primarily a language of symbols and formulas. It is extremely precise, clear, and extremely laconic, thanks to formulas using algebraic designations. The algebraic symbol in mathematics, like the word in conversation, generalizes; moreover, its generalizations are extraordinarily broad, highly convincing, and very economical. For example, after working with concrete quantities, pupils come to the conclusion that: $3+4 = 4+3$; $5+2 = 2+5$. And after investigating and applying in practice a series of such equalities, the children naturally approach the generalization: $a+b = b+a$, which means that whatever numbers we take for the two items, the sum never changes as a result of reversing the position of the items. After this, it is sufficient to write down two letters in differing order, join them with "plus" and "equal" signs, and the children will see the commutative property of addition and sense the great generality of this property.

Three or four letters in the formulas $C + a \cdot b$ or $P = (a + b) \cdot 2$ replace extensive verbal formulations of the corresponding rules and relationships.

In mathematics lessons, even in the earliest grades, it is expedient to use algebraic symbols accessible to children's understanding. By the way, herein lies another means of bringing the school mathematics course closer to mathematical science.

Algebraic symbols are used in primary grades:

1) in transcribing the properties of operations; e.g., the commutative property of addition and multiplication: $a + b = b + a$; $a \cdot b = b \cdot a$; the combinative property of addition and multiplication: $a + b + c = (a + b) + c = a + (b + c)$; $a \cdot b \cdot c = (a \cdot b) \cdot c = a \cdot (b \cdot c)$; the distributive property of multiplication: $(a + b) \cdot k = a \cdot k + b \cdot k$;

2) in transcribing rules of various kinds; e.g., the rules of calculating the perimeter and area of a rectangle, etc.;

3) in drawing up algebraic formulas which express a relationship between quantities; e.g., $C = a \cdot b$ (to show the relationship between speed, time and distance);

4) in solving problems with algebraic data and problems solved by means of drawing up equations;

5) in finding the numerical value of such expressions as: "$a + 685$ if $a = 437$" and the numerical value of letters in such expressions as: "$a \cdot 18 = 1800$."

The use of algebraic symbols is only one aspect of algebraic propaedeutics. Another aspect of this section is teaching children to read and write correctly both numerical and algebraic expressions ($5 + 4$; $12 - 8$; $16 \cdot 3$; $20 : 4$; $a + b$; $e - k$; etc.), and to find their value. By comparing expressions and finding equalities and inequalities, children become acquainted with these concepts and with such elementary equations as equalities with one unknown, designated by a letter. With the help of drawing up equations, children learn how to solve certain types of problems.

Thus, the introduction of algebraic propaedeutics into the program facilitates studying arithmetic topics on a higher level of generalization, and trains children to use elements of mathematical language, thereby bringing the mathematics course closer to mathematical science.

The great importance of algebraic propaedeutics is that it makes it possible, as early as the primary grades, to build the mathematical apparatus (solution of elementary equations and inequalities) that permits certain problems to be solved by means of drawing up equations.

The part of the new program called "Geometric Material" has also been considerably improved. The new program avoids the inadequacies in this section of the present program, in which the geometry of measures (measuring segments, area, volume) was presented adequately, but the geometry of figures was weak. The children became more or less thoroughly familiar only with the rectangle (square) and learned its properties and how to calculate its perimeter and area. But this is insufficient. A great variety of figures are seen in the surrounding environment, and in their secondary school geometry course the children will encounter many geometric figures as objects of logical proofs. Taking this into account, the new program provides for students to be introduced to a broader range of geometric figures. During the study of the first ten numbers in grade 1, children are introduced to the polygon and to the names of its elements (sides, angles, and altitudes), which they use as material in calculations. From polygons they proceed to concentrate on quadrangles, of which the rectangle and square are singled out and the properties of their sides and angles are studied.

Triangles are important in grade 2; the children concentrate on the different types thereof.

The circle and circumference are presented in the program; the children become acquainted with the center, radius, and diameter of a circle, with how to draw it and divide it into equal parts.

Much work is done with line segments: drawing, measuring, comparing, and performing operations on them.

The following brief lines in the 2nd grade program deserve much attention: "Problems in dividing a given polygon into parts and the converse problems." For example, for a given diagram, the children must determine: a) the total number of triangles in a rectangle divided by two diagonals; b) what figures make up this diagram; c) out of two squares divided into triangles, make one triangle and a rectangle, etc.

It is easy to see that work of this kind is of great importance in developing the children's "geometric perception" of spatial concepts and their constructive thinking, and ultimately will better prepare them to study in the subsequent systematic geometry course.

A new feature in the section "Calculating Area" is the introduction of the template for measuring the area of any polygon. (The template is a very simple instrument: a transparent sheet of boxed paper.) This not only enables the children to measure the area of any plane figure, but it also helps the teacher to give them a correct understanding of the process of measuring area, which consists of counting the number of squares contained in a given figure. From there it is easy to proceed to an understanding of area as the number of squares with a side equal to a unit of length into which a given rectangle can be divided. Of course, there is no need to give children a definition of area at this stage, but the teacher should know what concept of area he is helping the children to develop.

Not only the content, but the system of teaching geometric material, has been changed. In the new program, this material is now distributed among all topics and studied throughout the entire course. This is necessitated by the need to establish a connection between geometric and arithmetic material. Segments, lines, and rectangles are often used as illustrative material; e.g., the concept of fractions is given by dividing segments and circles, the distributive property of multiplication is illustrated by calculating the perimeter of a rectangle, the commutative property of multiplication is demonstrated on a rectangle divided into squares, problems in motion are illustrated by segments, etc.

The program provides for teaching skills of measurement and drawing. The children learn to draw segments, right angles, rectangles

(squares), right-angled triangles on unlined paper, using a ruler and drawing triangle, to measure straight lines on location, using a measuring chain and field compasses, and to construct right angles and rectangles on a plot of land, using a cross-staff.

The volume of concrete geometric concepts planned by the new program can be considered sufficient for serving as the basis for developing geometrical thinking and teaching the necessary knowledge and skills; it can also serve as a sound basis for mastering the systematic geometry course in secondary school.

Solving problems is of great importance in the new program. But more than in the existing program, problems are made to serve the overall aims of studying this subject, i.e., to form basic mathematical concepts, reveal and give concrete definition to different kinds of quantitative relationships, to apply theory in practice, to use different intellectual operations in the process of solving problems (analysis, synthesis, abstraction, generalization, etc.) that further the development of the children's logical thought. The explanatory note underlines the subordinate role of problems: they are not an end in themselves, but a major means of attaining the aims provided for by the mathematics program.

In accordance with this, the mathematical content of problems and the system of distributing them are determined by the content and system of the basic topics of the mathematics course. Thus, during the introduction to the properties of arithmetic operations, problems are solved in applying these properties; when the concept of the arithmetic average is taught, problems are solved in calculating the average value of magnitudes; etc.

Thus, what is important in the system of solving problems is their direct connection with those concepts which are formed with their help and applied to them.

Problems with dependent variables play an especially great role. In this connection, we must underline the deep meaning contained in the following brief lines of the program: "Examples of different relationships between quantities (price, cost and quantity, speed, time and distance, etc.), drawing up tables and formulas illustrating the dependences studied. The solution of problems on the basis of these dependences."

This refers to problems whose solution leads to an understanding of two types of functional dependency: direct and inverse ratios between quantities.

The interrelationship of these quantities is at first investigated in simple problems and expressed in verbal formulations; then it is fixed in algebraic formulas, by means of which one quantity is expressed by other quantities — e.g., cost by amount and price, amount by cost and price, price by amount and cost.

When studying dependent variables, the children learn to complete, read, and draw up tables in which the value of a third quantity is found from the given values of two other quantities.

The study of dependent variables requires a study of the nature of change in one quantity as it depends on change in the other quantities; e.g., how cost changes by several times when the amount changes if the price remains constant; how the amount changes if the price changes several times and the cost remains constant, etc.

Thus, the functional propaedeutics provided for by the new program is carried out to a considerable extent by solving problems with dependent variables.

"Simple problems" [prostye zadachi] occupy a large part of the new program. Their study in school practice, and presumably in the new textbooks, will be somewhat accelerated. Experimental research has shown convincingly that all the basic types of simple problems in direct and indirect form are fully accessible to children and can be studied in grades 1 and 2.

Complex problems of gradually increasing complexity are also introduced early. The program for grade 3 mentions complex problems in all four operations, with and without a limitation on the number of operations. The explanatory note warning against unwieldy problems mentions problems of three or four operations.

The new program has substantial changes in the methods of working with problems. A good deal of work in generalization is done as early as grade 1, in connection with solving simple problems, namely, when writing solutions to problems in the form of numerical formulas. The formula lacks a reference, and this makes it possible to draw up problems with varying concrete content from the same formula, as a result of which the children will see what different problems solved by the same operation have in common. Beginning in grade 2, problems are solved with algebraic data and algebraic formulas. This further facilitates an understanding of the fact that problems with varying concrete content can be solved by the same operation. For example, seven or eight types of simple problems in subtraction are solved by the formula $x = a - b$.

The problem also indicates formulas in connection with solving complex problems. The application of formulas is a valuable method of teaching children to solve problems. A skillful (somewhat limited) use of this method should exert great influence on the pupils' mathematical development. With drawing up numerical formulas as a preliminary to solving problems, the center of gravity shifts to logical work on the problem, i.e., to an analysis of the conditions of the problem and the drawing up of a plan to solve it. In the compact structure of the formula, the entire process of solving the problem is presented: the operations to be performed, the numbers to be used in the operations, and the sequence of the operations.

Drawing up numerical formulas serves as a good preparation for drawing up elementary equations of problems (the connection between numerical formulas and equations is so great that in some cases it is difficult to draw a line between them).

When studying the relationship between the components and results of operations, students learn how to solve elementary equations, and this knowledge can be applied to solving problems by means of drawing up equations. For example, problems in finding an unknown summand, subtrahend, or another component of an operation are solved by means of equations.

Later, pupils learn to solve more complex equations, which enables them to solve more complex problems. Thus, the grade 2 program contains an equation of the type $x + 3 \cdot 10 = 64$, by means of which the following problem, for example, can be solved: "A boy bought a book and 10 pencils at 3 kopecks a pencil. He paid 64 kopecks for his entire purchase. How much did the book cost?"

Thus, by introducing numerical formulas for solving problems which do or do not contain unknowns, the new program prepares primary school pupils to solve problems by means which they will encounter in secondary school.

An examination of the new program shows that it has applied the progressive ideas of contemporary mathematics teaching sufficiently fully and consistently. The new program has absorbed much of value from the experience of advanced teachers, the results of experimental research carried out by psychologists and methodologists, and the achievements of scientific pedagogical thought, while preserving a certain amount of continuity with the previous program.

The selection of new material was done with consideration of the actual conditions in which the regular school operates.

The new programs, as well as the new textbooks that have been compiled on the basis of those programs, open up broad possibilities for enhancing the level of mathematics education in the primary grades.

* * *

Matematika v shkole, 1967, No. 1

DRAFT OF THE SECONDARY SCHOOL MATHEMATICS PROGRAM*

The following took part in drawing up the program: V. G. Boltianskii, A. N. Kolmogorov, Iu. N. Makarychev, A. I. Markushevich, G. G. Maslova, K. I. Neshkov, A. D. Semushin, A. I. Fetisov, A. A. Shershevskii, and I. M. Iaglom.

The final editing of the explanatory note was done by A. N. Kolmogorov, A. I. Markushevich (introduction, arithmetic, algebra and elementary analysis) and I. M. Iaglom (geometry).

EXPLANATORY NOTE

General Principles

1. The programs published here represent a responsible stage in the radical improvement of mathematics teaching in the school, intended to be carried out over a series of years. These programs are to serve as a basis for writing new textbooks and for experimental teaching. Only after these textbooks have been approved and necessary changes in the program made will teaching according to these programs become obligatory in the general [massovaia] school.

Such a broad approach to the matter has per-

---

*The editors request that mathematics teachers, scientific workers, and teachers' methods societies express their comments and suggestions about the content of this draft for the mathematics program.

mitted us not to confine ourselves to temporary corrections, but to review anew, from general fundamental positions, the question of the content of the school mathematics course and the optimal ways of studying this content. At the same time this approach was also responsible for certain peculiarities in the published programs. The planners strove to define with sufficient clarity the content of teaching for each year. The explanatory note sometimes gives specific instructions regarding the level of difficulty of those problems which all students must learn to solve. At the same time, in order not to hamper excessively the work of the staffs of writers who will be working on new textbooks, and of the teachers in experimental schools, the planners avoided excessively detailed program instructions wherever they thought it desirable to leave some freedom for testing various possible systems of studying the material. In particular, one must bear in mind that for each topic (provided with a number and an indication of the number of hours) a systematized enumeration of the materials to be learned is given, which may not coincide with the order in which the material is studied within the topic. In cases where the planners believe the distribution of material among topics and the order of study of individual topics in the program are still subject to debate, this is indicated in the explanatory note.

It should be noted that the distribution of classroom hours among the topics was also subjected to exhaustive debate in the commission which prepared the programs. If it departs noticeably from the existing tradition, this reflects the views of the planners on the relative importance of individual topics.

In its general features, the structure of the school mathematics programs which have been in effect until now represents the achievement of pedagogical thought at the end of the nineteenth century, when there arose the idea of the need to introduce elements of "functional thought" into the algebra course. In contrast to almost all foreign countries, our general school programs have until recently lacked the beginning of differential and integral calculus.

With great regard for the valuable experience accumulated in school work, we must seek new ways of radically improving the content of school mathematics education in the direction of bringing school instruction closer to the structure of mathematical science and to the demands of related sciences and technology. We must combine raising the logical level of instruction with increasing its clarity and orientation toward an organic link with an absorbing natural-science interpretation of mathematical facts.

The new program introduces elementary concepts of differential calculus in the 9th grade and makes wide use of them in subsequent chapters of the mathematics course. Given a sufficiently clear exposition based on geometric and physical concepts, this material is not difficult for the 9th grade. It has been studied in 9th grade classes in the general school. It is precisely in this grade that it serves to simplify the study of traditional matters such as function analysis, etc. Integrals are introduced in the 10th grade and are then used to calculate volumes.

The program takes a different approach to the introduction of elements of mathematical logic and the theory of sets. The program recommends only a gradual and very cautious introduction of elementary terms and definitions from this field, e.g., in connection with explaining the principles of operation of computers (in grade 7).

2. The pedagogically correct combination of inductive and deductive methods is of great importance in the successful teaching of mathemat-ics. Inductive, and especially experimental, methods of establishing facts, including the use of the pupils' direct practical experience, should play a basic role in the lower grades. In geometry, for example, a wider use of cutting figures from paper, etc., should be made for this purpose.

Experience has shown that an interesting and understandable inductive establishment of the facts — rather than the formal deductive method — permits material to be learned more deeply and firmly at an early stage of study. Too early an introduction of deductive proofs usually committed to memory not only does not further the development of the pupils' logical thinking, but as a rule artificially retards it, often for a lengthy period.

The program proposes that the habits of deductive thought be taught at all stages of study. The concept of the deductive structure of the scientific discipline should be formed more gradually and cautiously.

At first the laws studied (when necessary, for example, the criteria of divisibility, the properties of vertical angles) are deduced from individual concrete examples in the form of explanations not intended for memorization. Deductive proofs only appear as an independent element of mathematical theory when the material studied enables the pupils to perceive their necessity.

The role of the deductive method is subsequently increased. The mathematics program creates favorable conditions for developing a need for deductive proofs and a correct concept of the structure of deductive scientific theory, the axiomatic system of the structure of science, over a sufficiently long period of time. The clear demonstration of the essence of the axiomatic method in geometry and algebra should be the culminating moment in the overall system of the mathematical preparation of the students.

3. The program takes account of numerous ties with related disciplines and vocational training. Early introduction of negative numbers and elementary algebraic formulas (grades 4 - 5) greatly helps the beginning of the physics course in the 6th grade. The equation of uniform motion ($s = vt$) and the graphic solution of motion prob-

lems in mathematics lessons anticipate the study of mechanics in physics lessons. The velocity of free fall is introduced in physics lessons somewhat earlier than derivatives are introduced in mathematics lessons, making it possible to solve a series of problems with physical content in mathematics lessons. Harmonic oscillations are studied in mathematics after the topic "Vibrations and Waves" is studied in physics. This interaction of two subjects, without avoiding the solution of physics problems in mathematics lessons and while anticipating certain new mathematical concepts in physics lessons, seems to the program planners not only permissible, but in many cases more desirable.

The program provides for systematic use of the slide rule in calculations (without investigating the principles of its operation) in grade 7 (topic 7), where it finds wide application.

An acquaintance with the slide rule may also begin in grade 6 after topic 2, which will create more favorable conditions for the study of algebra and geometry, since the calculations aspect of the mathematics course can be considerably simplified in this case.

An acquaintance with calculations from formulas in grade 5, the solution of systems of linear equations at the end of grade 6, and the use of the slide rule beginning with grade 7 can serve the needs of related subjects — physics, chemistry and vocational training. An acquaintance with logarithmic and semi-logarithmic graphs at the end of grade 8 opens up possibilities for broad practice in the mathematical processing of empirical data from any sectors of the natural and social sciences (e.g., semi-log graphs of industrial growth). Essential for links with other disciplines and vocational training is the increased attention to approximate calculations which the program provides for in grade 7.

Local practice in surveying the geodesy is not clearly indicated in the program, but it is desirable as early as grade 4. There are especially broad opportunities for this at the end of grade 7 (plane-table survey, the precise measurement of areas) and the beginning of grade 8 (the application of trigonometric functions, the solution of triangles).

4. Given universal education, the material studied should be comprehensible to everyone on all levels of study. Mastery of an expanded range of ideas demands not only very great clarity in logical formulations, but also a rejection of the drive, very widespread in school practice, for the appearance of "rigor" and system in the deductive structure of the course (often quite illusory). Considerably wider use is to be made of directly indicating that individual facts, which can be proven but are intuitively obvious, are accepted in school without proof.

5. Skills must be firmly mastered. For example, students must be able to perform arithmetic and geometric calculations without error. Students showing no heightened interest in mathematics must acquire these skills from a large number of sufficiently simple exercises and problems. In many instances the memorization of formulas should be replaced by creating the habit of using handbooks. It is inadmissible to subject the nature of general education, intended for all, to the interests of those students who will enter technical schools after the eight-year school or higher technical institutes after the 10th grade. However, we believe that the instructions below, which limit the difficulty of the problems to be solved, do not lower the level actually attained in the majority of schools at the present time.

6. The programs indicate several "talks by the teacher." These talks are intended to acquaint students with important scientific ideas, about which all students can be given only a general concept in the school, indicating to them the prospects of further mathematics study and its role in the natural sciences and technology. They should probably be expanded even more. (A series of visual aids and films can be of great help in acquainting students with the more difficult questions.)

The secondary school study plan allots hours for optional lessons beginning in the 7th grade (see the general explanatory note to the draft program). As a result of freeing part of the study time for optional lessons, the number of classroom hours for the study of mathematics in the two upper grades has been decreased from the presently operative 6 to 5. Programs for the optional mathematics courses are still being worked out. It is assumed that a two-hour course for grades 7-10, "Supplementary Chapters and Problems in Mathematics," will receive the widest distribution. An anticipated draft program for grades 9-10 is appended.

Probably, many 9th and 10th grade students will want to combine the supplementary mathematics lessons with supplementary lessons in drawing, physics, radio technology, etc. Such optional courses as "Computer Mathematics" and "Programming" can be added to the general course in "Supplementary Chapters and Problems in Mathematics." We believe that in one or another combination, the latter course will interest a considerable proportion of students in the upper grades. The introduction of this course should be recommended wherever there are several parallel upper grades in one school or several closely located schools. An experienced teacher can also organize lessons in "Supplementary Chapters and Problems in Mathematics" with small groups of 9th and 10th grade students.

The program planners consistently took the standpoint that in the general mathematics course, obligatory for all students, preference should be given to topics of the broadest general educational significance, the study of which would further the formation of a scientific outlook and show the place of mathematics in the system of sciences and in man's practical work. As a result of these considerations, elementary mathematical analysis occupies a large place in the program of the upper grades, and some space is allotted to elementary concepts of the theory of probability.

With much regret, the planners excluded the topic "Complex Numbers" from the general required program. But they believed it inadvisable to retain this topic in the abbreviated form in which it is presented in the present program (without the geometric interpretation of multiplication, De Moivre's formula, and its application to the extraction of roots). On the other hand, the course "Supplementary Chapters and Problems in Mathematics" introduces the topic

of complex numbers sufficiently early and uses them in a series of applications.

The arithmetic of natural numbers (elements of the theory of division with proof of the uniqueness of division into simple factors) is also studied in more depth in the course "Supplementary Chapters...." The supplementary course also contains a clear formulation of the principle of mathematical induction (naturally, concepts of induction are also cultivated in the general course).

The new program provides for a clear introduction to elementary geometric transformations in the eight-year school. The topic "Geometrical Transformations" enters the program of optional lessons in the upper grades. Here Challe's theorems are proven for a plane and for space, and a clear concept of a group of transformations is provided.

The program planners proceeded on the assumption that the required program of entrance examinations to higher educational institutions should correspond to the program of the basic mathematics course in secondary school.

A preliminary acquaintance in secondary school with elementary mathematical analysis will permit (university) students to better understand instruction in the basic natural-science and technical disciplines from the very beginning. We believe that this advantage fully compensates for the necessity to acquaint higher school students with complex numbers and formulate the principle of mathematical induction in higher schools, after the transition to the new programs in secondary school.

At the same time we do not close our eyes to the fact that the optional mathematics lessons in (secondary) school will provide additional training to those students who take them, and hence a certain real advantage in competitive higher school examinations. But even now those applicants who have spent sufficient effort on supplementary mathematics lessons enjoy an advantage in competitive exams. Introducing these helpful optional lessons in the general [massovaia] school will make the additional mathematics training, necessary for success in the competition, available to wider circles of young people.

<u>Explanations of the Structure of the Programs</u>

The programs require the following distribution of classroom time:

	Grade 4	Grade 5	Grade 6	Grade 7	Grade 8	Grade 9	Grade 10	Total
Arithmetic and elementary algebra	5	5	–	–	–	–	–	10
Algebra	–	–	4	3/4	4	–	–	11-1/2
Algebra and elementary analysis	–	–	–	–	–	3	3	6
Geometry	1*	1*	2	3/2	2	2	2	12-1/2
Total	6	6	6	6	6	5	5	40

The "Supplementary Chapters..." course for the 9th grade has a certain completeness. After taking this course, 10th graders can, instead of continuing it, elect optional lessons in computer mathematics, physics, etc.

The geometry hours in grades 4-5 (see * above) are included in the general mathematics course. Geometry is not taught as a separate subject until grade 6.

The content of the programs in the upper grades is expanded without decreasing the time spent on basic traditional subjects, partly by introducing elementary algebra and geometry in grades 4-5. Broad experimentation has proven the possibility of a greater intellectual load in these grades. The programs for the upper and intermediate grades have also been freed from a number of traditional, excessively specialized topics (see below, notes to individual points in the program).

The programs require systematic work throughout the entire school course, with a return to material learned earlier only in a brief repetition at the beginning of new topics. While following this "linear" system of constructing a mathematics course, however, the programs divide the course into distinctly separate finished stages. It is desirable that the students should also be conscious of this division. At the end of grade 5, arithmetic, in the sense of knowing how to perform operations with rational numbers, is

finished, and the systematic construction of algebra begins. At the beginning of grade 9, the students must understand that they are now (after propaedeutics in grade 7) first beginning the systematic study of limit processes, characteristic of "higher mathematics" in the traditional but still interesting sense. In accordance with this, there should be separate textbooks for grades 4-5, 6-8, and 9-10.

Without changing its name, the geometry course is divided into the same three stages. The first stage (grades 4-5) is propaedeutics in its logical level. Only gradually do proofs appear of isolated interesting theorems. However, all this material is not wholly repeated in grade 6, but is only partly reviewed, with certain proofs being performed during the study of topic 4. During the second stage (grades 6-8), the systematic study of plane geometry is completed and information about solid geometry is given in connection with drawing, which is extremely important for preparing students for practical work, as well as for those students who, after the 8th grade, will immediately proceed to learn some vocation connected with technology.

The third stage provides a systematic study of solid geometry with the use of vectors and co-ordinates, and a concept of the axiomatic approach to geometry.

The 9th grade geometry course is given as one topic, since it is precisely here that work on a new system of exposition is desirable (for the same reason, the material in topic 4 in grade 6 is not divided).

THE EIGHT-YEAR SCHOOL

Arithmetic and Elementary Algebra (Grades 4 - 5)

It is assumed that in the first three grades the students acquired firm skills in performing the four arithmetic operations with natural numbers and some experience in dealing with elementary fractions which enables them to perform "in their heads" operations of the type:

$$\frac{1}{2} - \frac{1}{3} = \frac{1}{6}; \frac{1}{5} \div 2 = \frac{1}{10}; \frac{1}{5} \cdot 2 = \frac{2}{5}; \text{ etc.}$$

The course in arithmetic and elementary algebra repeats and systematizes the information about natural numbers which the students learned earlier. The systematization is based on understanding the concept of "number" and the operations with numbers, while drawing in concepts of "set," "element in a set," and "membership in a set." The enumerated concepts are explained on the basis of various concrete examples of sets and are learned in the process of performing exercises.

The students gradually become familiar with the concepts of set, addition of sets, the "common part" or "intersection" of sets, and empty set and subset.

These concepts are used in the study of the divisibility of numbers, systems of equations and inequalities, and in forming the concept of functions, where the investigation of examples of finite sets and the correspondences among them are very useful.

By the end of the course, the technique of performing arithmetic operations should be perfected and secure enough to cope with calculations involving numbers of any size. As a rule, however, it is sufficient to confine calculations to 3-, 4-, and 5-place numbers, going beyond these limits only in occasional exercises.

The writing and solving of equations occupy a large place throughout the course. At first, equations are solved on the basis of dependencies among the components and the results of operations; later (in the second topic), certain rules are formulated, including the rule of sign change when transferring a term from one side of the equation to the other. Ultimately, the students should have no difficulty solving linear equations of the type: $0 \cdot 5x - 7 = 0 \cdot 3x - 15$.

Early introduction of equations permits the study of solving verbal problems to be organized in a new way. Sufficiently convincing examples reveal the advantages of the algebraic over the arithmetic method. Later the student himself is permitted to choose which method to use in solving a problem.

Identities are explained on the basis of the laws of arithmetic operations.

When the concept of an expression containing variables is introduced, the basis is laid for forming the concept of functions.

When the concept of a "formula" is introduced, the application of alphabetic letters is expanded. They are used to signify not only numbers, but expressions containing variables.

The inequality signs, familiar to the students from the elementary grades, are used throughout the course. Skills in dealing with inequalities are acquired gradually.

Explanations for Individual Topics

Topic 1. A description of the natural order appears in the first topic as the consecutive points on a ray.

The study of arithmetic operations develops and strengthens the students' calculation skills. Particular attention is paid to difficult cases of multiplication and division, and to operations with zero and 1.

It is useful to combine the repetition of the commutative and associative laws of multiplication with calculating the areas of rectangles and the volumes of rectangular parallelepipeds (the latter will be new to the students).

The arithmetic laws are applied to explaining operations with many-placed numbers and in the transformation of expressions. Exercises in setting up expressions are useful for a deeper understanding of the process of operations.

Topic 2. The topic "Whole Numbers" introduces the removal of brackets and the combining of like terms. The level of difficulty of the identities posed to the students should not exceed operations of the type: $(2x + 3) - (3x - 2) = -x + 5$.

The study of negative numbers and fractions is useful not only for solving equations but for strengthening skills at calculation: a new element, demanding thought, is included in the monotonous work of performing arithmetic operations (the strangeness of performing subtraction and addition, the necessity of determining the sign of the number). An acquaintance with negative numbers will prove useful in geography and nature study lessons.

Positive and negative numbers are introduced as characteristics of directed magnitudes and their changes. The line of real numbers serves as the basic means for studying the addition and subtraction of whole numbers. The modulus of a number is defined as the distance from the point representing the number to the point of origin.

Topic 3. Basic attention is paid to the addition and subtraction of decimals; skills are developed in multiplying and dividing decimals by whole numbers. Multiplying and dividing by fractions belongs to grade 5.

Topic 4. Number systems are studied in topic 4 after division with a remainder, since the operation of division with a remainder is applied in denoting numbers by the said system. Powers are utilized both to represent numbers in the said system, e.g., $50 = 2^5 + 2^4 + 2$, and to factor numbers: $48 = 2^4 \cdot 3$.

Topic 5. Multiplying a whole number by a fraction can be directly preceded by calculating the area of a rectangle.

The study of ordinary fractions should prepare students for the study of algebraic fractions.

Basic attention in topic 5 is concentrated on developing skills in operations with positive numbers. The first concept of the precision of approximate values is given. An elementary concept of the infinite decimal is given during the calculation of decimal approximations of an ordinary fraction.

Topic 6. In connection with the formula $s = vt$ and its graphic interpretation, it is desirable to study motion graphs (graph of the motion of trains with stops, etc.), which will help in the study of physics in the beginning of grade 6.

In general, this section makes broad use of algebraic transcriptions in the formulas: $S = 1/2\, ah$; $V = abc$, etc. The basic characteristics of operations are also transcribed:

$$a \cdot b = b \cdot a, (a \cdot b) \cdot c = a \cdot (b \cdot c), a \cdot (b + c) = a \cdot b + a \cdot c,$$

as well as the laws of operations with fractions:

$$\frac{a}{b} + \frac{c}{d} = \frac{a \cdot d + b \cdot c}{b \cdot d} ; \frac{a}{b} \cdot \frac{c}{d} = \frac{a \cdot c}{b \cdot d} ;$$

$$\frac{a}{b} : \frac{c}{d} = \frac{a \cdot d}{b \cdot c} .$$

Throughout this topic, skills in performing operations with any rational (not only positive) numbers are perfected.

Algebra (Grades 6 - 8)

The 1962 plan assigned 8 hours during the year to algebra in grades 6-8 (the teaching of algebra began in the second half of grade 6). In the new programs we have 11-1/2 hours each year. Moreover, when the new programs for grades 4 - 5 are implemented, students will enter grade 6 with considerable knowledge about algebra. Therefore, new topics can be included in grade 8 without reducing the overall number of hours for topics corresponding to the 1962 programs, as the table on page 24 shows.

In regard to the topics corresponding to the content of the 1962 programs, the following proposals are made:

1) The logical level of exposition is to be raised somewhat, by introducing elementary logic and the use (very cautious, however) of the corresponding symbolism.

1962 Program	No. of hours	New Program	No. of hours
6th grade topics: "Algebraic Expressions," "Rational Numbers. Equations"	36	Transferred to grades 4 - 5	
Remaining topics	240	Topics 1 - 5, 7 - 8	283
		Topics 9 - 11	90
Review	10	Review	20

2) Increased attention is to be paid to developing skills in calculation (approximate calculations, the use of tables). (1)

3) Demands for the performance of artificial complicated operations are to be decreased in comparison with the existing tradition. To clarify this matter, we give examples below, characterizing the level of demands to be made on all students.

We consider it essential to establish firmer demands in regard to the accurate performance of elementary operations, while recommending to students who show a superior interest in mathematics the solution of complicated problems demanding inventiveness or special skills.

The introduction of fractional exponents and exponential functions in the eight-year school lends a logical completeness to a series of generalizations, beginning with the introduction of negative exponents. The general educational interest of an acquaintance with geometrical progressions and exponential functions does not require lengthy explanations. The study of logarithmic functions permits an explanation of the working of the slide rule and expands the student's fund of calculating skills.

As was mentioned in the explanatory note to the program for grades 4 - 5, the students practice solving equations throughout the entire course. Topic 4 summarizes and systematizes the basic concepts pertaining to this. The study of functions and drawing the corresponding graphs also runs through the entire course. Special attention to the "field of a function" and the "field of its values" should be tied in with topic 5. During the study of topic 7, it is also useful to examine certain untraditional graphs, e.g.:

$$y = |x|; \ y = |x - a|; \ y = \frac{x}{|x|}$$

without becoming carried away by excessively complicated examples. In connection with decimal approximations, it is wise to introduce the term $[x]$ for whole values of x and $\{x\}$ for fractional values of x and to draw the corresponding graphs. As a result, the concepts of "characteristic" and "mantissa" will be ready ahead of time for the study of logarithmic calculations in topic 11.

The program explicitly indicates the functions:

$$y = ax + b; \ y = \frac{k}{x}; \ y = ax^2; \ y = ax^3;$$
$$y = \sqrt{x}; \ y = a^x; \ y = \log_a x; \ y = Ax^b.$$

The study of quadratic trinomials belongs in the 8th grade program, where it is connected with the concept of derivatives. This stock of functions is sufficient to develop skills in studying the relationship between the aspect of a graph and its parameters, and concepts of the connection between a function and its inverse.

The study of the dependence between the form of the graph of the fractional linear function

$$y = \frac{ax + b}{cx + d}$$

and its parameters can be recommended, but it does not enter the (required) program. The exponential function $y + Ax^b$ with an arbitrary exponent is referred to only at the very end of the program, when it is revealed that its graph on log paper is always a straight line. Study of the relationship between its form on ordinary graph paper and its exponent b should be investigated only as a possible exercise.

Explanatory Notes to Individual Topics

Topic 1. Here or earlier the signs of implication ($\Rightarrow$) and equivalence ($\Leftrightarrow$) of statements may be introduced. We believe that symbol representation will facilitate the understanding and utilization of the concept of equivalent equations. Somewhat later, in geometry, the principle of proof from the converse will be formulated. When the notation of the negative of a statement ($\overline{A}$) is introduced, one can write down the principle of proof from the converse in the form of a logical identity:

$$(A \Rightarrow B) \Leftrightarrow (\overline{B} \Rightarrow \overline{A}).$$

Topic 2. The algebra of rational monomials possesses a certain completeness and encompasses very many problems of practical importance.

It is sufficient to explain dimensionality by showing that the numerical expression of work changes $ml^2 t^{-2}$ times, if the units of mass, length, and time change respectively m, l, and t times, etc. But the principle of uniformity of formulas having an invariable geometric or physical meaning must be expressly formulated.

Topic 3. Here and later the programs underline the purpose of identities: to reduce expressions of a certain type to a standard form.

The purpose of factoring remains somewhat undefined. Therefore it is appropriate to show its application to the solution of equations and the reduction of fractions in this section, anticipating topics 4 and 5.

The common notation for the standard-form polynomial,

$$a_0 x^n + a_1 x^{n-1} + \ldots + a_n$$

would still be difficult. It is sufficient to write

out a finite number of the terms in the sequence of expressions:

$$a,$$
$$ax + b,$$
$$ax^2 + bx + c,$$
$$ax^3 + bx^2 + cx + d,$$
$$\ldots\ldots\ldots$$

Problems in factoring should not be difficult. Exercises of the type

$$x^3 + ax^2 - x - a = (x^2 - 1)(x + a) = (x - 1)(x + 1)(x + a),$$

are close to the limit for compulsory requirements.

Topic 4. This requires examples of quadratic equations which are solved by factoring, and examples of non-linear systems chosen so that their algebraic solution presents no difficulties, but whose corresponding geometric depictions are varied; e.g., four solutions of the system

$$x^2 + y^2 = 4,$$
$$x^2 - y^2 = 0$$

are depicted as the points of intersection of the circle and two straight lines, etc. Several problems in which the solution of non-linear systems can serve as a useful apparatus for actual geometric or physical problems can be solved later in topic 8, when, after a system is reduced to a quadratic equation, the equation is solved with the help of tables of square roots.

Topic 5. Examples of required transformations:

$$\frac{\dfrac{1}{x} - \dfrac{1}{y}}{\dfrac{1}{x} + \dfrac{1}{y}} = \frac{y - x}{y + x}; \quad \frac{x^2 + ax + bx + ab}{x^2 - a^2} = \frac{x + b}{x - a}$$

Topic 6. Special attention is given to the binary system of notation (including binary fractions). As a minimum, the structure of the binary adder is explained. It is desirable to investigate the technical means of realizing functions of one or two binary ("Boolean") variables and discuss the importance of these functions in mathematical logic.

Topic 7. In connection with the extraction of roots, the need first arises of clarifying concepts of the <u>algorithm</u> for obtaining approximations of any precision. Since time is insufficient, one can limit this to the "empirical method"; but it is advisable to pose the problem of a more effective algorithm and to recommend the analysis of the iterative algorithm for calculating $\sqrt{x}$:

$$ y_{n+1} = \frac{1}{2}\left(y_n + \frac{x}{y_n}\right). $$

An acquaintance with the binary system of notation in topic 6 provides another opportunity to show a very simple but effective algorithm for deriving a square root (and without much additional difficulty, a cube root).

The technique of evaluating errors is fully clarified. The derivation of the most difficult formula

$$ \Delta(a:b) = \frac{b\,\Delta a - a\,\Delta b}{b\,(b+\Delta b)} $$

is possible after topic 5. By replacing $b+\Delta b$ with b, we obtain

$$ \frac{\Delta(a:b)}{a:b} \approx \frac{\Delta a}{a} - \frac{\Delta b}{b}. $$

It becomes even easier to evaluate sum, difference, and product.

In the 9th grade, new light is shed on linear interpolation after an acquaintance with derivatives. Therefore at this point a purely practical approach is possible. Neither proofs nor the memorization of formulas is required in the calculation of surfaces and volumes of geometric shapes; it is far more important to develop an ability to work with a handbook.

Topic 8. Quadratic trinomials are studied in the 9th grade by use of the concept of derivatives. In solving systems, it is useful to state that a system of a quadratic and a linear equation with two unknowns can be reduced to a quadratic equation with one unknown. Examples should not be complex. The material studied is applied in solving inequalities.

Topic 9. Only the formulas for arithmetic and geometric progression explicitly stated in the program are required. However, a sufficient number of examples should be used to illustrate the technique of calculating by recurrent formulas. Especially desirable are exercises with differences of higher orders, for deducing formulas of the sum of squares and the sum of cubes (not for memorization!). A practical acquaintance with inductive proofs is desirable (without a compulsory verbal formula of the "principle of mathematical induction").

Topic 10. Examples of irrational equations for compulsory quizzes:

$$ \frac{x}{\sqrt{1+x^2}} = a; \quad \sqrt{1+x} + \sqrt{1-x} = 1\text{-}1/2 $$

Topic 11. The concept of irrational numbers is not included in the 8th grade program. This does not prevent the teacher from explaining why $\sqrt{2}$ cannot be rational, and to tell in a general way that in all the problems with which the 8th grade student will be concerned, operations with irrational numbers can be replaced by operations with their rational approximate values. The exponential function a^x, $a \geq 0$ was already defined for rational values of x in topic 10. It remains only to treat it precisely like a function — in particular, to examine its graph. Curious students who raise this question are informed without proof that the definition in its basic features also extends to irrational values of x.

The program indicates the minimum stock of formulas that permit an understanding of the basic applications of exponential functions and the laws of logarithmic calculations with the given definition of logarithms.

Geometry (Grades 4 - 8)

The hours allotted to geometry in grades 4 - 5 are distributed throughout the year at the discretion of the teacher. The overall number of hours (65) is sufficient for the pupils to learn the program material and to acquire certain skills in geometrical constructions.

1962 Program	No. of hours	New Program	No. of hours
6th grade topics "Basic Concepts," "Trangles"	46	Transferred to grades 4 - 5	
Remaining topics	188	Topics 4, 6, 8 - 11	193
		New topics 5, 7	20
Review	12	Review	15

In these grades, geometry is constructed as a natural-science discipline which generalizes observations about the surrounding world. Toward the end of grade 5, the importance of the logical element in the teaching of geometry increases.

The above table gives an approximate comparison of the number of hours allotted to geometry in the eight-year school in the past and present programs.

One should bear in mind that in a number of respects the plane geometry course has been simplified. Thus, students are no longer required to expound the proofs of the criteria for the congruence of triangles, but may state the fact and refer to the equality of corresponding parts; the program no longer includes the theorems of metrical correspondences in a circle, the points of intersection of medians and the height of triangles, inscribed and circumscribed rectangles, segments containing a given angle, Geron's formula, etc. (Many of the theorems that were dropped will appear in the course as "problems for proof.")

The properties of continuity, order [poriadok] and motion appear as they are needed and are accepted without proof. The basic axiom about the degree of mobility of plane figures (the position of a figure in a plane is given by indicating a point, a ray extending from it and its locus) is taught only in grade 7 (during topic 7).

The program allows for considerable attention to geometric transformations, whereby the mastery of the relevant concepts proceeds in several stages. Grades 4 - 5 require an experimental approach to geometric transformations; in the study of axial symmetry, wide use is made of folding paper, while the introduction to central symmetry and rotation utilizes the turning of a figure fastened by a pin. In the 6th grade topic "Parallels and Perpendiculars. Axial and Central Symmetry," the basic properties of symmetry (already partly known to students from grades 4 - 5) are established; subsequently, references to these properties replace resorting to experiment. Parallel transfer is investigated in the last section of grade 6 (topic 5). Rotation appears in topic 6 (grade 7), and all forms of motion are compared in topic 7. Transformations of similarity are examined in topic 8, in particular, central homothety.

In the eight-year school, geometrical transformations are regarded only as transformations of figures.

Explanatory Notes to Individual Topics

Topic 1. In the 4th grade, geometry is primarily visual. Broad use is made of cutting shapes from paper and cardboard and folding pieces of paper. The use of graph paper plays a large role; along with this, only gradually do the rules and protractor begin to be used. The compass first appears in connection with measuring segments, and later in connection with drawing circles, when it is also shown that the diameter of a circle is its axis of symmetry. At the end of the 4th grade program, the hypothesis of the equality of vertical angles is given as a theorem, perhaps the first in the whole geometry course.

Topic 2. In the 5th grade the logical element in the geometry course increases, but the number of theorems should still remain very modest: theorem of the sum of angles in a triangle, theorems of the area of a parallelogram, triangle and trapezoid, the Pythagorean theorem. The criteria of congruence of triangles are deduced from constructing triangles from their elements. Thus, if two circles with centers A and B, AB = c, and radii b and a respectively, intersect at two points C and C_1 symmetrical to line AB (in other words, ABC and ABC_1 are congruent, as shown by folding a piece of paper along line AB), then it follows that two triangles with corresponding equal sides are congruent.

The operational side of 5th grade geometry consists in forming elementary skills in geometrical drawing. It is very important that pupils receive a good set of drawing equipment (if possible, including a drawing board and T-square).

In solving problems of construction, the pupils begin systematic use of a set of instruments: ruler, compass, protractor. The choice of construction problems has not been fixed by the program, but the overall number of problems solved should be sufficient to form permanent skills. In establishing the correctness of various constructions ("bisect a segment," "draw a perpendicular through a given point to a given line," "bisect an angle," etc.), it is natural to utilize the concepts of symmetry.

The concept of direction arises in connection with drawing parallel lines. The direct drawing of a great number of parallels (with the aid of ruler and protractor) shows convincingly that a grid of parallel lines covers a plane completely, or, in other words, it illustrates the axiom of parallelism and facilitates the introduction of an angle between directions. (Two directions are distinguished in the pencil of parallel lines, so that the angle between two directions is defined uniquely.) The concept of the parallelogram can easily be connected with the study of segments of parallel lines enclosed between parallels; at this point it is also appropriate to discuss the distance between parallel lines.

Topic 3. The Pythagorean theorem may, for example, be established by the Hindu method, by means of cutting four right triangles with legs a and b out of a square with side a + b.

Topics 4 and 5. In the 6th grade, the students' attention is drawn to the problem of the systematic construction of geometry, the isolation of initial unproven assumptions, and the efficient proof of subsequent theorems. The basic concern is to establish a supplementary "system of axioms" (although it is still insufficient for a purely deductive construction of all of geometry). From this point on, experiment ceases to be the basic tool of knowledge and serves only to illustrate and test (reinforce) the correctness of deductions. The word "axiom" is not mentioned as such in the eight-year school program, since the list of assumptions accepted here without proof is so great that it would be difficult to call them all axioms. However, in the teacher's discussion of the history of geometry at the beginning of grade 6, it is perfectly appropriate to tell about the role of axioms in geometry and to give examples of axioms, while pointing out that a satisfactory axiomatic construction of geometry was not completed until the very end of the nineteenth century.

The idea of a consistently logical construction of geometry should not be stated in the 6th grade, but should arise in the process of learning new facts, rather than precede the study of facts. The general logical concepts indicated in the 6th grade program should be introduced very cautiously and gradually, and only at that stage of the course where the accumulated material will provide a base for the generalizations that are examined; thus, the concept of the converse of a theorem should follow the first examples of reciprocally converse theorems rather than precede them. The process of mastering the general concepts listed at the end of the topic can also be continued beyond grade 6.

Topic 5 may also be studied directly after the first part of topic 4 (parallelism). The matter of choosing the order of exposition throughout the 6th grade remains open.

The ability to construct proofs, acquired in the 6th grade, should be brought up to the level of freely using the concepts of symmetry; problems of the type: "Given the isosceles triangle ABC, prove the equality of the line segments

AM and BM, where M is a point on the altitude (axis of symmetry of the triangle!) CD," should not cause the students any difficulties.

Topic 6 has been considerably shortened by consigning a number of secondary theorems and constructions to (homework) problems. Directed angles and arcs are introduced in connection with rotation. The program does not fix the meaning of the term "directed angle"; many values of directed angles can be included between −180° and +180° or between − ∞ and + ∞; however, the second definition of the term "directed angle" seems preferable to us.

Topic 7. The inclusion of this generalizing section is connected with completing the study of different types of motion (axial and central symmetry, parallel transfer, rotation).

Topic 8. The traditional exposition has been greatly reduced. All theorems about proportional segments are deduced from a single theorem about the intersection of three parallel lines by two arbitrary transversals. The subject of measuring segments has a natural connection with algebraic material. Since the concept of real numbers is lacking at this stage of mathematical study, refinements regarding the commensurability or incommensurability of segments are left out.

The study of similarity begins with a discussion of the general concept of similarity in arbitrary shapes. After proving the criteria of similarity in triangles, it is established that similarity (proportionality of linear measurements) entails conformity (equality of corresponding angles). The similarity of polygons is regarded as a particular case of the general concept of similarity. Central homothety is introduced only in connection with the construction of similar shapes.

Topic 9 does not provide for any proofs of stereometric theorems; its aim is only to systematize somewhat the basic ideas received at drawing lessons about planes, lines in space, and elementary solids.

Topic 10. A precise definition of the length of a curve is not required here (it should be given during topic 1 in the 9th grade course "Algebra and Elementary Analysis"). On the in-

tuitive level, similarity permits us to establish that the circumference ["length"] of a circle is proportional to the radius ($1 = 2\pi R$), and the area ["space"] is proportional to the square of the radius ($S = \pi R^2$). The coincidence of the factor π in both cases is explained by breaking the circle into a great number of sectors. A survey of the formulas for the volumes of geometric solids is given.

The concept of similarity is used to establish the nature of the relationship between the surface area (S) and volumes (V) of geometrical solids and their linear dimensions. The concept of dimensionality is given.

Interested students may optionally perform proofs using Cavalieri's principle.

Topic 11 requires some practice in using tables of trigonometric functions; it is recommended that graphs of these functions be constructed (for the degree values of the angle). The proof of the theorem of cosines can be connected with the formula for the distance between two points given by their coordinates: if vertex A of triangle ABC coincides with the origin, while vertex B lies on the abscissa, then the coordinates of points B and C are (c, 0) and (b cos A, b sin A), and consequently,

$$a^2 = BC^2 = (b \cos A - c)^2 + (b \sin A)^2 = \\ = b^2 + c^2 - 2bc \cos A.$$

Considerable practice in solving scalene triangles is not required.

Topic 12. Neither the proof nor the memorization of the formulas for the surfaces and volumes of circular solids is required. It is far more important to develop skill in working with a handbook.

UPPER GRADES OF SECONDARY SCHOOL
(9 - 10)

Algebra and Elementary Analysis

The essential feature of the course in "Algebra and Elementary Analysis" is the inclusion of derivatives, integrals, and elementary probability theory.

The concept of derivatives, which is visually extremely simple and essentially already known from physics (velocity), is introduced in the first half of the 9th grade in order to utilize it systematically when studying quadratic trinomials and exponential and trigonometric functions.

The concept of integrals is introduced in the 10th grade. Students become acquainted with its elementary aspects in the section "Elementary Theory of Probability."

The course concludes by acquainting the students with elementary information about electronic computers.

Explanatory Notes to Individual Topics

Topic 1. Here it seems appropriate (if this was not done earlier) to make use of the terminology of set theory: the set of solutions of a system is the intersection of the sets of the solutions of the equations it contains. It is also good to analyze examples requiring a concept of union of sets: the set of solutions to the equation $x^2 - y^2$ is the union of sets of solutions to the equations $x + y = 0$ and $x - y = 0$.

In studying a system of two first-degree equations with two unknowns and a determinant equal to zero, it is sufficient to establish, on the basis of geometric interpretation, that in this case the system either has no solutions or is equal to one first-degree equation. It is useful to analyze several other examples of systems of equations with algebraic coefficients.

Topic 2. Here it is desirable to give a proof of the irrationality of $\sqrt{2}$. No systematically expounded theory of irrational numbers is required. A somewhat more detailed explanation can enter the optional course, "Supplementary Chapters and Problems in Mathematics."

The volume of facts of a purely informative nature depends on the discretion of the teacher. Only the final conclusion must be learned and memorized: in the expanded system of numbers, the theorem of the existence of the limit of a bounded monotonic sequence holds true, the usual properties of arithmetic operations and inequalities hold true, and any real number with

any given value approaches the rational numbers.

Topic 3. For elementary functions (e.g., $y = x^2$), students must learn to find, with x_0 and $\epsilon > 0$, that $\delta > 0$ for which $|x - x_0|$ δ yields $|y - y_0| < \epsilon$. After studying the evaluation of error in the 7th grade, this does not present great difficulty.

The heuristic concept of derivatives may appear in the first lessons of this section (see the article by A. N. Kolmogorov in the journal Matematika v shkole, 1965, No. 6).

Topic 4 contains material traditionally studied in school. A new subject is the deduction of derivatives of trigonometric functions, prepared for by examining the formulas of sine and cosine with sums and differences for arguments.

Topic 5. Study of the law of exponential growth requires an examination of examples from economics, biology, etc.

Topic 6. The concept of integrals is introduced by way of the relation of an integral to the area on the graph of a function — without strict proof.

Assuming (without proof) that there exists

$$\lim_{\Delta \to 0} \frac{a^\Delta - 1}{\Delta} = c,$$

it is easy to establish the formula $(a^x)' = c\, a^x$. The number e may appear as a base, whereby the coefficient c is equal to 1.

The application of integrals to calculating volumes and areas belongs to the geometry course.

Topic 7. In the field of solving trigonometric equations, the program requires only a few examples.

In finding the derivative of

$$y = c \cos (kx + \Theta)$$

(which is necessary for understanding harmonic oscillations), the formula of a function derived from a function may be applied (with a heuristic, non-rigorous deduction). The fact that (1) gives a general solution to the equation $y'' = -k^2 y$ is not proven (although it is desirable to discuss this problem with elementary conditions for this equation). It is assumed that geometric illustrations are applied in explaining the addition of harmonic vibrations.

Topic 8. The elements of combinatorial theory are subordinated to the study of elementary probability theory. Their independent study and the introduction of terms from the theory of permutations and combinations remain optional.

The course ends with a talk by the teacher about the application of electronic computers in science and the national economy (topic 9). Where possible, the program provides for an excursion to a computer center. An acquaintance with the working principles of electronic computers and programming is carried out in optional lessons.

Geometry

The geometry course for grades 9 - 10 differs from the traditional one in its broad application of vectors and coordinates. The well-known advantages of analytical methods over purely synthetic ones permit us to simplify many sections of the program — e.g., the use of scalar products facilitates the deduction of theorems about the perpendicularity of lines and planes. (In particular, if the perpendicularity of a line to a plane is defined by changing to zero the scalar products Ia and Ib, where I is the vector of the line, and a and b are the vectors defining the plane — then the theorem of two perpendiculars from the traditional geometry course becomes almost self-evident.)

The program leaves undecided whether to begin the exposition of elementary solid geometry by listing the spatial axioms of intersection or whether to rely on visual concepts to formulate the properties of vector operations, which will then serve as basic assumptions (axioms) on which to base the subsequent deductive construction of the course. In any event, the proof of the distributive property of scalar multiplication utilizes elementary facts of solid geometry.

The formulas for the volumes of elementary solids are deduced by the methods of integral calculus.

Explanatory Notes to Individual Topics

Topic 1. It is assumed that students are already familiar with the basic facts pertaining to the mutual distribution of lines and planes in space from their drawing exercises and from the geometry course in the eight-year school. Now the information received earlier is systematized. The theorem of three perpendiculars can be formulated in terms of orthogonal projections: a projection on a plane, and the subsequent projection on a line lying in this plane, lead to the same result as a direct projection on the line.

The program refrains from an excessively detailed listing of theorems, since it is based on a selective system of expounding solid geometry.

The program includes the application of parallel projections to the depiction of solids because of the following considerations. Sketches and drawings used in proving solid geometry theorems and in analyzing solid geometry problems are usually made with an "arbitary" parallel projection. A full analysis of the degree of their arbitrariness goes beyond the limits of the required program. However, the problem of assumptions made in the depiction of elementary geometric figures should be made clear to the students.

The concept of scalar products leads naturally back to the theorem of cosines.

Topic 2. This topic is a direct continuation of the preceding one. The theory of polyhedral angles and the problem of measuring polyhedral angles are conveniently combined with the study of elementary spherical geometry; however, such a method of exposition requires additional time and cannot be recommended as obligatory.

The program does not provide for defining the general concept of right polyhedrons or for posing the problem of enumerating such polyhedrons; the students can become acquainted with a right octahedron (but not with dodecahedrons or isosahedrons!) in the process of solving problems.

Formulas for the volumes of solids are deduced by means of integral calculus (using the concept of primitive functions).

The geometry course concludes with a talk about the axiomatic method in geometry; here, Lobachevskii's non-Euclidean geometry and the unprovability of the axiom of parallels may be examined.

OUTLINE OF THE MATHEMATICS PROGRAM

I. The Eight-Year School

Arithmetic and Elementary Algebra (grades 4 - 5)

Grade 4   (6 hours a week, a total of 210 hrs., including 30 hrs. for geometry)

Topics	Hours
1. Natural numbers	85
2. Whole numbers	45
3. Decimals	50

Grade 5   (6 hrs. a week, a total of 210 hrs., including 35 hrs. for geometry)

4. Divisibility of numbers	20
5. Operations with common fractions and decimals	85
6. Rational numbers. Formulas and coordinates	70

Algebra (Grades 6 - 8)

Grade 6   (4 hrs. a week, total of 140 hrs.)

1. Systematization of concepts of algebraic problems acquired in grades 4 - 5	12
2. Ratios, proportions, monomials	40
3. Integral expressions	48
4. Equations and systems of equations	40

Grade 7   (3 hrs. a week in the first semester, 4 hrs. a week in the second, a total of 122 hrs.)

5. Rational expressions	40
6. Systems of notation. Arithmetical mechanisms of computers	10
7. Inequalities. Approximate computations. Extraction of roots	72

Grade 8   (4 hrs. a week, total of 140 hrs.)

8. Quadratic equations	30
9. Numerical sequences. Arithmetic and geometric progressions	25
10. Fractional exponents	30
11. Exponential and logarithmic functions	35
Review	20

Geometry   (Grades 4 - 8)

Grade 4   (30 hrs., distributed throughout the year)

1. Basic geometric concepts	30

Grade 5   (35 hrs., distributed throughout the year)

2. Geometric constructions	25
3. Areas	10

Grade 6   (2 hrs. a week, total of 70 hrs.)

4. Parallelism and perpendicularity. Axial and central symmetry	60
5. Parallel transfer	10

Grade 7   (3 hrs. a week in the first semester, 2 hrs. a week in the second, a total of 88 hrs.)

6. Circle and rotation	30
7. Motions	10
8. Proportionality of segments. Similarity of shapes	36
9. Systematization of information about solid geometry drawing lessons (distributed throughout the year)	12

Grade 8   (2 hrs. a week, total of 70 hrs.)

10. Measurement of area and volume	25
11. Metrical ratios in the triangle. Trigonometric functions	30
Review	15

II. The Upper Grades (9 - 10) of Secondary School

Algebra and Elementary Analysis

Grade 9   (3 hrs. a week, total of 105 hrs.)

1. Systems of equations and inequalities	15
2. Infinite sequences and limits	15
3. Continuous functions, limit of a function, derivatives	45
4. Trigonometric functions, their graphs and derivatives	30

Grade 10   (3 hrs. a week, total of 105 hrs.)

5. Derivative of an exponential function and a logarithm	8
6. Integrals	12
7. Trigonometric functions (continuation)	40
8. Elementary theory of probability	23
9. Information about electronic	

computers   2
   Review   20

Geometry
Grade 9   (2 hrs. a week, total of 70 hrs.)
   1. Distribution of lines and planes.
Coordinates and vectors in space   70
  Grade 10   (2 hrs. a week, total of 70 hrs.)
   2. Polyhedrons and solids of revo-
lution   50
   Review   20

THE MATHEMATICS PROGRAM FOR THE EIGHT-YEAR SCHOOL

Arithmetic and Elementary Algebra
Grade 4   (6 hrs. a week, total of 210 hrs., including 30 hrs. for geometry)
   1. Natural numbers — 85 hrs.

The reading and writing of many-placed numbers. Depiction of numbers as points on a ray. Comparison of numbers.

The arithmetic laws: commutation, association and distribution. Addition, subtraction, multiplication and division of many-placed numbers.

Numerical expressions. Expressions containing variables. The numerical value of an expression. The transformation of expressions on the basis of the arithmetic laws.

Note: The concept of volume of a right-angled parallelepiped is introduced in connection with study of the arithmetic laws.

   2. Whole numbers — 45 hrs.

Positive and negative numbers. The depiction of numbers as points on a line (the line of real numbers). Modulus of a number. Comparison of numbers.

Addition. Laws of addition. Role of zero in addition. Opposite numbers. Subtraction. Distance between two points on the real line. Algebraic sum. Multiplication. Laws of multiplication. Law of signs during multiplication. Role of one during multiplication. Division.

Reduction of expressions: removing parentheses, taking out the common factor, combining like terms.

   3. Decimals — 50 hrs.

Measuring magnitudes. The decimal system of measurement. The decimal.

Depiction of decimals as points on a line. Comparison of decimals.

Addition and subtraction. Multiplication and division by a whole number.

Grade 5   (6 hrs. a week, total of 210 hrs., including 35 hrs. for geometry)
   4. Divisibility of numbers — 20 hrs.

Concept of degree. Division with a remainder. Number systems (decimal, binary). Factors of a number. Simple and complex numbers. Criteria of the divisibility of numbers. Factoring of numbers. Largest common denominator. Reciprocally simple numbers. Least common multiple.

   5. Operations with common fractions and decimals — 85 hrs.

The common fraction. Depiction of fractions as points on a line. Reducing fractions to a common denominator. Simplification of fractions. Comparison of fractions.

The four arithmetic operations with common fractions and decimals. Laws of operations. Approximate value of a number. Margin of error. Rounding off numbers. Decimal approximations of common fractions. Percentages.

   6. Rational numbers. Formulas and coordinates — 70 hrs.

Operations with rational numbers of either sign.

Calculating from formulas. The formula $s = vt$. Formulas of the circumference of a circle, area of a rectangle, triangle, and circle, volume of a right-angled parallelepiped. Formulas of the area of a square and volume of a cube. Formula of percentages. Intermediate arithmetic.

Axes of coordinates. Abscissa and ordinate of a point in a plane. Construction of a point from its coordinates.

Graphs of motion. Graphs of temperature, cost, etc.

Algebra
Grade 6   (4 hrs. a week, total of 140 hrs.)
   1. Systematization of algebraic concepts

acquired in grades 4 - 5 — 12 hrs.

Use of letters in algebra. Equations and identities. The concept of a function.

2. Ratios, proportions, monomials — 40 hrs.

Ratios of magnitudes and numbers. Proportions. Basic property of a proportion. Finding the unknown term in a proportion. Direct and inverse proportionality. Graphs of $y = kx$; $y = k/x$.

Degrees with whole-number exponents (positive, negative and zero). The formulas: $a^m \cdot a^n = a^{m+n}$; $(a^m)^n = a^{mn}$.

Monomials and their reduction to the standard form: $kx^l y^m z^n$. Writing large and small numbers in the form: $k \cdot 10^n$.

The dimensionality of geometric and physical formulas.

3. Integral expressions — 48 hrs.

The reduction of any integral expression into a polynomial (sum of integral monomials). The standard form of a polynomial with one variable.

Factoring and formulas of factoring:
$(a \pm b)^2$; $(a \pm b)^3$; $(a+b)(a-b)$.

Graphs of linear functions and of the functions ax^2, ax^3. Examples of graphs of other second- and third-degree polynomials.

4. Equations and systems of equations — 48 hrs.

Properties of equalities. Set of solutions of a system of equations and its geometric depiction in the case of one or two unknowns.

Solution of systems of linear equations.

Grade 7 (3 hrs. a week in the first semester and 4 hrs. a week in the second, a total of 122 hrs.)

5. Rational expressions — 40 hrs.

The transformation of any rational expression into a ratio of two polynomials. Simplifying algebraic fractions by factoring the numerator and denominator.

Examples of equations with an unknown in the denominator.

6. Arithmetic mechanisms of computers — 10 hrs.

The binary system of notation — the arithmetic basis of electronic computers. Convert-

ing whole numbers and fractions from the binary system to the decimal system and back (give examples).

Binary arithmetic. Binary addition on the binary adder (the basic element of the arithmetic mechanism of computers).

7. Inequalities. Approximate computations. Extraction of roots — 72 hrs.

Properties of inequalities. Operations with inequalities. The inequality:
$$|a+b| \leq |a| + |b|.$$

First-degree inequalities with one and two unknowns, their geometric meaning. The set of solutions of inequalities; equivalency of inequalities.

Absolute and relative error. Evaluation of error in the sum, difference, product and quotient of approximate numbers.

Rules of dropping places in approximate calculations. The slide rule.

Inverse functions. Graph of the function $y = \sqrt{x}$.

Finding a square root by graph, table, slide-rule and by means of the algorithm giving an approximation of any desired precision. The concept of extracting roots of any degree.

Tables of squares, cubes, quadratic and cube roots.

Linear interpolation.

Calculating (from formulas) the volumes and areas of prisms, pyramids, cylinders, cones and spheres.

Grade 8 (4 hrs. a week, total of 140 hrs.)

8. Quadratic equations — 30 hrs.

General formula of solution. Viète's theorem and its inverse. Examples of equations and systems reduced to quadratic.

9. Numerical sequences. Arithmetic and geometric progressions — 25 hrs.

Recurrent definitions of sequences. Formula of a general term and the sum n of the terms of an arithmetic or geometric progression.

10. Fractional exponents — 30 hrs.

Reducing expressions containing only the signs of multiplication, division, power or root to the standard form: $kx^\alpha y^\beta z^\gamma$.

Examples of more complex transformations of

irrational expressions and solutions of irrational equations.

11. Exponential and logarithmic functions — 35 hrs.

Exponential function. Formulas: $a^x \cdot a^y = a^{x+y}$; $(a^x)^y = a^{xy}$.

Graph of the exponential function. Logarithmic function and its graph. Formulas:

$$\log_a(xy) = \log_a x + \log_a y;$$

$$\log \frac{x}{y} = \log_a x - \log_a y;$$

$$\log_a x^c = c \log_a x; \quad \log_b x = \frac{\log_a x}{\log_a b}.$$

Tables of logarithms and "antilogarithms." Examples of calculations using tables.

Graph of the exponential function $y = Ax^b$ on log paper; graph of the exponential function on semi-log paper.

Review — 20 hrs.

Geometry

Grade 4   (30 hrs., distributed throughout the year)

1. Basic geometric concepts — 30 hrs.

Geometric figure, surface, line. Straight line, radius, segment. Broken line; its length. Comparison of the length of a broken line with the length of a segment uniting its ends. Ratio between the sides of a triangle.

Angles. Comparison of angles. Bisector of an angle. Adjacent and vertical angles. The right angle and its construction by means of a protractor. Types of triangles.

Perpendicular to a line and its construction by means of a protractor. Distance from a point to a line. Axial symmetry.

Circle, center, radius, diameter, chord, arc. Measuring the degrees of an angle. The protractor. Adjacent and vertical angles.

Grade 5   (35 hrs., distributed throughout the year)

2. Geometrical constructions — 25 hrs.

Construction with a compass and ruler: basic constructions; constructing figures symmetrical to a given figure in regard to a line or a point. Construction of figures turned at a given angle.

Construction of parallel lines with a ruler,

protractor, T-square. Pencil of parallel lines; direction. The parallelogram and its center of symmetry.

The triangle and its parts. The sum of angles in a triangle. The construction of triangles from three parts (four cases). Criteria for congruence of triangles. Construction of right triangles. Criteria for congruence of right triangles.

3. Areas — 10 hrs.

Finding areas by cutting out shapes and rearranging them. Area of a parallelogram, triangle, trapezoid. The Pythagorean theorem.

Note: Formulas for the circumference and area of a circle (without proof) are included in the 5th grade course of arithmetic and elementary algebra.

Grade 6   (2 hrs. a week, total of 70 hrs.)

4. Parallelism and perpendicularity. Axial and central symmetry — 60 hrs.

The properties of angles formed by parallel lines and a transversal (the theorem and its converse). The parallelogram, rhombus, rectangle, square, and their properties.

Convex figures. Convex polyhedrons. Sums of the internal and external angles of a convex polyhedron.

Ratios between the sides and angles of a triangle.

The inclined plane and its projection. Properties of the perpendicular and the inclined plane. Properties of a perpendicular passing through the center of a segment. Properties of the bisector of an angle. The isosceles triangle.

Properties of axial and central symmetry.

The theorem, assumptions and conclusions. Converse and antithesis. Method of proving from the antithesis.

5. Parallel transfer — 10 hrs.

Definition of parallel transfer. The equality of figures derived one from the other by parallel transfer. The solution of problems in parallel transfer.

Grade 7   (3 hrs. a week in the first semester, 2 hrs. a week in the second, a total of 88 hrs.)

6. Circles and circumferences — 30 hrs.

Circumference and circle. Line tangent to a circle; secant.

Intersecting and tangential circles; internal

and external tangency.

Directed angles and arcs. Rotation and its properties.

Relation between chords, arcs, and central angles of the same circle. Measurement of angles and arcs. Properties of a diameter perpendicular to a chord. Properties of arcs contained between parallel chords. Inscribed angles.

Circles inscribed in a triangle and circumscribing a triangle. Rectilinear polygons.

7. Transfers — 10 hrs.

Transfers and their properties. Concept of orientation. Proper and improper transfers.

Types of symmetry of figures. Figures having several axes of symmetry.

8. Proportionality of segments. Similarity of figures — 36 hrs.

Measurement of segments. Ratio of segments. Proportionality of segments cut off by transversals across parallel lines.

Similarity. Coefficient of similarity. Criteria for the similarity of triangles.

Homothety as a method of constructing similar figures. Plane-table surveying.

9. Systematization of information about solid geometry obtained in drawing lessons (distributed throughout the year) — 12 hrs.

Parallelism and perpendicularity of lines and planes. Angles between lines and planes.

Development of the prism, pyramid, cylinder, and cone.

Grade 8 (2 hrs. a week, total of 70 hrs.)

10. Measurement of areas and volumes — 25 hrs.

Measurement of areas on graph paper. Ratio of the areas of similar figures. Area of a rectangle, parallelogram, triangle, trapezoid. Area of a polygon.

Circumference and area of a circle.

Concept of volume. Concept of similarity in space, ratio of volumes of similar bodies.

11. Metrical ratios in the triangle. Trigonometric functions — 30 hrs.

Metrical ratios in the right triangle. Pythagorean theorem. Calculation of the distance between two points given by their coordinates. Equation of a circle.

Trigonometric functions of acute and obtuse angles: sine, cosine and tangent. Change in trigonometric functions when the argument is changed from 0° to 180°. Values of trigonometric functions for angles of 0, 30, 45, 60 and 90 degrees.

Tables of trigonometric functions. Identities:

$$\sin^2 \alpha + \cos^2 \alpha = 1; \ \text{tg}\,\alpha = \frac{\sin\alpha}{\cos\alpha} ;$$

$$\sin (90° - \alpha) = \cos\alpha; \ \cos (90° - \alpha) = \sin \alpha;$$
$$\sin (180° - \alpha) = \sin\alpha; \ \cos (180° - \alpha) = -\cos \alpha.$$

The solution of right triangles. Theorem of cosines, formula for the area of a triangle, theorem of sines. Solution of acute triangles.

Review — 15 hrs.

MATHEMATICS PROGRAM FOR UPPER GRADES OF SECONDARY SCHOOL (Grades 9 - 10)

Algebra and Elementary Analysis
Grade 9 (3 hrs. a week, total of 105 hrs.)

1. Systems of equations and inequalities — 15 hrs.

Clarifying the concepts of the set of solutions to a system of inequations or inequalities and the equivalence of systems of equations and inequalities.

Study of a system of two first-degree equations with two unknowns.

2. Infinite sequences and limits — 15 hrs.

Definition of a limit. Sum of an infinitely decreasing geometric progression. Repeating decimals.

Irrational numbers as non-repeating decimals. Proof of the irrationality of $\sqrt{2}$. Existence of a limit in a bounded monotonic sequence (without proof). Circumference of a circle and the number π.

Infinitesimals. Theorems of the limits of a sum, product, and quotient.

3. Continuous functions, limit of a function. Derivatives — 45 hrs.

Definition of continuity. Continuity of rational functions in every point of their field of definition. Derivatives.

Derivatives of a sum, product, quotient, x^n for whole values of n, inverse function.

Increase and decrease of functions; maximums and minimums.

Study of quadratic trinomials.

Application of derivatives in geometry (tangents) and physics (velocity, acceleration).

4. Trigonometric functions, their graphs and derivatives — 30 hrs.

Generalization of the concept of angles. Radian measurement of angles and arcs. Limit of the relation of a chord to an arc.

Trigonometric functions with a numerical argument, their graphs, evenness and oddness, periodicity. Sine and cosine of sum and difference. Continuity of trigonometric functions; their derivatives.

Grade 10 (3 hrs. a week, total of 105 hrs.)

5. Derivatives of exponential functions and logarithms — 8 hrs.

Derivative of an exponential function. Equation of exponential increase. Derivative of a logarithm.

6. Integrals — 12 hrs.

Primitive functions. The definite integral and its application in determining the area under a curve. The formulas of Newton and Leibniz.

7. Trigonometric functions (continuation) — 40 hrs.

Reduction formulas.

Ratios between trigonometric functions of the same argument.

Trigonometric functions of the sum and difference of doubled and halved arguments.

Concept of inverse trigonometric functions.

Harmonic oscillations; the equation $y'' = -k^2 y$. Addition of harmonic vibrations with a common period.

8. Elementary probability theory — 23 hrs.

Concept of probability. Calculating probability as the ratio of the number of favorable cases to the overall number of cases. Independent experiments. Bernoulli's solution. Pascal's triangle. The formulas:

$$C_{n+1}^{m+1} = C_n^m + C_n^{m+1}; \ C_n^m = C_n^{n-m};$$

$$C_n^0 + C_n^1 + \dots + C_n^n = 2^n.$$

Newton's binomial.

Discussion by the teacher about the law of large numbers and statistical laws.

9. Application of electronic computers in science and the national economy — 2 hrs.

Discussion by the teacher.

Excursion to a computer center.

Review — 20 hrs.

Geometry

Grade 9 (2 hrs.) a week, total of 70 hrs.)

1. Analysis of lines and planes; coordinates and vectors in space — 70 hrs.

The logical structure of geometry (definitions, axioms, theorems).

Parallelism of lines and planes in space. Pencil of parallel lines. Direction. Vectors in a plane and in space and parallel transfers. Addition of vectors, their multiplication by a number. Analysis of a vector into three directions.

Parallel projection (on a plane). Application to the construction of depictions of three-dimensional figures.

Perpendicularity of lines and planes. Orthogonal projection on a plane and on a line.

Angles between lines and planes.

Area of projection. Theorem of three perpendiculars.

Coordinates of a vector and a point in a right-angled system of coordinates. Scalar multiplication, its expression by means of coordinates, properties of scalar multiplication. Distance between two points in space.

Grade 10 (2 hrs. a week, total of 70 hrs.)

2. Polyhedrons and solids of revolution — 50 hrs.

Polyhedral angles. Plane and dihedral angles of a polyhedral angle.

Prism and parallelepiped. Pyramid. Truncated pyramid. Cube and right tetrahedron. Surfaces of the prism and pyramid. Surfaces of revolution and bodies of revolution.

Concept of volume. Volume of the parallelepiped, prism, cylinder, pyramid, cone, spherical segment, and sphere. Surfaces of circular solids (cylinder, cone, spherical segment, sphere). Problems in surface areas and volumes.

A closing talk by the teacher about the axiomatic method in geometry.

Review — 20 hrs.

OPTIONAL COURSES

Supplementary Chapters and Problems in Mathematics

Grade 9   (2 hrs. a week, total of 70 hrs.)

1. Sets and operations on them (8 hrs.).

Covered in connection with the study of systems and inequalities in the required program.

2. Natural numbers and the principle of mathematical induction (8 hrs.).

Divisibility, factoring (proof of uniqueness). Principle of mathematical induction. Supplementary problems in numerical sequences.

3. Generalization of the concept of number. Complex numbers (12 hrs.).

The field of rational numbers. Irrational numbers. The field of real numbers. Complex numbers and their geometric interpretation.

4. Algebraic equations of any degree (12 hrs.)

Factorability of polynomials, Bezout's theorem, theorem of the existence of a root (without proof), linear factoring of polynomials. Solution of problems in drawing up equations and systems of equations.

5. Problems and supplementary questions about differential calculus (8 hrs.).

In particular — the derivative of a function from a function. Solution of problems using the concept of derivatives.

6. Geometric transformations (22 hrs.).

Chall's theorem in a plane and in space. Transformations of similarity in a plane and in space. Projections and affine transformations of a plane. The concept of a group of transformations. Solution of geometric problems.

Grade 10.   (2 hrs. a week, total of 70 hrs.)

1. Integrals (10 hrs.).

The integral as the limit of a sum. Applications in geometry and mechanics.

The natural logarithm as $\int \frac{dx}{x}$. The number e and the exponential function e^x for real values of x.

2. Complex numbers and trigonometry (14 hrs.).

The trigonometric form of a complex number. Operations on complex numbers in trigonometric form. De Moivre's formula. Roots of one and binomial equations.

e^{ix} for real values of x and Euler's formulas. Applications to the theory of oscillations.

Solving problems in all sections of the course (34 hrs.).   (This time may be concentrated or broken up in accordance with the material in the general course.) Special attention is given to problems in solid geometry for developing spatial concepts.

Topics to be chosen by the instructor (12 hrs.), e. g., "Differential Equations and Their Importance in Natural Sciences" (12 hrs.).

The geometric interpretation of the first-degree equation (directional field). Concept of problems with initial conditions. Theorems of existence and uniqueness. Examples of differential equations.

"Supplementary Problems in the Theory of Probability" (12 hrs.). Mathematical expectancy. Dispersion and the law of large numbers (proof in the form of Chebyshev's theorem).

"The Concept of Non-Euclidean Geometries and the Axiomatic Method in Geometry" (12 hrs.), e. g., selected theorems in the geometry of the sphere, including proofs, and a talk by the teacher about Lobachevskii's geometry and other systems of geometry.

Footnote

1) In grades 6 - 8, one should not neglect the development of skills in making rough estimates of the expected results of arithmetic operations.

Matematika v shkole, 1967, No. 2

A. N. Kolmogorov

NEW PROGRAMS AND SOME BASIC QUESTIONS ABOUT IMPROVING

THE MATHEMATICS COURSE IN THE SECONDARY SCHOOL

I

The first version of the draft program published in issue No. 1 of Matematika v shkole was drawn up in 1965; 4,000 copies were printed, which permitted rather broad debate, in the spring of 1966, among groups of teachers, workers in institutes of teacher improvement and teacher training, in universities, and in the Academy of Sciences of the USSR. Many requests expressed during the debate were acknowledged by those who planned the programs. In a number of sections, the programs were considerably simplified. But in some matters such basic differences of opinion were expressed that the planners and the central commission for the content of secondary education cannot expect unanimous approval of the choice made. I will begin with a survey of the basic differences of opinion expressed during the debate.

1. There was not complete unanimity in regard to the desirability of an earlier coverage of a number of subjects in the eight-year school. Even though our proposals were approved by the majority of participants in the debate, I will briefly repeat the reasons for our proposals.

We believe that the introduction of subject teaching [predmetnoe prepodavanie] from the 4th grade on will expedite the earlier introduction of algebraic ideas (negative numbers, equations, alphabetic symbols, the numerical axis and numerical plane, and elementary functions in the 4th and 5th grades). I will say in this regard that those who planned the program for the 4th and 5th grades approached the evaluation of the expected results of the study of arithmetic in the first three grades very cautiously. Our 4th and 5th grade programs do not fully utilize the material included in the new programs planned for grades 1 - 3 (which, in my personal opinion, are in need of some simplification).

An earlier introduction to algebra permits the 8th grade program to carry geometric progression and exponential and logarithmic functions without being overloaded with new ideas. Since the final draft adds an extra hour to the 8th grade mathematics course (6 hours a week instead of the present 5), objections to this proposal become even less justified. I will say a few words later about the methods aspect of the question.

2. The final text of the draft preserves instructions limiting the level of difficulty of compulsory exercises for all students. This drew many attacks from adherents of "developing

skills" [vyrabotka navykov]. I will emphasize once more that, as is stated in the explanations to the programs, this is not a matter of lowering requirements for firm, clear knowledge and the habit of correct solution of algebraic problems, etc., but only an effort to prevent a tendency to drilling in the solution of purely academic problems. I will return to this question later, and for the moment will confine myself to the following. There is no doubt that skills in performing certain basic, constantly met operations should be automatic. This pertains not only to the four rules of arithmetic, but to elementary algebraic transformations and to the drawing of diagrams (by hand, without drafting instruments!) of elementary geometric figures. But the range of these automatic and rapid skills should be very limited. For example, there is no reason why they should include finding logarithms and antilogarithms of intricate academic expressions, etc. I will also return to these questions later.

3. An organic and sufficiently early (9th grade) introduction of the elements of mathematical analysis into the secondary school course was approved by the majority of participants in the debate. But many teachers expressed doubts about the accessibility of this material, and certain officials of higher educational institutions flatly opposed any introduction. However, the introduction of elements of mathematical analysis into the secondary school program was approved by the council of mathematics teaching methods in the Ministry of Higher and Specialized Secondary Education of the USSR, consisting mainly of workers in higher technical schools.

Of no less importance, from the standpoint of the influence of the mathematics course in molding the students' overall scientific outlook, is the introduction of elementary concepts of the theory of probability in the secondary school course. This did not draw open objections during the debate on the first version of the program, but it remained in the background. The program planners do not doubt the possibility of its implementation, since they have in mind very simple and graphic material. But here, in contrast to the elements of mathematical analysis, we have no experience in teaching the subject in the general school. It will be possible to accumulate such experience in the next few years by means of optional lessons.

4. Many participants in the debate sharply criticized the clear reference in the first version of the programs to elementary concepts and definitions of the theory of sets, mathematical logic and elements of abstract algebra (the concepts of groups, rings, fields). The planners regarded this not as the inclusion of additional material in the program, but mainly as a more modern (and essentially simpler and more intelligible) exposition of questions that are implied in the traditional course in an unclear form. In comparison with the beginnings of introducing the elements of "modern mathematics," which have become widespread in the school practice of a number of other countries, our proposals were very modest. Nonetheless the debate revealed that our proposals had not been preceded by sufficiently broad propagation of the ideas of "modern mathematics." It is curious that our proposals encountered particularly sharp objections among authoritative representatives of related sciences — physics and mechanics.

In the published final draft program, some of our proposals relating to elements of set theory and mathematical logic have been transferred from the basic text, containing compulsory requirements, to the recommendations made in the program supplements; others have been transferred to the program of optional lessons. The authors of the program yielded in this regard partly out of fear that in unskilled hands any attempts to modernize the logical structure of the school course might do more harm than good.

5. Many attacks were made on the formulation (found in the explanations to the program) regarding the logical level of the geometry course in grades 6 - 8. However, I believe that these attacks are largely the result of misunderstanding. In proposing that the criteria for the equality of triangles be accepted without proof, and by saying that an axiomatic development of geometry, in the strict sense of the word, is not feasible in a course beginning in the 6th grade, we are only trying to combat the widespread tendency to create the appearance of strict develop-

214

ment in the school exposition. I will also return to this matter later.

II

Having completed my survey of the 1966 discussions, I shall attempt to clarify the general aims of the program planners, after analyzing a few individual cases for the sake of example.

We considered the attainment of ideological consistency in the secondary school mathematics course to be one of our basic aims. By this I have in mind the following requirements: 1) wherever possible, the students must be led along direct routes toward modern, rational methods of solving problems; 2) the transition to a new range of ideas must be motivated, insofar as possible, in a manner that students understand; 3) every topic in the student's work, once begun, must be carried out to those minimal results which will actually justify it; the school should not be concerned with filling students' memories with preparations that will not be used in the school course, in the hope that they will come in handy some day.

The first of these requirements motivated the planners' recommendation of an earlier introduction of algebra in writing down general formulas for solving model problems and equations. The programs recommend an earlier introduction of negative numbers for the same reason.

Attempts were made to acquaint students with negative numbers even earlier. The program planners settled on the 4th grade because subject teaching is introduced then and, naturally, mathematics instructors are better prepared to make innovations in the teaching of arithmetic and the rules of algebra.

From the logical standpoint, this is the natural order of beginning a systematic course in arithmetic: natural numbers, followed by the complete system of whole numbers ($..., -2, -1, 0, 1, 2, 3, ...$). As a result, the depiction of numbers as points on a "numerical straight line" precedes the systematic study of fractions. But pupils learn about the simplest fractions as early as the first three grades. They have no difficulty in finding the points marked 37-1/10 or 37-2/10

on a thermometer. In drawing graphs of the temperature change of air (included in the program of the first three grades), they will naturally depict the course of temperature as a continuous line and will not be surprised that the transition from negative to positive temperatures can fall at 7-1/2 a.m. on the graph, etc. These skills are merely systematized and generalized in the last topic of the 4th grade (which directly indicates "depiction of decimals as points on a straight line").

To illustrate the second general requirement, let us examine topics 9, 10, and 11 of the 8th grade program. They enable students to see the historical road of mathematical development which led to the modern definition of exponential and logarithmic functions. When covering topic 9, it becomes possible to contrast the arithmetic progression $(0, a, 2a, 3a, ...)$ with the geometric progression $(1, b, b^2, b^3, ...)$. Then, when it is seen that multiplying the factors of the second progression corresponds to adding the factors of the first progression, one can discuss the first tables of logarithms.

In covering topic 10, it is useful to set the problem of interpolating the geometrical progression: $(1, 10, 100, 1000, ...)$. For example, if one sets

$$b = 10^{0.0001} = \sqrt[10000]{10}$$

and compares the progression

$$1, b, b^2, ..., b^{1000} = 10$$

with the progression

$$0; 0.0001; 0.0002; ...,$$

one obtains nothing less than the four-place table of antilogarithms in Bradis's collection. It is useful to use this table without delay to prepare a large-scale graph of the function

$$y = b^n \text{ from } x = 0.001 \cdot n.$$

A formally irreproachable introduction of exponential functions is impossible without introducing irrational numbers, but does not require any developed theory of them. One need only remember that for rational r and s in topic 10 it was proven that for $a > 1$, if $r < s$, then $a^r < a^s$; then show, by using the graph of $y = 10^x$, that this inequality represents the monotonicity of the function a^x <u>for all rational values of x</u>; then accept without proof that there exists a single monotonic function a^x <u>for all values of x</u>, which for rational values of x receives the definitions:

$$a^x = a^{\frac{p}{q}} = \sqrt[q]{a^p}, \quad \text{if} \quad x = \frac{p}{q}$$

and

$$a^x = a^{-\frac{p}{q}} = \frac{1}{\sqrt[q]{a^p}}, \quad \text{if} \quad x = -\frac{p}{q}.$$

I imagine that in a superior [sil'nyi] class, a discussion of irrational numbers would inevitably arise as early as the 7th grade (the irrationality of $\sqrt{2}$, $\sqrt{3}$, etc.). In such a class, the above method of introducing exponential functions should be applied in the 8th grade. But if the 8th graders feel no need to investigate the matter of whether each point on a straight line corresponds to a rational number, this formulation can be given in the first topic of the 10th grade, with an inevitable repetition of the characteristics of exponential functions. Nothing more than this formulation should be required in secondary school. The presently accepted definition (see, e.g., §174 of the second part of the textbook by E. S. Kochetkov and E. S. Kochetkova) would be advantageous only if it were used to derive the characteristics of powers with irrational exponents. But if the latter are accepted without proof, then the gain in comparison with our method of definition proves illusory.

In accordance with our second basic requirement, the formal introduction of irrational numbers as non-repeating decimals is postponed until the need for it has sufficiently matured. It is not because of the authors' carelessness, but in order that the necessity of this step may be more fully comprehended, that the definition of the limit of a sequence precedes the formal introduction of irrational numbers. The limit

$$\lim_{n \to \infty} \left(\frac{1}{10} + \frac{1}{10^2} + \dots + \frac{1}{10^n} \right) = \frac{1}{9}$$

exists in the system of rational numbers, but the limit of approximate decimal places does not exist because $\sqrt{2}$ is lacking in the system of rational numbers, etc. This sequence, however, is not supposed to be obligatory. Different versions of the formal definition of the sum and product of arbitrary real numbers should be given in the textbook, but the proof of the characteristics of arithmetic operations on real numbers is not only not provided for in the program, but its exclusion from the obligatory material (even in a strong class) is expressly recommended.

The aims formulated above also explain the early introduction of derivatives. Calculating the ratio of increments

$$\frac{\Delta y}{\Delta x} = \frac{(x + \Delta x)^2 - x^2}{\Delta x} = 2x + \Delta x$$

for the function $y = x^2$ is so simple that it can even precede the definition of the limit of a function — serving as a justification for the latter. It is also logical not to postpone the investigation and application of the formula for the speed of a falling body (calculating the ratio of the distance covered to the square of the time by an empirically discovered law, as was actually done by Galileo).

The whole topic of the increase and decrease, the upper and lower limits, of functions is covered with the help of derivatives, beginning with the trinomial raised to the second power. The great attention given to this subject in school is completely sensible; but the concept should not be complicated for the students by excessively general definitions that are superfluous in studying elementary functions. In my opinion, in secondary school it is sufficient to define the "point of the local maximum" as the point at which increase changes to decrease.

I will say in regard to this that by limiting ourselves to the functions defined on segment [a, b] which fulfill "Dirichlet's condition" (the segment is divided into a finite number of segments), we can formulate the theorem: the absolute maximum on segment [a, b] is reached either at one of the ends or at one of the points of the local upper limit.

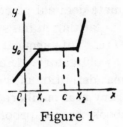

Figure 1

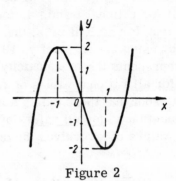

Figure 2

But the definition of the points of "local maximum" and "local minimum" accepted in most analyses inevitably leads to the need to explain to students that at point c, which lies inside the continuous interval of the function (see Figure 1), a duplication of figure 275 in part two of E. S. Kochetkov's and E. S. Kochetkova's textbook), the function simultaneously has a local maximum and a local minimum. At this stage, comprehension of this seemingly paradoxical statement, although it is a good exercise in formal logic, distracts the students' attention too much from the simple, clear picture of the change from segments of increase to segments of decrease of the function, the only change they will meet with in problems of real interest to them.

A completely incongruous situation has been created in the 10th grade this year, when the textbook of E. S. Kochetkov and E. S. Kochetkova, written for the study of derivatives, is already in mass use, but the subject itself has been dropped. In classes where the large print of the textbook is pedantically followed, students will waste their efforts in learning the general university definition of the points of local maximum and local minimum and will try to figure out the above-mentioned paradox; but they will not be able to find the local maximums and minimums of the function $y = x^3 - 3x$ (see Figure 2) after finding its derivative ($y' = 3x^2 - 3$) and solving the equation $3x^2 - 3 = 0$.

A great sacrifice resulting from decreasing the overall number of mandatory mathematics exercises in the upper grades is the exclusion of complex numbers from the mandatory program in the draft now being published. But I must say, in respect to this, that, following the third above-mentioned requirement for planning

the school course, we consider it senseless to keep the topic "Complex Numbers" in the present programs now that the trigonometric form of complex numbers is studied — for example, but the addition of arguments in multiplication is excluded. An idea of that minimal volume of information about complex numbers which would make the study of them productive is given in our program of optional lessons, in which complex numbers are introduced in the 9th grade and widely utilized both in their purely algebraic aspect and in connection with trigonometry and oscillations.

III

The introduction of elements of analysis and the theory of probability in the secondary school program merely reflects the improvements in the structure of mathematics itself in the 17th and 18th centuries. But the attitude of mathematicians toward the foundations of their science has changed considerably during the last few decades. Even at the beginning of the 20th century, the theory of sets and mathematical logic, and the study of arbitrary (then called "abstract") groups, rings, and fields, multi-dimensional geometry and Riemannian geometry, were regarded merely as important additions to the structure of "classical mathematics" and explained only in special lectures for advanced university students, or they formed part of the programs of preparation for master's exams by young people "aspiring to the rank of professor." But now there is an ever increasing tendency to begin a serious introduction to mathematics with a generalized study of the basic types of mathematical structures: sequence structures, the algebraic structures of groups, rings and fields, topological structures, etc. The structures of classical mathematics arise in the capacity of natural particular cases; for example, the structure of real numbers is the structure of Archimedes' ordered field with the axiom of completeness.

There have been widely publicized efforts by mathematicians in many countries to systematically cultivate such an approach "from above" (from logically elementary structures to those most useful to their specialties in the beginning) in secondary and even in primary school; evidently, these attempts contain a great deal that stems from fashions and temporary novelties. It is curious that, in our country, mathematicians who are not occupied with concrete mathematical work, but with "the foundations of mathematics," mathematical logic, general ideas of cybernetics, semantics, semiotics, etc., and learned methods specialists are particularly inclined to get carried away by experiments of this sort.

Not adhering to these fashionable enthusiasms, the planners of the first version of the program drew what they considered to be a very moderate outline for introducing into the school course elements of the contemporary approach to basic mathematical concepts. In their final plan the authors were more cautious than they would have liked to be. But such great caution evidently accords with the actual situation in the preparation not only of teachers, but of methodologists and instructors in pedagogical institutes.

How great the danger is of unsuccessful attempts to introduce concepts new to school practice can be seen from a recent attempt to introduce elementary set-theory concepts into a geometry textbook for grades 6-8 (K. S. Barybin, Geometry, "Prosveshchenie," 1966). This book says that "a set is finite if it has a final element." The author deduced from this that the set of natural numbers is infinite. But what is one to do with the set of whole negative numbers? The theoretical set expression $a \cap b$ is

introduced for the intersection of geometric figures. The expression $a \cap b = M$ is interpreted as meaning that lines a and b intersect at point M. It is not explained what one is to do with lines which intersect at two points; $a \cap b$ is simply read: "the lines a and b intersect" — which is not a definition of the set, but a way of saying $a \cap b \neq \emptyset$.

But we believe that as early as the 7th and 8th grades an optional course program should be worked out in which the principles of mathematical logic, a necessary prerequisite for understanding the construction of modern computers and set theory (mainly finite!), will receive a sufficiently broad development, and the principles of abstract [obshchaia] algebra will be understood on the basis of calculations according to modulus m (in particular, modulus 2).

In the spirit of our original recommendations, the program of "Supplementary Chapters and Problems of Mathematics" is retained for the 9th grade, which begins with the small topic "Sets and Set Operations" and closes with the concept of groups of geometric transformations. Thanks to a fuller clarification of the problem of consecutive stages of generalization of the concept of numbers than in the basic course, here it will be appropriate to give examples not of numerical rings and fields (the rings and fields calculated by modulus m, mentioned above), but rather to settle for the general ("abstract") concept of group. In 10th grade optional exercises, it is natural to examine problems of groups and the theory of probability in terms of the theory of finite sets, and to use all the concepts acquired in order to clarify the question of the axiomatic method in geometry.

IV

In conclusion I shall return to the matter of skill development and training in solving problems. In this regard there exists at present a very great divergence between the actual state of things in the majority of schools and the recommendations based on the experience of the "strictest" teachers. Investigations show that students are unable to perform the most elementary operations without errors or to correctly read the simplest graphs, not to mention drawing the more complicated ones. Yet the Moscow City Institute of Teacher Improvement recommends that all students become skilled in the rapid performance of the most complicated transformations and the rapid solution of tricky (though essentially trivial) problems.

In this institute's didactic materials for the 10th grade (1966), examination variants are arranged in order of difficulty. Variant No. 1 of each examination is intended for weak students.

Test No. 12 (20 minutes)

Variant No. 1

Find the logarithm of:

1) $x = \dfrac{(a^2 + b^2)^3 \, tg^2\alpha}{(a-b)^2 \, tg^2\beta} \sqrt[3]{\dfrac{tg^2 2\beta}{a^2 - b^2}}.$

2) $x = \dfrac{1}{2a} \sqrt[4]{\dfrac{1}{ab^2 \sqrt[3]{c^2}}}.$

3) Find the antilogarithm of:

$$\log x = -\frac{1}{7} \log \sec^2\alpha + $$
$$+ 3\left(\frac{1}{3} \log c - \frac{2}{21} \log \cos \alpha\right).$$

4) Is it possible to calculate log sin 300° ?

The attainment of speed in performing algebraic operations is necessary for productive, conscious work. For example, when covering the topic "Derivatives," the calculation

$$\frac{\Delta y}{\Delta x} = \frac{(x + \Delta x)^3 - x^3}{\Delta x} = 3x^2 + 3x\Delta x + (\Delta x)^2$$

should be made automatically, without diverting attention from understanding its result. But reasonable requirements which can be applied here to those students for whom the study of mathe-

matics is only an element of general education are, in my opinion, very far from the requirements desired by the Moscow Institute of Teacher Improvement.

One can hope, however, that the general aims of the new programs will presently receive great attention, in the light of recent decisions by the CPSU Central Committee and the Council of Ministers regarding the secondary school. The introduction of optional lessons in grades 7 - 10 is a necessary supplement to the emphatically general educational nature of the basic course in mathematics in the upper grades.

In principle, everyone agrees that teaching should not be subject to the interests of those students who intend to enter higher educational institutions after school. In spite of that, many statements were addressed to the tasks of continuing the study of mathematics in technological and physics-and-mathematics higher educational institutions, and even more to the special task of preparing students to pass the competitive college examinations. Both themes played a large role in the debate. Recently, the situation has developed in which the work of a mathematics teacher in the upper grades has begun to be judged to a significant extent by the success of his students in the competitive examinations for the most difficult higher educational institutions. It is very doubtful that the exaggerated attention paid to learning the special techniques of solving competitive-exam problems is useful even for the insignificant minority of students who will enter these difficult colleges. In any case there is no doubt that for the majority of students this tendency greatly decreases the practical results of covering the school mathematics course: artificial details are forgotten, while the basic concepts remain vague and incomplete.

Of course, the interests of those students who will enter higher educational institutions immediately after school or a few years later should not be forgotten. Our view is based on the assumption that the entrance exams to higher educational institutions will include only material from the mandatory school program. To make our conclusions sufficiently concrete, we will examine the interests of the majority of technical higher schools and pedagogical institutes — which at present accept students without much competition — separately from the interests of higher educational institutions with high requirements and much competition for enrollment. In regard to the latter, it is hypocritical to speak of their accessibility to students unable or unwilling to spend extra effort on the study of mathematics. Naturally, these institutions will in practice accept mainly students who, in addition to serious mastery of the obligatory school course, will do the more difficult optional work; and this situation will only be just if they are helped in this by the school, not by private tutors. We believe that this is one of the tasks in the broad organization of optional studies.

As for the larger group of higher educational institutions, they are not presently suffering from the secondary school graduates' inability to solve ingenious exponential and trigonometric equations, but rather from their lack of overall mathematical development, including the absence of any conception of evaluating absolute and relative error in approximate calculations. Yet a clear understanding of such basic concepts as the concept of derivatives will create new opportunities for constructing courses in physics and other natural-science and technical disciplines in higher educational institutions of the most different kinds.

Finally, we believe that the planned expansion of the semantic content of the school mathematics course will be especially useful to those students who will enter higher schools not directly after school, but after practical working experience. Interesting general mathematical concepts, connected with important applications and reinforced by a selection of sufficiently simple and natural examples, will be better retained and more helpful when returning to theoretical studies in higher educational institutions after a few years, than quickly forgotten, narrowly specialized skills pertaining to individual, specialized types of problems.

For highly competitive higher schools, the expansion of the programs' semantic content will also prove useful, even from the standpoint of more rational entrance exams, since it will be-

come possible to test fully the ability for conscious mastery of ideas and expand the basis for choosing problems "to test intelligence."

V

It is assumed that the new programs will be introduced in the following way:

Grades	4	5	6	7	8	9	10
In entirety	69	70	71	72	73	74	75
With certain simplifications	—	—	—	—	69	70	71

One should bear in mind that, in comparison with other subjects, mathematics occupies last place in its timetable for introducing new programs. Evidently this is because until now the content of secondary school mathematics has been the most archaic and lagged most behind the demands of the time. This timetable permits completely new textbooks to be created before the new programs are introduced; individual chapters will be tested experimentally in the school as they are written.

We believe that our draft program is a healthy basis for such experiments. (1) It is possible that the suggestions of the textbook authors and the school experimenters will lead to certain shifts in the distribution of the material, sometimes even from one class to another. But the overall structure of the course should not be greatly changed as a result.

For example, an argument is still going on about the order in which an acquaintance with negative numbers, ordinary fractions, and decimals should begin in the 4th and 5th grades. The authors of the programs have expressed their own opinion in this matter, but in order to work on textbooks for grades 6 - 8, the essential thing is only a general consensus that 6th grade students will enter with already formed elementary concepts about the system of all rational numbers (which will be systematized in the beginning of grade 6), the use of letters, and the solution of equations. Arguments are possible about the study of exponential and logarithmic functions in the 8th or 9th grade, but the essen-

220

tial thing is a consensus regarding the need to include elementary analysis (the first concepts of derivatives and integrals) and the theory of probability in the 9th and 10th grade program.

A possible alternative to the draft program is to transfer the limit of a sequence (with the sum of an infinitely decreasing geometric progression and the conversion of repeating decimals into simple ones), the concept of real numbers (with even greater simplification of this topic), and a section on "Systems of Equations and Inequalities," suitable for reviewing the whole course of the eight-year school, into the 8th grade. In that case the 9th grade program could begin with the topic "Exponential and Logarithmic Functions."

Personally, however, what attracts me in the program we have planned is the possibility of a direct transition from fractional exponents to exponential functions, or essentially even the blending of these two topics into one. I think that such an approach can lead to a considerable saving in time and in students' energy.

In posing the question of what meaning to assign to the expression a^x for different values of x for which this expression was previously meaningless, it is completely natural to consider x the variable and gradually construct a graph of the function $y = a^x$.

Of course, to do this the students must be taught ahead of time that a function can be defined for any set — in particular, for a finite set or the set of natural numbers. But this is exactly what the authors of the program have in mind. It is assumed that the sequence $y_1, y_2, \ldots, y_n,$ $\ldots$ will be regarded from the very beginning as the function $y_n = f(n)$, which is defined only for natural values, and that in covering the topic "Numerical Sequences" the students will learn to graph sequences and to regard these graphs as a particular case of the graphs of functions (see Figure 3).

VI

If I have called the present program archaic, this pertains especially to geometry. Here the program planners found themselves in a difficult

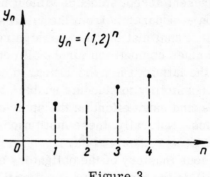

Figure 3

position, since they should actually have begun not with drawing up new programs, but with clarifying the desired logical structure for a school geometry course. We had to orient ourselves primarily by foreign experience, while national experimental work in the schools could only be applied to the lower grades.

The basic currents in restructuring the school geometry course, which have presently found the widest recognition, can be formulated in three points:

1) The formulation of elementary geometric concepts takes place in the lower grades.

2) The logical structure of a systematic geometry course in the intermediate grades is considerably simplified in comparison with the Euclidean tradition. The development of the habit of strict logical proofs is combined at this stage with an open recognition of the right to accept a supplementary system of assumptions without proof.

3) The geometry course in the upper grades is based on vector concepts. This naturally entails a use of the coordinate method (but in an auxiliary capacity, since the exposition does not become any less "geometric" from this reference).

The first of these points is obviously sufficiently well recognized in our methods literature, although at present it is still not sufficiently realized in the general school. I believe that our draft program on the whole correctly defines the stock of geometric concepts that should be accumulated before the beginning of the 7th grade geometry course.

The draft program requires that the systematic study of geometry begin in the 6th grade. The 6th grade course is conceived not in the spirit of the Euclidean tradition, but in accordance with the second point formulated above. In my opinion, a good model for realizing this concept is still the French textbook of Emile Borel, written in 1905. Such an understanding of the systematic geometry course in the intermediate grades would make it reasonable to begin somewhat earlier — e.g., in the second half of the 5th grade. The possibility of beginning the systematic geometry course from the very beginning of the 5th grade was maintained by several members of the commission.

This course can be constructed not with less, but with considerably more, "logical rigor" than is presently accepted, if one supplements the list of assumptions made openly without proof (it is not so important whether they are called "axioms"), approximately as follows:

1) The properties of order [poriadok] on a straight line are accepted without proof. It is accepted without proof (but in a clear formulation) that a line, a pair of radii with a common origin, and a simple closed polygon divide a plane surface into two parts.

2) The axiom of parallel lines is accepted at the very beginning of the course in its strong form: through a point passes one and only one straight line parallel to the given straight line.

3) Parallel transfer is defined as the transfer of all the points of a figure in one and the same direction to one and the same distance. It is postulated that a parallel transfer is a movement, i.e., it preserves the length of segments and the size of angles.

4) Sufficient movability of figures is postulated: in addition to that shown in point (3), the possibility of turning a plane around a center and symmetrical reflection relative to a straight line.

5) The characteristics of the orientation of plane figures are postulated (preservation of orientation during transfers and turns and change to the opposite in axial symmetry).

6) The characteristics of the intersection of a straight line and a circle and of two circles are postulated without proof (which makes the deduction of the third criterion of congruence of triangles trivial).

7) Similarity is <u>defined</u> as the equality of relations of corresponding segments. It is postulated: a) there exist figures similar to the given one, with arbitrary coefficients of similarity, b) the corresponding angles in similar figures are equal.

The postulates 7(a) and 7(b) permit us to avoid, in particular, the difficulties arising in the topic of "Similarity" from a lack of clear concepts of irrational numbers. For example, the <u>theorem</u> — "Triangles whose corresponding angles are equal are similar," — receives a very simple proof.

Let the corresponding angles of $\triangle ABC$ and $\triangle A'B'C'$ be equal. Construct $\triangle A''B''C''$ similar to $\triangle ABC$, with $\dfrac{A''B''}{AB} = \dfrac{A'B'}{AB}$. Since $A''B'' = A'B'$, then, according to the second sign of equality of triangles, $\triangle A''B''C''$ equals $\triangle A'B'C'$ and hence is similar to $\triangle ABC$.

I realize that these hasty notes are insufficient. But the task of creating for intermediate classes a sufficiently simple, and at the same time logically correct, geometry course on a radically changed basis seems to me one of the most important in the whole ongoing reform of the school mathematics course. I could not pass over it in silence.

The program planners were unanimous about the need for sufficiently developed elements of solid geometry in the eight-year school. It would be an inadmissible violation of the practical orientation of all secondary school teaching if the geometry course in grades 6 - 8 remained completely isolated from the drawing course, which in the new study plan is fully covered in grades 7 - 8 and whose geometric content basically amounts to the study of projections of spatial figures, which requires rather clear conceptions about the respective location of lines and planes in space and the angles between them. In our opinion, topic 9 of the draft program for the 7th grade cannot be dropped, but the time allotted to it can instead be increased. Simplifying the logical structure of the plane geometry course in grades 5 - 7 may permit this to be done.

The distribution of material planned for topic 10 also seems subject to debate, but not its mandatory requirement in the eight-year school. After all, almost all this material is covered in grades 4 - 5 in contemporary experimental teaching.

In discussing the possibilities of expounding the elements of solid geometry in the eight-year school, one should bear in mind that the basic content of chapter one, part two, of A. P. Kiselev's textbook permits a logically correct, extremely simple exposition by expanding somewhat the number of assumptions accepted without proof.

For example, one can:

a) postulate the transitivity of parallel lines in space;

b) postulate the equality of figures derived one from the other by parallel transfer, after extending the above definition;

c) accept without proof that a plane is obtained by turning a line intersecting an axis at a right angle to a straight line, after postulating the possibility of turning a figure around an axis (which is done in A. P. Kiselev's textbook).

Without great difficulty, the reader can verify how simple the proof of the remaining theorems about the relative location of lines and planes in space becomes, if he allows these basic hypotheses to be simply accepted as additional axioms. Naturally, this does not prevent assigning superior or more interested students the problem of proving them.

VII

One should distinguish between the problem of introducing vector concepts into the school course and constructing the geometry course in the upper grades on the basis of vectors. The program planners argued a great deal about where vectors should first appear in the program. At first the final geometric topic in the 6th grade was called "Parallel Transfers and Vectors." For the sake of simplification, the mention of vectors in this place was dropped. It was debated whether to introduce vectors in the beginning of the 8th grade, which would make it possible from the very beginning to combine trigonometric functions with a study of vectors and their projections. Finally, vectors were kept only in the 9th grade program.

The published draft program was drawn up before the structure of the physics course had taken final shape. In its final version, the physics course was divided into two parts [kontsentr]: the first in grades 6 - 7, the second in grades 8 - 10. The second part begins with mechanics and a systematic cultivation of vector concepts, for which reason the possible appearance of vectors in the beginning of the 8th grade mathematics course also deserves renewed debate.

Our explanatory note speaks of the possibility of constructing the 9th and 10th grade geometry course on the basis of vectors. The inclusion, in the secondary school program, of the concept of "vector space," with a formulation of its characteristics as axioms, would have very great significance; it would combine and illuminate a significant part of the mathematics and physics courses in a new way. One should think that the presentation of the system of scalar quantities as "one-dimensional vector space," the system of vectors in a plane as "two-dimensional vector space," and the practically and intuitively natural "three-dimensional vector space" would in principle be completely accessible to the average student in the upper grades; the general educational effect of such an expansion of the mathematical concepts obligatory for all upper-grade students would be enormous.

In countries where the secondary school course is completed not at the age of seventeen, but at eighteen, it is now generally accepted that such a broad acquaintance with the concept of vector space is necessary. The new official French programs require the study of vectors in a plane in grade 4 (in the French system), i.e., at the age of 13 to 14. The more progressive textbooks already in fairly wide use take this program requirement to mean that the concepts of "vector space" and its "dimensions" should be formed in grade 2 [sic] (at the age of 15 to 16).

However, one must realize that the axiomatic

postulation of the basic properties of vectors should be preceded by visual acquaintance and lengthy practice in dealing with them. It is difficult to accommodate both this visual acquaint- with vectors and a systematic exposition of the concept of vector space in the 9th grade. Everything would be easily solved if the first introduction to vectors could take place in the 8th grade. Then one could confidently recommend the obligatory construction of the final geometry course in grades 9 - 10 by the vector system. As noted above, in France such a transition to the vector standpoint is considered realizable even with students younger than those in our 9th and 10th grades.

Thus, I believe that the final elaboration of our draft program for geometry should go not in the direction of dropping the goals expressed above, but in the direction of implementing them more consistently and uniformly. When I said that, in the opinion of the authors, the published draft program was a healthy basis to follow in writing textbooks, it was not by accident that I confined this assertion to textbooks for grades 4 - 5 and to textbooks in algebra and elementary analysis for grades 6 - 10. In order to work calmly and confidently on new geometry textbooks, preliminary work would have to be done: one or several collectives of scholars and teachers, utilizing foreign experience, would have to draw up and publish a draft (or several drafts) for a "logical skeleton" of a school geometry course (the basic hypotheses and the basic series of theorems to be proven) in a form suitable for criticism and for experimental use by sufficiently experienced teachers.

VIII

In conclusion I wish to emphasize that we are not concerned with the usual piecemeal reform of programs, but with a decisive transition to an essentially new and higher level of mathematics teaching in our schools. The published draft program plan is only the first step in that direction. Further work, particularly on textbooks, can only be brought to a successful conclusion, given the closest cooperation between teachers, methodologists, and prominent mathematicians. It is assumed that several teams of authors will work on textbooks for each grade and each subject simultaneously. It is very important that each of them have a balanced representation of teaching experience and an understanding of the scientific principles of a rational construction of the school course. One supposes that in their final form the textbooks written by different teams of authors will retain distinct individual features. But one must hope that the work of these teams will not be completely independent, and that even in its primary and intermediate stages it will serve to make all program requirements gradually more precise.

Footnote

1) In any event, for mathematics courses in grades 4 - 5, algebra in grades 6 - 8, and algebra with elementary analysis in grades 9 - 10. As regards geometry in grades 6 - 10, see below.

Genetics Education

Biologiia v shkole, 1965, No. 4

M. D. Golubovskii

ON THE DEVELOPMENT OF GENETICS IN OUR COUNTRY AND SCIENTIFIC TRUTH

(From the Pages of the Newspapers and Journals)

An abnormal situation has been created in biology during the last twenty years. Its essence was accurately expressed by the President of the Academy of Sciences of the USSR, M. V. Keldysh. "The development of biology," he wrote in the newspaper Pravda, "was affected to a large extent by the exclusive position of a group of scientists headed by T. D. Lysenko, who denied a number of the most important trends of biological science and instilled their own viewpoints, which often did not correspond to the modern level of the science . . . . A number of scientists were removed from work in their specialties; the subjects of scientific institutions were limited; and the most important achievements of the science were excluded from the programs of the schools and higher educational institutions" (15).* The reasons for the abnor-

---

The author is associated with the Institute of Cytology and Genetics of the Siberian Branch of the USSR Academy of Sciences.

*Here and throughout, the numerals refer to articles in the list cited at the end of the survey.

mal development of biology and, above all, of genetics in our country are analyzed in numerous articles that have appeared in the central newspapers and journals since the October (1964) Plenum of the Central Committee of the CPSU.

The division of the united science of life into two opposed, mutually hostile biologies — "bourgeois" and "Michurinist" — and the corresponding division of genetics into "Morganist" and "Michurinist" has inflicted great harm. Science in itself is objective, and the laws established by it are operative throughout the world. Academician N. N. Semenov (25), the eminent geneticists M. E. Lobashev (17), Zh. Medvedev and V. Kirpichnikov (18), and others write about this. The paths to cognition of scientific truth are complex; dozens of hypotheses are enlisted to explain one and the same phenomenon, and at times they all turn out to be incorrect. Experience is the criterion of the objectivity and correctness of a given hypothesis; only when dozens of correctly organized experiments, which take into consideration all the possible mistakes, give the same result can a hypothesis or theory be accepted. But if new facts appear that contradict the accepted ideas, the scientist is obligated to accept his error openly and bravely, without any subterfuges, no matter how humiliating this seems to him (N. Semenov).

Any scientist is always wrong about something, is always mistaken in something; therefore, what has validity in science is not what some scientist has said, but what the facts of modern science are.

It is well known that the great Russian chemist D. I. Mendeleev did not understand the revolution in physics and rejected the teachings about electrons and about the divisibility of the atom. But his opinion turned out to be mistaken, and the physicists did not take it into consideration (B. Kedrov, 14). A similar example can be taken from biology too. Often, in order to prove the inheritance of characteristics acquired in the course of individual development, the works of Lamarck, Darwin and Michurin are quoted, but this idea has been abandoned by modern geneticists, as not confirmed by the facts. Dogmatism begins when the statements and opinions of individual persons are accepted without proof in all cases in life.

T. D. Lysenko built his theory "on sand," completely ignoring the factual data from genetics. Flat denial of the experiments and theories of previous science is one of the characteristics of any kind of pseudoscientific generalization (N. Semenov). What is new in science is never a simple denial of the old, but only its essential deepening or change. This is the law governing any cognition, and it is well observed in the history of genetics.

Genetics is a young science. It began to develop only at the beginning of our century, after the rediscovery of Mendel's laws. Mendel's laws and the life of this remarkable Czech scientist are recounted in numerous articles (3, 6, 14), and also in the journal Biologiia v shkole (B. Sokolovskaia, 27) and the article in this issue (V. V. Sakharov, 32). Mendel did not study heredity in general, but the nature of the inheritance of individual characteristics in a number of generations. All the results of

crossing were calculated quantitatively. The regularities found by Mendel constitute a firmly established fact in biology, corroborated by thousands of experiments at all levels of the organization of living matter — from viruses, bacteria and plants up to man.

If genetics is indebted to Mendel for the establishment of the laws of inheritance, it is obligated to the German scientist August Weismann for the idea that the hereditary characteristics have their material bearer in the structures of the cell nucleus (the "germ plasm"). This idea — the cornerstone of all genetics — was corroborated more and more as science penetrated more deeply into the subcellular and molecular levels of the organization of matter. Some of Weismann's hypothetical assumptions (for example, about the absolute contrast of germ cells and body cells or about the connection of hereditary determinants with the processes of differentiation) have not proven true and have been abandoned by scientists. The shortcomings in Weismann's views are natural and are explained by the low level of development of biology in the last century. Geneticists have found exceptions even to Mendel's laws: the linked [sovmestnoe] inheritance of characteristics, incomplete dominance, interaction of hereditary factors, sex-linkage, and so forth.

Progress in a science consists precisely of the fact that the deepened study of a subject limits the sphere in which previously discovered principles operate; a new theory appears that organically embraces the old theory and all the exceptions. In genetics, the chromosome theory of inheritance, postulated by the American biologist Thomas Morgan, is such a theory. Morgan established that hereditary dispositions, or genes, are distributed in a linear order on the chromosomes and that the position of the genes together on the chromosomes conditions the linked inheritance of many characteristics, each of which is determined by the genes. Independent inheritance of characteristics is explained by the accidental nature of the cleavage of chromosomes in the process of sex cell formation.

Morgan's theory tied together the material

cytological processes and the nature of the inheritance of characteristics with crossing. The genuine triumph of this theory was that many facts of chromosome behavior were predicted at first by geneticists and then were confirmed by cytologists. Morgan's theory was accepted throughout the entire world. The declaration that "Weismannism-Morganism" is idealistic bourgeois doctrine is either an inadmissible distortion of scientific truth or the grossest delusion (D. K. Beliaev, 4).

After the discovery of the chromosome theory of inheritance, genetics began to move ahead swiftly in the cognition of the nature of chromosomes and genes. In 1927 it was first shown, by exact quantitative methods, that radiation causes hereditary changes of the genes — mutations. Scientists began to study the hereditary substance of the cell nucleus by the methods of physics and chemistry. The history and results of these investigations are expounded excellently in the article by Professor S. Alikhanian — "What Is the Gene: Its Chemical Nature?" [Chto takoe gen: ego khimicheskaia priroda?] (2).

Genes, according to modern ideas, are strands of nucleic acids (DNA or RNA), which are responsible for the synthesis of a certain protein and which, in the final stage, determine the properties and characteristics of an organism. The latter are not contained in the genes in ready-made form, just as the sketch of a machine is not the machine itself. The genes determine only the possibility for the development of properties and characteristics in a strict sequence and under strictly determined conditions of the external environment.

Nucleic acids, their genetic role and modern notions of protein synthesis are discussed in an article by A. S. Spirin and K. P. Kazanskaia, published in the journal Biologiia v shkole (28). Nucleic acids, which contain hereditary information, are self-reproducing and are passed on from generation to generation; they determine species specificity. Proteins cannot construct copies of themselves or reproduce themselves; they are synthesized anew each time, with the help of nucleic acids. This information has given us a more profound understanding of the

essence and origin of life, which can exist only where there are substances that are capable of self-reproduction (nucleic acids). Modern genetics is introducing refinements into the definition of life as of a means for the existence of protein substances.

Inasmuch as the mode of development of each species is written down in a program, spasmodic transformations of one species into another are impossible (36). Such notions of the sudden transformations of species were widespread in the Middle Ages, and this is natural. But only a complete denial of scientific data and the profanation of science can explain the fact that information on the transformation of wheat into rye or barley, of nightingales into cuckoos, etc., began to appear in the works of Lysenko and his adherents and was passed off as an achievement of world science!

How did it ever come to pass that genetics, which studies the basic properties of life and has made such striking advances, was considered in this country to be idealistic and reactionary? In order to understand this, it is necessary to trace the development of genetics in our country. Many articles will help one to examine this problem, including the articles by M. Vasil'ev (6), Zh. Medvedev and V. Kirpichnikov (18), B. Kedrov (14), N. Semenov (25), O. Pisarzhevskii (21), M. Popovskii (22, 23), and A. Sharov (30).

In the Soviet Union, genetics began to develop only at the beginning of the twenties, and our country immediately occupied one of the leading positions in world genetics. The laboratories of N. I. Vavilov, N. K. Kol'tsov, Iu. A. Filipchenko, A. S. Serebrovskii, S. G. Navashin, I. V. Michurin, G. D. Karpechenko, and others were transformed into whole scientific schools. Genetics collectives, which were first-rate as regards their scientific level, were founded: the All-Union Institute of Plant-Growing, the Genetics Laboratory, and then the Institute of Genetics of the USSR Academy of Sciences, the Institute of Experimental Biology, the Medical and Genetics Institute, and departments in a number of universities. Intensive scientific activity was begun.

Academician N. I. Vavilov substantiated the law of homologous series of variability in plants and the doctrine of the centers of origin of cultivated plants. Together with his students, he created in the Soviet Union a world collection of cultivated plants, which served as source material for finding new productive varieties. A. S. Serebrovskii and his students (N. P. Dubinin, I. Agol, and others) first showed the complexity of the gene's structure. Now, thirty years later, this discovery of Soviet geneticists has found confirmation on the molecular level and is highly evaluated by world science.

The Soviet scientists S. S. Chetverikov, N. V. Timofeev-Resovskii, N. P. Dubinin, R. L. Berg, and others theoretically and experimentally elaborated a whole section of genetics — population genetics. These investigations raised the study of evolution to a new stage (the newspaper Komsomol'skaia pravda related the discoveries of N. P. Dubinin and his extraordinary fate [9]). Academician N. K. Kol'tsov, head of the Institute of Experimental Biology, expressed bold ideas on the ability of chromosomes to reproduce themselves and on the ways to influence the hereditary material so as to cause mutations. These ideas were justified by the development of science, and the Soviet scientists V. V. Sakharov, M. E. Lobashev and I. A. Rapoport experimentally discovered the action of chemical mutagens (24). N. V. Timofeev-Resovskii laid the bases of radiation genetics and biophysics.

I. V. Michurin, having generalized his many years of selection work, elaborated ways of guiding the phenomenon of genetic dominance in ontogenesis and successfully applied a number of new methods in distant hybridization. G. D. Karpechenko also did work of world significance on the problem of distant hybridization. He showed that the cause of sterility in distant hybrids often is the disturbance of chromosome behavior during the formation of sex cells and that, with the help of polyploidy, it is possible to restore fertility.

The combination of distant hybridization with polyploidy is a new powerful method in selection. The articles by P. M. Zhukovskii (13), M. I. Khadzhinov (29), V. S. Andreev (1), and others describe how it is utilized now for the creation of new varieties of potatoes, of valuable wheat-rye and wheat-couch grass hybrids, and other cultures.

On the basis of the high level of genetics in our country in the thirties, substantial results in selection were achieved. In 1936 about 20 million hectares were occupied by varieties of plants created on the basis of the Virovskii stock, and more than three hundred varieties of grain, industrial, fodder, vegetable and fruit crops were raised.

Soviet theoretical and applied genetics developed comprehensively and fruitfully, but we entered a period, well-known to everyone, in which many of the now rehabilitated trends in philosophy, economics and the natural sciences were declared hostile and even destructive. In 1936 a debate was imposed on genetics by T. D. Lysenko, I. I. Prezent, and a number of other persons who were not experienced in science. They rejected the basic positions of genetics and the major role of the chromosome in the transmission of heredity; they arbitrarily assumed that the property of heredity equally saturates all the "grains of living matter." This "new" direction again raised the problem, which had long ago been solved in principle by science of the inheritance of characteristics acquired in the course of ontogenesis. N. I. Vavilov wrote that the denial of the role of chromosomes and of the distinctions between hereditary and non-hereditary variability returned science to the first half of the 19th century. The majority of authoritative scientists — Academicians N. I. Vavilov, P. N. Lisitsyn, P. N. Konstantinov, M. M. Zavadovskii, and others — spoke out against the views of Lysenko and his adherents at the special session of the All-Union Academy of Agricultural Sciences in 1936. Unfortunately, in that period objective scientific criticism and facts frequently were not taken into consideration. Stalin supported Lysenko, and he and his associates, "utilizing the conditions of the cult of the personality, transferred the struggle with those of a different view from the plane of scientific discussion to the plane of demagogy and political accusations, and they succeeded in this"

(N. Semenov). Adherents of the chromosome theory of heredity were declared anti-Darwinists, reactionaries, and accomplices of fascism. The eminent Soviet geneticists I. Agol, G. A. Levitskii, S. G. Levit, G. D. Karpechenko, and many others were subjected to repression. The leaders of a number of institutes were removed as being destructive. After this, in 1938, Lysenko occupied the post of president of the Lenin All-Union Academy of Agricultural Sciences (VASKhNIL). The administrative inculcation of his "innovatory" ideas and reprisals against those who had different views began. N. I. Vavilov's honest and principled position became a serious obstacle in the path of the dissemination of pseudoscientific theories in biology. Nikolai Ivanovich enjoyed enormous prestige both in our country and abroad. He was the first director of the Institute of Genetics of the Academy of Sciences of the USSR, the first president of VASKhNIL, president of the Geographical Society of the USSR, and an honorary member of a number of academies in the world. In 1940 Vavilov was arrested and died in prison. This was a very great loss to Soviet science.

Despite the repression and the death of a number of talented researchers during the war years, Soviet genetics continued to develop in the first years after the war. However, in 1948 Soviet genetics was dealt a blow that arrested both its advance and that of biology as a whole for a long time. After the August session of VASKhNIL, Lysenko succeeded in obtaining the actual prohibition or curtailment of work on all the basic trends of modern genetics. Teaching of the fundamentals of genetics was discontinued in the higher educational institutions and the schools.

The establishment of a monopoly in biology, the impossibility of any kind of scientific criticism, the sharp lowering of the methodological level of research — all this led to a situation in which theories arose that could rest only on the profanation and falsification of scientific data: the teachings of Lepeshinskaia on the origin of cells from noncellular matter, on the generation of species, on the absence in nature of intraspecies struggle, the "law" of the trans-

formation of inanimate into living matter by means of living matter, and so forth. Such theories and laws, as Academician Semenov noted, belonged not to the 20th century, but to the distant past of science, when its development bore the imprint of metaphysics (25). The forcible introduction of Lysenko's recommendations into practice — vernalization, inner-variety breeding, sowing according to stubble, cluster planting of forests, methods of fertilizing fields and the treatment of soil, and others — turned out to be scientifically bankrupt or economically unprofitable.

It was only after October 1964 that, in our press, "a whole torrent of material gushed out, lifting the veil which covered the scandalously poor state of affairs in the field of biological science" (B. Kedrov, 14). Up to this time our society was deluded with respect to the fate of Lysenko's practical recommendations. Everyone remembers, for example, the great hubbub in connection with cluster planting. Lysenko, denying intraspecies struggle, "proved" that plants in a cluster will help one another. And how did things turn out in fact? From 1948 to 1953, more than twice as many forests were planted in our country than during the previous 250 years of our forest cultivation. However, by the autumn of 1956 only 4.3% of the trees of full value remained. And, indeed, these plantings were maintained because the collective farmers, despite the recommendations of the cluster method, took care of the plants weakened by the competitive struggle. The wasted resources constituted an enormous sum. (The facts cited were taken from the address of Academician V. N. Sukachev at the annual meeting of the Academy of Sciences of the USSR — Vestnik AN SSSR, 1965, No. 3.) The newspaper Sel'skaia zhizn' (V. Voronov, 7) tells of the bankruptcy of the widely publicized and generally introduced methods for raising the fat content of milk, which were proposed by Lysenko. Our country also sustained great losses from the fact that the introduction of the practical recommendations of modern genetics — hybrid corn, polyploidy and experimental mutagenesis — was delayed administratively (M. I. Khadzhinov, 29;

N. P. Dubinin and V. V. Khvostova, 10; M. Popovskii, 22).

The influence exerted by genetics on the practice of agriculture is enormous. As was noted in the article by Professor M. E. Lobashev (17), genetics transformed the art of selection into a science, introduced methods of appraisal according to the descendants in selection, substantiated the methods of individual selection, established the causes of sterility in distant hybrids and the ways of overcoming them, established the mechanism for determining sex and the ratio of the sexes, and so forth.

Genetic regularities are not always easily applied in selection work, for genetics has been in existence for several decades, but people have been occupied with selection for hundreds and thousands of years. Long before the birth of Michurin, methods for the application of mass and individual selection were elaborated in practical selection work. An analysis of the work of our most prominent selectionists, such as V. Ia. Iur'ev, V. S. Pustovoit, P. P. Luk'-ianenko and others, shows that they first of all applied those methods that had been tested by centuries of practice. But Lysenko and his followers, never remembering the failure of their views in practice, presented the matter as if the successes of our selectionists were due to the application of the principles of "Michurinist biology." In this way, protected by the name of Michurin, Lysenko's erroneous views were propagated. At the same time, the ways and methods of Michurin's work were intolerably distorted (N. Semenov). It is well known that Michurin regarded distant hybridization as a basic method of his work and also utilized spontaneous mutations. However, Lysenko not only did not develop efforts in the given direction, but hampered them in every way possible. Michurin's "followers" proclaimed vegetative hybridization as the basic method in selection (both of plants and of animals).

The time has come to think about the significance of the term "Michurinist biology." The well-known Soviet virologist, Professor V. Zhdanov, expressed the essence of the matter well: "Mendeleev's periodic system, Darwin's theory of evolution, and Einstein's theory of relativity are known to everyone. However, is it correct to speak about Mendeleevian chemistry, Darwinian biology, or Einsteinian physics? It is chemistry, biology and physics that exist — complex scientific disciplines in a constant state of development; and the immortal works of their founders have entered forever into their treasure houses. Is it possible for any, even the most brilliant, theory to exhaust the content of a developing science?" (12). Michurin made his contribution to the development of native biology. But his work did not exhaust all the problems of genetics and selection, let alone all the content of biology. During Michurin's life and afterwards, there arose such sections of genetics as radiation, chemical and molecular genetics, genetics of microorganisms, population genetics, immunology genetics and, finally, cosmic genetics. And, what is more, Michurin himself repeatedly warned of the impermissibility of establishing his personal views as dogma. In the article "Principles and Methods of Work" [Printsipy i metody raboty], he wrote: "I am in no way pretending to an exposition of new discoveries or the refutation of any laws established by scientific authorities. I am only presenting my conclusions and reasons on the basis of my personal practical work of many years in the matter of raising new varieties of fruit plants. It is very possible that in some cases I have fallen into error through an incorrect understanding of various phenomena in plant life and the application to them of even Mendel's laws and those of other scientists of recent times."

The ignoring of the most important achievements of biology and the propagation of subjective and unproven conceptions penetrated the school programs in biology. This is also dealt with in a number of articles published in recent times (8, 26). Academician B. E. Bykhovskii said: "When you become acquainted with the school textbooks in biology, you are simply frightened by what the children are being taught! And, indeed, these textbooks should give ideological training not only to future biologists, but to all students" (Vestnik AN SSSR, 1965, No. 3).

230

It is a task of state importance to bring biology teaching in the school into correspondence with the modern level of this science.

The October and March plenums of the Central Committee of the CPSU opened the doors for a revolution in biology. "A little time will pass, and Soviet science, which is proud of its successes in astronautics, physics, mathematics and chemistry, will also be proud of our Soviet biology" (N. Dubinin, 11).

In this survey of articles, naturally, it was impossible to reflect all their contents with sufficient completeness. And, indeed, we only succeeded in mentioning some of the articles. Our main purpose was to transmit the general essence of many articles and the identical aspiration of the authors to show the readers the most important aspects of the modern science and the basic direction of its development. We are attaching to the survey a list of articles (mentioned and unmentioned in the survey) that will be especially useful to biology teachers.

List of Articles

1. Andreev, V. S., "Poliploidiia v rastitel'-nom mire, " Biologiia v shkole, 1965, No. 1.

2. Alikhanian, S. I., "Chto takoe gen: ego khimicheskaia priroda?," Khimiia i zhizn', 1965, No. 1.

3. Atabekova, A., "Gregor Mendel' i zakon nasledovaniia priznakov," Nauka i zhizn', 1965, No. 2.

4. Beliaev, D., "Na osnove zakonov genetiki," Pravda, November 22, 1964.

5. Bianki, V., "Rytsar' nauki," Komsomol'-skaia pravda, February 6, 1965.

6. Vasil'ev, M., "Genetika: proshloe i nasto-iashchee," Uchitel'skaia gazeta, December 12, 1964.

7. Voronov, V., "K voprosu o zhirnomoloch-nosti," Sel'skaia zhizn', November 25, 1964.

8. Vorontsov, N. N., "Zhizn' toropit (Nuzhny sovremennye posobiia po biologii)," Komsomol'-skaia pravda, November 11, 1965.

9. Gubarev, V., "Dva poliusa zhizni," Komsomol'skaia pravda, February 27, 1965.

10. Dubinin, N. P. and Khvostova, V. V., "Atomnaia energiia i selektsiia," Priroda, 1965, No. 3.

11. Dubinin, N., "Rog izobiliia genetiki," Nedelia, 1965, No. 22.

12. Zhdanov, V., "Tsel' — upravliat' nasledstvennoi izmenchivost'iu," Meditsinskaia gazeta, February 2, 1965.

13. Zhukovskii, P., "O nekotorykh novykh metodakh prikladnoi genetiki," Sel'skaia zhizn', November 19, 1964.

14. Kedrov, B., "Puti poznaniia istiny," Novyi mir, 1965, No. 1.

15. Keldysh, M. V., "Sovetskaia nauka; itogi i perspektivy," Pravda, February 4, 1965.

16. Kerkis, Iu., "Chto takoe vegetativnaia gibridizatsiia," Uchitel'skaia gazeta, March 4, 1965.

17. Lobashev, M. E., "Genetika i sel'skokhozi-aistvennaia nauka," Zhivotnovodstvo, 1965, No. 3.

18. Medvedev, Zh. and Kirpichnikov, V., "Perspektivy sovetskoi genetiki," Neva, 1963, No. 3.

19. Mitiushin, V. M., "Sovremennye predstavleniia o strukture i funktsiiakh kletki," Biologiia v shkole, 1965, No. 1.

20. Mitiushin, V. M., "Stroenie i funktsii kletki v stadii deleniia," Biologiia v shkole, 1965, No. 2.

21. Pisarzhevskii, O., "Pust' uchenye sporiat . . . ," Literaturnaia gazeta, November 17, 1964.

22. Popovskii, M., "O chesti uchenogo," Sovetskaia Rossiia, February 4, 1965.

23. Popovskii, M., "Spor davnii, no ne zabytyi," Znanie — sila, 1965, No. 4.

24. Rapoport, I., "Khimicheskii mutagenez," Sel'skaia zhizn', October 22, 1964.

25. Semenov, N., "Nauka ne terpit sub'-ektivizma," Nauka i zhizn', 1965, No. 4.

26. Sokolovskaia, B., "O chem umolchal uchebnik . . . ," Uchitel'skaia gazeta, December 22, 1964.

27. Sokolovskaia, B. Kh., "Oznakomlenie uchashchikhsia s zakonami nasledstvennosti," Biologiia v shkole, 1965, No. 2.

28. Spirin, A. S. and Kazanskaia, K. P., "Nukleinovye kisloty i biosintez belka," Biologiia v shkole, 1965, No. 3.

29. Khadzhinov, M., "Genetika i problema gibridnykh rastenii," Sel'skaia zhizn', December 1, 1964.

30. Sharov, A., "Zametki o genetike," Znamia, 1965, No. 4.

31. Efroimson, V. and Medvedev, R., "Kriterii — praktika," Komsomol'skaia pravda, November 17, 1964.

32. Sakharov, V. V., "Gregor Mendel' — osnovopolozhnik nauki o nasledstvennosti," Biologiia v shkole, 1965, No. 4.

33. Mardashev, S., "Biologiia i meditsina," Pravda, June 11, 1965.

34. Polianskii, Iu., "Tsitologiia i shkol'naia biologiia," Uchitel'skaia gazeta, June 17, 1965.

35. Kerkis, Iu. Ia., "Eshche raz o vegetativnoi gibridizatsii," Uchitel'skaia gazeta, June 17, 1965.

36. Oganesian, M. G., "Priroda i znachenie mutatsii," Biologiia v shkole, 1965, No. 4.

Sovetskaia pedagogika, 1965, No. 3

V. F. Natali

PROBLEMS OF GENETICS IN THE SECONDARY SCHOOL COURSE

The 20th century is an atomic age, an age of rapid growth of the natural sciences (astronomy, physics, chemistry and biology). The youngest of the biological sciences — the science of heredity, genetics — achieved the greatest development during this time. From the first experimental work (by Mendel, De Vries, and others), genetics grew into a science conducted at the level of molecular research.

The first stages of the development of any science are rich in diverse, often hypothetical constructions. The first discoveries of new facts elicit explanations in the beginning that are far from the truth. Thus, for example, at the beginning of the 1900's the Dutch scientist, Hugo De Vries, obtained mutations for the first time while working with the plant Oenothera. Later research revealed that they represented mutations, now well known, in a number of chromosomes. However, De Vries could not explain or comprehend the mutational nature of these changes. He decided that the

The author is a Member of the RSFSR Academy of Pedagogical Sciences.

changed plants represented new species and gave them appropriate species names. De Vries believed that the Darwinian principle of the origin of species by means of natural selection, being too gradual a process of development, could not explain the origin of species, and he asserted that "species arise suddenly and discontinuously" (the viewpoint supported in our time by T. D. Lysenko).

Let us cite another example. As early as the end of the last century, scientists turned their attention to chromosomes and their behavior during cell division, and they expressed the proposition that it is precisely the chromosomes which determine the hereditary qualities of the organism. At the beginning of our century, when experimental research was begun (the rediscovery of Mendel's laws, the work of Correns, von Tschermak, and others), the concept of genes as the factors determining hereditary properties was advanced; it was believed then that the genes were located on the chromosomes. As we know now, this is a fundamentally correct position. However, at that time there was not yet any research as to what the genes were, and this concept of them bore the nature of a brilliant conjecture. Features were ascribed to them which they did not possess. It was thought that the genes were independent of any external influences and that if they did change, it was rare and under the influence of some internal causes (the theory of autogenesis). These mistaken theories were destroyed by the research of the twenties, in which it was shown that the genes represent definite locations on the chromosomes and that they are subjected to changes brought about by the most diverse external influences, both physical and chemical. In the same period, the linear arrangement of the genes on the chromosomes was established. During the twenties the science of heredity entered upon a strictly materialist path of development.

The research of the last twenty years constitutes a new and exceptionally important stage in the development of genetics. In this period, genetics was transformed from a purely biological science into a science closely connected with biochemistry, physics, and other sciences, and the invention of the electron microscope opened the way for the most refined microscopic research.

During this time the following things were proven:

1. Chromosomes consist of interconnected molecules of proteins and deoxyribonucleic acid (DNA).

2. Heredity is determined by the historically formed chemical structure of the DNA molecule, or, in the words of modern genetics, the DNA molecule carries all the hereditary information.

3. The genes represent definite locations on the long polymeric DNA molecule.

4. It is precisely the genes which determine the synthesis of specific proteins in the cell, and the proteins, as is well known, are the basis of all life processes which occur in the organism.

5. This process of synthesis of proteins occurs with the participation of ribonucleic acids, in a close interaction between the cytoplasm and the nucleus of the cell.

6. The influence of various forms of radiant energy and various chemical factors on the change of gene structure, which is reflected in heredity, was established by numerous experiments.

These are the most important achievements of genetic science; they have enormous significance for medicine and the practice of agriculture, and they have placed genetics in the position of the leading biological science.

Let us go on to the question of the position of biology in the school. There is general agreement that the fundamentals of the sciences should be taught in the secondary school. This, of course, is correct, but, unfortunately, this principle is not realized in the teaching of biology. During the past twenty years, the level of instruction in the biological subjects, and particularly in the 9th-grade course (Darwinism, general biology), has declined very sharply. Genetics, especially, has suffered in this process.

In the thirties the fundamentals of the science of heredity were expounded rather thoroughly in the textbooks of the course on Darwinism (for example, in the textbooks by M. N. Beliaev and V. F. Natali and in the textbook by M. I. Mel'nikov, A. A. Shibanov and A. A. Iakhontov). However, as early as the end of the thirties, material on heredity was eliminated from the syllabuses and the sole remaining textbook by Mel'nikov. This situation continued to exist in the forties and later. In the most recent years, 9th-graders have been using the textbook General Biology [Obshchaia biologiia] by E. A. Veselov. Although chromosomes are indeed mentioned in it during a description of cell division, all data of the most modern genetics are completely denied (above all, data concerning chromosomes as the bearers of heredity). At the same time, the criticism of present-day genetics is extremely subjective. Thus, the students can get only an incorrect notion of heredity from Veselov's textbook. It should be noted that the defects of this textbook are not limited to distortions in the elucidation of problems of heredity. The Darwinian theory set forth in the textbook is less similar to Darwinism than it is to the most rank Lamarckism of the beginning of the 19th century. The author actually denies one of Darwin's fundamental principles, the principle of divergency, as well as the whole Darwinian conception of the process of species formation. It is not by accident that the author of the textbook brings forth a false "hypothesis" of the sudden emergence of species as a counterweight to the Darwinian notion of constant evolution in the organic world.

And 9th-graders have used such textbooks to study general biology for more than sixteen years.

The teaching of biology in the secondary school is naturally dependent on the quality of the teachers' preparation. How do matters stand in this regard?

After the 1948 session of the Lenin All-Union Academy of Agricultural Sciences, the teaching of genetics was discontinued at the natural science departments of the teacher training institutes, and the students became acquainted with heredity in the course on Darwinism. But the syllabuses and textbooks for this course presented heredity in an incorrect and one-sided way. There is reason to believe that the preparation of biology students in the universities was not much better, with the exception, perhaps, of such universities as Leningrad and Moscow universities.

As a result of all that has been mentioned, a difficult situation with respect to biology arose in the school. It is necessary to raise the teaching of biology to a higher level and to purify the course of all matter that does not correspond to modern science. In order to fulfill these tasks we need new syllabuses, textbooks, and mainly (and especially urgently) — knowledgeable teachers.

What elements of genetics must be introduced into the general biology course?

I. First of all, it is necessary to give a correct presentation of the structure of the cell on a modern electron microscopic level. The students should know the difference between a microscope utilizing light and an electron microscope. Whereas the luminous microscope makes it possible to observe objects of magnitude as small as one micron (1 micron equals 0.001 mm.), the electron microscope magnifies up to 500,000 times and more, and allows us to see objects of a magnitude much, much less than one micron. In work with the electron microscope, other measures of magnitude are used, especially the angstrom (1 angstrom equals 0.0000001 mm.). It is clear that when one obtains such enlargements it is possible not only to see the smallest of living beings — the viruses — but also to photograph them and study their structure.

During a study of the cell on this level, it is necessary to talk about the structure of the nucleus and the presence of chromosomes and the nucleolus in it; the structure of the cytoplasm, and namely: the presence of mitochondria — the source of energy for all living processes, the network of little channels — the means of communication in the cytoplasm between the various parts of the cell, and the very smallest particles — ribosomes — in which protein synthesis occurs.

The apprehension may arise that it is impossible to show any of this. But the fact is that even formerly it was impossible, with the help of the ordinary luminous microscope, to show many parts of the cell, for example, the chromosomes. Moreover, the 9th-graders, who are slightly acquainted with atomic physics, are already capable of abstract thinking to a sufficient degree.

After a brief acquaintance with the structure of the cell, it is necessary to acquaint the students with the process of the karyokinetic division of the cell. The individual phases of this division can be demonstrated with the help of a good luminous microscope; for example, the division of a cell in the radicle of an onion may be shown if the appropriate preparations are made by the visual aid workshops. During an explanation of the individual stages of karyokinesis, or mitosis, special attention should be given to the longitudinal splitting of each chromosome and to the fact that each daughter cell receives the same number of chromosomes that the parent cell had. After the study of karyokinesis, one should go on to acquaint the students with the well-known propositions that, in the first place, in the development of an organism all the daughter cells receive the number of chromosomes characteristic for the species and, in the second place, each plant or animal species is characterized by a definite number of chromosomes which is typical for the species. Then the students should be briefly acquainted with the maturation of the sex cells, meiosis, as a result of which the number of chromosomes in the gametes is diminished by half.

II. The students should know the basic laws of heredity.

As early as 1865, the well-known scholar who worked in Brünn (Czechoslovakia), Gregor Mendel, published his research. This was the first experimental work in the field of the study of heredity. It long remained unknown to scholars, and, in essence, Mendel's conclusions were rediscovered in 1900 and published simultaneously by three scholars: Hugo De Vries, Correns, and von Tschermak.

The law of segregation. Mendel's basic experiment consisted of crossing two pure varieties of garden peas, one having yellow seeds, and the other — green. In the first generation all the seeds were yellow. This means that in this generation in the given case the yellow color dominates. (In genetics a trait is called dominant if it is expressed in the hybrid offspring; in contrast to the dominant yellow color, the green color is called recessive, i.e., not expressed.) The experiments of other scientists, Correns in particular, showed that incomplete dominance is observed in some plants of the first generation and that all the hybrids bear an intermediate character. Thus, crossing plants having red and white blossoms, Correns obtained plants with pink blossoms in the first generation. In Mendel's experiments, the plants from the first generation were crossed once more, and in the second generation the seeds were no longer uniform, but were segregated into three yellow and one green. True, it must be kept in mind that such a segregation is always obtained if a sufficiently large number of descendants is considered. Correspondingly, in Correns' experiments, when the hybrid plants with pink blossoms were crossed, in the second

generation a segregation in a different ratio was obtained: each plant with red blossoms was attended by two with pink blossoms and one with white.

At the time that these experiments were published they could not be explained with sufficient clarity. Now it has become known that the results obtained in these experiments — the regular segregation in the second generation — are explained by the fact that in all these experiments the traits whose development was connected with only one pair of chromosomes were successfully selected. This means that in the peas with yellow seeds this trait depends on two identical genes located in one pair of chromosomes, and that in the plants with green seeds it also depends on one pair of genes located in the same pair of chromosomes, as in the plants with yellow seeds. During the formation of the gametes, one chromosome of each pair of chromosomes remains. Then it is easy to conceive that with the union of gametes from the crossed individuals, a first generation will be obtained which will have a gene of yellow color in one of its pairs of chromosomes and a gene of green color in the other. As a case of complete dominance, in the pea, the gene of yellow color completely inhibits the effect of the gene of green color; in plants with red and white corollas, the gene of red color incompletely dominates the gene of white color.

Mendel's law of segregation should be set forth in that way.

The law of independent assortment. Mendel and other scientists were not restricted to crossing individuals differing in one pair of traits; they also crossed plants and animals which differed in two and more pairs of traits. As a result, it was discovered that during the cross each pair of traits is inherited independently of the others, and as a result of this in the second generation a very complex segregation occurs and different combinations of traits of the first and second pairs appear. This regularity received the name of the law of independent assortment. It should be kept in mind that this law is revealed only in those cases in which the various pairs of genes — yellow-green, tall-short, red-white — are distributed not on one pair of chromosomes, but by pairs all on different pairs of chromosomes, since in the opposite case the inheritance would occur differently.

The mutational process. At the very beginning of the development of genetic research, it became known that during the breeding of some animals and plants, changes in some of the traits were revealed in their descendants. These changes, called mutations, turned out to be hereditary. Since mutations were rarely manifested under ordinary, normal conditions of breeding, scientists formed the incorrect opinion that they arose independently of any external forces, under the influence of certain internal causes. However, as early as the beginning of the century, studies began to appear which indicated that there was an incorrect understanding of the causes for the origin of mutations. Gerasimov pointed this out as early as 1898, and later Soviet scientists, using radium emanations and X-rays on living organisms, showed that very diverse mutations appeared under their influence. Soon it was shown in other works that the influence of various chemical factors on an organism also causes the appearance of mutations. The work of Rappoport and Sakharov is especially interesting in this respect. In 1927 the work of the American scientist, Muller, appeared. It demonstrated the origin of mutations in the fruit fly, Drosophila, under the influence of X-rays. The study of mutations demanded great efforts, since the mutations were not easily discovered. What do mutations represent?

In the first place, it turned out that the majority of mutations are recessive, i.e., are not manifested in the first generation, and therefore it is necessary to make further crosses of the descendants of individuals who have been exposed to the influence of external conditions. Second, not all mutations are expressed in changes of observable traits. Geneticists know of a significant number of mutations which are expressed only in the fact that the descendants of individuals who have been exposed to certain influences are not viable. Such mutations are

called lethal. Apparently, they are explained by the fact that mutational changes of the gene substantially disrupt the basic life processes.

All mutations, as hereditary changes, are connected with certain changes in the chromosomes. The basic category of mutations is genic mutations. They involve changes in the individual genes which are contained in the chromosomes. Another group of mutations involves changes in the number and structure of the chromosomes. They are called chromosomal aberrations. In contrast to the genic mutations, these changes in the chromosomes can be observed under a microscope. Chromosomal aberrations can consist either of changes in the number of chromosomes or changes in the observable structure of the individual chromosomes. The students should be acquainted with the so-called polyploidic mutations, in which the number of chromosomes is increased by a multiple of their normal number, i.e., instead of pairs of chromosomes, there are three or four identical chromosomes; for example, if the chromosome number is 12, or 6 pairs, there can be 18, or 6 groups of three, or 24, or 5 groups of four. As is well known, such polyploidic mutations are of particular significance in practice.

The law of linkage, or the linear distribution of genes. At the beginning of the twenties, T. H. Morgan convincingly demonstrated in experiments with Drosophila that the various mutated genes are normally inherited together if they are situated on one chromosome. This regularity received the name of the law of the linkage of genes located on one chromosome. Then, with the aid of Morgan's brilliant experiments, it was shown that genes located on one chromosome occupy definite positions and are distributed in a linear order. Some interesting facts lie at the basis of these regularities. When the sex cells mature, at definite stages of meiosis, the chromosome pairs are completely uncoiled and are joined together. This process long ago received the name of the conjugation of chromosome pairs. Observations showed that at the time of conjugation the chromosome pairs can break in various places and interchange parts. It is easy to imagine that if we know some of the mutated genes in a heterozygous individual, i.e., an individual in whom these genes are located in one of the chromosomes, then through the transfer of these genes from one chromosome to the other we will be able to determine where they are located on the chromosome. This phenomenon received the name of crossing over. Use of this method led Morgan to the construction of the first mappings of chromosomes.

III. Special attention should be concentrated on the achievements of molecular genetics. It should be emphasized that the huge successes achieved by this science in a comparatively short period of time are connected with the development of the electron microscope, the joint research of biologists, biochemists and physicists, and the development of radiobiology and, in particular, radiogenetics.

What are the most important discoveries of this period?

It was established that the chromosomes consist of two substances: molecules of protein and molecules of a particular deoxynucleic acid (DNA). As is known, proteins exist in all cells, and all basic life processes are connected with them. There are also proteins in the nucleus and in the cytoplasm of the cells. It turns out that DNA is contained almost entirely in the chromosomes of the nucleus, although in a large quantity. The nucleus and the cytoplasm contain other nucleic acids which are called by the general name of ribonucleic acids (RNA).

The facts that were discovered directed the attention of geneticists to the study of the chemical structure of the DNA molecule. Biochemical research established that the DNA molecule is a very large polymeric molecule. Its molecular weight is measured in millions and more. The DNA molecule consists of repeated links of chains of the so-called nucleotides. An association automatically arises with the linear arrangement of genes established by Morgan. The nucleotides are arranged in a definite order, and carbohydrate, deoxyribose, and the residuum of phosphoric acid constitute the backbone of the whole chain.

It was proven by many investigators, including Watson and Crick, that autoreproduction, i.e.,

self-reproduction, is characteristic of the DNA molecule. It consists in exactly the same molecule being formed along the whole DNA molecule. Autoreproduction should be thought of as a process in which the individual links of the DNA molecule attract to themselves exactly the same compounds in the form of nitrous bases which are found in the surrounding medium and are formed as a result of the metabolism that takes place in the cell.

The basis of life processes and, first of all, of metabolism in the organism is proteins. These are the most complex of the organic compounds, but they are formed from chains of simpler compounds — the amino acids. There are twenty amino acids. All or some of them, in various combinations, can enter into the composition of the protein, but the number of molecules of amino acids which make up the proteins, in particular the complex proteins, is enormous. There can be several hundred in one molecule of protein.

It has been established that the synthesis of all proteins occurs in the cytoplasm of living cells and that the DNA molecules play an important role in this process. It may be considered as proven that the DNA molecule, which consists of genes, bears in itself the code of all the hereditary information, and the individual parts of this molecule, i.e., the various genes, determine the synthesis of different proteins and, consequently, the processes of activity in the organism that are connected with these proteins.

Just how do the DNA molecules, which enter into the composition of chromosomes and are found in the nucleus, program the synthesis of proteins in the cytoplasm? This remained unknown for a long time. It is now clear that this occurs with the participation of ribonucleic acid (RNA). We know of three different ribonucleic acids, which fulfill different functions. One of them (it is called soluble RNA), using the energy of specific particles found in the cytoplasm (mitochondria), activates the amino acids in the cytoplasm, which makes them capable of combining together. Another RNA (called messenger RNA) is distinguished by the fact that its molecules are formed side by side with the various parts of the DNA molecules in the chromosome, and then are transported to the ribosome particles, where the activated amino acids also are found. And here it transmits its information during the formation of the molecule of the corresponding protein, while the very process of the formation of the protein molecule occurs under the influence of a third RNA, which is found permanently in the ribosomes.

These discoveries resulted from persistent, painstaking work by geneticists and biochemists. Some of them were made quite recently. Thus, for example, it was only in 1961 that the messenger RNA was discovered and its role established.

IV. The students should know the enormous significance of advances in genetics in the practice of agriculture and medicine. The achievements of genetics make it possible to obtain more productive breeds of cattle and more productive varieties of agricultural plants, to create effective antibiotics, and to explain the causes of hereditary diseases, which opens up possibilities for elaborating methods of preventing and treating these diseases.

Here are some examples that show the practical significance of the science of genetics. The well-known selectionists Sapegin, Delone and others, using X-rays and ultraviolet rays, obtained varieties of wheat with upright stalks and larger grains which were drought resistant. Sakharov, Lobashov and others worked out methods for obtaining mutations by means of various chemical substances. Sakharov, through the use of colchicine, obtained polyploidic buckwheat, which is distinguished by its larger grains. Lutkov (in Novosibirsk) and Turbin (in Belorussia) obtained a triploidic beet that gives 20 percent more sugar than normal. American geneticists elaborated an effective method for obtaining hybrid seeds of corn, and this significantly raised the yield of this crop. This method has also been applied in the Soviet Union in recent years. Under the guidance of Beliaev (Institute of Genetics of the Siberian Branch of the Academy of Sciences of the USSR), new varieties of mink with different colors of fur (brown, blue, beige) have been raised.

The achievements in the area of obtaining more effective antibiotics and their sources are especially interesting. (Thus, the source of penicillin is the penicillium mold.) Through various influences on the culture of the mold, experimenters succeeded in raising its productivity 500 times. At the I. V. Kurchatov Institute, the antibiotic erythromycin was obtained; it acts on forms of pathogens that are resistant to penicillin.

It must be emphasized that inclusion of the fundamentals of genetics in the 9th-grade course necessitates a corresponding revision of the 8th-grade course, which can give the students information to prepare them for perception of the more complex material of the 9th grade. Thus, for example, in the 8th-grade course if would be possible to give a more extensive presentation of the cell, even on the electron microscopic level. It is necessary to introduce a description of the karyokinetic division of the cell and to mention the number of chromosomes in man and their role in heredity. Further, when the question is one of the synthesis of proteins, it would be possible to mention briefly that this synthesis is accomplished in the cell, in the interaction of the cytoplasm and the nucleus. In general, this course should be seriously corrected and freed of a superfluity of various details and of unclear formulations.

* * *

Programmed Instruction

Sovetskaia pedagogika, 1967, No. 7

THE CURRENT STAGE OF WORK ON THE PROBLEM OF PROGRAMMED INSTRUCTION

Programmed instruction, as a possible means of increasing the efficiency of the educational process in the most varied types of educational institutions, continues to attract the attention of officials in public education, scholars, engineers and technologists, and wide circles of the teaching profession and pedagogical society. The agendas of scientific conferences and many conventions, where problems of improving training and instruction in our country are discussed, always include questions about what programmed instruction essentially consists of, how efficient it is; how it should be incorporated into the media, methods, and organizational forms of teaching established in Soviet secondary and higher schools; what are the development trends and the prospects for its use.

The First All-Union Conference on Programmed Instruction, which took place in the spring of 1966, demonstrated the great interest of the most varied groups and categories of scientific and practical workers in solving this problem, and revealed the representatives of all links in the public education system as united in scientific research: representatives of different educational institutions — technical, military, pedagogical, medical, agricultural, and other higher educational institutions, schools [shkoly], and secondary specialized and vocational-technical schools took an active part in the conference. About 500 reports were made in all. These reports, as well as the literature and media of programmed instruction presented at the conference, showed that the problem is being worked on from a great variety of standpoints: new ways and approaches to working out its theoretical bases are being sought and defined, significant work is being done to create technical devices of programmed instruction and to find ways of penetrating more deeply the cognitive mechanisms of the students. Still, a very significant number of actual programs was presented at the conference: these were programming aids both for nonmechanized and for mechanized programmed instruction; very little was said about the pedagogical functions of the teaching devices and the methods of organizing lessons, applying the basic devices of programmed instruction.

After the conference, a year passed, essentially completing a five-year period of work on the problem of programmed instruction in our country. What has the experience shown?

The first stage, which began with the conference of the Council on Cybernetics in the summer of 1962, was a period of adjusting to the very idea and principles of programmed instruction. The representatives of pedagogical science and workers in the most varied sectors of public education were confronted with the task of understanding what programmed instruction was, whether it was worthwhile to study it, whether it had long-range prospects and, if so, what were to be its role and place in the system of other means and methods of teaching.

A scientific hypothesis was advanced that the new teaching devices — teaching machines and programmed textbooks which applied certain new principles — could promote individualization and a general rise in teaching efficiency. The principles forming an organic part of this scientific hypothesis were:

presenting study material to the student in small amounts;

including instructions for testing the mastery of each given amount;

providing the student with means of self-checking;

making the reception of instructions for subsequent work dependent upon the results of a test of the mastery of the given amount of information.

During this period an intensive search went on for ways to define the scientific approach to solving problems, taking account of the level of development of pedagogical and related sciences and of the specific conditions of instruction and training in our country.

The idea of control based on feedback was taken as the theoretical basis for work on the practical implementation and testing of the efficiency of these principles in teaching. Feedback in programmed instruction was then understood as the reception of information by the teacher as to how the students' cognitive activity. was proceeding. Later, the concept of feedback was developed and refined to take account of the two-sided nature of the educational process, in which the student is seen not as a passive object of control, but as an active participant who inter-

acts complexly with the control system; as a result, the concepts of internal and external feedback were introduced. The reception by the teacher of information regarding the course of the student's cognition came to be called external feedback, while the reception by the student himself of information regarding how accurately he had mastered study material came to be called internal feedback.

Psychologists also joined in working out the theoretical bases of this problem — in particular, psychologists who studied the problem of the efficiency of teaching on the basis of the theory of the stage formation of mental operations (A. N. Leont'ev, P. Ia. Gal'perin, and others), the theory of the establishment of associative connections (Iu. A. Samarin and others), and the application of algorithmic prescriptions and teaching algorithms in instruction (L. N. Landa and others).

Extensive use also began to be made of the theoretical achievements of Soviet didactics, particularly with respect to the role and place of independent work in the educational process, and the activization and individualization of learning (B. P. Esipov, I. T. Ogorodnikov, and others).

The work which began during this period on creating the first programmed materials and technical devices of programmed instruction and their experimental testing showed that programmed instruction has a certain positive effect even when only very imperfect programmed materials and teaching machines are applied; in other words, the original hypothesis of the potentials of programmed instruction for increasing teaching effectiveness was upheld. The majority of articles and publications during this period were devoted to proving the effectiveness of programmed teaching or to developing more precise and reliable methods of conducting experimental work for the purpose of obtaining sufficiently objective indices and results.

Naturally, in the course of experimental testing of the basic hypothesis, corrections were made both in the very principles of creating programmed materials and machines and in the methods of applying them. The principles of linear and multiple programming were refined and developed, new variants of combining them arose, corrections were made in the recommendations of American specialists and in their rigid demands based on behavioristic psychological conceptions of learning. New types of programmed materials and original models of machines appeared, such as programmed supplements to existing textbooks, workbooks, collections of multiple-choice questions, and test cards for teaching machines. Machines of the "repetitor" and "ekzamenator" type, almost unknown in the USA and the West, began to be built and applied to reinforce and test information. There was a change of opinion about the possibility of individualized teaching by means of programmed instruction devices alone. It appeared that in a situation of mass teaching requiring a combination of individual and collective forms of work, a gap in the volume and speed of covering material between strong and weak students was inexpedient. This matter became particularly critical in schools where lengthy individual independent work with programmed materials for a series of lessons proved completely inapplicable, primarily because collective forms of work are essential in school instruction and the age characteristics of children require a frequent change in types of activity, firmer guidance from the teacher, and closer interaction with one another. This was a period of trials and searches, a period for testing the theoretical tenets and concepts of programmed teaching in practice.

In the course of this work there arose new scientific theories and new personal hypotheses regarding the improvement both of programming principles and the methods of including programmed instruction in the educational process; at the same time the first conclusions and generalizations were also drawn.

Thus, while the first period could be called a period of studying the ideas and principles of programmed instruction and defining the theoretical approach to the solution of this problem in our situation, the second period can be called a period of intensive experimental testing of the ways of implementing these ideas and principles in practice.

During the five years of work, of course, tremendous and varied experience was accumulated, a great number of interesting and varied experimental data were collected and published. The task of analyzing and understanding this experience for application to methods theory appeared on the agenda. Therefore the third, namely, the present stage of work in the field of programmed instruction, is the stage of further elaboration of the scientific methods principles of programmed teaching on the basis of careful and profound understanding and generalization of experience, i.e., elaboration of the basic fundamental scientific and methods principles and recommendations.

It must first be stated that certain changes have occurred in the very understanding of the tasks of solving the problem of programmed instruction. Our understanding of the essence of programmed instruction has gone beyond the boundaries of its original treatment as a means of effective self-teaching, stimulated by step-reinforcement. At present, programmed instruction is regarded primarily as a means of introducing the principles and methods of the scientific organization of labor into education. The ideas and principles of the scientific organization of labor (SOL), as a system of scientifically justified measures and improvements that increase the overall productivity and efficiency of labor, promote a more efficient use of cadres, material means, and time, and can undoubtedly also find a certain application in the methods of programmed instruction. Therefore the further working out of the problem presupposes a broader use of the most important principles of SOL, including, above all, the following:

1. Standardization of labor, by which is meant not only setting the time allotted to a given work, but a precise indication of the volume of work and demands on the quality of its performance. The methods of programmed instruction, as we know, also require a precise description of the ultimate aims of instruction and an administration of study material by doses.

2. The principle of division of labor (in teaching, the pedagogical labor of the teacher and the cognitive labor of the students) into operations

or elements. This requires analysis of these elements from the standpoint of their necessity for attaining the ultimate aims; selection and isolation of the most important and essential elements and their distribution in rational order; determination of the most efficient methods of performing each operation and, for this purpose, study and selection of the best methods and techniques, using means of mechanized labor processes (including technical teaching devices).

3. Teaching the worker (in the system of education, the teacher) these selected scientifically justified methods of work, including those requiring the use of mechanical devices; this requires careful instruction and working out a system of precepts (methods instructions) for performing the given volume of work.

4. The correct placement [rasstanovka] of people with regard to their qualifications; their distribution, cooperation, and clear-cut interrelations in the process of joint activity. This can include the correct spacing of teachers by classes; the division of duties among teachers teaching one subject; the rational organization of the educational process, using individual and collective forms of work; the combining of students' independent work with the teacher's explanations, etc.

5. The principle of uninterrupted supply of everything needed for production. In the school situation, this means providing the teacher with a full complement of visual aids, a sufficient number of problems and exercises, and all the other materials for organizing the students' uninterrupted work at all stages of the educational process.

6. The principle of organizing working areas and their servicing (including the equipment of classrooms with the necessary teaching aids and technical devices of organization, maintaining language labs in working order, automated classrooms, teaching machines for individual use, etc.).

7. The introduction of rational graphs of labor and rest schedules. As applied to schools, this can mean drafting a pedagogically competent description of lessons, defining the length of changes, the sequence of period of study and holidays, etc.

8. Looking for and making correct use of incentives to activity, including the cognitive activity of students.

Of course, not all the principles listed here are or can be subsequently implemented in the methods of programmed instruction. But setting the task of using the principles of SOL in the schools undoubtedly gives a partially new orientation to the solution of the whole problem of programmed instruction and strengthens its scientific basis.

The broader direction which was given to research on this problem in the Ukraine also appears to have long-range possibilities. Here, programming in the broad sense, so-called general programming, came to be understood as the control of the process of training a specialist in accordance with the changing demands of production. The results of work in this area received their fullest generalization in the methods brochure Some Questions About the Scientific Organization of the Educational Process in Technical Schools [Nekotorye voprosy nauchnoi organizatsii uchebnogo protsessa v tekhnicheskikh vuzakh], prepared by the Ministry of Higher and Secondary Specialized Education of the Ukrainian SSR, and in the report entitled "Scientific Problems of Programmed Teaching and Paths of Their Development" [Nauchnye problemy programmirovannogo obucheniia i puti ikh razvitiia], by V. M. Glushkov, G. S. Kostiuk, G. A. Ball, A. M. Doviallo, E. I. Mashbits, and E. L. Iushchenko. These materials emphasize that programmed instruction can undoubtedly play a great role in the scientific planning of the training of cadres and in the scientific organization of the educational process in educational institutions.

The analytical program approach to matters of organizing educational work, characteristic of the methods of programmed teaching, undoubtedly helps the researcher to find more rational methods of solving a great range of problems connected with establishing the relationship between the productive functions of specialists under real production circumstances and the content of instruction. The starting point in this work is to define the total amount of information, skills, and habits needed to perform each of the specialist's productive functions and, on this basis, to define the aim and content of instruction — i.e., a more precise elaboration of the curriculum. Later work includes establishing a logical connection between the subjects, the composition of the student's program of study operations, taking full account of the required expenditures of time in performing each study operation and a number of other operations directed at organizing the control of the student's study. This approach gives the authors reason to define programmed instruction as "a type of instruction which is carried on in accordance with a teaching program framed beforehand, describing in detail both the final and intermediate products of instruction, and the process of obtaining them, i.e., the study activity of the students, organized in a certain way."

Of course, this general expanded interpretation of programmed instruction reflects primarily the specific nature of the preparation of specialists in higher educational institutions (including pedagogical), since in this work the chief problem is to maintain control of the specialist's training by the timely introduction of changes in the content of instruction, to establish the relationship between subjects, and to define their relative weight in accordance with the nature of changes in the development of production, science, technology, and culture. However, the fundamental bases of this approach can also be extended to other educational institutions, including schools where the content of education and the framing of the curriculum must likewise be determined on the basis of a more precise consideration of the demands made by life on contemporary secondary education.

At the same time one cannot ignore the fact that the trend toward an excessive expansion of the concept of programmed teaching, going so far as to depart from the concept of the scientific organization of labor or the scientific basis of planning the training of cadres as a whole, is incorrect, since these problems go beyond the range not only of programmed teaching but of teaching in general. Therefore it is advisable

to separate the field of programmed instruction per se from these broad national economic problems and tasks. The field of programmed teaching is the field of educational labor — by the teacher and student — and the main task of programmed instruction is to increase the efficiency of this labor by those special devices and methods of organizing the educational process which the idea of the programmed control of the student's cognitive activity gave rise to.

It should be noted that at present the very concept of control of the student's cognition has become more profound. This control is carried out both along the line of implementing the basic principles of programming contained in the teaching programs for machines or in programmed aids, and along the line of creating systems of programmed and other educational and methods materials and aids which enable one to guide the students' work at all stages of the educational process. The latter direction in the interpretation of the idea of controlling the student's cognition by the devices of programmed instruction is primarily connected with an acknowledgment of the necessity of combining programmed instruction methods with other devices and methods. This approach finds its practical realization in the work of a number of collectives, including that of the laboratory of programmed instruction in the V. I. Lenin Moscow State Pedagogical Institute [MGPI], where complexes of teaching materials are worked out which include systems of programmed aids of various didactic purposes to be used both with and without teaching machines, combined with a methods aid for the teacher. This methods aid helps the teacher to rationally combine the devices and methods of programmed teaching with the most successful traditional methods, and to make more effective use of the visual aids developed for the course. The article by Z. S. Khar'kovskii in this issue of our journal discusses the experiment.

Thus, at the present stage, the development of programmed teaching is typified by a new, broader approach to elaborating its scientific bases and by a transition from the problem of "programmed instruction" to the problem of "how to program instruction," which essentially means the development of a scientific system of organizing teaching, using the idea, principles, and basic means of programmed instruction.

At the same time a great lag has now appeared in working out questions of the programmed instruction methods and of creating study aids for programmed instruction. There is still not a single programmed textbook or other aid which has been subjected to sufficiently broad experimental testing and has been recommended for practical use in any educational institutions, although various staffs of researchers have already created a whole series of experimental materials for the most varied disciplines — for schools, technical schools, and colleges. They include teaching aids for mathematics (algebra for grades 6 and 8, geometry for grade 9 — in the V. I. Lenin Moscow State Pedagogical Institute [MGPI]; algebra for grade 9 — in the Scientific Research Institute for Pedagogy of the Ukrainian SSR; geometry for grade 8 — in the Cheliabinsk Pedagogical Institute; algebra and geometry for different grades — in School No. 123 in Kuibyshev, etc.); in physics (for grade 10 — the Odessa Pedagogical Institute; for grade 9 — the USSR Academy of Pedagogical Sciences and the Lenin MGPI); in chemistry (the Lenin MGPI, the Cheliabinsk Pedagogical Institute); in history (the Lenin MGPI); in Russian as a foreign language (Kiev University); in Russian as a native language (the USSR Academy of Pedagogical Sciences, the Lenin MGPI, the Tiumen Institute for Teacher Improvement); in geography (the Tiumen ITI, the Cheliabinsk Pedagogical Institute); and in several other subjects and disciplines.

It should be noted that although many of these teaching aids use the basic principles of programming and certain techniques of technical formulation borrowed from methods theory abroad, these first programmed aids are distinguished by great variety and a freer use of the principles and techniques of programming. The very range of types of programmed aids is broader in our country than in the United States, where only programmed textbooks or chapters of them, as well as aids for individual topics or

sections of courses, are being developed.

The methods commission of the International Scientific Council on the Problem of Programmed Instruction, after analyzing and evaluating the basic methodological principles of constructing different programmed aids and their didactic possibilities, agreed to distinguish the following basic groups of types of these aids:

programmed textbooks which pace the presentation of information, reinforce it, and develop the required skills and habits;

collections of programmed problems and exercises which only reinforce knowledge and develop skills and habits;

aids which contain only programs of control of learning.

Present-day theoretical and methods concepts of programmed instruction and the study of foreign and national experience in drafting programmed aids enable us to make certain generalizations and to distinguish the basic principles in the methods of developing each given type of programmed aid. The articles printed below expound the methods principles of developing experimental aids for different didactic purposes.

At the same time it must be noted that up to the present we still lack centralized supervision of the work of creating and publishing programmed aids. Textbooks and teaching aids are published locally without the competent judgment of specialists. They do not always fulfill strict requirements in regard to scientific content; nor are the general methodological requirements worked out for programmed aids of different types and purposes, by which authors and publishers could be guided.

Questions of the methods of programming are extremely complex. However, subsequent work can be made somewhat easier if certain generalizations are drawn on the basis of studying the early experience of their development and the experimental testing of programmed aids with regard to all the defects and inadequacies that have come to light.

The need to create special scientific methods aids, both about the general principles of programming methodology and about the application of these general principles to the practice of creating programmed aids for individual subjects, has undoubtedly become urgent. In this regard it is interesting to become acquainted with foreign experience in drawing up such aids for the general principles of programming (see the resumé of the American guide to programming methods in this journal), and with the experience in using these methods to create popular-science books (see the book Systems of Network Planning and Control [Moscow, "Mir" Publishing House, 1965], translated from the English, written in the form of a programmed aid that uses the principle of branched [razvetvlennoe] programming).

The solution to methods problems in creating programmed aids is also closely connected with developing technical devices of programmed instruction. It should be noted that at present the evaluation of the pedagogical possibilities of teaching machines has become more sensible and differentiated. The great creative and constructive work that evolved during the first years of work on the problem led to the creation of a tremendous number of different technical devices of programmed instruction, beginning with elementary electromechanical machines for individual use, and ending with complex automated classrooms. At the first stage, this freedom of technical search and creativity was undoubtedly permissible, useful, and even desirable. Now, however, the moment has arrived when further designing work and technical research should be directed into a certain channel. Above all, thanks to the existence of a considerable number of technical devices of various types and purposes, it is becoming possible to select the best models, those which are pedagogically most efficient and economically most sensible, and to concentrate our efforts on duplicating and mastering them.

Analysis of the functions of the machines already built and discovery of the errors made in designing them help us to define the basic possible areas of using technical devices in the teaching process and to formulate a few pedagogical requirements for technical devices for different didactic purposes.

An analysis of the teaching machines presently developed from the standpoint of the pedagogical functions they perform shows that technical devices which inform only the student himself of the degree of correctness of his cognitive operations are the simplest. Most of them lack means of presenting information or even stating problems, and are intended only to receive answers and give reinforcement. Provided that they work reliably, such machines are extremely useful since they stimulate the students' active participation, create additional motivation for learning, maintain self-testing, relieve the teacher, and increase the efficiency of work on reinforcing study material. Such technical devices can be comparatively cheap, and the most varied types of educational institutions can be provided with them. The chief technical problems here are: simplifying the input of answers (reducing students' operations for input to a minimum) and increasing the machine's memory capacity (i.e., the capacity for response: reinforcing a great number of questions without the need for frequent change of programs). As a rule, these machines work according to a linear program; practically speaking, they lack means for adaptation. The more complex machines of this type, which work according to a diversified program, usually include giving out differentiated information and blocking the flow of information in case of an incorrect answer. These machines are more expensive, but they are more adaptable for use in teaching with simple electromechanical devices.

The improvement of machines of this type and the drafting of programs for them represent a very important and noteworthy direction in the work on creating technical devices for programmed teaching, especially because in the long run the working out of programs of this type can serve as a good basis for developing programs for electronic computers used for purposes of research into the learning process.

In order for the teacher to obtain information about the progress of every student's work, more complex technical devices are needed — above all, automated classrooms with a control panel for the teacher and devices for sending the teacher information about how each student is working on each question. Only then can the teacher effectively enter the learning process and give individual help to the student or, in other words, control this process. Since it is very important that the teacher receive this information during the course of the learning process itself, simple devices of signaling and registering the students' answers are all that are needed here, even if the instructor must later process these entries in order to analyze the learning activity of each student and give him a grade. The classrooms and machines used for such purposes should, as far as is possible, be simple, inexpensive, and accessible to the most varied types of educational institutions.

Automated classrooms or machines for individual use that permit an analysis of the course of each student's cognition after the end of lessons should be more complex — that is, they should have means of registering this process throughout the entire lesson (including the time spent on cogitation, the number of requests for help, etc.). This is extremely important for the authors of the program, since it permits them to take account of the special features in the work of students of differing ability in covering all sections of the program.

On the other hand, there is no need to provide those classrooms and machines with which the ordinary teacher works with all these devices for registering the student's behavior. The ordinary teacher needs only an overall picture of the student's work; he should not conduct a comprehensive depth analysis of all aspects of the student's educational activity, as must the author of a teaching aid or an experimental researcher. Special attention must be paid to this, since attempts are being made to introduce rather expensive multifunctional automated classrooms of this type into ordinary educational institutions, whereas they are really only needed in experimental laboratory schools and in those educational institutions where special research on programmed instruction is being conducted.

Undoubtedly, for the needs of such specialized scientific research, even more expensive and complex technical complexes can and should be built, including electronic computers that will permit detailed observation of the work of each individual student. Technical devices for this purpose should aid researchers to penetrate more deeply the mechanism of the students'

cognitive activity and to carry on research primarily rather than teaching functions. Incidentally, it should be noted that in our country too little attention is still being paid to using programmed instruction devices for purposes of a deeper study of students' cognition. Abroad, however (in the USA, England, France), while the advertising clamor to introduce programmed teaching in the schools to replace the teacher has died down, research on using the devices of programmed teaching (including very complex and expensive teaching machines) to penetrate the mechanisms of students' cognitive activity has increased significantly.

Working out the methods of organizing the educational process, applying the basic printed and technical aids of programmed teaching, is a special field. These problems should be solved with reference to the conditions of teaching specific academic disciplines.

In the articles in the present issue of our journal, one can find descriptions of examples of organizing the educational process in various disciplines through the use of programmed materials and certain technical teaching aids. One thing is common to these experiments and to all the work in this field: it is wise to combine programmed teaching with the other media and methods of teaching and to conduct it under the instructor's supervision. Therefore it would seem extremely desirable to write teaching aids which, as it were, would program the instructor's work in organizing lessons, applying different teaching devices. These methods instructions should prompt the teacher as to where, when, and how to apply programmed aids and teaching machines, and how best to combine individual work with collective forms of lessons. Such instructions, of course, should not hamper the initiative of the teacher who works creatively; on the other hand, they ease the work of the less experienced pedagogue.

Thus, along with working out the general psychological and pedagogical principles of programmed teaching, the task of working out its methodology acquires ever increasing importance. This methodology includes:

drawing up programmed teaching aids and programs for teaching machines of different didactic purposes (the methods of programming);

working out pedagogical requirements for the technical devices of programmed teaching;

working out the methods of organizing the educational process, using the devices of programmed teaching in combination with other devices and methods.

Communist Upbringing

Pravda, August 22, 1967

ON MEASURES FOR THE FURTHER DEVELOPMENT OF THE SOCIAL

SCIENCES AND FOR INCREASING THEIR ROLE IN COMMUNIST CONSTRUCTION

(In the Central Committee of the CPSU)

In response to the tasks set by the 23rd Party Congress, the CPSU Central Committee has adopted a resolution, "On Measures for the Further Development of the Social Sciences and for Increasing Their Role in Communist Construction."

The resolution notes that the present stage of communist construction in the USSR — namely, the enlistment of the broadest masses of the workers in active social participation — the transition from capitalism to socialism being made in our time, the powerful national liberation movement of peoples, the ongoing scientific and technological revolution, the sharp ideological struggle, and other processes of world development require continued and comprehensive analysis and theoretical deductions from the standpoints of Marxism-Leninism. In this situation the importance of Marxist-Leninist theory and the role of the social sciences increase even more.

Marxism-Leninism is the basis for guiding the development of socialist society, a powerful weapon for the understanding and revolutionary transformation of the world. The theory marks out a road for practice and ensures a scientific approach to defining party policy in all realms of social life.

As a great international doctrine, Marxism-Leninism represents the ideological basis of the international communist movement and the unity of this movement. Only under the guidance of Marxism-Leninism is it possible to solve correctly the theoretical and practical problems raised by the present course of world events and the revolutionary movement. Creative work in the field of theory must be increased in the interest of strengthening the political, economic, and cultural cooperation of socialist countries, and determining the most effective ways and means of ensuring the victory of socialism over capitalism. The development of theory is essential for a successful struggle against bourgeois ideology, against contemporary anticommunism, against right and "left" revisionism, to win the minds and hearts of the broad working masses of the world.

The whole history of our party and the heroic achievements of the Soviet people during the half-century since the victory of the Great October Socialist Revolution affirm the mighty strength of revolutionary theory and testify to the fact that the CPSU has always manifested and continues to manifest unshakable fidelity to Marxism-Leninism and conducts an endless struggle with its enemies. The party faithfully follows the precept of V. I. Lenin: ". . .Only the party, guided by advanced theory, can fulfill the role of a vanguard fighter."

In its theoretical and practical activity, the CPSU undeviatingly observes the Leninist principle of combining the continuity of revolutionary experience of the past with a creative approach to and solution of new problems; it constantly concerns itself with elaborating theory, with developing all the component parts of Marxist-Leninist doctrine — philosophy, political economy, and scientific communism. On the basis of analyzing tremendous practical experience, the party has developed and enriched Marxist doctrines on the socialist revolution, on the dictatorship of the proletariat, and on the construction of socialism; it has solved theoretical problems of the industrialization of the country, the collectivization of agriculture, the cultural revolution, the development of Soviet democracy, the socialist nations and the multinational Soviet state; it has discovered the basic laws and motive forces in the development of socialist society and defined the chief tasks and prerequisites for the gradual transformation of socialism into communism.

Together with the other Marxist-Leninist parties, the CPSU has made its contribution to defining the nature of the present-day era, the motive forces and long-range prospects of the world revolutionary process; to working out the strategy and tactics of the international communist, workers', and national liberation movement, the scientific principles of relations between socialist states; and to establishing the ways by which different countries and peoples convert to socialism under modern conditions.

The party regards the creative development of Marxist-Leninist theory as its chief obligation, as the prerequisite to fulfilling the tasks posed in the CPSU Program for creating the material and technical base of communism, improving social relationships, and enriching the spiritual culture of the Soviet people and the communist education of the workers. Theoretical work, in connection with practice, is called upon to maintain high rates of development of the productive forces, the fullest and most rational use of the advantages of the socialist order, our natural wealth, and the achievements of science and technology in the interest of building communism.

The highly qualified, party-trained scientific and professional pedagogical cadres of philosophers, economists, historians, and representatives of other social sciences play an enormous role in the theoretical activity of the CPSU, in raising the level of the ideological and political education of the workers, and in propagandizing Marxism-Leninism. With the active participation of scientists, propagandists, and all ideological cadres, the party has done significant work in disseminating the ideological heritage of Marx, Engels, and Lenin. Publication of the second edition of the Works of K. Marx and F. Engels and of V. I. Lenin's Complete Works is of tremendous significance. For the first time a multivolume scientific edition of the history of the Communist Party of the Soviet Union has been undertaken. A series of profound studies in the field of philosophy, on economic and legal matters, on national and world history has been prepared and published by the institutes of the Academy of Sciences of the USSR and the academies of sciences of the union republics, and by other scientific institutions and departments of higher educational institutions. Scholars are paying increased attention to solving the pressing problems of modern life; their role in solving national economic problems has increased. The party highly values the achievements of the social sciences and their contribution to socialist and communist construction.

Measures to overcome the results of the cult

of personality, subjectivism, and voluntarism have had a positive influence on the development of the social sciences. The October (1964) Plenary Meeting of the CPSU Central Committee and the 23rd Party Congress showed what tremendous importance theory has in the present stage of communist construction and emphasized the necessity for scientific guidance of the development of society.

In the past few years, more favorable conditions have been created for the development of the social sciences. The state and prospects of research in the fields of philosophical, economic, historical, and other social sciences were discussed in party organizations and by collectives of scholars. Basic changes were made in the plans of scientific research. New programs in the social sciences have been elaborated for higher educational institutions, and standard teaching aids are being prepared. Measures have been taken to improve the system of political education.

At the same time the CPSU Central Committee believes that the increased problems of communist construction and the ideological struggle taking place in the modern world demand further development of theoretical thought, deeper analysis of socialist development, and a new increase in the level of the Marxist-Leninist education of cadres.

The scientific research in the humanities institutes of the Academy of Sciences of the USSR and in the academies of sciences of the union republics, as well as in other scientific institutions and departments of social science, does not always provide a profound and objective analysis of the actual processes of social life, thus hindering a correct evaluation of the history and future prospects of our society.

A lag is observed in research on fundamental theoretical problems which reveal all aspects of the mechanism of the action of the laws of contemporary social development. Theoretical questions on the political economy of socialism, on raising the efficiency of social production, and on implementing economic policy at the present stage are not analyzed in sufficient depth and breadth. Little attention is paid to the qual-

ity and profundity of philosophical analyses of modern achievements in the natural sciences, to study of problems of social psychology, of the collective and the individual, of society and the state, and of the development of socialist democracy during communist construction. Until recently, concretely defined social research projects were insufficiently developed and their scientific and methodological base remains extremely empirical. Many projects contain no new conclusions and recommendations of serious theoretical and practical importance.

Works on the history of the CPSU do not sufficiently show the all-encompassing nature of the party's leadership role. There is insufficient work on creating general fundamental works that would demonstrate the contribution of the CPSU to the theory of the construction of socialism and communism, its role in the international development of Marxism-Leninism during the fifty years since the October Revolution, and would profoundly reveal the struggle of the CPSU with the Mensheviks, Trotskyites, right-wing opportunists, national-deviationists, and other groups and movements hostile to the party.

Although in recent years quite a few valuable books have been published which concretely analyze the world development and the socioeconomic, political, and ideological currents of modern capitalism, the struggle of the working class against monopoly capitalism, and the peoples' struggle against imperialism and neocolonialism, many aspects and problems of capitalist society and the national liberation movement still await study in depth and breadth. The organization of such research is not being sufficiently goal-oriented.

Ideological integrity and firmness in the struggle against imperialist ideology, against bourgeois and reformist falsifiers of Marxism-Leninism, are demanded from workers in the social sciences. It is a major responsibility of Soviet scholars to expose the professional anti-Soviets [antisovetchiki] and anticommunists who are active in the field of "studying" the problems of the history of the USSR and CPSU, the world communist, workers', and national liberation movement. A responsible role belongs to Soviet scholars in the struggle against revisionism and nationalism, against the great-power anti-Soviet ideology of Mao Tse-tungism.

The theoretical level and effectiveness of scientific research are lowered because the academies of sciences of the USSR and the union republics make insufficient use of new forms of organizing, planning, and coordinating scientific research in the field of the social sciences. The state of scientific information in the field of the social sciences seriously lags behind modern requirements. The scientific institutions of the USSR Academy of Sciences are inadequately equipped with modern technical devices. In a number of cases, institutes and departments of the humanities wastefully duplicate one another or become confined to a range of petty topics, which leads to a diffusion of strength and puts a brake on bold scientific research. The fact that a number of scientific institutions seldom conduct fruitful discussions and have no adequately developed criticism and self-criticism also has a negative effect on the development of the social sciences.

Party organizations and the leaders of certain scientific research institutes often ignore these defects, pay insufficient attention to ideological education, fail to react quickly enough to instances of violation of scientific ethics, and do not strive to create a genuinely creative atmosphere in scientific staffs and a situation of high party exactingness and ideological integrity.

The teaching of social sciences in the educational institutions of the country requires further improvement. The ministries of higher and secondary specialized education of the USSR and other ministries and departments responsible for the training of specialists have not yet ensured the required level of social science teaching and of the political training of college youth. The leadership and party organizations of a number of scientific institutions and higher schools do not show proper concern for the growth and advancement of young scientific cadres.

The CPSU Central Committee has proposed to the central committees of the communist parties of the union republics, the territorial, re-

gional, city, and district party committees, party organizations, the Academy of Sciences of the USSR, and the Ministry of Higher and Secondary Specialized Education of the USSR that they adopt effective measures to eliminate the defects noted in the resolution, improve the state of scientific research, ensure a creative solution to theoretical problems in close connection with the concrete tasks of communist construction, and raise the level of social science teaching and the whole question of the Marxist-Leninist education of cadres.

The efforts of scholars should be subordinate, above all, to solving the problems posed by the CPSU Program and the 23rd Party Congress, to actively participating in work on the further development of the country's economy, strengthening its defensive capacity, raising the level of the people's material welfare and culture, and directed to the communist training of Soviet people and the struggle against bourgeois ideology.

The resolution of the CPSU Central Committee directs the attention of scientific research institutes, party organizations, and staffs of scholars working in the fields of philosophy, economics, scientific communism, history, law, esthetics, pedagogy, psychology, and other social sciences to the necessity for a more effective and comprehensive solution of major theoretical problems for the creation of theoretical works on pressing problems in the development of society and modern scientific knowledge, and for further improvement of the quality and efficiency of scientific research.

The present stage of social development and the progress of scientific knowledge demand that scientific research in the social sciences be directed primarily along the following lines:

in the field of philosophical sciences — further elaboration of materialist dialectics, the theory of knowledge and logic, methodological problems of the social, natural, and technical sciences; study of the dialectics of socialist society and the contradictions of modern capitalism, the relationships between objective and subjective factors of social development; development of historical materialism as an overall sociological theory, concrete social research; solution to problems of the social structure of society, improvement of socialist social relationships and their development into communist ones; research on the laws of social consciousness; theoretical solution to the problems of the individual and the collective, society and the state, socialist humanism, ethics, and esthetics;

in the field of economic sciences — thorough investigation of the laws and categories of the political economy of socialism and the mechanism of their operation; research on economic problems in creating the material and technical base of communism and developing communist production relationships; development of scientific recommendations for implementing the new principles of economic policy at the present stage, increasing the efficiency of social production, rational distribution of productive capacities, and use of the country's labor resources; study of the economic problems of technical progress, developing the theory and methods of optimal planning and functioning of the socialist people's society; problems of commodity-money relations under socialism; broad use of computers in the field of economics of individual sectors of the national economy; socioeconomic research in the field of demography; research on the form and methods of economic cooperation among socialist countries, the ways of reinforcing the world system of socialism, the discovery of new phenomena in the economics of contemporary capitalism, research on the socioeconomic contradictions of imperialism, on new forms of the imperialist struggle to control the world, etc.; study of the economic, social, and political problems of the developing countries which have been freed from colonial dependency;

in the field of scientific communism — development of Lenin's theory of socialist revolution as applied to the present time; discovery of the laws of development of the world revolutionary process, analysis of the class struggle of the international proletariat and of problems of the national liberation movement, of the struggle against imperialism; solution to theoretical problems of the international communist movement at the present time; study of the problems of war and peace; profound analysis of the an-

tagonistic contradictions between socialism and capitalism; comprehensive study of the sociopolitical problems in the development of socialism and its transition to communism; elucidation of the social results of the scientific and technological revolution; research on ways and forms of more closely approximating the working, living, and cultural conditions of the city and country, and on organically combining mental and physical labor in productive activity; solution to problems in the development of international relations; development of methods of scientific control of social processes; analysis of the content and forms of work in communist indoctrination, ways of overcoming private-property, religious, and other survivals in the consciousness and life of the workers; research on the processes and problems of improving the state organization and socialist democracy, on inculcating patriotism and internationalism; study of the history of building socialism in other countries;

in the field of the history of the CPSU and other historical sciences — analysis of the history of the CPSU in the struggle for victory of the socialist revolution and establishment of the dictatorship of the proletariat, for implementation of the Leninist plan of constructing socialism; research on the laws of development of the party and the growth in its leadership role in communist construction, on the activity of the CPSU in elaborating the revolutionary theory, strategy, and tactics of the working class; study of the theory and practice of party construction, the forms and methods of the work of party organizations; elucidation of the struggle of the CPSU for the ideological and organizational unity of its ranks against anti-Leninist groups and currents, for the unity of the international communist movement; elucidation of the decisive role of the broad masses in history, the struggle of the workers against social and national oppression, the great liberating mission of the working class; demonstrating the heroism of the Soviet people in defense of the achievements of the Great October Revolution, in the struggle for the socialist industrialization of the country, the collectivization of agriculture and the cultural revolution, in the routing of fascism during World War II; analysis of the history of strengthening the alliance between the working class and the peasantry, the friendship of peoples, the creation and development of the multinational Soviet state; study of the foreign policy of the USSR and international relations, the history of the international workers' and communist movement;

in the field of legal sciences — research on the pressing problems of governmental organization, the development of socialist democracy; solution to problems of the organization and activity of soviets of workers' deputies, the scientific bases of government control and legislative regulation of economic life and social relations; development of measures to prevent and eliminate criminality and other infringements of the law, reinforcement of legality and lawfulness in the country; preparation of scientific recommendations for improving Soviet legislation; exposure of the reactionary essence of modern imperialist state and law; study of the problems of international law.

The needs of science and practice, the resolution points out, create the need to organize complex research along all basic lines in the development of the social sciences. Primary attention in research should be given to Marxist-Leninist methodology, to the principles of a class-party, concrete-historical approach to social phenomena.

A major task of the social sciences is to conduct a systematic attack against anticommunism, to criticize in detail modern bourgeois philosophy, sociology, historiography, law, and the economic theories of apologists for capitalism; to expose falsifiers of the ideas of Marxism-Leninism, the history of social development, the communist and workers' movement; to decisively reject instances of right-wing and "left-wing" revisionism and national limitations — both in theory and policy.

More light must be shed on the universal, international meaning of Marxism-Leninism; using specific examples, one must show the superiority of communist over bourgeois ideology, the all-conquering force of the ideas of scientific communism.

In their work, the scientific research institutes of social sciences must conduct more extensive and comradely discussions on disputed or insufficiently clear questions.

The CPSU Central Committee has entrusted the State Planning Committee of the USSR, the State Committee of the USSR Council of Ministers on Science and Technology, the USSR Academy of Sciences, and the Ministry of Higher and Secondary Specialized Education with preparing and submitting for the consideration of the CPSU Central Committee, by January 1, 1968, suggestions for radical improvement in the organization, planning, and financing of research in the field of the social sciences, for the purpose of defining the real long-range prospects of basic and applied research on basic scientific problems, bringing the system of humanities institutes into accord with the demands of science and the problems of communist construction, correctly combining collective and individual forms of work, of experienced cadres and young scholars, and strengthening the material base of social science institutes.

The resolution of the CPSU Central Committee charges the Institute of Marxism-Leninism of the CPSU Central Committee (as the center of study of the ideological heritage of Marx, Engels, and Lenin) with the coordination of all research in the field of party history. The institute's attention is concentrated on solving pressing problems in the history of the CPSU and party organization, scientific communism, the international communist movement, and on organizing scientific information in these fields. In this connection, corresponding changes in the work plans, structure, and staffs of the institute and its affiliates are provided for.

Measures should be taken to further improve the theoretical training of the leadership cadres and ideological workers of the party in the Academy of Social Sciences and the Higher Party School of the CPSU Central Committee, as well as in local party schools.

The CPSU Central Committee has directed the attention of the USSR Academy of Sciences, the Institute of Marxism-Leninism, the Higher

Party School, and the Institute of Social Sciences of the CPSU Central Committee to the necessity of maintaining comprehensive study of the development of Marxist thought abroad; of supporting constant contact with the scientific institutions of socialist states and fraternal communist parties so as to coordinate research with them in the field of the social sciences, to coordinate the development of forms and methods of aggressive propaganda against anticommunist ideology; of systematically conducting joint scientific conferences on major problems of Marxist-Leninist theory, socialist and communist construction, the world revolutionary movement, and the pressing problems of history.

For the purpose of radically improving the system of scientific information and the further expansion of the documentary base of the social sciences, the USSR Council of Ministers' State Committee on Science and Technology, the USSR Academy of Sciences, and the USSR Ministry of Higher and Secondary Specialized Education have been entrusted with preparing suggestions for organizing the Institute of Scientific Information; the Institute of Marxism-Leninism of the CPSU Central Committee and the Main Archives Department of the USSR Council of Ministers have been entrusted with taking measures to supplement and make better use of archive materials, preserve state and party archives by modern technical means of reproducing documentary materials; the Central Statistical Administration of the USSR Council of Ministers, the USSR State Planning Committee, and the USSR Academy of Sciences are entrusted with developing a scientific system of the statistical data needed for social research and with expanding and centralizing the publication of these data.

The resolution provides for a series of measures to improve social science teaching in higher educational institutions and technical schools, and to intensify the communist training of students. A major task of the social science departments and party organizations of higher and technical schools is to inculcate specialists with a Marxist-Leninist outlook, with communist consciousness and high moral qualities, and to train them as active builders of communism,

innovators in production, patriots, and internationalists.

The central committees of the communist parties of the union republics, the territorial, regional, city, and district party committees, the USSR Ministry of Higher and Secondary Specialized Education, and the presidium of the USSR Academy of Sciences have been requested to eliminate defects in planning the preparation and distribution of scientific cadres, to bring about an improvement in the qualitative composition of scientific workers and teachers in the social sciences, and a further increase in their ideological level. For this purpose they must work out suggestions for the improvement of certification and recertification of social science teachers and workers in humanities institutes, the system of competitive staffing of higher school departments and scientific research institutes, by increasing demands on the level of scientific qualifications of specialists working in the social sciences; expand the training of pedagogical cadres in the social sciences, systematically improve their pedagogical skill, and give attention to improving the selection of graduate students.

The CPSU Central Committee, the resolution points out, attributes tremendous importance to the mastery by party and government cadres of Marxist-Leninist theory, the Leninist method, scientific forms and methods of work, the art of political indoctrination and organization of the masses. The party assumes that mastery of Marxism-Leninism is essential for all Communists and for officials in any sector of governmental, economic, and social activity. Party organizations should maintain more effective control over the political studies of Communists, the study of the classics of Marxism-Leninism, the history of the CPSU, philosophy, political economy, scientific communism, domestic and foreign party policy; they should pay particular attention to the ideological tempering of young Communists and Komsomol members, to training them in the spirit of communism and the revolutionary, patriotic, and labor traditions of the Soviet people; [they should] more broadly enlist social science workers in disseminating

Marxist-Leninist theory, the heroic history of the Communist Party, the glorious revolutionary traditions of the peoples of the Soviet Union; [they should] increase the role of houses and special rooms [kabinety] of political enlightenment connected with the territorial, regional, city, and district committees of the CPSU and of the party committees in the Marxist-Leninist education of cadres, in organizing scientific methods work, and in analyzing successes in Marxist-Leninist propaganda.

The CPSU Central Committee has entrusted the Press Committee of the USSR Council of Ministers and the central and local publishing houses with providing a large edition, for the mass reading public, of the works of Marx, Engels, and Lenin; sufficiently large editions of scientific works, textbooks, and methods and visual aids for the social sciences with respect to the fields of specialization of educational institutions and the needs of the system of political education; and publication of special series and libraries of scientific literature intended for certain categories of party and soviet activists, the intelligentsia, and workers in industrial and agricultural production. The role and responsibility of scientific institutions and publishing houses for the ideological and scientific content of social science publications must be increased, measures must be taken to improve the selection of editorial cadres and to increase their theoretical level and qualifications; the scientific level and quality of publications must be raised so that they arouse great interest and enjoy wide demand.

The editorial boards of social science and scientific journals, the editorial offices of central, republic, territorial, and regional newspapers, and the Committee on Radio and Television Broadcasting of the USSR Council of Ministers have been requested to work out measures to strengthen the dissemination of Marxist-Leninist theory and the achievements of the social sciences, while paying particular attention to raising the quality of published materials and of radio and television broadcasts.

The resolution of the CPSU Central Committee requires that the central committees of the communist parties of the union republics and the territorial, regional, city, and district party committees improve the supervision of party organizations over research and educational institutions, and give them constant help in selecting, placing, and training cadres. Party organizations should devote particular attention to training young scientific workers and teachers in the field of social sciences. An atmosphere of high responsibility must be constantly maintained in the staffs of scientists and teachers; their creative activity, mutual exactingness, criticism, and self-criticism must be developed, and professional pedagogical cadres must be inculcated with the spirit of the Communist Party.

It is the duty of representatives of the social sciences to develop broad scientific and propaganda work based on the decisions of the 23rd Party Congress.

The CPSU Central Committee expresses confidence that social science personnel and the entire ideological vanguard will achieve new successes in the creative development and dissemination of Marxist-Leninist theory, and will make their contribution to implementing the decisions of the 23rd Party Congress in the cause of building communism.

* * *

Sovetskaia pedagogika, 1963, No. 6

A. M. Netylko

CONCERNING AN INDIVIDUAL APPROACH IN THE ATHEISTIC

UPBRINGING OF PUPILS

Communist ethics and the fundamentals of a dialectical materialist world outlook are formed, and the rounded development of schoolchildren is achieved, at the lesson and in organized out-of-class activities. One of the most important principles of Soviet pedagogy, that of rearing children in the collective and through the collective, also concerns the development of atheistic convictions in schoolchildren. Experience has convincingly demonstrated that in a friendly, active children's collective, religiosity as a rule is a rare phenomenon.

As the pupils' collective becomes stronger, the moral staunchness and public activity of the schoolchildren rise to a higher level. And the conditions are thereby created for the development of atheistic views in the children. Active participation in the work of clubs, in large-scale out-of-class activities, in socially useful work, and in the life of the entire school collec-

---

The author is associated with the Tambov Teacher Training Institute.

tive contributes to a scientific, objective understanding of the surrounding world, which is incompatible with religious dogma. N.K. Krupskaya frequently stressed the great importance of collective work in atheistic upbringing. In an article entitled "On Antireligious Upbringing" [Ob antireligioznom vospitanii], she said that "it is necessary to extend the collective aspects of the children's life. We must enrich the life of the children as much as possible with new experiences. This does not mean taking them more often to the theater or on distant excursions. It means teaching them to read the surrounding world, to understand and create it. Then the child will not feel alone, and he will not have any need of religion" (1, p. 202). Consequently, one of the important factors in atheistic upbringing is the organization of purposeful collective activity for the children. This, however, does not exclude the need for individual work with each pupil.

School experience has shown that it is impossible to achieve success in instilling scientific atheism in the pupils without a good knowledge of their psychology, the conditions of their home upbringing, and the nature of the views that are being formed in them. "If pedagogy wishes to rear a person in all respects," K.D. Ushinsky wrote, "it must first understand him in all respects as well" (2, p. 23). It is especially important to bear this in mind in the process of atheistic upbringing. A good knowledge of the children is a most important condition for individualizing the methods of influencing them. We come to know the psychology of the schoolchild chiefly by attentively observing him at lessons, during varied out-of-class activities and socially useful work, and in individual talks. There are no special methods of studying the children for the purpose of atheistic upbringing. The use of questionnaires and the like in order to ascertain the pupil's attitude toward religion is absolutely out of the question. Similarly, other methods that may directly or indirectly offend or humiliate the pupil must not be employed.

Individual work enables us to penetrate more deeply into the spiritual world of the schoolchild, to determine the reasons for and sources of his religiosity, and to check on the efficacy of the methods used in rearing him. To employ an individual approach in the process of atheistic upbringing means to employ pedagogical methods of influencing the personality of the pupil which take into consideration his psychological traits, the conditions of his home upbringing, his experience in life, and the level of his development. Experience has shown that the degree and character of the religiosity of schoolchildren differ greatly. We sometimes find children and adolescents who are profoundly religious, who believe in God, in supernatural forces, and who read religious books. They do not participate in the social life of their collective, are not interested in literature, do not go to the movies or the theater, avoid socially useful work, and carefully evade talks, reports, and questions on antireligious themes. There are also children who do not believe in God, but believe in fate, in "prophetic dreams," and omens. The religiosity of some schoolchildren consists in

their taking part, together with their parents, in religious rites and in their going to church. However, we must emphasize that the absolute majority of schoolchildren are free from religious prejudices and are not affected by believers and superstitious people.

Naturally, antireligious measures cannot have the same effect on all children, no matter how carefully they are prepared or how ideal the method of conducting them. "A child reacts to measures of upbringing in different ways, depending on a number of conditions," says L.S. Slavina. "These conditions are: the traits of his personality which have already been formed, the reason prompting an action toward which that influence is directed, the relations between the child and his teacher and others around him, and his attitude toward the given method of rearing him.... The influence of the teacher is always expressed through the pupil's personality" (3, p. 3). When employing an individual approach to the schoolchildren in the process of their atheistic upbringing, it is important to remember that children who have recently come under the influence of religious prejudices are not indifferent to the opinion of their collective. One of the effective means of antireligious upbringing is to make an attentive study of the psychology of each such pupil, to ascertain the positive aspects of his personality, and to utilize them for support. The author of this article had an opportunity to be convinced of this when he studied how atheistic upbringing is organized in the schools of the Iaroslavl and Tambov Regions and in the Komi ASSR.

Yuri A., an 8th-grade pupil, and his brother Nikolai, a 9th-grade pupil, in a secondary school in the city of Rybinsk, were brought up in a religious atmosphere from preschool age. They read the Holy Scripture, regularly went to church, and performed religious rites. The boys were well-read and strong-willed, and received marks of "4" and "5" in their studies. However, it was not difficult to detect the pernicious influence of religious morality in their behavior: their superficial good breeding concealed such negative traits as individualism, insincerity, and hypocrisy. The brothers

258

fulfilled unquestioningly the social tasks they were asked to perform, but without manifesting any initiative and interest. They did not associate with other children of their age. The teachers realized that the antireligious work conducted with all the schoolchildren was not enough as far as Yuri and Nikolai were concerned, and that additional educational means in accord with their individual traits would have to be employed. It was also clear that one could not expect quick success in their case. The teachers decided that the first thing to be done was to draw these pupils into the life of the collective, to interest them in social and out-of-class activities, and to fill their leisure with such attractions as sports, excursions, movies, the theater, and the like. They began inviting the boys regularly to interesting out-of-class activities, and gave them social tasks whose fulfillment required creative activity and initiative. At the lessons the teachers periodically gave them individual problems to solve that involved relating the study material to the life around them. The teachers recommended, for out-of-class reading, books and articles in magazines and newspapers which proved how contradictory, scientifically unfounded and harmful religion is. The school principal, the secretary of the party organization, and the grade teachers had many private talks with the boys in an unconstrained atmosphere. And this long, persistent work on the part of the teachers' and pupils' collectives produced positive results: the boys succeeded in freeing themselves from the religious impressions of their childhood.

The need for an individual approach to schoolchildren during their atheistic upbringing is also conditioned by their age and psychological characteristics. We can speak frankly to some about their attitude toward religion, convince them of the absurdity of believing in the supernatural, and suggest that they read a number of books. With others, on the contrary, we must be extremely careful. We must first win them over, get them to be friends with good comrades, interest them in public, athletic, and out-of-class activities, and draw them into the life of the collective. Whenever problems of atheistic upbring-

ing must be solved, it is important to get the pupil to have faith in the teacher, the teaching staff as a whole, and in his comrades.

An individual approach in atheistic work presupposes an attentive, responsive attitude toward the personal life of the pupil, a readiness to help him in surmounting difficulties. A number of instances could be cited of children who are opposed to religious prejudices, but who, because of their parents' insistence, go to church, wear crosses, and observe the religious holidays. Those pupils upon whom parents and relatives exert a religious influence require not only patient explanatory work, but also the friendly moral support of the entire collective. Religiosity in children is rooted either in weakness of will or in their being isolated from the life of the class and the school.

From a talk with 9th-grade pupil Valya G., her grade teacher learned that the girl's relations with her mother, who was religious and had brought her daughter up in the same spirit from early childhood, were very strained. When the girl was of preschool and primary school age, she obediently did everything her mother demanded: she wore a cross, said her prayers, and observed the religious holidays. However, her piety was purely superficial. The school and Valya's friends exerted a greater influence on her than her mother. Valya joined the Komsomol in the 8th grade and flatly refused to take part in religious rites. The result was a family conflict. The mother stopped talking with her daughter. Valya began to study poorly and did not know how to conduct herself at home. Her grade teacher had some warm, friendly talks with Valya and explained to her that for many years the church had dulled the mind of her mother and that it was now difficult for the woman, who was no longer young, to immediately renounce the views so deeply implanted in her. He advised Valya to be tactful in her relations with her mother and not to offend her religious feelings. The teacher also did much work with Valya's mother in order to convince her that she was causing her daughter great harm and was depriving her of real human happiness. In long, personal talks with the religious woman, he showed her how life in the country-side had changed during the years of Soviet government, and how the spiritual make-up of those people whom she herself knew very well had changed. Thanks to the persistence of the grade teacher, normal relations were restored in the family.

Here is another illustration. Galina Sh., a 9th-grade pupil, decided to join the Komsomol. But she knew she would have to be very careful when speaking about this to her mother, who was a Baptist. Finally, after long hesitation, Galina told her mother of her decision. The mother immediately flew into a rage, and before Galina had a chance to find warm words to appease her fury, she began striking her daughter in the face. This religious mother beat her seventeen-year-old daughter mercilessly. How did the school react to this? The teachers realized that even the most painstaking work with this confirmed Baptist would not quickly produce a break in her fanatic convictions. The teachers and the Komsomol, having surrounded the young girl with concern and attention, suggested that she make up with her mother and not offend her religious feelings. At the end of the school year Galina was accepted into the Komsomol. Acting on the advice of her grade teacher, she did not say anything about it to her mother. A year later Galina finished school and took a job. She is a good worker, participates actively in public activities, and is preparing for entrance examinations into an institute. Her relations with her mother have become normal. Was her grade teacher right in advising her pupil to hide from her mother the fact that she had joined the Komsomol? We feel that under the circumstances there was nothing else she could do: it was impossible to get the religious woman to change her views in such a short time, and to tell her of her daughter's disobedience would mean aggravating the family conflict even more.

There are cases in which a father and mother are deprived of their parental rights by special decision of a court because they prevent their children from attending school and force them to observe religious rites. In the case discussed above such extreme measures were not neces-

sary. The school found the right solution, one that corresponded to the individual traits of the pupil and the conditions in her family.

We know that in many religious families the children grow up as atheists. This shows that the school exerts a decisive influence on the formation of the pupils' world outlook. But not all children "open their eyes" with age and protest against the attempt of their parents to rear them in the spirit of religious dogma. We must not forget that until the age of seven many children are under the influence of the family, which leaves its trace for a long time. In many cases only the long, systematic educational work of the school helps the pupils to become atheists.

As a rule, pupils who are under the religious influence of their parents hide the fact and feel uncomfortable in the presence of their comrades and teachers. Much is said in the press and over the radio about the reactionary role of the church and the need to combat religious ideology. If not enough atheistic work is conducted, schoolchildren sometimes begin to ridicule and criticize other children of their age who are religiously inclined. The teachers and grade teachers cannot assume a neutral position in such cases. They must constantly attend to the relations between the pupils and not permit anyone to be rude or tactless with those children who have come under religious influence.

Who should conduct the work with such pupils? That is a very important question. In school it is usually the grade teacher or the principal who occupies himself with them. Purely pedagogical measures are frequently supplemented by administrative measures, and this leads to an undesirable state of affairs: the children become reserved, their silence expressing their inner protest against the educational influence being exerted upon them. It must be said that the schools rarely draw the pupils' collectives into the struggle against the religious prejudices of children. And yet it is their peers who frequently are most successful in accomplishing these difficult tasks, under the guidance of a teacher, of course.

Here is a typical example. It became known that Alik Kh., an upper-grade pupil and a member of the Komsomol, went to church and performed religious rites. He was a passive and weak-willed youth with a weak character. Yet he was very industrious and truthful. He did not feel oppressed by the class collective, readily performed various tasks assigned to him, and took part in out-of-class activities, although he never displayed initiative in anything. The teachers, taking into consideration Alik's specific traits, set the Komsomol organization the task of helping him to overcome his religious prejudices. The Komsomol group was told to be tactful in its attitude toward the comrade, not to offend his religious feelings, and to try to draw him into the social life of the school. It is important to note that, having given this important task to the Komsomol, the teachers kept a constant eye on what it did, and the latter, in turn, regularly informed the teachers of the work it had done and turned to them for advice.

The upper-grade pupils had been working for two months on a production of Gogol's play The Inspector General, in which Alik was assigned the role of Osip. He worked very hard over this role and performed it excellently. One Sunday on which the boy was planning to go to church, the physical education teacher asked him to help in judging the ski contests. Alik could not refuse and, of course, did not go to church. Then the Komsomol members of his class invited him to the birthday party of Liuda K. Although he had intended to go to church on that day, he gave in to his comrades and spent the evening in their friendly circle. Alik became increasingly interested in public activities, which occupied his free time and attention. The affairs of the collective became so important for him that in the end he broke with religion.

The teachers selected the right way to free this pupil from his religious fetters. And at the same time another important task was accomplished: in the process of re-educating their comrade, the atheistic convictions of the collective as a whole were strengthened. The Komsomol members acquired definite experience in combating religious prejudices. This example shows that involvement of the pupils' collective in the atheistic education of individual schoolchildren is one of the most effective methods in such work.

It is quite understandable that schoolchildren who have come under the influence of religious parents are also under the unremitting observation and influence of other believers and ministers of religion. In order to employ an individual approach to such children, it is first of all necessary to ascertain who it is that exerts an influence on them and how they succeed in keeping these children within the meshes of religious prejudices. A knowledge of these facts will help the school to determine correctly how it should conduct its work in its struggle for the child's soul. In some cases it will be necessary first to expose the unlawful activity of sectarian preachers and priests among the pupils; in other cases it will be necessary to influence the parents and grandparents. Many children, as we know, observe religious rites, go to church, and refuse to join the Young Pioneer and Komsomol organizations not because they are religious, but because ministers of religion and other believers compel them to. For instance, sectarian Maria K., who works in a mine in the city of Vorkuta, composed religious, mystic letters and got some schoolchildren to distribute them. Fifth-grade pupils Kolya Z. and Borya P. were her helpers in this work. When their grade teacher learned of this from the pupils, she went to the parents of Kolya and Borya to ascertain what influence was exerted upon them in the family. She learned that their parents had no religious prejudices and that the children were being reared as atheists. Later the teacher discovered that the sectarian paid the schoolchildren generously for distributing her religious concoctions and that the two Young Pioneers could not resist the temptation. The grade teacher considered it sufficient to have a personal talk with the boys about the wrongness of their action, and convinced them not to do it any more. This incident also served as the occasion for a talk with the entire class on the theme: "The Principles of a Young Pioneer." The given illustration also shows that atheistic upbringing must be conducted with an awareness of how and by what means religion influences them.

At times many teachers, instead of employing an individual approach to the schoolchild, resort to talks involving moralization, exhortation, good wishes to "think things over seriously," "not to listen to the parents and not to submit to their influence," "to think of the honor and moral make-up of the Soviet schoolchild," etc. Such "methods" of atheistic upbringing, it is clear, will not produce positive results. Unsubstantiated talks about religion and the attempt to "re-educate" immediately will produce nothing but harm. As a rule, such admonitions merely serve to strengthen the child's religious fanaticism and to estrange him from his collective.

It is important to emphasize that atheistic talks cannot be a panacea for all troubles. They can have a positive influence on the formation of atheistic convictions only if the teacher knows why the child has come under the influence of churchgoers and what his attitude is toward the collective and his parents. The content and methods for such talks must take into consideration the individual traits of the children, their inner worlds, interests, and inclinations, their attitude toward religion, and the conditions of their home upbringing.

The development of atheistic views is a complex and long process and it is frequently accompanied by doubts and vacillation, an intense inner struggle, and profound emotional experiences for the schoolchildren who have been subjected to religious prejudices. This process involves the changing of some views and the establishment of others. During his talks with pupils, it is important that the teacher arouse a feeling of doubt in them, make them think, and help them, with the aid of scientific knowledge, to overcome religious dogma and find the truth.

The school should conduct all work connected with atheistic upbringing in close contact with the family. This is necessary not only to ensure unity in the pedagogical influence of the family and the school, but also because the source of the children's religiosity is, as a rule, the family. If the school does not conduct appropri-

ate work with the parents, its efforts often prove futile. An individual approach to the pupils necessarily implies individual work with the parents, whose religiosity and superstition sometimes come close to fanaticism. It is very difficult to re-educate such parents quickly. In these cases the teachers must direct their efforts toward showing the parents what harm they are causing their children by rearing them in a religious spirit. It is necessary to convince the parents that they are crippling their children, that they are instilling hypocrisy, deceitfulness, and slavish morals, and that they are impeding the children's learning.

Frequently, parents who do not believe in God still believe in omens, observe religious rites in accordance with established traditions, and have icons in their homes. As a rule, no conscious, deliberate religious influence is exerted upon the children in such families. However, this atmosphere leaves its impress on the world outlook of the schoolchildren. It is from such families that the children come to school burdened by these home superstitions. And the school must conduct systematic, persistent work with such parents. We can talk with them more straightforwardly and concretely about their superstitiousness and the harm they are causing their children. Thoughtful atheistic propaganda must also be conducted among those parents who are free from religious prejudices themselves, but do not pay attention to their children, as a result of which the children come under the influence of religious relatives and even outsiders.

When stressing the importance of individual work in the atheistic upbringing of the pupils, we must remember that only the totality of means and methods, in a carefully considered system, will make it possible to solve successfully the task of the atheistic upbringing of the young generation. This system presupposes the use of all the different forms, means and methods, the conducting of atheistic upbringing in all links of the educational process — at the lessons, in out-of-class activities, in the Young Pioneer and Komsomol organizations — and also atheistic propaganda among the parents. The

262

persistent and systematic work of each subject teacher and grade teacher and of every Young Pioneer leader is necessary. The system of atheistic upbringing presupposes an organic tie between antireligious educational work and life, and the participation of the schoolchildren themselves in scientific-atheistic propaganda to the extent of their ability.

Works Cited

1) N. K. Krupskaya, Soch., Vol. 3.
2) K. D. Ushinsky, Soch., Vol. 8. Moscow, RSFSR Academy of Pedagogical Sciences, 1960.
3) L. S. Slavina, Individual'nyi podkhod k neuspevaiushchim i nedistsiplinirovannym uchenikam, Moscow, RSFSR Academy of Pedagogical Sciences, 1958.

Economics of Education

Narodnoe obrazovanie, 1966, No. 12

V. Basov

THE DEVELOPMENT OF PUBLIC EDUCATION AND THE BUDGET

During the years of Soviet power our country has achieved enormous success in the development of public education. More than half of the working population has a higher or secondary education. Around 70,000,000 persons are engaged in various forms of study, including more than 47,000,000 students who study in the general education schools. The Soviet state annually appropriates large sums from the state budget for the development of public education. At the present time about one-half of all appropriations for education are expended on the current upkeep (excluding expenditures for capital construction, repair, and the acquisition of equipment) of the institutions of public education. During the Seven-Year Plan period these expenditures more than doubled, and a sum of 8,303,000,000 rubles is provided in the budget for 1966.

Concern for children, their health, upbringing and education has always been a primary task of our state. The public care and support of

children is a noble and humane concern that is in keeping with the lofty ideals of the socialist system. In our country everything is done to assure a happy childhood for Soviet children.

In tsarist Russia before the Revolution there were 275 kindergartens and playgrounds that served 7,000 children. At the beginning of 1966 there were some 90,000 kindergartens and nurseries maintained by the state, and 7,300,000 children were being educated in them. Attaching important socio-economic significance to the further development of children's preschool institutions, the plan for 1966 provides for an increase of the number of children in these institutions to 8,500,000. In 1966 alone the total enrollment of children in kindergartens and nurseries grew by 900,000. Approximately 26% of all children of preschool age will be included in children's preschool institutions.

Funds for the maintenance of children's preschool institutions come from state resources and payments by parents. The payments of parents into kindergartens make up 25% of the total amount of allocations, that is, the state budget carries the basic part of the expenses. The allotment per child is increasing from year

The author is Chief of the Department for the Financing of Education, USSR Ministry of Finance.

to year. Thus, if in 1958 the average expenditure per child in a kindergarten came to 256 rubles, in 1964 it reached 262 rubles. In 1966 it is planned to spend 1,886,000,000 rubles on the kindergartens, or an average of 295 rubles per child.

In the 1914/15 school year there were 123,700 schools in Russia, and 9,700,000 students were studying in them. Only about one-fifth of the children of school age were being taught. An average of 63 kopecks per person was expended for the maintenance of schools. The school had a pronounced class character: children of workers and peasants were permitted to receive only a primary education. More than 96% of the schools were primary schools. Now, however, universal compulsory eight-year education has been introduced in our country, and we are successfully carrying out measures for the transition to universal secondary education. In 1966 around 43,000,000 students are studying in the universal education schools, and more than 70% of the graduates of the 8th grade were accepted into the 9th. The average expenditure per pupil is constantly increasing. In 1958 it was 82 rubles, whereas in 1966 it was equivalent to 107 rubles.

The schools and groups with a prolonged day received nationwide approval in our country. These institutions correspond to the interests of the family and the state and are the most economic form for the social upbringing of children. In 1966 the number of students being educated in groups with a prolonged day will increase to 3,000,000. In addition to the expenditures on instruction, the state spends around 52 rubles a year on each pupil who is on the prolonged-day program. In 1966, 136,000,000 rubles were allocated for the prolonged day program.

In order to effectuate universal compulsory eight-year education and to create the conditions for the schooling of children who live far from schools, dormitories are being opened at the schools. At the beginning of 1966 there were 28,000 dormitories attached to schools, and 1,300,000 pupils resided in them. This year the number of pupils in school dormitories will increase to 1,600,000, and 215,200,000 rubles will be appropriated for them.

An extensive network of out-of-school children's institutions has been created in our country. At the beginning of 1966 there were 2,834 children's music and art schools, 1,451 sports schools, 3,416 Pioneer Homes and Palaces, 855 children's technical stations, stations for young naturalists and excursion-tourist stations, and approximately 200 children's parks of rest and culture. This year appropriations totaling 26,300,000 rubles have been planned for these institutions.

Great attention is paid in our country to the general educational preparation of working youth. In 1966 the number of pupils in these schools should reach 5,300,000, and 411,100,000 rubles, or an average of 82 rubles per pupil, was appropriated for their schooling. (This is three times greater than in 1958.)

Thus, a large network of institutions for the social upbringing and education of children is maintained at the state's expense. The budget creates a firm material basis for the development of public education in our country. Effectuation of the measures envisaged in the CPSU Program calls for a significant increase in budget appropriations for the maintenance of the institutions of public education. In connection with this, the problem of the effectiveness of the utilization of state resources allotted to public education is acquiring great significance.

* * *

Up to now, unfortunately, questions of efficiency have been treated in the economics literature mainly from the point of view of maintenance of a policy of economy at enterprises in the sphere of material production. After the September (1965) Plenary Meeting of the Central Committee of the CPSU, the attitude toward the economics of public education changed sharply. It is now generally recognized that the problem of the effectiveness of the utilization of funds in the sphere of services has the same important socio-economic significance as it does for enterprises and organizations that create material wealth. This was convincingly proven by the Scientific Conference on Problems of the Economics of Public Education, which was conducted in December 1965 at the Moscow (Lenin) State Teacher Training Institute.

The efficiency of public education involves not only a struggle for the rational utilization of state funds, but also a struggle for the fuller satisfaction of the needs of the working people. It is a struggle to obtain the greatest results with the least expenditures. There must be a constant search for economical forms of social upbringing and instruction that will bring the greatest national economic effect and at the same time guarantee the saving of public funds.

Study of the economic questions of public education must begin with a definition of its national economic significance from the point of view of raising the social productivity of labor. This problem has received sufficient elucidation in the Soviet economics literature. Public education undoubtedly plays an important role in the creation of the national income and in the development of the economy and culture of the country. Nevertheless, there are still many unresolved problems in this area.

The first attempts to calculate the economic effectiveness of public education were made by Academician S. Strumilin. He estimated that 33,700,000,000 rubles, or 23% of the national income, were obtained in 1960 as a result of raising the qualifications of employed persons. And the expenditures on public education for that year totaled only 10,300,000,000 rubles, that is, a profit of 23,400,000,000 rubles was obtained and the profitability was better than 227%. According to the calculations of Professor Zhamin, the investment of funds in public education in 1962 had the effect of creating 27% of the national income.

It is important to establish which socio-economic aspects of the reproduction of the skilled labor force are influenced by the educational level of working people. A study of the tie between the level of education and the results of labor, which was conducted by the Laboratory of Socio-Economic Research of the Lenin Teacher Training Institute at the "Dynamo" and

"Vladimir Il'ich" plants in Moscow, showed that in the majority of instances the labor productivity of workers rises with an increase in their general educational training. Thus, among machinist-toolmakers of the fourth skill category, with five years of work service, the workers with an eight-year education fulfill the output norm 35% more than workers with a five-year education. And the labor productivity of workers who have finished secondary school is 25% higher than that of workers who have completed eight years of schooling. A higher general educational level permits a significant reduction in the period needed for the mastery of a given specialty. Each grade of general educational preparation (from the 6th to the 10th) accelerates the mastery of new types of work by an average of 50%. Workers with a secondary education master new technology twice as fast as those having a five-year education.

Education is thus an important factor in raising the qualifications of workers. Thus, an average of five years is needed to raise a machinist-toolmaker with a five- or six-year education one pay grade higher, while from two to three years are needed when he has an eight-year education, and one year when he has a secondary education. The same kind of relationship manifests itself with respect to the rationalizing activity of the workers. The proportion of rationalizers among workers with a five- or six-year education is 3%; among those having an education through the 8th grade it is 11%, and among those with a secondary education — 23%. More than 83% of the total economies that are obtained by the introduction of rationalizing proposals are accounted for by workers with an education through the 9th and 10th grades. As the level of the workers' education rises, they permit less spoilage in production, less stoppage of machinery, and less breakage of instruments and equipment. Competent workers stick with their jobs, have a high degree of labor discipline, and take an active part in the social life of their collectives.

What are the ways of raising the efficiency of public education? The fundamental ones are improvement of the quality of instruction of the pupils and enhancement of the qualifications of teaching personnel. However, in this article we are going to dwell on other possibilities.

There are many ways to raise the economic efficiency of public education — the amalgamation of small schools, the rational utilization of classrooms, adherence to the established quota for classes, the selection of optimal periods of time for instruction, elimination of the phenomena of dropouts and grade repeating, improvement of the organization of the students' production training, the carrying out of a strict policy of economy, perfection of the system of planning and financing for the institutions of public education, and others.

Amalgamation of the small schools, especially the understaffed schools where teachers teach more than one grade at the same time, is an urgent task for the public education agencies. Since the pedagogical and economic inexpediency of maintaining understaffed schools has already been noted more than once, we will not repeat what has been well known for a long time. Let us note only that the maintenance of understaffed schools creates additional complications with respect to teaching personnel. It is sufficient to say that in the RSFSR alone some 50,000 teachers are inefficiently utilized for this reason. The elimination of understaffed schools would make it possible not only to decrease the shortage of teaching personnel, but also to secure in some measure a fuller work load for teachers of special disciplines in eight-year and secondary schools, in particular, teachers of singing and physical education. The economic aspect of this question also has considerable significance. Whereas the cost of schooling for one pupil in the primary grades of the eight-year and secondary schools is, on the average, 50 rubles per year, in the understaffed schools it fluctuates between 100 and 250 rubles. Recently the public education bodies have done much to amalgamate small schools and this has produced positive results. In comparison with the 1958/59 school year, the number of primary schools in the 1965/66 school year was reduced by almost 15,000, and approximately 40,000,000 rubles were released thereby. However, this is not enough.

The pupil quota in primary schools is still extremely small. In the 1965/66 school year there were, on the average, 41 pupils per primary school. Of the total number of primary schools in the RSFSR, 6% have up to 10 pupils and 12% have from 10 to 15 pupils, and in more than 71% of the primary schools the number of pupils does not exceed 40. But the work of eliminating the understaffed schools must be done thoughtfully, on the basis of a plan conceived beforehand, taking into account the concrete peculiarities of each region, city, and district.

The amalgamation of small schools must not be carried out at the expense of putting too many children into classes, increasing the number of shifts, or eliminating study rooms. Therefore, it is first necessary to create the corresponding material facilities. It is possible to solve this problem in two ways: by expanding the existing schools (adding additional classrooms to them) and also by building new schools. Authorization was given to construct classroom annexes starting in October 1965 at the expense of capital repair, funds released as a result of the elimination of understaffed schools, and overfulfillment of the budget income. Thus, the financial side of the problem has now been completely solved. In the construction of new schools we must take into account whether pupils from the understaffed schools will be transferred into them. In general, the development of the network of schools must conform to general economic development. It is inexpedient to dissipate state resources on the construction of understaffed schools in population centers where there is not a sufficient number of pupils. It is better to allocate these funds for strengthening the material facilities of eight-year and secondary schools that are situated in promising economic regions. It is also necessary to develop the most economical and optimal designs for school buildings, and these should be done separately for urban and rural areas.

In many cases the availability of free class space does not provide grounds for affirming that all the necessary conditions have been created for the elimination of understaffed schools.

If the pupils live three or more kilometers from the base schools, it is necessary to see to it that regular transportation is organized. It is important to determine in good time the number of pupils needing transportation, to plan the transport routes, to provide facilities at the places where the pupils assemble, to assign the necessary amount of transport, and so forth. The success of this work will depend to a great extent on how actively the public education bodies take part in it. We should also study the positive experience gained in the Baltic republics in organizing free transportation for pupils. They have been engaged in this practice for several years. In those places where it is impossible to organize transportation for pupils, it is necessary to create boarding facilities at the schools. Notwithstanding the great significance of dormitories in fulfilling the law on universal education and in improving the quality of instruction and upbringing, the plan for the construction of school dormitories is regularly unfulfilled.

One of the most important problems of the economics of public education is the study of ways to utilize school buildings efficiently. According to data of the Central Statistical Administration of the USSR, the area of classroom space is 47 million square meters, that is, 1.58 square meters per pupil (studying in the first shift), with a norm of 1.25 square meters. The rational utilization of classrooms depends in the first instance on the size of classes. It has been established that in the 1st through 8th grades of the universal education schools there should not be more than 40 pupils, in the 10th and 11th grades — not more than 35, and in the evening (shift) schools — 20 to 25 persons. However, the actual size of classes in schools is considerably below the established norms. Thus, in the RSFSR in the 1965/66 school year there were 34 pupils per class in the urban schools, 23 in the rural schools, 22 in the schools for young workers, and 17 in the schools for rural youth. There are schools where the size of classes does not exceed 5 to 10 persons. A low quota of pupils per class prevents the efficient utilization of school space, the elimination of school shifts, and the expansion of out-of-class work, and leads

to a significant rise in the cost of instruction. Thus, a reduction of the average size of classes by only one pupil demands an additional 166,000,000 rubles from the budget.

We must make a reservation at once: we are against an unreasonable solution of the question of class size in which the number of pupils in a class reaches 45 to 50 persons. Such a class size brings nothing but harm. It is simply impossible to permit the existence of classes (and, even more so, to open new ones) that have 5 to 10 pupils, especially when there are parallel classes. Raising the size of classes is not a simple task, and it must not be solved by a short-term campaign, but systematically and after definite preparatory work. In particular, it appears expedient to us to widen the radius of school districts, to open schools with a single language of instruction, to enlarge the area of classrooms, and so forth.

At present about 70% of the schools operate in one shift, and this means that approximately 800,000 classrooms are free after school sessions. With the transfer of all schools to one-shift sessions, the problem of the efficient utilization of school space will become even more pressing. It is necessary to give thought right now to the problem of how best to utilize these areas.

Out-of-class work with pupils is organized both in schools and in out-of-school institutions. Of the total appropriations assigned in the budget for club activities, 75% goes to schools and 25% goes to out-of-school institutions. From the economic standpoint it seems more expedient to make maximum use of school buildings for out-of-class work rather than to expand the existing network of out-of-school institutions. Large reserves for increasing the efficiency of public education are provided by improved utilization of the existing network of institutions of public education. However, there are still major shortcomings in this area. One of them is the shortening of working time in kindergartens and boarding schools.

From 1958 through 1964 the number of days of attendance by children in kindergartens decreased from 271 to 257, and the number of days of residence by pupils in boarding schools declined from 270 to 241 (with a norm of 307 days per year). Thus, the kindergartens are underutilized to the extent of 16%, and boarding schools — 21%, of the time per year, which in the final analysis leads to a rise in the average cost of maintaining one child in these institutions. Moreover, the fact that the kindergartens, for example, do not work at full capacity means in essence that 1,360,000 children do not attend kindergarten for a whole year and that 700,000 mothers do not work in production for this reason. The national economic significance of the efficient utilization of the network of institutions of public education demands a considerable improvement of medical services for children, the major repair of buildings in good time, and the correct organization of their work and staffing.

Improvement of the housekeeping services provided to institutions of public education can release large amounts of state funds. Thus, the majority of kindergartens, boarding schools, children's homes, and dormitories attached to schools generally do their own laundry and repair of small equipment. For this purpose each institution creates miniature laundries, acquires sewing and washing machines, and puts seamstresses and laundresses on the staff. Meanwhile, all these forms of work will cost much less if they are performed by communal service enterprises. Instead of each institution hauling its supplies independently, it is expedient to organize a centralized delivery network. According to rough estimates this will make it possible to cut expenses for the delivery of food products almost in half. The Moldavian SSR's experience in forming groups for centralized housekeeping services and in the accounting of expenditures for the maintenance of universal education schools in the rural areas is worthy of attention. The schools of that republic were freed of functions that were inappropriate for them; their housekeeping services improved considerably; their accounting and reporting became more precise, and their funds were expended more economically.

A program of economy is an important condition of proper economic management and of cautious and rational utilization of state funds. With the enormous growth of expenditures for public education, even a small measure of economy offers millions of rubles in savings. Strengthening the program of economy presupposes the elimination of mismanagement, excesses and misuse, the conservation of monetary and material values, and enhanced responsibility on the part of leaders of institutions of public education for the proper expenditure of state funds entrusted to them. Unfortunately, in practice one still encounters many instances in which proper significance is not attached to questions of economizing, budget appropriations are spent unproductively, and violations of financial estimates are permitted. Let us present several examples as evidence of this.

The state annually appropriates large sums for the purchase of school equipment and inventory. Thus in 1966 approximately 180,000,000 rubles were provided in the budget for this purpose, including 87,000,000 rubles for the schools. However, these funds are often used inefficiently. Some institutions of public education purchase expensive, unwarranted or completely unnecessary equipment, which becomes dead capital. Thus, the Partupinsk Kindergarten of the Kamchatka Region bought a refrigerator for 584 rubles that is not being used owing to the absence of electric power. The Khutor Boarding School, instead of purchasing the tables and school desks provided for in the estimate, concluded a contract with the Khabarovsk Art Fund for the latter to make 10 pictures and one panel for 2,400 rubles. An especially large number of financial violations are permitted at the end of the year. For example, Special Boarding School No. 30 of Moscow, using funds allotted for physiotherapy equipment, at the end of the year purchased expensive furniture for 2,600 rubles, including 9 sofa beds, 34 Gobelin chairs, 20 magazine tables, and crystal vases. In December, Boarding School No. 8 of L'vov bought 85 dining tables for 1,900 rubles even though the tables it had purchased five years ago at a cost of 1,300 rubles were lying in the storeroom unused.

A checkup by financial agencies has established that some institutions of public education permit such things as the maintenance of super-numerary posts, incorrect wage scales for school personnel, violations of the legislation on holding two jobs at the same time, and other violations of financial discipline.

* * *

The basic tasks in the planning of public education are: the correct determination of needs in the network of institutions of public education, the achievement of proportionality in the development of their individual types, and the securing of their rational distribution in terms of economic regions. The correct solution of these problems requires constant improvement of the methods of planning the expenditures for public education. Expenditures on the universal education schools are determined in summary plans according to average norms for a class, and therefore it is very important to correctly establish the transitional [perekhodrashchaia] network of classes. In a number of places it is adopted according to the actual fulfillment at the beginning of the school year. In such a situation the interest in a rational filling [komplektovenie] of classes is reduced considerably and the significance of the national economic plan is under-estimated. In our opinion it is better to determine the number of classes at the beginning of the year being planned on the basis of the actual number of pupils at the last accounting date and the class size established in the national economic plan.

The summary plans also determine the annual average number of classes. To the number existing at the beginning of the year is added an annual average increase, which is taken as equivalent to one-third of the absolute increase. Calculated in this way, the annual average number of classes is taken as the basis both for calculating educational, housekeeping and other expenditures and for determining expenditures for teachers' salaries. Some economists hold that in planning the expenditures for teachers' salaries in urban schools one should take 29.2% of

the absolute increase as the annual average of classes, since the teachers of these schools receive salaries up to the first of September for 8.5 months according to the number of rates designated on January 1, and up to the end of the year for 3.5 months according to the number of rates established on the first of September (for the second half of December salaries are paid in the following budget year). It seems to us that only the annual average number of teaching pay rates should be calculated by this method. Its use to determine the annual average number of classes leads to considerable complications in calculation, great inaccuracies, and errors.

Establishing the number of teaching pay rates has still more serious significance. This index is determined by proceeding from the number of hours stipulated in the curriculum for each class and the teaching load of the teacher for whom the pay rate was established. However, the number of teaching hours is generally much greater than that established in the curriculum. In order to take account of all these factors for each group of classes, detailed calculations are made that, while giving only approximate data, take away much time from personnel in public education bodies and planning and financial agencies. In our opinion, the number of teaching pay rates per class in the summary plans should be arrived at in accordance with the estimates of individual schools, with consideration of the changes made in the curriculums. This makes it possible to simplify considerably the calculation of the number of pay rates and in no way decreases its accuracy.

The appropriations for general education schools are determined separately for urban and rural schools. There are also two paragraphs for children's preschool institutions and boarding schools — one for urban schools and another for rural schools. However, the calculation of expenditures for their maintenance is done on an aggregate basis in the summary plan. It seems to us that in time the same procedure should be used to calculate the appropriations for general education schools, since the report data show that the size of classes, the number of teaching pay rates per class, the amount of the average rate, and the average expenses for individual expenditure items change in the same direction in both the urban and rural schools.

The summary planning of expenditures for other institutions and undertakings of public education is done in terms of an overall sum without distributing them according to separate types of institutions and undertakings. It is understandable that such planning is not at all economically substantiated. It seems expedient to plan expenditures for other institutions and undertakings of public education separately in terms of each group of these institutions and undertakings and to single out the basic kinds of expenditures: wages, housekeeping expenses, educational expenditures and other expenses. In the forest-sanitorium schools, sports schools, and music and art schools (seven-year schools), the student should be taken as the index of planning; in the other out-of-school and methodological institutions, the institution should be taken as the index; and in other undertakings of public education — the actual expenses of preceding years.

Centralization of the accounting of institutions of public education has recently received wide dissemination in the country. The posts of bookkeepers and accountants were eliminated from the staffs of small institutions, current accounts were closed, and the performance of accounting and the release of funds for their support were transferred to united (centralized) accounting offices that were established especially for this purpose under the principal credit authorities. Not having their own current accounts and the right of signature on bank documents, the heads of schools, kindergartens, etc., that are served by centralized accounting are practically deprived of the rights of managers of credit. This was furthered by the fact that with the centralization of accounting, the right of chief managers of credit to change during the year the appropriations for separate institutions within the limits of each paragraph became essentially unlimited. In order to observe formalities, however, in the centralized accounting offices a separate estimate is made for each institution and a separate accounting is performed, that is, extensive work is carried out that is practically of no use to anyone. In our opinion the institutions served by centralized accounting should compile a summary estimate and do a general accounting.

Uniform methodology is an indispensable condition for the economically competent planning of expenditures for public education. It permits uniformity in methods of calculation, significantly lightens the work of drawing up calculations, and contributes to raising its economic level.

At present the Ministry of Finance of the USSR is developing methodological instructions for the planning of expenditures for maintaining institutions of public education. In addition, it is planned to put out practical manuals on individual financial questions for the personnel in public education bodies.

The increased attention of scholars, economists, and personnel in the field of education to questions of the economics of public education will undoubtedly contribute to a more effective utilization of state funds and, in the final analysis, will improve the quality of the pupils' instruction and upbringing.

* * *

Vestnik vysshei shkoly, 1964, No. 4

L. I. Tul'chinskii

ECONOMICS OF HIGHER EDUCATION

The Soviet higher school of today is not only an educational and research institution; it is also a large and diversified economy that has many links with the commodity and monetary system. A number of higher schools, such as the Moscow and Leningrad universities, the Kiev, Urals and Kharkov polytechnical institutes, the Moscow Higher Technical School, the Moscow Power Institute, and the Leningrad Electrical Engineering Institute, dispose of vast material values that are worth far more than the fixed assets of many industrial enterprises. The higher schools have thousands of educational, research and production buildings, and hundreds of complex and costly machine-tools and machines on their balance sheets. They have jurisdiction over substantial dwellings, communal facilities, subsidiary farm enterprises, polyclinics, school experimental fields, and training grounds.

The higher educational institutions have an annual monetary turnover that exceeds one billion rubles. Wages are paid twice a month to hundreds of thousands of teacher, auxiliary and managerial personnel. Each month almost a million students and postgraduates are given stipends.

All this taken together comprises the economics of higher education,[*] and defines its economic and financial activity.

The head of every higher school can dispose of the financial assets and facilities of the institution entrusted to him at his discretion. This right must naturally be used in the interests of the state, and it is subordinated to the basic task of achieving the greatest results in the training of specialists and the performance of scientific research with the least outlays of financial, material, and labor resources.

The socialist economic system presupposes rational, scientifically substantiated economies in expenditures on minor requirements and rejects all unnecessary economies — the incomplete use of appropriations for essential, urgent

---

The author is associated with the Finance Research Institute of the USSR Ministry of Finance.

[*]Under the concept "economics of higher education" we include a complex of issues concerned with the management and internal structure of the higher schools, their material, technical, educational and research facilities, questions of labor and wages, finances, the system of planning, financing, accounting, and reporting.

needs. In the first instance, the economies are one way of effectively utilizing funds, in the second — they damage higher education.

Proper management of the economy of higher education implies improving, simplifying and reducing the cost of the administrative apparatus over and within the higher schools; rationally and effectively employing the labor of higher school personnel and the wage fund; thriftily and ably disposing of the material values; properly and economically organizing instruction; rationally using financial resources; eliminating nonproductive expenditures connected with "spoilage" in instruction, research, and upbringing.

The Finance Research Institute of the USSR Ministry of Finance has made a study of some of the problems involved in the economics of higher education in 96 higher schools (2,600 departments) of 14 union republics. The results, in our opinion, are of definite interest to higher school personnel.

The investigation has revealed that many higher schools (for example, Azerbaijan University, the Murmansk Higher Marine School, the Leningrad Conservatory, the Moscow Institute of Geological Prospecting, the Novosibirsk Institute of Construction Engineering, the Tashkent Textile Institute, the Belorussian Technological Institute, the Daghestan Agricultural Institute, the Armenian Teacher Training Institute, the Kirghiz Medical Institute, the Kharkov Stomatology Institute, the Rostov Institute of Farm Machinery, etc.) devote little attention to economic problems. The established view here is that monetary and financial problems, estimates and bookkeeping reports are the business only of the bookkeeping, planning and financial bodies. Council meetings rarely consider the results of the financial and economic activity of the higher school, the economic problems that arise in connection with the repeating of courses by students, with the dismissal of students, with administrative shortcomings within the higher school, etc.

And yet these problems are of considerable practical interest.

During the 1961/62 academic year, for example, in the higher schools of Rostov Region (where these questions were studied in greater detail), more than 1,200 students dropped out, mainly because of poor progress, and about 8,000, chiefly correspondence students, had to repeat a given course. Rough calculations for 1961/62, which took into account the relationship between the number of students and the cost of education in the day, evening and correspondence divisions, show that the expenditures arising from the dismissal of students who had not finished the course of instruction and from the repeating of courses amounted to a considerable sum involving several million rubles.

Needless to say, this colossal waste should not be eliminated by lowering standards. Laxity and undeserved satisfactory marks for idlers and lazy students will lead to the turning out of inadequate specialists. Therefore, only the industrious, capable youth, young people with searching minds, who know life and have an ardent desire to learn, should be admitted. And that should be established during the entrance examinations.

Let us discuss the question of improving the system of administration in the higher schools and, above all, of the proper organization of the departments. A study of the problem in 2,400 departments of 81 institutes showed that instruction, research, and methodological work is conducted best when there is a good teaching staff as regards both quantity and qualifications. However, there are still many inadequately staffed departments. Thirty-nine of the number studied had, on the average, a staff of only 1.5; 119 had 2-2.5, 328 — 3-3.5, and 340 departments had 4-4.5. The largest number of small departments belong to agricultural and medical institutes (43 and 49 per cent respectively) and the physical culture and sports institutes (48 per cent). The Omsk and Georgian veterinary institutes, the Erevan and Kirghiz medical institutes, and the Kharkov Stomatology Institute have departments functioning with 1.5-2 staff members. Such departments are formal entities and are formed, as a rule, for purely "financial" considerations. Naturally, small departments cannot perform the functions assigned to them.

If identical and related departments were

merged and the regulations requiring that departments should generally have a staff of five scientific workers, of whom two at least have academic degrees or titles, were strictly observed, that would considerably improve education and research and save a great deal of money.

Another pressing problem is that of a more rational organization of the work of teaching staffs. Its solution requires, above all, that their number should be fixed correctly on a scientific basis. During the years that the Soviet higher school has existed, the system for determining the numerical strength of teaching staffs has changed several times in accordance with the development of the material and educational facilities, the improved qualifications and larger number of teachers, and the different objectives in the training of highly skilled specialists.

A common feature of all these changes was that teaching staffs were to be determined, as a rule, on the basis of data on the curriculum and the standard teaching load. This system made it possible to coordinate the number of teachers employed with the requirements of the curriculum and to regulate the teaching load. The drawback was that the results of the teacher's work were determined only by the quantity of hours worked. The main indexes — the number of specialists trained and the quality of the scientific work done — were not taken into account. Moreover, the process of planning teaching staffs and the wage fund was very cumbersome and laborious. Each higher school had to submit calculations to the planning and financial bodies on every department and practically every teacher.

Beginning with the 1956/57 school year, a new method was introduced for determining teaching staffs. This system was based on the average number of students per teacher. In 1959, uniform norms for determining teaching staffs in the correspondence and evening institutes and departments were worked out for the first time. But no such norms have been elaborated for the day higher schools, with the result that some of the schools had norms that

were substantially below what they should have been. And this meant that more teachers were engaged than was necessary, that they had light teaching loads, and that the wage fund was used irrationally. In other cases, especially in small or provincial higher schools, the norms were excessively high: each teacher had a heavy teaching load.

An investigation of the problem in 58 higher schools revealed the following. The average norm for the engineering institutes surveyed is 12.6 students per teacher: in the Rostov Construction Engineering Institute, for example, it is only 11.3 per teacher, while in the Kharkov Engineering Institute of Municipal Construction it is 13.3. The average norm for the universities is 10.7. But in Azerbaijan University it is only 9.8, and in Daghestan University — 11.3. The norms are subject to especially marked fluctuations in the higher schools under the branch ministries of the union republics. In the day departments of the teacher training institutes, the average norm is 10.9 students per teacher, while in the Armenian Teacher Training Institute it is 10.4; at the same time, there are 12 students per teacher at the Azerbaijan Teacher Training Institute. In the medical institutes, the average norm is 9.2, but in the Tbilisi Medical Institute it is 7.3, and in the Turkmen Medical Institute — 10.

The All-Union Conference of Higher School Personnel (1961) recommended that uniform norms be worked out for the teaching staffs of similar groups of day higher schools, departments, and divisions. For the present, we suggest the following norms: for engineering, hydrometeorological, industrial-arts, engineering and melioration higher schools, for institutes of the mechanization and electrification of agriculture and for higher marine schools, where students combine instruction with production training — 13; for the departments catering to all the remaining students — 12; for the engineering-economics, economic, law, library, and historical archives institutes — 15 and 14, respectively; for universities — 10; agricultural and fruit and vegetable institutes — 11; teacher training institutes — 11; medical institutes — 9;

higher schools of art -- 5; physical culture and sports institutes -- 7.

In drafting these norms, we took into consideration the existing average norms (planned and reported) in the day higher schools (at the departments) as of January 1, 1963, the average teaching load in the 1961/62 academic year, and the planned teaching load for the 1962/63 academic year. Due account was also taken of the need to adjust the teaching loads in the higher schools of different specialties, of the special conditions in the training of students who combine instruction with productive labor, of the reduction in the number of students in foreign language study groups at the universities and institutes training foreign language teachers and specialists, and of the increase in the number of lecture hours in foreign language study to 240 per year.

The introduction of uniform norms for the day higher schools will make it possible properly to apply the system adopted in the 1956/57 academic year for determining teaching staffs, to improve research work and instruction, to create equal conditions in a given field for all higher schools, to bring order into the expenditures for wages, and to improve substantially the economic indexes of the work of the higher schools.

The very system of determining teaching staffs on the basis of the student body became less cumbersone and complex; it expanded the rights of the rectors, deans and department heads and helped to improve research work. However, this system does not take into account the positive aspect of the old procedure — the dependence of the size of the teaching staff on the curriculum.

At present the teaching staff for each higher school is established by the ministry or department on the basis of the total number of students and postgraduates, without regard for the curriculum or the leaching load per teacher. However, the size of the teaching staff of a given department has to be planned without consideration of the number of students, and only on the basis of the teaching hours allotted in the curriculum and the average load for one teacher. As a re-sult of this discrepancy in planning (both by the department and the higher school), the teachers in the different departments of one and the same school frequently have varying teaching loads.

A study of teaching loads at 2,592 departments of 91 higher schools showed that about 40 per cent of the departments (excluding the social science departments) have a teaching load of less than 720 hours a year per teacher. Most of these departments are in the departmental higher schools — medical institutes (57 per cent), agricultural institutes (54 per cent), and teacher training institutes (43 per cent). In some (the Kharkov Aviation Institute, the Azerbaijan Oil and Chemistry Institute, the Armenian Teacher Training Institute, the Grodno Medical Institute, the Kharkov Stomatology Institute, and the Armenian Physical Culture and Sports Institute), the staffs of 60 to 90 per cent of the departments have this low average teaching load.

Of the 1,050 departments whose teachers have less than 780 teaching hours a year, in the case of 5 departments it is below 260 hours, that is, one hour a day; in 11 departments it is from 261 to 390 hours, in 72 — from 391 to 520, and in 230 it is 650 hours; in the remaining 732 departments, the teachers carry a load of from 651 to 780 hours a year. These figures show that a large number of teachers in many higher schools devote no more than one to two and a half hours a day to teaching. This is the direct outcome of bad planning that does not take the curriculum into account and does not provide firm, obligatory minimum norms for each teacher. At present, a firm annual norm exists only for the social science departments — 550 hours for teachers and 420 hours for department heads. The establishment of such norms for all teachers, irrespective of their scientific degrees and titles, will undoubtedly serve as the point of departure for an even distribution of teaching, research, and methodological work within the higher school.

It would seem advisable to fix a minimum standard teaching load for all higher school teachers on the basis of a six-hour working day, that is, an average of 1,848 working hours a year. If we exclude 48 days (or 288 hours) for vacations, we get an annual load of 1,560 working hours. And if we consider that at least 50 per cent of this time should be devoted to instruction, the average teaching load will be 780, and the minimum — 720 hours. The rest of the time should be devoted to research and methodological work. Provision should also be made for increasing the teaching hours of those teachers who are not doing any research or methodological work. This should be done at the discretion of the rector and the department head.

Considering that the teaching load for some teachers (for instance, in foreign language and physical culture departments) who do no research will amount to more than 780 hours a year, the average for each institute should be 840 hours per teacher. Moreover, as we know, the six-hour working day for a teacher does not include preparing for classes (for example, lecture notes, etc.), lecturing at different courses, reviewing dissertations, scientific papers, books, fulfilling the assignments of public organizations — reports, lectures, and so forth.

One of the prerequisites for a more efficient organization of the teachers' work is unification of the existing, and elaboration of new, uniform norms for teaching loads. Norms can be established for all types of educational work, and the Ministry of Higher and Specialized Secondary Education of the USSR should issue a manual on uniform norms, especially since some norms have been in operation since 1930 and are now outdated. The new norms should stimulate teachers to do more complex and difficult types of educational work, such as lectures, for example. Is it right to equate one hour of lecture time in the day division with one hour of practical or laboratory work? We believe that one hour of lecture time in the day division should be equated with two and a half hours of practical or laboratory work.

The introduction of unified norms will make it possible to measure the various types of teaching work in terms of their complexity and the required ability and skills.

One of the most complex and difficult aspects of the work of the higher schools is the training of specialists who are holding down jobs while they study. Some researchers abroad think that the all-out expansion of this system in the USSR at the present time stems solely from a desire to cut state expenditures on the training of specialists. It cannot be denied that correspondence education costs less than the training of specialists in the day divisions. The expenditure on teachers' salaries, for instance, is only a quarter of the expenditure in the day divisions. The average number of students per teacher in the correspondence divisions is 50, as compared with 12 in the day divisions. The cost of maintaining auxiliary and managerial staffs per student is approximately one and a half times less than in the day institutes. The correspondence students are not given stipends, and much less is spent on the maintenance of dormitories. We should add that the correspondence and evening students who are employed in the sphere of material production create output and a part of the national income, and that those employed in the nonproductive sphere provide social, cultural, and other services. Hence, the correspondence and evening students engage in socially useful labor even while they are being trained and thus help the national economy. On the other hand, correspondence students are allowed paid leaves for tests, examinations, and the preparation of course and graduation projects at the expense of the factory or office.

However, the really important thing is not economic considerations, but the fact that favorable conditions are created for an increasing number of working people — workers, employees, and collective farmers — to study at a higher school without leaving their jobs. The system also ensures the training of more skilled engineers and technicians who have a sounder theoretical and practical background. This policy is in complete accord with the tasks of the present phase of the comprehensive building of communism.

Correspondence and evening instruction is one of the reliable and tested methods of training personnel. The existence of three forms of instruction (day, correspondence, and evening) in each higher school makes it possible to utilize fully the working time of teachers, to improve the methods and quality of instruction, more rationally to use the educational premises, laboratories, and equipment, and to eliminate supplementary outlays of state funds on the travel of correspondence students to cities that have correspondence schools.

The party and the government have set the task of increasing the number of students in the evening and correspondence divisions to 2,260,000 by 1965. This number exceeds that of the day divisions by almost 30 per cent. To accomplish this, it would be economically advisable to establish evening and correspondence divisions or departments in all the day higher schools, and only evening divisions in the medical institutes, since it is hardly possible to train doctors by correspondence.

Another important economic problem of higher correspondence education is that of reducing

costs by raising the quality of instruction, adhering strictly to terms of study, and eliminating instances in which students drop out of school.

Such are some of the economic problems of higher education. They emphasize the need for greater attention on the part of higher school personnel to questions of economics, for more profound study of the economy of the higher school, for more complete financial estimates, and for learning to have a regard for public money and its rational expenditure.

* * *

From the Editors. The Editorial Board is publishing L. I. Tulchinskii's article with a view to attracting the attention of higher school personnel to the problems of higher school economics. Although some of the author's suggestions are problematic, there can be no doubt as to the timeliness of the problem he raises.

Statistics

Narodnoe obrazovanie, 1967, No. 12, Supplement

M. Poluboiarinov

PUBLIC EDUCATION IN THE USSR IN FIGURES (A BRIEF SURVEY)

Note

The 1925-1939 data adduced in this article
pertain to the territorial bounds of the USSR as
of September 17, 1939, while those for 1914, as
well as for 1940-1967, pertain to the USSR within
its present boundaries. In certain cases the 1966
and 1967 data are preliminary and may undergo
modification.

* * *

One of the most important and fundamental indices characterizing the achievements of the cultural revolution in our country in the fifty years
of Soviet government is provided by the statistical data on the broad and comprehensive development of public education.

The figures that detail the scale and success
of the work done to eliminate illiteracy, and to
develop schools and higher and secondary specialized educational institutions, as well as the

The author is Assistant Chief of the Culture
Division, Central Statistical Administration,
attached to the USSR Council of Ministers.

increase in scientific and scholarly personnel
during the half-century, demonstrate the depth
and complexity of the social and cultural changes
that have occurred in the lives of all the peoples
in the Soviet Union.

Today we rejoice in the significant successes
scored during the Soviet years in the work of
public education in the USSR, inasmuch as the
scale of the work in this field among the peoples
of our country has been enormous. Let us recall
that in prerevolutionary Russia nearly three-
quarters of the population aged nine and above
was utterly illiterate. At that time four out of
five children and teen-agers had no opportunity
to go to school. Moreover, many of the nationalities inhabiting the borderlands of tsarist Russia
were almost universally illiterate. Prior to the
October Revolution, more than forty of the peoples of the USSR did not even have their own written languages.

According to the data of the Russian statistical
annual for 1915, the 1897 census showed 27%
literacy in Russia; but in Central Asia (Turkestan)
the figure was 6%, in the Caucasus — 17%, and
in Siberia — 16%. Only 17% of the women were
literate, while in Central Asia that figure was

277

only 3%, in Siberia — 7%, and in the Caucasus — 8%. Literacy was still lower in such areas as Semirech'e, where literacy among the female population over nine years of age did not exceed 1%, in Turgai Region it was 2%, in the Trans-Caspian Region — 3%, and in the Samarkand and Fergana regions — less than 1%.

Socialism has brought education and enlightenment to the Soviet people, and has immeasurably elevated and enriched the spiritual life of society. The Soviet years have seen the country take an enormous step forward in the development of education. But in the first years after the triumph of the October Revolution it was necessary to start almost from zero, for the most important task of the young Soviet state was to eliminate illiteracy. It had to teach millions of people to read and write. At enterprises, in organizations, schools, and clubs, tens of thousands of courses and illiteracy elimination centers were organized. This was a truly unprecedented crusade for knowledge by the millions. During the twenty prewar years, 1921-1940, as many as 60 million persons learned to read and write, not counting those of limited literacy who continued to study. The progress of eliminating illiteracy is indicated by Table 1 on the numbers of adults studying in schools and groups for elimination of illiteracy and semiliteracy (the figures are for the numbers studying at the beginning of each year, in thousands).

At present, over 73 million persons, or more than one-third of the country's population, are engaged in study of one kind or another, not including children in the preschool age group. This is nearly seven times as many as in 1914. The manner in which the number of persons enrolled in educational institutions of various types varied in different periods is indicated in Table 2.

It is clear that elimination of illiteracy was on a particularly broad scale during the First Five-Year Plan, when the industrialization of the economy and the collectivization of agriculture were under way. In 1932 alone, the number of persons attending illiteracy elimination courses exceeded 14 million, or more than ten times as many as in 1925.

Along with the elimination of illiteracy there was a universal expansion of the network of general education schools and an increase in enrollment. The network of schools grew with particular rapidity after the adoption, in 1930, of the law on universal primary education. Table 3 presents figures descriptive of the development of the school network during the First Five-Year Plan, and indicates the number of day-session general education schools and the enrollment in them (in thousands) in various years.

During the First Five-Year Plan, the number of schools rose from 119,000 in 1927 to 166,000 in 1932, i.e., an increase of over 47,000. During the same period, enrollment increased by 10 million, nearly doubling. That period showed a particular increase in enrollment in rural schools: 8 million.

The Soviet people fulfilled the goals of the Second Five-Year Plan in education, too, where a further development of schooling was provided for. The years of the Second Five-Year Plan showed a continuation in the growth of the number of schools and their enrollment, while the network of incomplete secondary and secondary schools increased, as did that of the primary schools; and the planning of schooling was improved. Table 4 shows, in thousands, the changes in the number of general education day-session schools during the Second Five-Year Plan.

These data show that in 1937 (the final year of the Second Five-Year Plan) the number of schools had increased by 2,000 since 1932, and the number of pupils in them by more than 8 million, or 1.4 times.

Although the number of schools did not change greatly, there was a rapid growth in both urban and rural enrollment, a consequence of the fact that the years 1933-1937 witnessed the building of larger schools, particularly schools offering incomplete and complete secondary education. In 1932, for example, the number of such schools was somewhat over 28,000 (26,800 seven-year, and 1,300 secondary), while in 1937 they increased to 44,000 (34,200 seven-year and 9,900 secondary). In those years there was a considerable increase in the number of secondary schools, testifying to the expansion of secondary education at that time, particularly in rural local-

Table 1

Year	Total studying (thousands)	Of which: Illiterate	Semiliterate
1925	1,383.3	1,383.3	—
1926	1,615.9	1,615.9	—
1927	1,540.6	1,351.5	189.1
1928	1,466.2	1,247.5	218.7
1929	2,055.8	1,799.6	256.2
1930	6,764.0	5,771.5	992.5
1931	9,254.8	6,189.8	3,065.0
1932	14,245.7	7,663.6	6,582.1
1933	8,969.6	4,770.0	4,199.6
1934	8,417.8	4,659.8	3,758.0
1935	7,711.7	3,867.7	3,844.0
1936	7,105.5	3,329.6	3,775.9
1937	8,466.3	4,086.0	4,380.3
1938	7,455.1	3,830.8	3,624.3
1939	6,953.0	3,313.2	3,639.8

Table 2

Types of schooling	1914/15	1940/41	1960/61	1966/67
Total enrolled (thousands)	10,588	47,547	52,600	73,559
Of which				
In schools of all types for general education	9,656	35,552	36,187	48,170
Including: primary, incomplete secondary, and secondary schools	9,656	34,784	33,417	43,529
schools for working and farm youth and adult schools (including correspondence students)	—	768	2,770	4,641
In vocational and/or technical schools and trade schools (FZU)	106	717	1,113	1,961
In secondary specialized educational institutions	54	975	2,060	3,994
In higher educational institutions	127	812	2,396	4,123
Persons who learned new occupations or underwent upgrading on the job or in courses, and persons taking other forms of schooling	645	9,491	10,844	15,311

Table 3

	1928/29	1929/30	1930/31	1931/32	1932/33
Urban and rural:					
Number of schools	124.8	133.2	152.8	168.1	166.3
Number of pupils	12,068	13,516	17,614	20,933	21,397
Urban:					
Number of schools	11.3	11.4	11.1	11.5	11.3
Number of pupils	3,360	3,570	3,825	4,562	4,834
Rural:					
Number of schools	113.5	121.8	141.7	156.6	155.0
Number of pupils	8,708	9,946	13,789	16,371	16,563

Table 4

	1933/34	1934/35	1935/36	1936/37	1937/38
Urban and rural:					
Number of schools	166.5	163.1	164.1	164.8	168.4
Number of pupils	22,096	23,539	25,555	27,611	29,562
Urban:					
Number of schools	12.0	12.6	13.7	15.1	16.7
Number of pupils	5,228	6,062	6,971	7,841	8,680
Rural:					
Number of schools	154.5	150.5	150.4	149.7	151.7
Number of pupils	16,868	17,477	18,584	19,770	20,882

ities, where the number of secondary schools rose from 123 in 1932 to 4,561 in 1937. Table 5 shows that the substantial expansion of secondary general education (incomplete and complete) is also testified to by the rise in the number of students in upper grades (thousands, not including those in types of schools other than those listed here).

During the First Five-Year Plan, there was a steady rise in the number of pupils in the 5th through 7th grades; this led, subsequently, in the Second Five-Year Plan, to an increase in the enrollment in the 8th through 10th grades. In 1937 there were 8.7 million pupils in the 5th through 10th grades, as compared with only 1.5 million in 1927. Moreover, this included over 5 million in these grades in rural schools, which was 2.4 times as large as the number in 1932 and 12 times as large as in 1927. During the First and Second Five-Year Plans, the number of 8th through 10th graders in the countryside multiplied nearly 31 times (from 12,000 in 1927 to 373,000 in 1937). At the end of the Second Five-Year Plan, the number of pupils in grades 5 through 10 in rural schools came to one-fourth of all the pupils in day-session general education schools in the countryside.

Having reached the goals set in the Second Five-Year Plan in the field of development of culture, the Soviet people, under the leadership of the Communist Party, proceeded to implement the objectives of the Third Five-Year Plan. The goal set for that period was to substantially expand secondary education and, consequently, to enlarge the network of incomplete secondary and secondary schools both in the cities and the vil-

Table 5

	1927/28	1932/33	1937/38
Urban and rural:			
Total enrollment	11,369	21,257	29,446
In grades 1-4 and preparatory classes	9,910	17,675	20,755
In grades 5-7	1,332	3,515	7,677
In grades 8-10 (or 11)	127	67	1,014
Urban:			
Total enrollment	3,160	4,767	8,611
In grades 1-4	2,126	3,393	5,202
In grades 5-7	919	1,311	2,768
In grades 8-10 (or 11)	115	63	641
Rural:			
Total enrollment	8,209	16,490	20,835
In grades 1-4	7,784	14,282	15,553
In grades 5-7	413	2,204	4,909
In grades 8-10 (or 11)	12	4	373

lages. At the beginning of 1940/41 there were 191,600 schools in the country, of which 45,700 (or nearly one-fourth) offered seven-year courses, and 18,800 (or nearly one-tenth) were complete secondary schools.

The first years of the Third Five-Year Plan saw the successful solution of the tasks of preparing the conditions for attaining universal compulsory seven-year schooling, as is evidenced by the Table 6 data on increase in schooling in the years prior to World War II (figures in thousands).

As the figures show, in the three prewar years, there was a rapid increase in the number of schools providing secondary schooling (incomplete and complete). In 1940/41, there were about 25 million pupils in these schools, or about three-fourths of the total enrollment. For purposes of comparison, we note that in the 1927/28 school year, pupils in seven-year and secondary schools comprised only one-fourth of the total number in all day-session general education schools, while in 1914 they were a little more than 10%. These figures are a vivid confirmation of the fact that, on the eve of World War II, the work of implementing universal seven-year schooling was proceeding at full steam in the USSR, and that the network of secondary schools was being greatly expanded.

Unfortunately, the war prevented the Soviet people from implementing all that was projected by the Third Five-Year Plan. Lasting four years, the war stopped the development of public education for several years. During the war, particularly in the territory temporarily occupied by the fascist troops, a great number of schools, higher and secondary specialized educational institutions, libraries, clubs, and the like, were destroyed. In the report of the Extraordinary State Commission to Determine and Investigate the Atrocities of the German-Fascist Occupants, On the Material Losses Inflicted by the German-Fascist Occupants upon the State Enterprises and Institutions, Collective Farms, Public Organizations, and Citizens of the USSR [O material'nom ushcherbe, prichinennom nemetsko-fashistskimi zakhvatchikami gosudarstvennym predpriatiiam i uchrezhdeniiam kolkhozam, obshchestvennym organizatsiiam i grazhdanam SSSR] (1945), data are adduced describing the enormous damage done to cultural institutions, particularly to schools. Especially great damage was done to educational institutions in the RSFSR, the Ukraine, Belorussia, Moldavia, Lithuania, Latvia, and

Table 6

	1938/39		1939/40		1940/41	
	schools	pupils	schools	pupils	schools	pupils
Urban and rural districts:						
Total	171.6	31,517	172.7	32,186	191.5	34,784
Primary	121.7	10,646	116.7	9,518	125.9	9,786
Seven-year	36.3	11,712	39.2	11,705	45.7	12,525
Secondary	12.5	9,028	15.8	10,835	18.8	12,199
Other	1.1	131	1.0	128	1.1	274
Urban:						
Total	18.0	9,375	19.0	9,929	21.5	10,776
Primary	6.5	1,502	6.5	1,389	6.9	1,370
Seven-year	4.3	2,243	4.2	2,076	4.8	2,181
Secondary	6.4	5,554	7.5	6,382	8.9	7,117
Other	0.8	76	0.8	82	0.9	108
Rural:						
Total	153.6	22,142	153.7	22,257	170.0	24,008
Primary	115.2	9,144	110.2	8,129	119.0	8,416
Seven-year	32.0	9,469	35.0	9,629	40.9	10,344
Secondary	6.1	3,474	8.3	4,453	9.9	5,082
Other	0.3	55	0.2	46	0.2	166

Estonia: 84,000 schools were destroyed or wrecked, in which 15 million pupils had studied before the war, as well as 334 higher educational institutions where 233,000 had studied.

Upon victorious completion of the war in 1945, the Soviet people set to the rebuilding of the economy, including its schools. Much was done to make it possible for all school-age children to be able to study, even in the first postwar school year. As the result of tremendous efforts by the Soviet people and by party, soviet, and economic agencies, the number of schools at the start of the first postwar school year almost equalled the 1940/41 level. However, as a consequence of the wartime losses, the number of pupils was substantially below 1940. In 1945/46, a total of 187,000 day-session schools functioned in the USSR as a whole, of which 132,000 were primary schools. Enrollment in all schools at that time was somewhat over 26 million pupils, or over 8 million fewer children than in 1940/41. Changes in the number of schools and pupils in 1945 as compared to 1940 (for the individual constituent republics) can be seen in the comparative figures on day-session schools in Table 7.

Comparison of these figures shows that the number of pupils in the 1945/46 school year was 25% less than in the 1940/41 school year for the USSR as a whole, including a 26% loss in the RSFSR, Azerbaijan, and Turkmenia, and a loss of over 30% in Kazakhstan, 32% in Kirgizia, and 28% in Uzbekistan. In Estonia the number of pupils in school in 1945 was at virtually the same level as in 1940.

If we compare the schools by types, we find that the first postwar year saw an increase of nearly 6,000 primary schools over the prewar year, and a decline of 10,000 incomplete secondary and secondary schools. Also related to this was a sharp decline in enrollment in the number of pupils in the upper grades: from 10.8 million in 1940 to 5.2 million in 1945 in the 5th to 7th grades, and from 2.4 million to 975,000 in the 8th through 10th (11th) grades.

Table 7

	1940/41		1945/46	
	schools	pupils (thous.)	schools	pupils (thous.)
USSR	191,545	34,784	186,853	26,094
RSFSR	113,880	20,229	113,453	15,018
Ukrainian SSR	30,881	6,687	28,470	5,049
Belorussian SSR	11,844	1,691	10,915	1,337
Uzbek SSR	4,931	1,281	4,580	927
Kazakh SSR	7,734	1,129	7,812	785
Georgian SSR	4,511	743	4,114	593
Azerbaijan SSR	3,575	655	3,258	487
Lithuanian SSR	2,829	376	3,243	305
Moldavian SSR	1,839	437	1,825	353
Latvian SSR	1,586	237	1,448	221
Kirgiz SSR	1,645	329	1,537	223
Tadjik SSR	2,628	303	2,881	240
Armenian SSR	1,155	327	1,173	252
Turkmen SSR	1,254	240	1,089	178
Estonian SSR	1,253	120	1,055	126

Thanks to large-scale and intensive efforts, the school system was restored in a brief period of time. As early as 1947/48, there were 197,000 day-session schools functioning in the USSR as a whole, or somewhat more than in 1940/41. The number of pupils in school in 1949/50 had almost reached the number on the eve of the war. In subsequent years, the number of pupils declined somewhat because the entering grades were comprised of children born during the war; but by 1961 the number of pupils exceeded the prewar number and reached 35.8 million.

In 1958, the USSR Supreme Soviet adopted a law on the schools. In accordance with that law, 1959 saw the beginning of a transition from universal compulsory seven-year to universal compulsory eight-year schooling. This transition was completed everywhere in 1962, when all 7th graders were promoted to 8th grade for the following year so as to finish incomplete secondary schooling.

The data in Table 8 provide a sense of the change in the structure of the schools and the number of pupils (by groups of grades after 1958).

In the last few years there has been a decline in the network of primary schools and an increase in the number of eight-year and secondary schools, while in 1966/67 there was a considerable increase in the number of secondary schools. This increase is occurring in conjunction with the fact that the country is progressing toward a transition to universal complete secondary education, in accordance with the Directives of the 23rd Congress of the CPSU on the Five-Year Plan for Economic Development in 1966-1970.

Thus, the postwar years have witnessed a rise in public education in our country to a higher level. Universal compulsory eight-year schooling has been achieved, and in the current Five-Year Plan (1966-1970) it is planned, on the whole, to complete the transition to universal secondary schooling. In this connection, it seems to us to be of interest to trace the increase, in the course of 50 years, in the number of pupils in the 5th to

Table 8

	1958/59		1962/63		1966/67	
	schools, thous.	pupils, mill.	schools, thous.	pupils, mill.	schools, thous.	pupils, mill.
Total no. of schools	199.7	29.6	197.6	38.5	188.3	43.5
Primary	112.4	4.5	105.4	4.3	91.3	3.7
Seven-year	55.7	8.9	—	—	—	—
Eight-year	—	—	62.8	16.0	58.5	14.8
Secondary	30.7	16.1	28.1	18.0	36.7	24.7
Schools for children with mental or physical defects	0.9	0.1	1.3	0.2	1.8	0.3

Table 9

	1914/15	1940/41	1958/59	1966/67
Total enrollment (thousands)	9,656	35,552	31,483	48,170
In grades 1-4	9,031	21,483	17,779	20,577
In grades 5-8	523	12,506	10,571	20,013
Of which, in grade 8	51	1,281	1,633	4,777
In grades 9-11	102	1,290	3,022	7,295
In schools for children with mental or physical defects	—	273	111	285

10th grades in general education schools of all types (including evening school students) (Table 9).

The figures show that at present there are over 48 million pupils in general education schools of all types — five times as many as in 1914. Moreover, there are now over 27 million pupils in the 5th through 10th (or 11th) grades (44 times as many as were enrolled in these grades before the October Revolution); among these more than 7 million are obtaining a complete secondary education in the 9th and 10th (or 11th) grades. This is 72 times as many as studied in these grades in 1914.

Before the Revolution, many nationalities had no schools, and in the schools that did exist, education was conducted, as a general rule, in the Russian language. Today every republic, region, and district has a widely ramified network of general education schools, in which instruction is in the native tongue. At present, school instruction is given in the USSR in 57 languages.

All the constituent republics have seen a considerable increase in the number of pupils — in some of them to levels ten or even hundreds of times greater than in the prerevolutionary past. Table 10 enables one to form a judgment on this.

Since the first years of its existence, the Soviet government has manifested and continues to manifest very great concern for improving the level of education of the adult population. Toward that end, a network of evening (shift) and correspondence schools has been established so that youth who did not acquire secondary education in their school years are able to obtain it without giving up their jobs. During the 1966/67 school

Table 10

	1914/15	1966/67
USSR	9,656	48,170
RSFSR	5,684	26,187
Ukrainian SSR	2,607	8,468
Belorussian SSR	489	1,769
Uzbek SSR	18	2,592
Kazakh SSR	105	2,866
Georgian SSR	157	928
Azerbaijan SSR	73	1,199
Lithuanian SSR	118	562
Moldavian SSR	92	763
Latvian SSR	172	343
Kirgiz SSR	7	657
Tadjik SSR	0.4	613
Armenian SSR	35	553
Turkmen SSR	7	455
Estonian SSR	92	215

year, 4.6 million persons were attending such schools, or six times as many as in 1940.

The data in Table 11 present an idea of the changes in the network of evening schools, and include those general education day schools at which classes have been organized for urban and rural working youth, plus data on independent correspondence schools.

Recent years have seen an increase in the enrollment in evening schools in the 5th through 11th grades — particularly in the 9th to 11th grades, where the 1966 attendance was nearly 30 times as high as in 1940, while in grades 5 through 8 it was 2.7 times as high.

With the expansion of the school network and the increase in the number of pupils, there has also been an increase in the number of teachers. In 1966/67 there were 2.5 million teachers in all general education schools. In 1914 there were only 280,000 teachers in the schools. Today a majority of the teachers have higher or incomplete higher education, as is evident from the Table 12 data on the level of education of teachers in day schools (at the beginning of the school year, in percentages).

During the past fifteen years there has been a sharp rise in the level of teachers' general education: from 14.2% with higher education in 1950 to 42.9% in 1966. There has been a corresponding decline in the number of teachers with incomplete higher and secondary education, as well as in the percentage of those lacking complete secondary education.

In the years of Soviet power there has been large-scale construction of schools. Thus, from 1918-1967, government and cooperative enterprises and agencies (not counting collective farms) have built general education schools with a total of more than 28 million pupil places (of which about one-half were in rural places) (see Table 13).

In addition, 50,000 schools, with a capacity of more than 6 million pupils, have been built on the initiative and with the funds of the collective farms in the postwar period (1946-1966).

In the very first years after the Revolution, when the young Soviet republic was waging the Civil War, school construction was begun. By 1929, nearly 8,000 schools, with a capacity of over a million pupils, had been built. School construction has proceeded at a particularly rapid pace since 1955. During the past twelve years

Table 11

	1940/41	1958/59	1960/61	1966/67
Total no. of schools	7,276	15,493	25,229	21,903
Of which, independent	—	9,947	12,331	12,547
Enrollment (including correspondence students), thousands	768	1,916	2,770	4,641
In grades 1-4	107	51	54	66
In grades 5-8	551	1,048	1,655	1,467
In grades 9-11	110	817	1,061	3,108

Table 12

% of teachers (with indicated level of education)	1950	1955	1958	1966
Higher	14.2	23.5	28.9	42.9
Teachers' institutes and equivalent institutions	20.4	26.9	23.1	13.4
Secondary, including pedagogical	58.9	47.6	46.4	42.2
Secondary pedagogical	46.9	41.0	41.3	33.1
Less than complete secondary education	6.5	2.0	1.6	1.5

(1956-1967), schools with a total of nearly 12 million places have been built.

From the very first days of the existence of the Soviet government, one of its principal concerns has been for children, for their health and upbringing. Let us recall that the decrees of the Soviet government adopted during the first years after the triumph of the October Revolution included decrees on feeding children and on placing homeless children.

The party ascribes particularly high significance to the role of society in the rearing of children today. The system of preschool institutions born of the October Revolution is being expanded. This is evidenced by the establishment of a large network of nurseries and kindergartens. Within ten years after the Revolution, over 2,000 permanent kindergartens had been established for over 107,000 children, while by 1940 the number of kindergartens had reached 24,000 and the number of children in them exceeded a million. In 1966 there were 8.2 million young children in all preschool institutions, 4.2 times as many as in 1940. Moreover, in addition to the permanent nurseries and kindergartens, seasonal nurseries and playgrounds are organized everywhere during the summer. In 1966 alone these served over 4 million children.

The data in Table 14 reflect the increase in the number of children in preschool institutions in the years of Soviet power.

The constant increase in the network of preschool institutions has been accompanied by a considerable increase in the rate of construction of kindergartens and nurseries. The years 1918-1967 have seen the building and functioning of preschool institutions with a capacity of 4.8 million, taking into consideration only those built at government expense. Particularly rapid rates of construction of these institutions are characteristic of the postwar period and the last few years. Thus, in 1965 alone, kindergartens and nurseries with a capacity of 435,000 were opened, over four times as many as during the entire Fourth Five-Year Plan.

Children's institutions are also built in our

Table 13

Years	No. of schools	Pupil places (thousands)
Total built and put into use, 1918-1967	91,569	28,166
1918-1928	7,780	1,061
1929-1932 (First Five-Year Plan)	13,128	3,771
1933-1937 (Second Five-Year Plan)	18,778	5,576
1938-1940 (Third Five-Year Plan)	5,325	1,593
1941-1945 (war years, data from July 1, 1941 to Jan. 1, 1946)	8,412	1,177
1946-1950 (Fourth Five-Year Plan)	4,345	1,181
1951-1955 (Fifth Five-Year Plan)	5,819	1,912
1956-1960	9,510	3,175
1961-1965	14,088	6,460
1966	2,224	1,203
1967 (estimate)	2,160	1,057

Table 14

	1914*	1940	1960	1966
No. of children in permanent children's nurseries, kindergartens, and combinations of both (thous.) of which:	4.55	1,953	4,428	8,192
Urban	4.55	1,422	3,565	6,597
Rural	—	531	863	1,595

*In the boundaries prior to September 17, 1939.

country by collective farms. From 1956 to 1966, institutions with a capacity of 1.3 million children have been put into operation by such local initiative.

We have a variety of types of preschool institutions. In some, the children are placed for the entire day and night or even a full week, while in others they are kept only during the day, with the parents taking the children home in the evening. The government meets the bulk of the costs involved in keeping children in kindergartens and nurseries. Payments by parents presently comprise only an insignificant part of those costs.

The development of the system of children's institutions and the increase in the numbers they care for have a major influence not only upon the rearing of children and the maintenance of their health; this also raises the living standard of the people to some degree, as real income is increased out of public funds.

It would have been impossible to create a broad network of children's institutions if the corresponding construction of premises for kindergartens and nurseries had not occurred. The government spares no funds toward that end and annually increases the opening of new preschool institutions.

The rates of expansion of construction of the network of children's preschool institutions from funds of government and cooperative enter-

288

Table 15

Total built and opened, 1918-1967 (thousands of accommodations)	4,754.4
1918-1928	22.7
First Five-Year Plan	38.2
Second Five-Year Plan	183.5
3 1/2 years of the Third Five-Year Plan	236.8
July 1, 1941-January 1, 1946	56.9
Fourth Five-Year Plan	101.8
Fifth Five-Year Plan	416.5
1956-1960	925.0
1961-1965	1,846.3
1966	427.7
1967 (plan)	500.0

Table 16

	1913	1928	Jan. 1, 1941	Dec. 1, 1960	Nov. 15, 1966
Total (thous.)	190	521	2,401	8,784	12,924
Of which:					
with higher education	136	233	909	3,545	5,227
with secondary specialized education	54	288	1,492	5,239	7,697

prises and organizations other than collective farms are indicated in Table 15 (in thousands of accommodations).

As is evident from the data cited, nurseries and kindergartens with places for nearly 5 million children have been built in the years 1918-1967; of this total, 2.8 million, or more than 58%, were built in the past seven years.

The elimination of illiteracy and semiliteracy, and the extensive development of schooling, have created all the prerequisites for improving higher and secondary specialized education. Lenin pointed out that without the guidance of specialists in various branches of knowledge, without techniques and experience, the transition to socialism is impossible because socialism requires a conscious and mass-scale forward movement to a higher labor productivity than capitalism can offer.

* * *

Questions of training of highly qualified personnel for all branches of the economy and culture have always been central to the attention of the Communist Party and the Soviet government. A decree of the Council of People's Commissars in 1918, elaborated and signed by Lenin, proclaimed the reorganization of higher education on new principles. This decree of Lenin's brought about a genuine overturn: the doors of higher educational institutions were opened to the toiling masses for the first time in history; instruction in higher educational institutions not only became free, but students were provided with material assistance by the state.

A majority of the students in our higher educational institutions receive stipends and have the right to free use of textbooks, study aids, books,

Table 17

Years	Graduation from higher educational institutions		Graduation from secondary specialized educational institutions	
	Total	Annual average	Total	Annual average
1914	12	12.0	7	
1918-1928	340	30.9	198	18.0
1929-1932	170	42.5	291	72.8
1933-1937	370	74.0	623	124.6
1938-1940	328	109.3	678	226.0
1941-1945	302	60.4	540	108.0
1946-1950	652	130.4	1,278	255.7
1951-1955	1,121	224.3	1,560	311.9
1956-1960	1,498	299.6	2,577	515.4
1961-1965	1,732	346.3	2,572	514.4
1966	432	—	685	—
1918-1966	6,945	—	11,001	—

etc. Those students who study and work in industry at the same time are granted extra paid vacations.

Between 1918 and 1966, higher and secondary specialized educational institutions trained nearly 18 million persons: engineers and technologists, agronomists, physicians, teachers, economists, etc., including 6.9 million with higher education. All this has made it possible to provide the national economy with qualified specialists. As of November 15, 1966, about 13 million persons with higher and specialized secondary education were employed in the USSR (excluding the military), including 5.2 million with higher education and 7.7 million with secondary specialized education. The data in Table 16 show how the number of such persons has changed with the years.

The development of higher and secondary specialized education made it possible to create an army of millions of persons performing mental labor. Before the Revolution, according to the 1897 census, the number of persons engaged primarily in mental work was 870,000. In 1926 the USSR already counted 2.9 million persons engaged in mental labor; by the beginning of 1967 there were more than 27 million engaged chiefly

in mental labor, or nearly ten times as many as in 1926. The rapid rate of development of the system of higher and secondary specialized education is evidenced by the annually increasing graduations of experts from higher and secondary specialized educational institutions in the years from 1918 to 1966 (in thousands) (see Table 17).

In 1914, somewhat more than 180,000 persons were studying in the country's higher educational institutions and technical schools. Moreover, there were none of the former in Belorussia, Azerbaijan, Lithuania, Armenia, Moldavia, the Central Asian republics, and Kazakhstan. Today the training of persons of the highest qualifications, and the training of national cadres, are proceeding in all the republics. In the 1966/67 school year, there were more than 8 million persons studying in higher and secondary specialized educational institutions, 45 times as many as in 1914. An idea of the manner in which the number of educational institutions and their enrollments have changed may be obtained by familiarizing oneself with certain comparative data in Table 18.

Although the number of educational institutions declined somewhat from 1940 to 1966, the num-

Table 18

	1914/15	1940/41	1960/61	1966/67
Number of higher educational institutions	105	817	739	767
Number of students (thousands)	127	812	2,396	4,123
Of which:				
In day sessions	127	558	1,156	1,740
In evening sessions	—	27	245	618
By correspondence	—	227	995	1,765
Number of secondary specialized educational institutions	450	3,773	3,328	3,980
Number studying in them (thousands)	54	975	2,060	3,994
Of which:				
In day sessions	54	787	1,091	2,111
In evening sessions	—	32	370	677
By correspondence	—	156	599	1,206

Table 19

	1940	1945	1960	1966
Graduated from higher educational institutions (thous.)	126.1	54.6	343.3	431.9
Of which, from institutions specializing in:				
Industry and construction	24.2	8.5	95.2	149.5
Transport and communications	5.9	1.6	16.1	20.2
Agriculture	10.3	2.9	34.7	35.0
Economics and law	5.7	2.4	25.0	35.1
Health, physical culture, and sports	17.4	6.6	30.7	32.5
Education	61.6	32.0	139.1	155.1
Arts and the cinema	1.0	0.6	2.5	4.5
Graduated from secondary specialized educational institutions (thous.)	236.8	118.1	483.5	683.7
Of which, from institutions specializing in:				
Industry and construction	21.7	16.0	189.9	271.4
Transport and communications	8.3	3.5	36.6	57.5
Agriculture	21.5	19.8	80.2	92.7
Economics and law	7.2	8.2	56.5	91.7
Health, physical culture, and sports	90.4	32.5	64.2	79.9
Education	85.7	37.2	48.9	75.1
Arts and the cinema	2.0	0.9	7.2	15.4

Table 20

	1914/15		1960/61		1966/67	
	Institu-tions	Students (thous.)	Institu-tions	Students (thous.)	Institu-tions	Students (thous.)
Total (thousand persons)	105	127.4	739	2,395.5	767	4,123.2
Of which, by groups of institutions:						
Industry, construction, transport, communications	18	24.9	206	1,019.3	227	1,855.8
Agriculture	14	4.6	96	246.4	98	398.8
Economics and law	15	11.4	51	161.9	43	294.7
Education, art, and cinema	52	81.5	288	779.0	301	1,314.3
Health, physical culture, and sports	6	5.0	98	188.9	98	259.6

Table 21

	Students in higher educational institutions			Students in secondary specialized educational institutions		
	1927	1960	1966	1927	1960	1966
Total (thousands)	168.5	2,396.1	4,123.2	189.4	2,059.5	3,993.9
By nationality:						
Russians	94.5	1,480.1	2,494.7	105.1	1,302.3	2,536.4
Ukrainians	24.6	343.6	590.2	21.0	331.6	610.5
Belorussians	4.9	63.7	122.6	4.5	66.0	141.0
Uzbeks	0.5	53.5	112.4	3.6	28.0	68.6
Kazakhs	0.3	40.8	75.9	2.5	28.3	55.6
Georgians	4.0	48.5	77.0	5.7	22.6	37.1
Azerbaijanians	1.9	28.5	63.9	5.7	21.4	50.0
Lithuanians	—	25.8	46.0	—	28.8	52.7
Moldavians	0.2	12.0	26.4	0.1	10.1	23.9
Latvians	—	16.5	22.7	—	16.7	21.7
Kirgiz	0.1	9.9	18.7	0.4	6.4	11.3
Tadjiks	0.1	11.9	19.9	0.3	6.4	13.6
Armenians	3.4	36.7	67.7	3.6	21.7	49.1
Turkmenians	0.1	9.5	17.8	0.6	6.3	12.2
Estonians	—	12.9	18.8	—	12.6	17.9

Table 22

	1914/15	1940/41	1960/61	1966/67
USSR	127.4	811.7	2,396.1	4,123.2
RSFSR	86.5	478.1	1,496.7	2,470.5
Ukrainian SSR	35.2	196.8	417.7	739.1
Belorussian SSR	–	21.5	59.3	115.9
Uzbek SSR	–	19.1	101.3	188.3
Kazakh SSR	–	10.4	77.1	163.1
Georgian SSR	0.3	28.5	56.3	81.4
Azerbaijan SSR	–	14.6	36.0	78.3
Lithuanian SSR	–	6.0	26.7	50.7
Moldavian SSR	–	2.5	19.2	40.6
Latvian SSR	2.1	9.9	21.6	36.0
Kirgiz SSR	–	3.1	17.4	36.7
Tadjik SSR	–	2.3	20.0	34.7
Armenian SSR	–	11.1	20.2	43.3
Turkmen SSR	–	3.0	13.1	22.7
Estonian SSR	3.3	4.8	13.5	21.9

ber of students increased very sharply: more than fourfold. This is evidence of the fact that the size of higher educational institutions has become larger in recent years. While the average enrollment at a higher educational institution was less than 1,000 in 1940, it was over 5,000 in 1966.

As we know, the USSR trains personnel of higher and secondary qualifications for all branches of the economy. The comparative data in Table 19 demonstrate the growth and change in graduation from higher and secondary specialized educational institutions by groups of institutions, by branches of the economy (in thousands), at various times in the development of the economy.

It is evident that, in the overwhelming majority of cases, the 1966 data vastly exceed the data for both the postwar and prewar years. This contrast is even sharper upon comparison of data (see Table 20) characterizing the numbers and enrollment in higher educational institutions in recent years and prior to the October Revolution.

Let us recall that in the first months subsequent to the triumph of the October Revolution, the capitalist class of the entire world asserted repeatedly that the downfall of the Soviet system was inevitable, inasmuch as at that time Russia was essentially an illiterate country and the working class did not have its own specialists capable of directing the machinery of government and the country's economy. However, life refuted these assertions and confirmed the correctness of Lenin's words to the effect that the Revolution would awaken the people's initiative and that the Soviet government would develop leaders and organizers from among the masses, that the workers and peasants, having taken power, would learn how to rule the state and master all the achievements of science and technology.

Today all can see how the Soviet people, under the leadership of the Communist Party, is confidently moving forward and, thanks to the triumph of socialism and the most far-reaching changes in our economic, political, and cultural life, has not only caught up to but in many respects has left the capitalist countries far behind.

The Great October Revolution has opened up access to education to the laboring people of all nationalities. The USSR has provided broad op-

201 0 1968

Table 23

	1914/15	1940/41	1960/61	1966/67
USSR	54.3	974.8	2,059.5	3,993.9
RSFSR	35.4	594.0	1,260.3	2,423.9
Ukrainian SSR	12.5	196.2	398.2	718.7
Belorussian SSR	1.4	35.0	62.6	134.8
Uzbek SSR	0.1	25.1	53.3	122.0
Kazakh SSR	0.3	30.3	86.0	193.4
Georgian SSR	0.5	26.1	26.3	43.2
Azerbaijan SSR	0.5	17.4	27.0	65.0
Lithuanian SSR	1.5	6.4	32.3	60.9
Moldavian SSR	0.5	4.1	17.2	39.8
Latvian SSR	1.3	9.6	24.7	41.2
Kirgiz SSR	—	6.0	17.2	35.4
Tadjik SSR	—	5.9	11.9	27.2
Armenian SSR	0.1	8.9	14.8	36.0
Turkmen SSR	—	7.7	12.3	25.3
Estonian SSR	0.2	2.1	15.4	27.1

Table 24

	1914/15	1940/41	1950/51	1958/59	1966/67
USSR	8	41	69	104	176
RSFSR	10	43	77	116	194
Ukrainian SSR	10	47	54	91	161
Belorussian SSR	—	24	41	71	133
Uzbek SSR	—	28	65	107	173
Kazakh SSR	—	16	46	71	131
Georgian SSR	1	77	98	119	177
Azerbaijan SSR	—	44	98	97	163
Lithuanian SSR	—	20	45	90	168
Moldavian SSR	—	10	36	56	119
Latvian SSR	8	52	73	88	157
Kirgiz SSR	—	19	49	77	133
Tadjik SSR	—	15	46	92	131
Armenian SSR	—	82	111	111	192
Turkmen SSR	—	22	54	85	115
Estonian SSR	35	46	80	101	169

Table 25

	1914/15	1940/41	1950/51	1958/59	1966/67
USSR	3	50	71	90	170
RSFSR	4	53	79	98	190
Ukrainian SSR	4	47	61	84	156
Belorussian SSR	2	39	54	69	154
Uzbek SSR	0.2	37	62	67	112
Kazakh SSR	0.5	48	62	82	156
Georgian SSR	2	71	67	66	94
Azerbaijan SSR	2	52	69	71	135
Lithuanian SSR	5	22	45	87	201
Moldavian SSR	2	17	54	55	116
Latvian SSR	5	50	91	112	180
Kirgiz SSR	—	38	60	76	129
Tadjik SSR	—	38	69	61	102
Armenian SSR	1	66	75	80	160
Turkmen SSR	—	57	62	88	128
Estonian	2	20	94	105	210

portunities to all the people to attain higher and secondary specialized education. National cadres are being trained in the higher educational institutions and technical schools of every republic. The numbers of students in higher educational institutions and in technical schools have grown very substantially everywhere in the years of Soviet power, particularly the numbers of students of various nationalities in the country — tens and hundreds of times. This is evidenced by the data (in thousands of persons) in Table 21.

Figures on the enrollment (in thousands of students) at higher educational institutions, within the territories of today's republics — in the pre-revolutionary years and today (for the beginning of the school year) — provide a striking contrast (see Table 22).

The fifty years have seen a sharp increase in students in the USSR as a whole: 32-fold. The postwar years have seen an increase in the number of students in all the constituent republics, particularly in the Kirgiz SSR (12-fold), in the Uzbek SSR (nearly 10-fold), in the Kazakh SSR (15.7-fold), and in the Turkmen SSR (7.6-fold).

There has also been a considerable increase in the numbers of university and technical school students in the republics of the Baltic states, which became part of the USSR in 1940. In the Lithuanian SSR the number of students in higher educational institutions increased 8.5-fold from 1940 to 1966, and those in secondary specialized educational institutions — 9.6-fold; in the Latvian SSR the number of students has risen, correspondingly, 3.6-fold and 4.3-fold; in Estonia, 4.6-fold and 12.8-fold.

The figures in Table 23 bear witness to the changes in enrollment in technical and other secondary specialized educational institutions (in thousands, at the beginning of the school year).

In the country as a whole, therefore, the number of students in technical secondary schools grew almost 74-fold in the Soviet period. The increase in numbers of students in secondary specialized educational institutions in Uzbekistan, Kazakhstan, Armenia, Azerbaijan, Estonia, and other republics increased beyond all comparison with the past. Further, as compared with 1940, the number of such students increased by a factor of 4.1 for the USSR as a whole, whereas in Moldavia and Lithuania the rise was 9.6-fold, in Estonia — 12.8-fold, in the RSFSR —

6.9-fold, and in Kazakhstan — 6.4-fold.

If we examine the successes in the development of higher education from the standpoint of the number of students per 10,000 population, we find that there are 176 per 10,000 at present, while in 1914 there were 8. In Georgia, the respective figures are 177 and 1, in Latvia — 157 and 8, in the RSFSR — 194 and 10, and in the Ukraine — 161 and 10.

In 1966 there were 170 students in technicums per 10,000 population, while in 1914 there were only 3. The corresponding figures for Estonia were 210 and 2, for Armenia — 160 and 1, and for Kazakhstan — 156 and less than 1. Significant comparative data in this respect are cited in Tables 24 and 25 on the numbers of students in higher educational institutions per 10,000 population (as of the beginning of the school year).

The number of students in technicums and other secondary specialized educational institutions per 10,000 population (at the beginning of the school year) is shown in Table 25.

The fiftieth anniversary of Soviet power is characterized by tremendous achievements in science. The broad development of higher and secondary education created the necessary conditions for training a large army of scientific personnel. The development of science became an object of constant concern of the party from the very first years after the triumph of the October Revolution. The Soviet government is doing everything possible to create a broad network of research institutions and to train scientific and teaching personnel capable of resolving complex problems in the natural, technical, and social sciences. As early as 1940, there were 98,300 research scientists in the USSR, while in 1914 they had numbered only 11,600. Within two years after the close of World War II (by 1947), the number of research scholars had reached 146,000, including 45,000 with doctoral or candidate's degrees. By the beginning of 1967, the research institutions, higher educational institutions, and other Soviet agencies counted 712,000 scientific and scholarly teaching personnel, or one-fourth of the world total. They include over 150,000 candidates and about 17,000 doctors. As compared to 1914, the total number of scientific personnel has increased 61 times.

It is important to note that in the course of the years of Soviet power, each constituent republic has trained its own national personnel. The following data testify to the increase in scholarly personnel of various nationalities: from 1939 to 1966 the total number of scientific personnel in the USSR as a whole increased 7-fold, while the figure for the Kirgiz SSR is 32, the Kazakh SSR — 19, the Turkmen SSR — 18, the Uzbek SSR — 17, the Tadjik SSR — 12, the Azerbaijan SSR — 11, the Georgian SSR — over 7, the Belorussian SSR — 8, and the Ukrainian SSR — 8.

The data cited in the present article are vivid evidence of the fact that in the fifty years of Soviet power the well-known postulates of Marxism-Leninism have been fully confirmed to the effect that the socialist revolution is an obligatory condition for and a reliable guarantee of a cultural revolution.

* * *